# SOCIOLOGY

## OF

# SPORT

## AND

# PHYSICAL ACTIVITY

---

## SECOND EDITION

# SOCIOLOGY

OF

# SPORT

AND

# PHYSICAL ACTIVITY

SECOND EDITION

*Edited by*:

George B. Cunningham and John N. Singer

Center for Sport Management Research and Education
Texas A&M University
College Station, Texas

# DEDICATIONS

For Melissa, Harper, and Maggie
*GBC*

For all my students — past, present, and future
*JNS*

# CONTRIBUTORS

## EDITORS
### George B. Cunningham
George B. Cunningham (PhD, The Ohio State University) is a Professor, Associate Dean for Academic Affairs, and the Marilyn Kent Byrne Chair for Student Success in the College of Education and Human Development at Texas A&M University. He also serves as the Director for the Laboratory for Diversity in Sport. Author of over 150 articles and book chapters, Cunningham's research is in the areas of diversity, group processes, and employee attitudes. He is author the award winning book, *Diversity in Sport Organizations* and is the former president of the North American Society for Sport Management.

### John N. Singer
John N. Singer (PhD, The Ohio State University) is an Associate Professor with the Division of Sport Management in the Department of Health and Kinesiology at Texas A&M University. His research, scholarship, and teaching interests have been in the areas of diversity and social justice, ethics and legal issues, race and ethnicity, and qualitative inquiry in the field. Singer's sport industry experience includes work as a marketing intern with the PGA Tour, a football operations intern with an NFL team, and a deputy coordinator and graduate assistant working with African American male athletes in a university summer bridge program.

***

## AUTHORS
### Mike Newhouse-Bailey
Mike Newhouse Bailey is a doctoral student at The University of Texas at Austin. He began his career in sport in intercollegiate athletics, with experience ranging from marketing, facilities, and communications. His research focuses on youth sport and the family.

### Brandon Brown
*Brandon Brown* is a Sport Management Doctoral student at Texas A&M University. After receiving his Bachelor's degree in Sport Management at Florida State University, he went on to receive both a Master's degree in Business Administration and Sport Business Management. Prior to attending Texas A&M University, Brandon worked as a Sales Associate

for the New York Mets in Queens, New York. His current line of study focuses on Sport Marketing.

**Ted Burden**
Ted Burden is a doctoral student of Sport Management at The University of Texas at Austin. Prior to starting his PhD, he was a high school varsity coach at various high schools throughout Texas. He has coached youth (interscholastic/community) sports for over 25 years. Mr. Burden's primary research interests include youth sport withdrawal and intramural sport program development, as well as coach training and certification.

**Akilah R. Carter-Francique**
Akilah R. Carter-Francique (Ph.D., University of Georgia) is an Assistant Professor in the Department of Health and Kinesiology at Texas A&M University. Her research and scholarship, teaching, and service focus on race, gender, and sport and physical activity. As a former collegiate athlete and sport administrator, current issues of diversity and social justice, participation and representation, and access and opportunity continue to influence and shape her work.

**Jonathan M. Casper**
Jonathan M. Casper (PhD, University of Northern Colorado) is an assistant professor in the Department of Parks, Recreation and Tourism Management at North Carolina State University. Dr. Casper's research interests include social and psychological aspects of youth and adult sport participation, sports' role within active living and quality of life, and participant and fan consumer behavior.

**Kenneth Sean Chaplin**
Kenneth Sean Chaplin is a lecturer at the University of Texas at Dallas. His areas of interests include sport, education, and race and ethnicity.

**Adam Cohen**
Adam Cohen is a second year doctoral student and research assistant at Texas A&M University. Before returning to graduate school, he was involved in advocacy initiatives in the non-profit community for six years including a year of service with Americorps VISTA. His research is focused on the field of sport-for-development and social justice initiatives with sport components, as well as on non-traditional sports and their impact on participants.

## Marlene A. Dixon

Marlene Dixon (PhD, The Ohio State University) is an Associate Professor and Fellow in the M.G. Seay Centennial Professorship for Education at The University of Texas at Austin. Her primary research interests include the multilevel factors that impact the work-family interface and enduring involvement in sport careers. Her work has been published in a variety of journals including the *Journal of Sport Management*, *Sport Management Review*, *Research Quarterly for Exercise and Sport*, and *Quest*.

## Michael B. Edwards

Michael B. Edwards (PhD, North Carolina State University) is an assistant professor in the Department of Recreation, Park and Tourism Sciences at Texas A&M University. His research interests center on social inequality in children's access to spaces and programs for physically active leisure and recreation. He is particularly interested in the policy- and community-level barriers to sport and recreation participation for minority and low-income children and adolescents living in rural areas.

## Michael Hutchinson

Michael Hutchinson (PhD, Texas A&M University) is an Assistant Professor at the University of Memphis. His academic research interests include branding and internal marketing strategy, and he has received external funding from various sources, including the Knight Foundation and the North American Society for Sport Management.

## Chanho Kang

*Chanho Kang* is a doctoral student in the Division of Sport Management at Texas A&M University, where he also received his master's degree in Sport Management. Before he came to U.S to study, he was a sport marketer for 5 years in Korea. His primary research interests are in the areas of marketing and consumer behavior.

## Woojun Lee

*Woojun Lee* is a doctoral student at Texas A&M University, where he also received his Master's degree in Sport Management. He serves as a graduate assistant in the Laboratory for Diversity in Sport. His academic research interests include diversity in sport and recreation organizations, with a primary focus on race and gender issues in sport.

## Brian P. McCullough
Brian McCullough (PhD, Texas A&M University) is an Assistant Professor of Sport Management at Bowling Green State University. His research interests are in the areas of organizational behavior and institutional theory, with primary focus on the environmental management and impact of sport organizations.

## E. Nicole Melton
E. Nicole Melton (PhD, Texas A&M University) is an assistant professor at Seattle University. Her research interests include gender and sport, specifically the gendered nature of sport organizations and its consequences.

## Calvin Nite
Calvin Nite (PhD, Texas A&M University) is an Assistant Professor of Sport Management at Texas Tech University. His primary research interests focus on management issues in intercollegiate athletics and how those issues affect student-athletes.

## Michael Regan
Michael Regan is a doctoral student in the Department of Sociology at Texas A&M University, having previously earned two degrees at California State University-Hayward. His research is in the area of diversity, with a particular emphasis on gender and race.

## Melanie L. Sartore-Baldwin
Melanie L. Sartore-Baldwin (PhD, Texas A&M University) is an Assistant Professor of Sport Management at East Carolina where she teaches courses in Sport Management and Sport Studies. Her primary areas of research are that of sex and gender issues, sexual orientation and sexual prejudice, and weight discrimination.

## Emily Sparvero
Emily Sparvero (PhD, The University of Texas at Austin) is an assistant professor in the School of Tourism and Hospitality Management at Temple University. Her research is focused on the ways in which communities can leverage sport events and teams to achieve public policy goals. She has also studied the economic impact of sport events, with a particular emphasis on marathons and other mass participation sport events.

## D. Scott Waltemyer

D. Scott Waltemyer (PhD, Texas A&M University) is an Assistant Professor in the Department of Health and Human Performance at Texas A&M University-Commerce. His research interests span the areas of organizational behavior and organizational theory within sport organizations, with a focus in the area of small group processes and performance, leadership, and group member attitudes.

## Stacy Warner

Stacy Warner (PhD, The University of Texas at Austin) is an Assistant Professor of Sport Management at East Carolina University. Her research is primarily focused on the roles that sport and sport culture play in the lives of individuals through communities, families, social networks, and work environments. Additionally, Warner has acquired work experience in many facets of the sports industry. She often utilizes these experiences to critically examine sport and consider how sport *can* have a positive impact on the life quality of individuals.

## Jon Welty Peachey

Jon Welty Peachey (PhD, University of Connecticut) is an Assistant Professor of sport management at Texas A&M University. His research centers upon sport for social change and development, organizational change, and developing effective and inclusive leadership strategies for sport organizations. He has over 12 years of experience working in the international sport context, including serving as vice president of international operations with the Institute for International Sport, a worldwide non-profit organization using sport to effect positive social change.

# TABLE OF CONTENTS

# PREFACE

Sport and physical activity are wildly popular in North America, and for that matter, around the world. For evidence, simply go to a university's recreation center on any given evening. Inside, you will witness hundreds of students exercising on treadmills, lifting weights, playing pick-up basketball games, challenging one another in squash and racquetball, climbing rock walls, running on the track, participating in spin classes, swimming laps in a pool, and taking part in yoga or Pilates. Outside, you might observe people playing water volleyball, participating in a game of beach volleyball, or taking part in any number of intramural contests — ranging from flag football to Frisbee golf. Or, as another example, simply drive by athletic fields on a given weekend, and you will see children — both girls and boys — participating in soccer, baseball, flag football, or other contests. Not only are the children participating, but their parents, siblings, friends, and neighbors are oftentimes cheering for them on the sidelines.

As these examples illustrate, sport and physical activity have become central parts of our daily lives. Not only do people actively participate in sport and physical activity, but we are also inundated with information about such activities in newspapers, on the Internet, in magazines, and on television. The primacy of sport and physical activity has resulted in the academic study of those endeavors, including the management of, psychological dynamics associated with, and sociological analysis of sport and physical activity. The focus of this book, *Sociology of Sport and Physical Activity (2nd ed.)*, is on the latter academic pursuit.

We have expanded this edition of the book, including a variety of chapters authored by scholars from around the world. The first several chapters focus on introductory material, with a discussion of the foundations of the sociology of sport and physical activity (Cunningham and Welty Peachey), sociological theory and research (Cunningham), and ethics (Singer). We then move into a examination of sport and physical activity in society, with chapters concentrating on sport and health (Edwards and Casper), sport and the economy (Sparvero), international sport (Broan, Kang, and Lee), sport and the media (Melton), the environmental impact of sport and physical activity (McCullough), sport for social change and development (Welty Peachey and Cohen), and deviance (Waltemyer). This section is followed by chapters focusing on sport and institutions, including sport and community (Warner), youth sport (Dixon, Burden, and Newhouse-Bailey), and intercollegiate sport (Nite). In the final section, the authors investigate the relationship among sport, physical activity, and culture, including chapters focusing on race (Singer), gender (Sartore-Baldwin), social class (Chaplin), power (Carter-Francique and Regan), and religion (Nite and Hutchinson). The book is intended for upper-level undergraduate and graduate students. We also expect, though, that coaches, administrators, fitness instructors, physical education teachers, and any other person who is involved in sport or physical activity will benefit from the text's information.

## Special Features

Each chapter has several features that should aid in the learning process. These include (a) *learning objectives* at the beginning of each chapter, (b) *discussion questions* that instructors can use to stimulate conversations concerning the chapter topic, and (c) *supplemental readings*, which people can consult to gain a deeper understanding of the chapter content.

## Acknowledgements

Anyone who has written or edited a book knows that many people contribute to the final product. Such is certainly the case with this book. We are thankful to the many colleagues who agreed to write chapters for the book. Not only have they been a joy with whom to work, but their keen insights and gripping analyses of sport and physical activity make for engaging reading. We are also thankful to the many students with whom we have worked over the years. Not only have we enjoyed our interactions with them in the classroom, our offices, and labs, but we have learned much from them. These interactions have certainly informed our writings in this book. Finally, we thank the many persons who helped review and edit the chapters, including Kylie Easterling and Mandy Pryor.

George B. Cunningham & John N. Singer

*Editors*

# CHAPTER 1

# FOUNDATIONS OF THE SOCIOLOGY OF SPORT AND PHYSICAL ACTIVITY

George B. Cunningham and Jon Welty Peachey

*\*\*\**

**Learning Objectives**

After reading this chapter, you should be able to:

1. Define sport, physical activity, and sociology.
2. Differentiate between sociology and other related disciplines.
3. Discuss the ways in which sport is a microcosm of society.

## INTRODUCTION

Sport and physical activity are deeply embedded in American society. People routinely engage in these activities, either as participants, by talking about them with friends and family, or by watching them as spectators. Sport's cultural significance in the US is perhaps best illustrated by examining people's behaviors during mega-events, like the Super Bowl. According to Stephen Messenger (2010), 20 million Americans attend Super Bowl parties. These get-togethers take time to plan, as evidenced by the data showing that people plan their Super Bowl parties over 1 month in advance, and an average of 17 people attend each gathering. But, not all of these people are necessarily football fans; instead, 40% of all Super Bowl viewers are not football fans at all, but attend the events for social reasons. Finally, people collectively spend 10 million hours preparing food for the big game.

As this example illustrates, sport and physical activity represent some of the most pervasive cultural phenomena in North America, and they represent the focus of this book. Specifically, we adopt a sociological focus to critically examine the role of sport and physical activity in society and the role they play in people's lives. The purpose of this chapter is to provide a foundation of that discussion. In doing so, define key constructs, outline to utility of adopting a sociological lens to study sport and physi-

1

cal activity, and close by discussing the ways in which sport and physical activity represent a microcosm of society.

## KEY TERMS AND DEFINITIONS

### Sport and Physical Activity

People oftentimes have their own implicit definition of sport. By this, we mean that though they might not have formal classification schemes in place, they have a general understanding of what activities they consider sport. After all, sport represents a prominent institution, and people engage in, read about, discuss, or view it on a nearly daily basis. Despite this general understanding, few people have a formal definition of sport, and because of this, disagreements often emerge concerning what is a sport and what is not. For instance, while most people consider soccer a sport, the water becomes murkier when considering other activities, like horseracing, racecar driving, rhythmic gymnastics, or professional wrestling. In fact, television channels devoted to sports news and programming, like ESPN, will televise events that few might consider sport, like Spelling Bee competitions. So in what process does one engage to demarcate some of these activities as sport, but others as something else? For that matter, if soccer is considered a sport, is this true across all contexts? Certainly one would consider elite soccer competitions, such as those that occur at the FIFA World Cup, as sport, but what about 5 year-olds kicking the soccer ball in their back yard?

Questions such as these have prompted scholars to develop formal definitions of sport. According to these authors:

- *Sport* is "an institutionalized competitive activity involving two or more opponents and stressing physical exertion by serious competitors who represent or are part of formally organized associations" (Nixon, 1984 p. 13).
- *Sport* is "a competitive activity involving at least two competitors, requiring physical skill, following formal rules, and occurring within a formal organizational framework" (LeUnes, 2008, p. 5).
- *Sport* represents "well-established, officially governed competitive physical activities in which participants are motivated by internal and external rewards" (Coakley, 2009, p. 6).

2

We can draw several points from these definitions. First, sport is physical in nature. It involves physical exertion and participants demonstrating physical skill. This requirement rules out some activities that might be observed on sport-focused television programming, such as playing chess or competing in a spelling bee. Second, sport involves at least two people. Thus, a woman who runs 6 miles each morning before starting her day is not engaging in sport because she is not competing against others. Third, and related to the previous point, sport involves competition. This element not only excludes the woman who starts each day with a morning run, but it also excludes non-competitive forms of physical activity, such as professional wrestling. Fourth, sport is bound by formal rules of competition. The types and universality of rules might vary, ranging from guidelines set by international governing bodies to those set by a local parks and recreation department for their leagues. In either case, the rules and policies shape the nature of participation and provide boundaries for appropriate behaviors. This means that persons competing in the adult kickball league sponsored by the Austin Recreation Center are engaging in sport, while children causally kicking a ball to one another in their front yard are not.

In addition to considering the definition of sport, it is also instructive to examine other forms of movement. Consider the following:

- *Physical activity* refers to "any body movement produced by skeletal muscles and resulting in a substantial increase over the resting energy expenditure" (Carron et al., 2003, p. 9)
- *Exercise* represents "a form of leisure physical activity (as opposed to occupational or household physical activity) that is undertaken in order to achieve a particular objective (e.g., improved appearance, improved cardiovascular fitness, reduced stress, fun) (Lox et al., 2010, p. 4).

Inclusion of these terms allows for a broader investigation of how people are physically active and how doing so impacts their lives. That is, rather than limiting the examination to formal, competitive physical activities involving two or more people (i.e., focusing exclusively on sport), considering physical activity and exercise allows for examination into a variety of ways in which people are active. This includes teenagers playing a game of pick-up basketball, a girl swimming laps in the evenings, or an older adult who participates in Pilates three times a week. All of these represent certain forms of physical activity and warrant sociological analysis. As such, the chapters in this book evaluate the influence of both sport and physical activity in society.

## Prevalence of Sport and Physical Activity

Sport is one of the most popular institutions in American society. As one illustrative example, consider the media attention devoted to major sport events, like the Super Bowl, Olympics, and World Cup, among others. According to the Nielson Company, an organization that tracks how many Americans watch different televisions shows, the 2010, 2011, and 2012 Super Bowls were the most watched broadcasts in US history. The prevalence of televised sport is seen elsewhere, too: multiple television stations are solely devoted to covering sports, and the major broadcast stations in the US (ABC, CBS, FOX, and NBC) all dedicate much of their weekend programming to sports.

But television represents just one element of sports' media reach. Thousands of Internet websites focus exclusively on an array of sport and physical activity topics, including official team information, player profiles, education (e.g., swimming techniques, coaching strategies), college recruiting, and fantasy sports, to name but a few. As a testament to the popularity of these sites, Dwyer and Kim (2011) report that there are over 20 million fantasy sports users. Finally, large portions of print media are committed to sport and physical activity. As one well-known example, the *USA Today*, which has the largest circulation in America, reserves a quarter of the news coverage to sport and physical activity.

Not only is the media coverage substantial, but so too is the amount spent on sport and physical activity. As noted in Chapter 5, Milano and Chelladurai (2011) calculated what consumers spent for products and services related to sport and physical activity in the US. They estimated that this spending, what they term the gross domestic sport product, ranged from $168.5 to $207.5 billion in 2005. This makes sport one of the top industries in the nation. Furthermore, most of the economic activity comes from physical activity and exercise endeavors, or what Chelladurai (2009) refers to as participant sport. The latter point further illustrates the importance of considering the influence of both sport *and* physical activity in society.

## Sociology

The focus of this book is to examine sport and physical activity from a sociological perspective, and therefore it is important to define "sociology." Several definitions are available:

- *Sociology* "is the scientific discipline that describes and explains human social organization" (Eitzen & Sage, 2009, p. 3).
- *Sociology* "is the study of social worlds that people create, organize, maintain, and change through their relationships with one another" (Coakley, 2009, p. 4).
- *Sociology* "is the analysis of the structure of social relationships as constituted by social interaction" (Abercrombie et al., 2000, p. 333).

Several themes appear in these definitions. First, sociology is an academic discipline aimed at scientifically studying phenomena. Second, sociologists examine people and the institutions these people create. By institutions, we are referring to the practices that are continually repeated, that are shaped by prevailing norms, values, and standards, and that have special meaning to those in a particular context. Finally, and related to the previous point, researchers adopting a sociological lens primarily study social issues and the manner in which people engage and interact with one another.

Sociology is distinct from other, related scientific disciplines, such as biology and psychology. Biologists frequently focus on people and their behaviors but do so by examining factors internal to the individual, such as their genetics or physiological makeup. Psychologists, on the other hand, also examine people, their attitudes, and behaviors, but do so by focusing on mental processes and how these influence people's attitudes, values, and actions.

To better understand the nature of these differences, let us consider how biologists, psychologists, and sociologists might study a common topic in sport: sexual orientation. The biologist might examine this topic by considering how genetic and physiological factors are associated with one's sexual orientation. For instance, Hamer et al. (1993) observed that DNA markers on the X chromosome genetically influenced men's sexual orientation. Psychologists might approach the topic by focusing on people's attitudes and different mental processes. For instance, some researchers have argued that conceptualizing sexual orientation as only reflective of one's sexual partners is overly limited and does not take into account other, meaningful factors. Instead, they suggest that one's sexual orientation is multidimensional, consisting of behaviors, attractions, fantasies, and self-image (Gosiorek & Weinrich, 1991). Finally, unlike biological and psychological examinations of sexual orientation, with a focus on factors internal to the individual, a sociological approach would draw attention to cultural, environmental, and societal factors. For instance, Sartore and Cunningham (2010) observed how an organization's culture, policies, history, and leadership all served to stigmatize lesbians and heterosexual women presumed to be lesbian.

To better understand the nature of sociology, consider the three basic assumptions that undergird sociologists' outlook toward the world (Eitzen & Sage, 2009). First, sociologists view people as social beings by their very nature. Consider that children enter the world completely dependent upon others for their survival and that throughout time, people have routinely found it more advantageous to cooperate with one another in order to provide basic functions, such as defense, food, and shelter. Second, maintain that people are largely socially determined, as they are products of their social environment. Various socialization agents, including friends, family, the church, and the media, among others, shape people's attitudes and their behaviors. Third, sociologists suggest that people create, shape, and challenge the social contexts in which they are situated. That is, social groups of all types, such as families, corporations, and societies, are formed by their members. As the group members interact with one another, they continually sustain and, through human agency, change their social environments.

## Sociology of Sport and Physical Activity

Given this background, we can define the *sociology of sport and physical activity* as a subsection of sociology that studies sport and physical activity as social phenomena. Research in the sociology of sport and physical activity seeks to answer a number of questions, including:

- Why are some sports valued and promoted, while others are not? How does this vary by society?
- What are some of the ethical issues associated with sport and physical activity? How does these issues impact subsequent participation opportunities?
- What is the economic significance of sport and physical activity, and how does sport serve to reinforce classism?

- How do the media shape people's perceptions of sport and physical activity?
- How do sport and sport participants affect the environment, and what can they do to lessen any negative impact?
- What is the influence of being physically active on people's development, health, and well-being?
- How does sport and physical activity impact one's notion of masculinity and femininity, sexual orientation, class, race, religion, and politics?

These questions, and others like them, are more easily addressed by considering sport and physical activity as social constructions, or "parts of the social world that are created by people as they interact with one another under particular social, political, and economic conditions" (Coakley, 2009, p. 12). By adopting such a lens, one comes to see that participants, spectators, coaches, administrators, and all other persons involved collectively shape notions of sport and physical activity. How people think about sport and physical activity is not static; instead, these notions are created and recreated within a particular cultural milieu and, thus, intersect with other portions of society.

In short, studying sport and physical activity from a sociological perspective requires people to thoughtfully and critically analyze these social phenomena. It means moving beyond simply analyzing box scores or win-loss records to consider how sport, as a social construction, shapes people's lives and influences their well-being. It also means identifying prevalent issues within sport and physical activity and considering the controversies embedded in this context. In doing so, people can be better informed about the impact of sport and physical activity on society.

Adopting such a lens, while fruitful, is not always comfortable. Sport and physical activity are highly valued in society, and in many ways, represent microcosms of society — a point we highlight in the following section. People are also strongly attached to sport, and this means that they might see the articulation of sport's faults or shortcomings as a personal affront. As an illustrative example, there is considerable evidence that, relative to boys and men, girls and women are under-represented in sport, receive fewer resources for their athletic endeavors, and are trivialized in the media, with an emphasis on their physical appearance rather than their athletic talents (for an overview, see Acosta & Carpenter, 2012; Cunningham & Sagas, 2008). These patterns suggest that structural changes are needed: not only should girls and women receive more re-sources and participation opportunities, but perhaps more importantly, people's beliefs about who should and *should not* participate in sport and physical activity require alteration. This position, while embraced by some, is frequently dismissed by men. After all, sport was created by men, for men, and men have historically had the most power and privi-lege in this context. Thus, it is hardly surprising that men will oftentimes point to alternative explanations (e.g., women have little interest in sport and physical activity) to justify the current structure and distribution of resources.

As the previous example illustrates, adopting a sociological perspective can spur controversies and debate. But while sometimes making people feel uneasy, these discussions are fruitful, as they bring to light the social implications of sport and physical activity and how these activities influ-ence participants and spectators. In the following section, we continue this dialogue by considering the ways in which sport and physical activi-ty serve as a microcosm of society.

## SPORT AND PHYSICAL ACTIVITY AS A MICROCOSM OF SOCIETY

As we previously mentioned, sport is a microcosm of society. By this, we mean that sport is a window into, or a mirror which reflects the underly-ing values, beliefs and assumptions of a cultural group. Sport shows us what we as a society are committed to, and what our motivations are (Fahey, 2008). As an institution, sport provides a convenient laboratory, in many ways, for researchers to examine societal values, socialization, bureaucracy and other structures and processes that exist at the societal level. Whether examining the attitudes and behavior of professional sport fans, or the behavior of parents at youth soccer league matches, the types of sports, the way in which they are organized, who participates and who is excluded, all offer clues about the nature of society (Eitzen & Sage, 2009).

### Sport and Societal Values

Sports are an integral aspect of the social and cultural contexts in which people live, and they engage more people in a shared experience than any other institution or cultural activity today (Coakley, 2009). Since the 19th century, academicians have contended that modern sport is infused with societal values, and that sport then promotes and reinforces these value systems (Breivik, 1998; Digel, 1988). As Coakley (2009) commented, "American values clearly affect American sport" (p. 58). Values are "the criteria people use to select and justify actions and to evaluate people (including the self) and events" (Schwartz, 1992, p. 1). They (a) are beliefs that transcend specific situations, (b) pertain to desirable end states or behaviors, (c) guide selection or evaluation of behavior or events, and (d) vary in terms of relative importance (Schwartz, 1992). They are what we deem to be worthwhile, interesting, excellent, desirable and important (DeSensi & Rosenberg, 2003).

Essentially, the moral values that are the constitutive elements of sport are expressions and reflections of the basic moral values of society (Russell, 2007). Our values are a social construction of reality, whereby our value systems are not independent and eternal, but ever changing, and created by human interaction in societies (Berger & Luckman, 1966). It follows that individuals in a society are then socialized through sports, as the structure and values of sport influence individuals' development and moral attitudes, for good or bad (Nucci & Young-Shim, 2005). As such, the sociology of sport and physical activity is important because people use sport to reaffirm ideas and beliefs that are important to them and widely held by others (Coakley, 2009). Because of this, an attack upon sport is often viewed as an attack upon society itself (Eitzen & Sage, 2009).

Our focus here will be on the predominant American values that are mirrored in sport, consistent with Eitzen and Sage (2009). These values are success, competition, valued means to achieve, progress, materialism, and external conformity. It must be recognized that values are culturally derived, and sport will mirror values reflective of the society in which it operates. In other words, the American culture places a high degree of value on competition and materialism, which are not emphasized as much in more cooperative Asian cultures such as Japan and Korea. Thus, the values which sport mirrors may be different in America than in more cooperative societies. We must also note that because sport reflects society, society and its values will influence sport in both good and bad ways (Breivik, 1998). Both good and bad actors and actions will be found in sport as they are in society. For instance, as will be described below, one of the negative consequences of American society's high value on competition is the win-at-all-costs mentality that pervades sport at all levels, resulting in deviance and various illegal activities and scandals. This win-at-all costs focus is at the root of the scandals involving performance enhancing drugs in professional sport, the recruiting violations in collegiate athletics, and the highly competitive professional sport model that is infiltrating youth sport resulting in parental misconduct and youth burnout. Nevertheless, for good or bad, sport is a microcosm of society, and because of this, the sociology of sport and physical activity is vitally important.

*Success*

In a competitive culture such as the U.S., society frames success and excellence as aspects that must be displayed and measured in the constant pursuit of human excellence (Russell, 2007). We value the self-made person, or the individual who has achieved money and status through his or her efforts in a highly competitive system (Eitzen & Sage, 2009). The metrics we use to gauge success are often economic in focus, such as income, personal wealth, and the amount of possessions that we attain. We idolize self-made figures in the business world such as Warren Buffet, Oprah Winfrey, and Samuel Walton, or National Basketball Association (NBA) athletes such as Shaquille O'Neil and the all-time great Michael Jordan, who have parleyed success on the field or court into material gain (e.g., luxury homes and cars, expensive jewelry). In fact, the most striking aspect of American culture could be that we identify standards of personal excellence with competitive occupational achievement (Williams, 1970).

The focus on competition and success is also seen in sport, where there is a preoccupation with winning (Woods, 2007). Americans want winners, whether they are in school, politics, business, sport, or any other endeavor, and this aim to win is reflective of society's value system (Russell, 2007). Thus, in sport, most persons who participate glorify winning. We oftentimes consider athletes and coaches who fail to win the "big" one as failures (Woods, 2007). Do we really ever remember who the runner-ups were in a given year in the Super Bowl, World Series, or National Collegiate Athletic Association (NCAA) men's and women's basketball championships? Coaches and sport administrators, then, make it a priority to socialize their athletes with the value of winning, and reinforce this with rewards, status, praise, honor, and "perks" (Eitzen & Sage, 2009). This demand for winners is found at all levels of sport, from professional to grass roots community recreation leagues for children and youth, as evidenced by the mammoth attention given to the Little League World Series, the Gatorade "Punt, Pass, and Kick" contests, and other national sport competitions for youth.

*Competition*

Going hand in hand with success, American society values competition as a means to succeed and achieve. The moral values associated with competition support, stand for, and express familiar values in all institutions that exist to promote human excellence, and hence reflect societal values (Russell, 2007). Competition infuses almost all aspects of American society, from the corporate world to schools to the Boy and Girl Scouts to our sporting pursuits, resulting in a "survival of the fittest" mentality. Competition selects out those not fit to succeed or achieve, and thus, becomes synonymous with American society. Within this environment, there is subsequently a tendency to evaluate individuals based on their accomplishments, rather than on their personality, character and other more human qualities (Eitzen & Sage, 2009). Competitive sport, as it evolved in the 20th century, came to embody our society's competitive spirit and values, which then had bearing on how sport in North America was organized (Breivik, 1998).

However, as a result of the competitive process and the "survival of the fittest" approach to life and sport, people oftentimes reward winning disproportionally. When winning thus becomes the end all and be all, when winning becomes everything, coaches and players can turn to forms of cheating and deviance to achieve success and consequently take advantage of others in order to win, just as individuals and businesses outside of sport engage in illegal activities fueled by the drive to win-at-all-costs (Eitzen & Sage, 2009). This win-at-all-costs philosophy distorts our sense of values, and individuals believe that the ends justify the means. When this happens, we see athletes tempted to use performance-enhancing drugs to gain a competitive edge, coaches engaging in illegal recruiting practices to sign the star prodigy, and parents pushing their children beyond what is normal to succeed so that they can secure that college athletics scholarship. Thus, in a competitive society, competition is what drives us in life and sport, and because we have difficulty coming in second, we often engage in illegal and inappropriate activities to ensure that we do indeed finish first.

*The Valued Means to Achieve*

A third manner in which sport mirrors societal values is that sport embodies the characteristics and mechanisms reflecting the desired means to achieve that permeate a given society. For instance, in American society, there are three related and highly valued means to succeed (Eitzen &

Sage, 2009). The first is the Puritan ideal of hard work. We value individuals who are industrious and make something of themselves out of nothing, such as the American story of an immigrant who came to this country with nothing and then through hard work and sacrifice, became a wealthy individual. On the other hand, we denigrate those who do not. Americans tend to believe that poor people deserve to be poor because they do not work as hard as middle- or upper- class individuals. Secondly, American society believes that a pathway to success is through continual striving for excellence. We believe that one should never give up, and that economic success is always possible (i.e., attainment of the American dream). Finally, deferred gratification is also valued as a means to achieve in American society. By this, we mean that individuals have a willingness to forsake immediate pleasure for the promise of later rewards. A successful individual in the U.S. is thus one who has the drive to stay in school, work two jobs, or go to night school for the prospect of attaining future rewards (Eitzen & Sage, 2009).

Sport, then, mirrors these societal values of means to achieve, as athletes presumably obtain individual achievements in sport through hard work, perseverance and sacrifice. Essentially, the American work ethic is the sport ethic (Eitzen & Sage, 2009). Sport embodies the most powerful principles of achievement-oriented, competitive societies. As Digel (1998) asserts, "The principle of achievement as it exists in the realm of sport permits an almost utopistically pure presentation of competitive achievement such as cannot be found in any other spheres of life" (p. 180). Sport symbolically represents both individual motivation and achievement, and it is this principle of achievement and continual striving for excellence, which is the mechanism for the distribution of rewards, both in society and in sport (Digel, 1988; Woods, 2007). The top performers in sport are fueled and rewarded by the societal demand for increased achievement, and coaches promote the conservative American values of hard work, discipline, perseverance, and respect for authority (Woods, 2007). As such, competitive sport is a window into the valued means to achieve in a society.

*Progress*

Another way in which sport reflects societal values is through its emphasis on progress. Societies will differ with regards to their focus on the past, present, or future. American society places paramount importance upon the future. While not totally devaluing the past or present, Americans give greater emphasis to the future and progress, to obtaining a better job, a brighter future, a bigger home in a nice neighborhood, a college education for the children, and the like (Eitzen & Sage, 2009). Americans are not satisfied with the status quo, and continually strive for growth (i.e.., bigger is better). However, while progress connotes change, there are some aspects of society which many feel should not be changed, such as the political system, economic system, and fundamental American values. Thus, many do not favor radical changes in the system.

Within the sport context, coaches, athletes, fans, the media and other stakeholders place a high degree of value on progress. Athletes and teams strive for continual improvement and progress towards goals, through setting records, winning more games and championships, or mastering new techniques to enhance performance. Society deems those who do not progress as failures, and thus we see coaches fired routinely for failing to have a winning record, or athletes traded because of poor performance in a given year. Therefore, the values of the sport system are rooted in society's focus on progress and on the rewards attainable to those who succeed and achieve.

*Materialism*

A fifth societal value mirrored in sport is the overwhelming emphasis on materialism. Americans believe that hard work and effort should result in increased economic standing, income, and in the acquisition and consumption of goods and services exceeding our basic needs of nutrition, medical care, shelter and transportation (Eitzen & Sage, 2009). All of this indicates measures of success in the competitive struggle, and are aspects of what Americans consider to be the "good life." The acceptance of materialism is synonymous with the American dream (McDorman et al., 2006). Thus, the goal for many is to accumulate possessions that bring status and provide for a better way of life. This is realized in several ways, including our choices of homes, clothing styles, boats, prestigious neighborhoods in which we live, season tickets, and country club memberships, among others (Eizten & Sage, 2009).

Sport, then, embodies this emphasis on materialism, is integrally tied to the material and economic conditions of society, and reinforces these materialistic value systems (Breivik, 1998; Coakley, 2009). In the 19th and 20th centuries, as sport became more businesslike, the corporate model began infiltrating the organization of sport franchises and governing bodies (Woods, 2007). We see this evidenced by the fact that college and professional teams are driven by money concerns, such as lucrative television deals, professional teams relocating to more economically viable cities, and by the focus on profit as the bottom line. Athletes are also motivated by material considerations, and accumulating more money, perks and other rewards seems to be the mercenary motivation of many athletes rather than a pure love of the game or loyalty to the team and fans (DeSensi & Rosenberg, 2003; Eitzen & Sage, 2009). Free agency has resulted in multi-million dollar contracts, and the appeal of materialism for athletes is expressed in symbols such as contractual bonuses and huge television endorsements. The problem here is that these large payouts may cause athletes to lose perspective on the meaning of money and even complain about their "meager" salaries as compared to others (McDorman et al., 2006). Fans, too, are not immune to the trappings of materialism, as we are attracted to plush stadiums with the latest amenities (such as the billion dollar Dallas Cowboys Stadium), and by athletes and teams playing in contests with huge sums of money at stake. As such, materialism is all pervasive, in American society as well as sport.

*External Conformity*

Finally, sport also mirrors society with regards to the value the institution places on external conformity. Societies cannot tolerate total freedom by individuals, so to avoid disorder, societies socialize individuals into acceptable beliefs and practices (Eitzen & Sage, 2009). As individuals strive to be successful in the eyes of others, they seek validation through shared standards of achievement or conformity. Society, then, expects conformity, and not deviance. We can segment conformity in American society into two levels. On one level, Americans conform to the official expectations of the nation, state or community through the customs and laws. Deviations from these expectations are punished. On another level, individuals conform to expectations of closely-knit groups, such as families, peers or work groups. However, the bureaucratic trend in American society also forces individuals to conform. Bureaucracy is rational and values conformity to rules and procedures in order to accomplish organizational objectives. The interests of the organization supersede those of the individual. In fact, the values that emerge from this hierarchal form of organization have become core values of American society (Eitzen & Sage, 2009).

Within the sport context, conformity is highly valued. Coaches expect behavioral conformity of athletes to promote team unity and achieve team objectives. Coaches demand that players dress and speak in certain ways, behave in certain ways, conduct themselves appropriately in front of the media or on social media outlets, and expect the subordination of the self to team success, just as in all bureaucratic structures which reflect society's value on external conformity. In addition, athletes and players are expected to accept the authority of the coach without question. Those who challenge the coach's authority are labeled as insubordinate and are soon traded or dismissed from the team. This is another aspect of external conformity found in sport (Eizten & Sage, 2009). Athletes should not challenge the systems, rules, and power structures of a coach or of sport in general, or they are considered deviant. Athletes are, in essence, viewed as instruments to achieve organizational goals, as a means to an end.

## The Power of Sport to Shape Values and Change

Before concluding, we must recognize the fact that sports also have the potential to affect and change societal values. The social environment shapes members of society, but they can also change that environment. This process of human agency occurs when individuals actively shape social life by adapting to, negotiating with, and changing social structures (Eitzen & Sage, 2009). Sport and its value systems can influence society in both good and bad ways (Breivik, 1998), and sport can be a platform to point for the need for change in society (Woods, 2007). For instance, there is evidence that sport can foster the development of social capital. Social capital is the "features of social organization such as networks, norms, and social trust that can facilitate coordination and cooperation for mutual benefit" (Putnam, 1995, p. 66). Bonding social capital occurs when individuals form relationships with similar others (e.g., with peers, neighbors, individuals of the same social strata), whereas bridging social capital is when relationships and networks are formed with dissimilar others (e.g., with individuals from different social strata). An example of bridging social capital is when the homeless individuals playing on a soccer team through an intervention designed to use sport to help them get back on their feet, form close friendships with their volunteer coaches. These bridging relationships then help link the homeless players to other social services, such as housing, education and jobs (Welty Peachey et al., 2011).

Sport has been found to increase social capital and the social mobility among disadvantaged youth in the Netherlands (Spaaij, 2009) and to increase the social capital of homeless soccer players in the Homeless World Cup (Sherry, 2010). In addition to developing social capital, sport has been used in Northern Ireland to promote interaction and break down barriers between Protestant and Catholic youth (Woods, 2007); in Israel to foster cross-cultural acceptance between Palestinians and Jews (Sugden, 2006); in Cyprus to foster peace and understanding between Greek and Turkish Cypriots on this divided island (Lyras & Welty Peachey, 2011); and as a vehicle to combat urban unrest and juvenile delinquency in the U.S. and England (Coakley & Dunning, 2004). Thus, sports have the potential to influence social worlds and value systems, which is another reason why the sociological study of sport and physical activity is so vitally important.

As has been shown, the American value system influences the structure, operation, and performance of sport, and sport in turn reinforces and mirrors these values. Sport also reaffirms our beliefs and ideas about gender, race and class, and can also serve as a site to challenge dominant ideologies and values of a given society, pointing to the need for change. Therefore, because sport is a microcosm of society and also a potential site for change, the sociological study of sport and physical activity is of high importance to academicians, students, practitioners, and all stakeholders involved in the production and consumption of contemporary sport and athletics.

## CHAPTER SUMMARY

The purpose of this chapter was to provide an overview of the sociology of sport and physical activity. To do so, we first defined and discussed key terms, including sport, physical activity, and sociology. We then discussed how sociology differs from other disciplines, including biology and psychology. The chapter next turned to an analysis of how adopting a sociological lens to study sport and physical activity, while challenging at times, can provide novel insights. In the final section, we provided an outline of how sport and physical activity oftentimes serve as a microcosm of society. To do so, we focused on several values particularly salient within U.S. culture: success, competition, the valued means to achieve, progress, materialism, and external conformity.

## DISCUSSION QUESTIONS

1. How do you define sport, and how does this definition impact whether you consider certain activities as sport?
2. Do you differentiate between sport and physical activity? Why or why not?

3. We provided several definitions of sociology. Which definition do you prefer and why?
4. How does sociology differ from other disciplines also aimed at understanding people's behaviors, such as biology and psychology?
5. In what ways do sport and physical activity serve as a microcosm of society?
6. Are there aspects of sport and physical activity that are unique to that context and not necessarily observed in other segments of society? If so, why is this the case?

## RECOMMENDED READINGS

Abercrombie, N., Hill, S., & Turner, B.S. (2000). *The Penguin dictionary of sociology* (4th ed.). New York: Penguin Books. (A thorough reference that provides an overview of many sociological key terms.)

Eitzen, D.S., & Sage, G.H. (2009). *Sociology of North American Sport.* Boulder, CO: Paradigm Publishers. (An extensive text devoted to the sociological study of sport; includes information pertaining to sociological theory, violence, societal values, gender, race, politics, and religion, among others.)

*Sociology of Sport Journal.* (The official publication of the North American Society for the Sociology of Sport; published by Human Kinetics, this journal offers contemporary research and analysis related to sport in society.)

## REFERENCES

Abercrombie, N., Hill, S., & Turner, B.S. (2000). *The Penguin dictionary of sociology* (4th ed.). New York: Penguin Books

Acosta, R.V., & Carpenter, L.J. (2012). *Women in intercollegiate sport: A longitudinal study – thirty-five year update – 1977–2012.* Unpublished manuscript, Brooklyn College, Brooklyn, NY.

Berger, P.L., & Luckman, T. (1966). *The social construction of reality.* Garden City, NY: Doubleday.

Breivik, G. (1998). Sport in high modernity: Sport as a carrier of social values. *Journal of the Philosophy of Sport, XXV*, 103–118.

Carron, A. V., Hausenblas, H. A., & Estabrooks, P. A. (2003). *The psychology of physical activity.* New York: McGraw Hill.

Chelladurai, P. (2009). *Managing organizations for sport and physical activity* (3rd ed.). Scottsdale, AZ: Holcomb-Hathaway.

Coakley, J. (2009). *Sports in society: Issues and controversies.* New York: McGraw-Hill.

Coakley, J., & Dunning, E. (Eds.). (2004). *Handbook of sports studies*. London: Sage Publications.

Cunningham, G. B., & Sagas, M. (2008). Gender and sex diversity in sport organizations: Introduction to a special issue. *Sex Roles, 58*, 3-9.

DeSensi, J., & Rosenberg, D. (2003). *Ethics and morality in sport management*. Morgantown, WV: Fitness Information Technology, Inc.

Digel, H. (1988). The prospects of modern competitive sport. *International Review for the Sociology of Sport, 23*, 177-191.

Dwyer, B., & Kim, Y. (2011). For love or money Developing and validating a motivational scale for fantasy football participation. *Journal of Sport Management, 25*, 70-83.

Eitzen, D.S., & Sage, G.H. (2009). *Sociology of North American Sport*. Boulder, CO: Paradigm Publishers.

Fahey, J.F. (2008). Sport: Mirror of society. *Play True, 2*, 1-2.

Gosiorek, J. C., & Weinrich, J. D. (1991). The definition and scope of sexual orientation. In J. C. Gonsiorek & J. D. Weinrich (Eds.), *Homosexuality: Research implications for public policy* (pp. 1-12). Newbury Park: Sage.

Hamer, D. H., Hu, S., Magnuson, V. L., Hu, N., & Pattatucci, A. M. (1993). A linkage between DNA markers on the X chromosome and male sexual orientation. *Science, 261*, 321-327.

LeUnes, A. (2008). *Sport psychology* (4th ed.). New York: Psychology Press.

Lox, C. L., Martin Ginnis, K. A., & Petruzzello, S. J. (2010). *The psychology of exercise: Integrating theory and practice* (3nd ed.). Scottsdale, AZ: Holcomb-Hathaway.

Lyras, A., & Welty Peachey, J. (2011). Integrating sport-for-development theory and praxis. *Sport Management Review, 14*, 311-326.

McDorman, T., Casper, K., Logan, A., & McGinley, A. (2006). Where have all the heroes gone? An exploration of cultural therapy in *Jerry Maguire, For Love of the Game*, and *Any Given Sunday. Journal of Sport and Social Issues, 30*, 197-218.

Messenger, S. (2010, February 5). By the numbers: Super Bowl facts and figures. Retrieved from www.treehugger.com.

Milano, M., & Chelladurai, P. (2011). Gross domestic sport product: The size of the sport industry in the United States. *Journal of Sport Management, 25*, 24-35.

Nixon, H. L. (1984). *Sport and the American dream*. New York: Leisure Press.

Nucci, C., & Young-Shim, K. (2005). Improving socialization through sport: An analytic review of literature on aggression and sportsmanship. *Physical Educator, 62*(3), 123-130.

Putnam, R. D. (1995). Bowling alone: America's declining social capital. *Journal of Democracy, 6*, 65-78.

Russell, J.S. (2007). Broad internalism and the moral foundations of sport. In W.J. Morgan (Ed.), *Ethics in Sport* (pp. 51 – 66). Champaign, IL: Human Kinetics.

Sartore, M. L., & Cunningham, G. B. (2010). The lesbian label as a component of women's stigmatization in sport organizations: A comparison of two health and kinesiology departments. *Journal of Sport Management, 24*, 481-501.

Schwartz, S. H. (1992). Universals in the content and structure of values: Theoretical advances and empirical tests in 20 countries. In M. Zanna (Ed.), *Advances in experimental social psychology*, Vol. 25, (pp.1–65). New York: Academic Press.

Sherry, E. (2010). (Re)engaging marginalized groups through sport: The Homeless World Cup. *International Review for the Sociology of Sport, 45*, 59-71.

Spaaij, R. (2009). Sport as a vehicle for social mobility and regulation of disadvantaged urban youth. *International Review for the Sociology of Sport, 44*, 247-264.

Sugden, J. (2006). Teaching and playing sport for conflict resolution and coexistence in Israel. *International Review for the Sociology of Sport, 41*, 221-240.

Welty Peachey, J., Cohen, A., Borland, J., & Lyras, A. (2011). Building social capital: Examining the impact of Street Soccer USA on its volunteers. *International Review for the Sociology of Sport*. Advance online publication. doi: 10.1177/1012690211432068

Williams, R.M., Jr. (1970). *American society: A sociological interpretation*. New York: Knopf.

Woods, R. (2007). *Social issues in sport*. Champaign, IL: Human Kinetics.

# CHAPTER 2

## SOCIOLOGICAL THEORY AND RESEARCH

### George B. Cunningham

***

**Learning Objectives**

After reading this chapter, you should be able to:

1. Define theory and discuss its applicability to the study of sport and physical activity.
2. Discuss the major theories used to understand sport and physical activity in society.
3. Identify the different research methods for examining sport and physical activity in society.


## INTRODUCTION

Social and behavioral scientists who study sport and physical activity in society are, in many ways, different from other people with an interest in the topic. They engage in a specialized form of inquiry called *research*, and in most cases, they draw from and seek to contribute to *theory* to help them better understand phenomena. The process in which they engage is more specialized than that of a journalist or reporter (who might also conduct research for an article) and also moves beyond common sense. Rather, researchers engage in science and scientific inquiry.

Kerlinger and Lee (2000) articulated five ways in which science and common sense differ:

1. **The use of theory**. To be sure, non-scientists commonly use "theories" to explain behaviors, but their theories differ from those scientists employ. Lay theories are frequently based on unfounded explanations not subjected to scrutiny. Scientists, on the other hand, systematically build theories, and theories are routinely subjected to scrutiny to determine their merit. Of course, some non-scientists do not sometimes implicitly use theory (e.g., Rhoden, 2006), but this is the exception rather than the norm.

2. **Systematic and empirical examination.** Non-scientists test theories in selective fashion and against their own predispositions. In this case, a supportive anecdote is seen as evidence, while disconfirming evidence is dismissed as an anomaly. Scientists, on the other hand, test predictions and theories in laboratory settings or field research, and their findings are subjected to scrutiny from others.

3. **Alternative explanations.** Scientists try to rule out factors that can provide alternative explanations for their findings. They might achieve this through the study design (e.g., have a control group and an experimental group) or statistically (e.g., by controlling for possible extraneous factors in their analyses). On the other hand, non-scientists will generally accept information in accord with their views and dismiss other factors. For instance, if they believe African Americans are genetically (naturally) more athletic than Whites, they will ignore or dismiss instances where this is not the case.

4. **Relationships among factors.** Social scientists are concerned with understanding and explaining how factors are related to one another, and as a result, they deliberately and systematically examine and scrutinize those relationships. Laypersons might also be interested in relationships, but they do not investigate them in any sort of controlled or precise fashion.

5. **Explanations of observed phenomena.** Scientists examine factors that can be readily observed and are not concerned with metaphysical explanations. For instance, to suggest that someone wins a boxing match because of God or that it is wrong to express a particular view is to speak metaphysically. They shy away from such discourse because these sentiments cannot be tested or observed. Non-scientists are not concerned with these limitations, and thus, frequently engage in such debates.

As these examples illustrate, social and behavioral scientists explore issues much differently than do other persons. These differences are largely a function of theory and scientific research. As such, the purpose of this chapter is to explore these issues in greater depth. To do so, I start with an explanation of theory and why it is important to understand phenomena. I then move to a discussion of the prevailing theories scientists use to understand sport and physical activity in society. In the final section, I offer an overview of the different approaches to conducting research and the steps scientists take to conduct their studies.

# THEORY

## Definitional Considerations

As I have articulated elsewhere (Cunningham, in press), theory represents "a statement of constructs and their relationships to one another that explain how, when, why, and under what conditions phenomena take place." There are several elements of this definition that warrant more attention. First, theory consists of constructs and propositions. Constructs are approximated units that cannot readily be observed, while propositions represent the expected relationships among those constructs (see also Bacharach, 1989). For instance, suppose a researcher is interested in sexual prejudice toward coaches, where sexual prejudice represents the bias people hold against lesbian, gay, bisexual, and transgender (LGBT) individuals. In developing the study, the researcher decides to examine the role of religious fundamentalism, sexism, and contact with LGBT persons as the key factors that might influence this prejudice. In this example, sexual prejudice toward coaches, religious fundamentalism, sexism, and contact all represent constructs. The relationships among the constructs (e.g., that as religious fundamentalism increases, so too will prejudice toward LGBT coaches) represent propositions.

Articulating constructs and their relationships with one another is just part of the story, though. As previously noted, theory is concerned with explaining how, when, why, and under what conditions different activities take place. Thus, with respect to the aforementioned relationship between religious fundamentalism and sexual prejudice, the theoretician might build the argument as follows. Religious fundamentalists generally (a) hold conservative views toward their religious beliefs and other elements in their lives, (b) express bias against people who are different than they are, and (c) maintain authoritarian beliefs (Altemeyer & Hunsberger, 1992; Cohen et al., 2009). Furthermore, fundamentalist religious organizations, like Focus on the Family, hold that homosexuality is a sin, maintain that LGBT individuals pose a threat to children, and that one's sexual orientation is a choice that can be altered (Schulte & Battle, 2004). All of these factors suggest that fundamentalists might see homosexuality as wrong, and because of this perspective, are likely to harbor bias against sexual minority coaches. Indeed, social psychological researchers who have studied this issue have offered supportive evidence (see

Herek, 2009). Furthermore, recent research suggests that religious fundamentalists are most likely to express prejudice when they have few friends who are LGBT (Cunningham & Melton, in press). This is because having friends who are different from the self allows one to re-think preconceived notions and see how those friends actually have many similarities to the self. The influence of intergroup contact answers some of the questions related to when and under what conditions phenomena occur.

## Applicability

Theory's utility is widespread, as it has the potential to influence research, teaching, service, and practice. Theory is the cornerstone of good research. In fact, Kerlinger and Lee (2000) suggested that theory represents the fundamental aim of science. It is both useful and testable (Bacharach, 1989; van Knippenberg, 2011) and allows researchers to frame their research questions, develop their research methods, analyze their data, and interpret their findings. Some scholars have persuasively argued that without theory, one's ability to advance scientific understanding is questionable (Sutton & Staw, 1995).

Theory's utility is not limited to research, though. Rather, it has the potential to inform teaching, service, and practice. Kurt Lewin perhaps best illustrated these sentiments when he wrote, "there is nothing more practical than a good theory" (1952, p. 169). Good theories help people make sense of the world around them. Rather than seeing each phenomena as a unique case or adopting a trial and error approach to solving problems, people can use theories to help understand activities they observe or phenomena that occur within their sport organizations. For instance, people have used theory to help them better engage with students during after school programs (Bruening et al., 2010), provide classroom instruction (Dixon & Bruening, 2006), or examine athletic departments to better understand the effects of diversity (Cunningham, 2009).

One way scholars effectively utilize theory is in their relationships with industry professionals (Irwin & Ryan, in press). Specifically, researchers will sometimes partner with practitioners to solve industry-related problems, and in doing so, the researchers bring their scientific expertise and knowledge of theory with them so they can better address the issues at hand. This partnership benefits sport managers, as they are able to draw from the most recent scientific advances to combat the issues facing them. But the relationship is not one-sided; instead, the researchers also develop keen understandings of new troubles facing the industry, as well as the limitations of their existing theories and research methods. As a result, the researchers can then take this new knowledge with them to refine and reformulate their theories to better encapsulate what is taking place in the sport industry.

## USING THEORY TO UNDERSTAND SPORT AND PHYSICAL ACTIVITY IN SOCIETY

Given this background, I now provide an overview of the predominant theories used to understand sport and physical activity in society. Most sociologists and sport sociology textbooks focus solely on sociological theories. In this chapter, while I will address the most common sociological theories, I also include social psychological theories and theories found in the physical activity and community health literature. Doing so allows for a more robust understanding of people's experiences in the sport and physical activity context.

### Sociological Theories

There are many sociological theories applicable to the study of sport and physical activity in society. However, rather than reviewing them all individually, I aggregate them into four large groups: functionalism theory, conflict theory, critical theory, and interactionist theory (see Table 2.1).

*Functionalism Theory*

According to Eitzen and Sage (2009), functionalism "attributes to societies the characteristics of cohesion, consensus, cooperation, reciprocity, stability, and persistence" (p. 10). From this perspective, society is seen as a system of interdependent parts working together. Sport and physical activity are seen as parts of this system and serve to bring about positive change in society. People adopting a functionalist viewpoint see sport and physical activity as positively contributing to society and benefiting participants through the development of better health and wellness, character development, and the ability to learn life lessons.

As one example, the National Federation of State High School Associations (see www.nfhs.org) published a document outlining potential benefits of participating in high school activities, including athletics. According to the report, high school athletics (and other extracurricular activities):

Table 2.1: Theories Used to Understand Sport and Physical Activity in Society

| Class | Theory | Description |
|---|---|---|
| Sociological | Functionalism theory | Sport and physical activity positively contribute to society through improved psychological and physical well-being |
| | Conflict theory | Because of competition for resources, sport and physical activity contexts are sites where power and class differences are heightened. |
| | Critical theories | Focus on power and power relations in the sport and physical activity contexts, with a particular emphasis on human agency. |
| | Interactionist theory | Focuses on how people interact with their social environments, including sport and physical activity, to form their identities. |
| Social Psychological | Social categorization framework | Stemming from the social categorization process, people have greater affect toward and provide more help for people similar to the self. |
| | Similarity-attraction paradigm | People who are similar to one another are likely to be attracted to and express liking toward one another. |
| Physical Activity/Health | Social ecological theory | Individuals, their social environments, the physical environment in which they live, and policies set at the local, state, and national levels all influence people's attitudes and behaviors. |

- Support the academic missions of the schools;
- Are fundamentally educational in nature;
- Are associated with later life success;
- Represent a valuable part of the overall high school experience;
- Have a positive association with academic success in other areas, such as grades;
- Help fulfill basic student needs and minimize dropout rates; and
- Teach important life lessons.

As another example, the Centers for Disease Control and Prevention list several benefits of regular physical activity, including:

- Weight control;
- Reduced risk of cardiovascular disease, Type 2 diabetes, and some cancers;
- Strengthening of bones and muscles; and
- Improved mental health, one's ability to engage in everyday activities, and the probability of living a long life.

As these examples illustrate, several people and agencies adopt a functionalist approach when discussing the role of sport and physical activity in society. While they might acknowledge the potential detriments associated with sport and physical activity participation, they either dismiss these shortcomings or argue that they are outweighed by the benefits.

*Conflict Theory*

Whereas functionalism focuses on the benefits of sport and physical activity to society, conflict theorists examine the social processes that result in disharmony, social discord, and conflict (Eitzen & Sage, 2009). Drawing heavily from Marx, conflict theory puts a primacy on power, status, and privilege, and holds that people tend toward competition, not cooperation. Consequently, the struggle for resources results in unrest in society and between groups. Conflict theorists argue that people use their resources and privilege as ways to secure their standing in society, as a consequence, to subjugate others; hence, social structures and class differences are highlighted. This reproduction of status and privilege is sometimes achieved explicitly, such as through force. In most other situations, though, the means are more implicit in nature. Here, media images and social institutions, such as churches and schools, are used to reinforce the social structures that privilege some and disadvantage others.

The use of social institutions to promote specific ideologies is particularly effective because people will adhere to those ideological tenets even if they are contrary to their best interests. Marx referred to this as false consciousness.

As one example, consider the structure and funding of schools in the US—something that affects spending on student learning initiatives and their extracurricular activities, like athletics. In most states, property taxes are used to finance schools, and this creates a system of "haves" and "have-nots." To illustrate, suppose two districts have the same number of students, but one is in a largely affluent suburb, while the other is a dilapidated inner-city setting. The property values in the suburban district are likely to be higher than those in the inner-city setting; thus, taxed at the same rate, monies-per-student will be higher in the former district relative to the latter. Poorer districts can choose to increase revenues by increasing tax rates, but this doubly hurts the residents in that area—people who might already have difficulty meeting the taxation needs. Thus, the prevailing school financing system—one seen throughout most of the US—serves to privilege the wealthy and penalize the poor. Some states have developed "Robin Hood" systems to share money from richer districts with poorer ones, but such systems are largely panned by residents as "unfair" or, in other cases, have been ruled as unconstitutional. In either case, this form of institutional classism (see Lott, 2002; Lott & Bullock, 2007) is maintained.

*Critical theories*

Social and behavioral scientists also employ critical theories to understand phenomena. Like the theories previously discussed, critical theories also focus on power and power relations. But, unlike those grand theories, which put an emphasis on societal norms and structures, critical theories also focus on human agency, or the choices people make. Critical theorists recognize the influence of society, but seek to understand how "individuals and groups exert human agency as they cope with, adapt to, and change existing power relationships" (Eitzen & Sage, 2009, p. 12). Researchers adopting a critical lens frequently employ one of three theories: hegemony theory, feminist theory, or critical race theory.

*Hegemony Theory.* In drawing from conflict theory, hegemony theory focuses on social class and power, but in doing so, also highlights issues of ideologies and culture. Hegemony theory focuses on the steps the powerful elite take to ensure that their privilege is maintained. As Sage (1998) notes:

> A critical social perspective invites us to step back from thinking about sport merely as a place of personal achievement and entertainment and study sport as a cultural practice embedded in political, economic, and ideological formations. Relevant issues involve how sport is related to social class, race, gender, and the control, production, and distribution of economic and cultural power in the commodified sport industry. (p. 11)

As one example, consider popular methods of funding sports arenas and stadiums. Crompton et al. (2003) illustrate that, historically, individual team owners and groups financed their stadiums and arenas. However, starting in the 1970's, the public began to contribute more monies to these venues, such that public-private partnerships are now the norm in terms of stadium financing. In this case, private owners split the costs of multi-million (or even billion) dollar stadiums with the host community. There are certainly some benefits to having a major league franchise in a city (Crompton, 2004), and having a quality stadium in which to play is a key ingredient in keeping and attracting teams. Nevertheless, these financing partnerships are largely one-sided in favor of the wealthy owners. In most cases, the city does not reap any of the monies generated from the venues, such as revenues from luxury boxes, personal seat licenses, and the like. Yet, it is the taxpayers in that area who provide half of the construction funds. Furthermore, even though taxpayers foot half of the construction bill, high ticket prices often preclude them from attending sporting events at the venue. As I have noted elsewhere (Cunningham, 2011), the cost of attending all home games for a particular season accounts for 5 to 23 percent of the average American's annual income, thereby pricing them out of attending the games. Thus, the current stadium financing structure is consistent with hegemony theory tenets: wealthy owners develop structures and processes that advantage them while subjugating less affluent and less powerful citizens.

*Feminist Theory.* Another perspective requiring a critical lens is feminist theory. Two fundamental assumptions undergird this theory. First, people's experiences in their life, whether at church, in the workplace, or while participating in sport, are gendered in nature. In the context of the current discussion, this means that sport and physical activity represents a site more welcoming to boys and men than to girls and women, and where activities, skills, and values considered "masculine" are praised and esteemed, while "feminine" ones are devalued and demeaned (Birrell, 2000). Second, because girls and women are continually devalued and subjugated in sport and physical activity settings, there is a need to change the underlying structures and processes. In doing so, women might become more empowered and thereby alter their social surroundings.

Social and behavioral scientists adopt a feminist approach to study a number of issues, including the depiction of women in the media. Researchers have shown, for instance, that women receive less coverage than do men across a variety of media forms, including newspapers, magazines, television, and the Internet. When they do receive coverage, it is frequently in less desirable locations (e.g., back page of the sports section) or their pictures are smaller. More fundamentally, though, *how* women and men are depicted also differs. The media regularly focuses on men's athletic accomplishments, photographs them during competition, and highlights their masculine characteristics and ruggedness. It is a much different story for women, though. In this case, the media are more likely to focus on their personal lives, such as their husbands or children (though rarely their partners in the event that the athlete or coach is lesbian or bisexual). When photographed, women are more likely to be posing or in supportive roles than they are to be engaged in athletic competition. Similarly, the stories about women, when compared to those of men, are less likely to focus on their athletic accomplishments. Finally, the types of sports that receive media coverage also vary. For instance, Olympics coverage is more likely to focus on sports where women's femininity is accentuated, such as figure skating or beach volleyball, than on sports where this is not the case, such as crew or hockey.

*Critical Race Theory.* Researchers might also adopt critical race theory to study sport and physical activity in society. According to Hylton (2009), this theory is guided by five central tenets, the first of which is that researchers centralize race and racism in their analysis of systems, processes, and individual behaviors. Second, critical race theorists question the legitimacy of meritocracy, color-blindness, equal opportunity, and racial equality. Third, researchers adopting this paradigm have a commitment to social justice, including a belief in egalitarianism and liberation. Fourth, critical race scholars seek out and centralize people who are otherwise marginalized and have had their voices silenced. Finally, critical race theorists embrace a multidisciplinary approach to their scholarship. In addition, other critical race theorists stress the principle of interest convergence, which notes that "the interest of blacks in achieving racial equality will be accommodated only when it converges with the interests of whites" (Bell, 1980, p. 523).

Critical race theory can be applied to the sport setting in a number of ways. Consider the case, for instance, of racial integration within Major League Baseball. Branch Rickey was the Brooklyn Dodgers owner who signed Jackie Robinson to a professional contract, thereby breaking the "color barrier" in baseball. From one perspective, Rickey is a pioneer and forward-thinking leader who bravely helped integrate Major League Baseball. From a different perspective, critical race theorists might suggest that Rickey might be forward-thinking, but his primary motivation was likely the good of the baseball club, not social justice. That is, if Robinson were not an exceptional player who could meaningfully help the club (he was Rookie of the Year, after all), then he would not have been signed, even with the social benefits of racial desegregation (for further discussion, see DeLorme & Singer, 2010). Such a position is consistent with Donnor's (2005) use of interest convergence (see the previous paragraph, Bell, 1980), and others who have presented similar arguments with respect to Paul "Bear" Bryant and Adolf Rupp integrating their collegiate sport teams (Ladson-Billings, 2004).

*Interactionist Theory*

Unlike many of the previous theories outlined in this chapter, interactionist theory focuses chiefly on how people interact with their environment to give meaning to their lives. As Eitzen and Sage (2009) note, people attach meanings to the symbols, behaviors, and attitudes of others with whom they interact in their environments. This process, which is on-going, helps people to make sense of their social worlds and develop their identities, as coaches, athletes, exercisers, and the like. In doing so, they socially construct their reality, while also forming, creating, and recreating their social identities.

A number of researchers have drawn from interactionist principles in their analysis of sport and physical activity, with a focus on topics such as the social construction of race (see Adair, 2011) or the experiences of women who coach (Sartore & Cunningham, 2007). Anderson (2008) provided an intriguing analysis of how heterosexual male cheerleaders socially constructed sexual orientation and masculinity. While some people maintain that men who sleep with other men are gay or bisexual, these cheerleaders rejected such notions. Rather, they constructed same-sex behaviors as either a form of sexual recreation or as a means of also engaging in sexual behaviors with women. Consistent with an interactionist perspective, these men constructed their sexual identities based on their social surroundings, others' behaviors, and the feedback they received from their cheerleading peers.

## Social Psychological Theories

As previously noted, most sociological texts and chapters focus on functionalism, conflict theory, critical theories, and interactionist theory, but do not address social psychological theories. This is an unfortunate omission for a number of reasons. First, while it certainly has psychological roots, social psychology is a sub-discipline of sociology. Second, social psychological theories can help explain people's behaviors in the sport and physical activity context. Finally, including social psychological theories brings a focus to the intersection of the individual within social contexts, and thus, with the possible exception of interactionist theory, provides a more inclusive understanding of how people operate in social settings than do other theories. Two theories are particularly relevant to the current discussion: the social categorization framework and the similarity-attraction paradigm.

### Social Categorization Framework

Two theories contribute to the social categorization framework: social identity theory (Tajfel & Turner, 1979) and self-categorization theory (Turner et al., 1987). These theories hold that people classify themselves and others into social groups based on salient characteristics. These might include one's race, sex, religion, sport fanship, and the like. Thus, they come to see the self and others in terms of a social identity. When the particular diversity dimension is salient and personally meaningful (among other factors), people will use these differences to evaluate the self and others. People with characteristics similar to the self are considered in-group members, while those different from the self are considered out-group members. *Ceteris paribus*, in-group members are liked more, receive more help, and garner more positive evaluations than do out-group members. Furthermore, these differential evaluations are likely to transfer from one situation to the next, thereby generating stereotypes.

The social categorization framework is useful in analyzing people's experiences in sport and physical activity. Consider, for instance, the case of people choosing an exercise club to join. The social categorization framework suggests that people will be more likely to engage in situations where they feel like they are an in-group member, or where they are surrounded by similar others. Thus, a novice exerciser is unlikely to join a fitness club that emphasizes bodybuilding, just as a woman might prefer to exercise at women-only clubs (like *Curves*). Reflective of these dynamics, Jennifer Woods and I have observed that most people, irrespective of their gender or exercise habits, feel they fit better with exercise gyms that emphasize health and wellness, as opposed to an appearance focus (Cunningham & Woods, 2011). Thus, the notions of fit and preferring to be around similar others impacts a number of decisions, including where people exercise.

*Similarity-Attraction Paradigm*

Another social psychological theory is the similarity-attraction paradigm (Byrne, 1971). From this perspective, people who are similar to one another are likely to also be attracted to and express liking toward one another. The similarities they share, particularly on visible characteristics (e.g., age, sex, race) might also lead them to assume that they share other commonalities, such as shared life experiences, congruent values, or similar world views. For instance, people who are the same age might also believe that they have common attitudes toward life or experiences (e.g., struggling through the Depression). Of course, these underlying similarities are not always present, but the perceptions of such likeness is important, as it is associated with greater interpersonal attraction, helping behaviors, and overall affect. Thus, while the underlying processes differ from the social categorization framework, the end result is the same: similarity breeds attraction and positive affect.

Researchers have used this theory less frequently than the social categorization framework, but there is evidence of its utility in understanding people's attitudes and behaviors in sport. For instance, in 2006, I conducted a study of college students enrolled in physical activity classes to determine how being different from others in the class impacted their overall satisfaction with the class (Cunningham, 2006). Consistent with similarity-attraction paradigm predictions, I found that students in the class perceived a link between demographic dissimilarity from others and subsequent differences based on values, attitudes, and beliefs. That is, if they thought they were different from others based on their race (for instance), then they were also likely to believe that they differed from others in the class based on more deep-level characteristics. The latter judgments were particularly important because the more people thought they differed from others based on values, attitudes, and beliefs, the less satisfied they were with the class. Thus, the similarity-attraction paradigm helps explain, at least in part, students' satisfaction (or lack thereof) with their physical activity experiences.

## Physical Activity and Health Theories

Most theories related to physical activity and health adopt a psychological approach. This is likely because of the notion that the amount of physical activity in which one engages or one's overall physical well being is largely a function of personal choices, attitudes, and behaviors. Thus, perspectives like Azjen's (1991) theory of planned behavior, Bandura's (1986) social cognitive theory, and Deci and Ryan's (2002) self-determination theory have, in many ways, dominated the exercise and health literature.

Increasingly, though, researchers have recognized the need for multilevel perspectives to understand health behavior. That is, one's attitudes and behaviors related to being physically active are shaped by individual factors, such as personality or motivation, but also by other elements, including their family, neighborhood, workplace, and community in which they live, to name a few. Therein lies the importance of ecological models of physical activity. As Sallis and colleagues (2006) note, ecological models recognize that individuals, their social environments, the physical environment in which they live, and policies set at the local, state, and national levels all influence people's attitudes and behaviors (see also McLeroy et al., 2003). As they note, "Rather than positing that behavior is influenced by a narrow range of psychological variables, ecological models incorporate a wide range of influences at multiple levels" (p. 299).

The ecological approach helps researchers to better understand what factors shape behaviors and also inform policy-makers decisions regarding physical activity interventions. That is, the most effect interventions are likely those that (a) target one's community spaces to ensure that they are safe and convenient places for exercise, (b) activate motivational and educational programs aimed at improving one's attitudes toward being active, and (c) use various means, such as the mass media or community-based initiatives, to change the norms and values related to being active (Sallis et al., 2006). Kahn et al. (2002), in their impressive review of physical activity interventions, recognized as much in advocating for physical activity interventions that took into account individual factors (e.g., motivation) with more macro-level factors, such as community-wide education campaigns, school-based PE interventions, and capacity building activities in the community.

Let us consider one example of how social ecological models might be used to understand physical activity in society. Research suggests that demographics are associated with physical activity behaviors, such that racial minorities, the poor, and the elderly are all less active than are their counterparts (see Lox et al., 2010). Psychological models would focus solely on issues related to motivation or their desire to be active. However, a social ecological approach would recognize that inactivity is due to both personal factors, such as those previously mentioned, and environmental factors. For instance, because they are more likely to work multiple jobs and have less autonomy in their work, the poor have less leisure time available to engage in exercise than do their more affluent counterparts. They are also less likely to have access to worksite physical activity programs—something that can meaningfully impact how frequently they exercise. Because their peers also experience similar constraints, social norms for physical activity are likely to be low. Finally, active living environments might also impact activity rates, such that well-lit, safe, attractive neighborhoods needed for leisure time physical activity are likely to be in short supply. As this brief example illustrates, social ecological models offer an encompassing perspective for understanding physical activity.

## RESEARCH METHODS

Having reviewed the primary theories used to understand sport and physical activity in society, I next turn to research methods. That the two topics are presented in different sections might suggest that they are completely distinct from one another. This is not the case; instead, the most effective researchers use theory to guide the entire research process, including how the data are collected, what questions are asked, the manner in which the data are analyzed, and the interpretation of the results. Thus, theory informs and is interwoven into every element of the research process (Cunningham, in press).

As Coakley (2009) notes, broadly speaking, researchers employ one of two research methods—quantitative and qualitative—by either observing people, asking people questions, or analyze existing documents (see Table 2.2). I explore these possibilities in greater depth in the following

Table 2.2: Researching sport and physical activity in society

| Data Source | Data Collection Method | |
| --- | --- | --- |
| | Quantitative | Qualitative |
| Participant Questions | Overview: Participants complete questionnaires or other measures where the data are recorded in numerical units | Overview: Participants respond to open-ended questions posed by the researcher |
| | Examples: Survey research involving questionnaires; experimental studies | Examples: In-depth personal interviews; focus groups |
| Observation | Overview: Researcher observes the activities of others and then converts the observations into numerical units | Overview: Researcher is deeply embedded in a social context and records feeling as well as the behaviors of others |
| | Examples: Observing a video of participants in an experiment; observing coaching behaviors at practice | Examples: Ethnographic research; autoethnographies |
| Secondary Data | Overview: Researcher retrieves quantitative data from existing source to explore research questions | Overview: Researcher retrieves qualitative data from existing source to explore research questions |
| | Examples: Using census data to explore physical activity patterns; drawing from longitudinal datasets | Examples: Conducting content analysis of magazines; analyzing international organizational documents |

space. In doing so, I present ways in which researchers could address a single research question—the under-representation of women in coaching and leadership positions—by employing any of the six research methods. Finally, while I present the different approaches separately, it is important to remember that (a) some researchers employ mixed methods approaches, where they conduct both quantitative and qualitative analyses, and (b) other researchers will use multiple forms of a particular research method within one study, such as when scientists conduct interviews, observe the workplace, and conduct textual analyses of workplace documents.

## Quantitative Research Methods

Social and behavioral scientists using quantitative research methods collect information about people in the sport and physical activity context, convert the information into numerical data, and then use statistical analyses to examine the relationships among the variables. Quantitative research usually entails large datasets with many people, or when experimental designs are employed, smaller datasets are used but with tighter control over possible extraneous variables.

One way of conducting quantitative research is by asking participants questions, either through surveys or experiments. As one example, Burton et al. (2009) asked participants to rate what type of characteristics were important for various jobs in an athletic department. Participants indicated that masculine roles (e.g., delegating, managing conflict) were most congruent with the athletic director position. These assumptions disadvantage women because, even though they can and frequently do engage in "masculine" behaviors, people frequently think that they cannot. Thus, when personnel directors think about who might be well suited for an athletic director role, they frequently envision people who stereotypically exude masculine characteristics: men.

Another way of conducting quantitative research is through observing participants, although this type of quantitative research occurs infrequently. As one possible example, researchers could videotape people discussing the pros and cons of different coaching applicants. They could then review the recordings and tally the number of positive or negative remarks made about women and men applying for leadership positions.

As a third possibility, scientists can also draw from existing data sources to examine issues of interest. Secondary data analysis represents a popular method. Sartore and Sagas (2007) engaged in this approach in their study of the representation of women coaching women's collegiate athletic teams. Specifically, they collected data from archival data sources, aggregated the data into a single file, and then conducted a trend analysis. That is, they explored whether certain trends or patterns emerged over time. The authors observed a significant decrease in the proportion of women coaching women's teams from 1977 to 2006.

## Qualitative Research Methods

When using qualitative research methods, social and behavioral scientists collect information about people and then analyze the data for emergent trends and themes. Relative to quantitative research, the sample sizes in qualitative research are usually smaller, with as few as 3 or 4 participants in the study. However, the method of inquiry usually allows for thicker, more in-depth description of the phenomena at hand.

Researchers frequently ask participants questions in qualitative research, such as through personal interviews or focus groups. As an illustrative example, Norman (2010) conducted interviews with six women coaching major sport teams in the UK, asking them about their background, their experiences coaching, the obstacles they encountered, and ideas for the development of future coaches. The interviews lasted between 60 and 120 minutes. Participants in Norman's study believed that many factors contributed to the under-representation of women in coaching, including the trivialization of women's accomplishments, the marginalization of women through the existing organizational and institutional structures, and various forms of prejudice.

In addition to conducting interviews, scientists can also observe people in the sport and physical activity context. Ethnography represents one way to achieve this end. Here, the researcher is immersed into the social setting and thus conducts observation and interviews while living "in the field." As an example, a researcher could spend extensive time (sometimes up to several years) as an athletic department employee. During that time, the researcher would attend meetings, engage in conversations with coworkers, and observe the day-to-day interactions and social processes of the workplace. Doing so would allow the researcher to better understand the lived experiences of the study participants.

Finally, social scientists adopting a qualitative approach might also analyze documents, artifacts, or media. As one example, Shaw (2006) examined the social processes within sport organizations that served to privilege men and disadvantage women. In addition to conducting personal interviews and observing workplace interactions, she also read through internal organizational documents. This data collection effort helped her better understand how subtle (and sometimes not so subtle) activities legitimated men's power and privilege in sport.

## CHAPTER SUMMARY

The purpose of this chapter was to explore theory and research methods commonly used to understand sport and physical activity in society. I defined theory as "a statement of constructs and their relationships to one another that explain how, when, why, and under what conditions phenomena take place" (Cunningham, in press) and illustrated how its applicability extends to research, teaching, services, and practice. The discussion then moved to the primary theories used to understand sport and physical activity in society, including sociological, social psychological, and physical activity and health theories. In the final section, I discussed different approaches to conducting research, including quantitative and qualitative analyses. Thus, the chapter provides a broad overview for understanding how social and behavioral scientists engage in the practice of scientific inquiry to better understand people's experiences in the sport and physical activity settings.

## DISCUSSION QUESTIONS

1. Using your own words, how do you define theory?
2. Why is theory useful in understanding sport and physical activity in society?
3. Which of the theories reviewed in this chapter do you most closely identify? Why?
4. With which of the theories reviewed in this chapter do you most disagree? Why?
5. Provide an overview of the different research methods social scientists can use to understand sport and physical activity.

## RECOMMENDED READINGS

Kerlinger, F. N., & Lee, H. B. (2000). *Foundations of behavioral research* (4th ed.). Fort Worth, TX: Harcourt College Publishers. (An exceptional research methods book that addresses issues related to theory, hypotheses, and research methods.)

*Sport Management Review*, Volume 16, Issue 1. (This journal issue provides a scholarly exchange focusing on theory and theory development in sport management.)

Lox, C. L., Martin Ginis, K. A., & Petruzzello, S. J. (2010). *The psychology of exercise: Integrating theory and practice* (3rd ed.). Scottsdale, AZ: Holcomb-Hathaway. (The authors provide an overview of the various theories used to understand sport and physical activity participation.)

## REFERENCES

Adair, D. (Ed.) (2011). *Sport, race, and ethnicity: Narratives of difference and diversity.* Morgantown, WV: Fitness Information Technology.

Ajzen, I. (1991). The theory of planned behavior. *Organizational Behavior and Human Decision Processes, 50,* 179-211

Altemeyer, B., & Hunsberger, B. (1992). Authoritarianism, religious fundamentalism, quest, and prejudice. *International Journal for the Psychology of Religion, 2,* 113-133.

Anderson, E. (2008). "Being masculine is not about who you sleep with…:" Heterosexual athletes contesting masculinity and the one-time rule of homosexuality. *Sex Roles, 58,* 104-115.

Bacharach, S. B. (1989). Organizational theories: Some criteria for evaluation. *Academy of Management Review, 14,* 496-515.

Bandura, A. (1986). *Social foundations of thought and action: A social cognitive theory.* Englewood Cliffs, NJ: Prentice Hall.

Bell, D. (1980). *Brown v. Board of Education* and the interest-convergence dilemma. *Harvard Law Review, 93,* 518-533.

Birrell, S. (2000). Feminist theories for sport. In J. Coakley & E. Dunning (Eds.), *Handbook of sports studies* (pp. 61-76). London: Sage.

Bruening, J. E., Madsen, R. M., Evanovich, J M., & Fuller, R. D. (2010). Discovery, integration, application, and teaching: Service learning through sport and physical activity. *Sport Management Education Journal, 4,* 31-48.

Burton, L. J., Barr, C. A., Fink, J. S., & Bruening, J. E. (2009). "Think athletic director, think masculine?": Examination of the gender typing of managerial subroles within athletic administration positions. *Sex Roles, 61,* 416-426.

Byrne, D. (1971). *The attraction paradigm.* New York: Academic Press.

Coakley, J. (2009). *Sports in society: Issues and controversies* (10th ed.). New York; McGraw Hill.

Cohen, A. B., Malka, A., Hill, E. D., Thoemmes, F., Hill, P. C., & Sundie, J. M. (2009). Race as a moderator of the relationship between religiosity and political alignment. *Personality and Social Psychology Bulletin, 35,* 271-282.

Crompton, J. (2004). Beyond economic impact: An alternative rationale for the public subsidy of major league sports facilities. *Journal of Sport Management, 18,* 40-58.

Crompton, J. L., Howard, D. R., & Var, T. (2003). Financing major league facilities: Status, evolution, and conflicting forces. *Journal of Sport Management, 17,* 156-184.

Cunningham, G. B. (2006). The influence of demographic dissimilarity on affective reactions to physical activity classes. *Journal of Sport and Exercise Psychology, 28,* 127-142.

Cunningham, G. B. (2009). Understanding the diversity-related change process: A field study. *Journal of Sport Management, 23,* 407-428.

Cunningham, G. B. (2011). *Diversity in sport organizations* (2nd ed.). Scottsdale, AZ: Holcomb-Hathaway.

Cunningham, G. B. (in press). Theory and theory development in sport management. *Sport Management Review.*

Cunningham, G. B., & Melton, E. N. (in press). Contact with lesbian and gay friends moderates the relationships among religious fundamentalism, sexism, and sexual prejudice. *The Journal of Sex Research.*

Cunningham, G. B., & Woods, J. (2011). For the health of it: Advertisement message and attraction to fitness clubs. *American Journal of Health Studies, 26,* 4-9.

Deci, E., & Ryan, R. (Eds.) (2002). *Handbook of self-determination research.* Rochester, NY: University of Rochester Press.

DeLorme, J., & Singer, J. N. (2010). The interest convergence principle and the integration of Major League Baseball. *Journal of Black Studies, 41,* 367-384.

Dixon, M. A., & Bruening, J. E. (2006). Retaining quality workers: A case study of work-family conflict. *Sport Management Review, 9,* 79-103.

Donnor, J. K. (2005). Towards an interest-convergence in the education of African-American student athletes in major college sports. *Race, Ethnicity and Education, 8,* 45-67.

Eitzen D.S., & Sage, G.H. (2009). *Sociology of North American sport* (8th ed.). Boulder, CO: Paradigm Publishers.

Herek, G. M. (2009). Sexual prejudice. In T. Nelson (Ed.), *Handbook of prejudice* (pp. 441-467). New York: Psychology Press.

Hylton, K. (2009). *"Race" and sport: Critical race theory.* New York: Routledge.

Irwin, R. L., & Ryan, T. D. (in press). Get real: Using engagement with practice to advance theory transfer and production. *Sport Management Review.*

Kahn, E. B., Ramsey, L. T., Brownson, R. C., Heath, G. W., Howze, E. H., Powell, K. E., ... et al. (2002). The effectiveness of interventions to increase physical activity: A systematic review. *American Journal of Preventive Medicine, 22* (Supplement), 73-107.

Kerlinger, F. N., & Lee, H. B. (2000). *Foundations of behavioral research* (4th ed.). Fort Worth, TX: Harcourt College Publishers.

Ladson-Billings, G. (2004). Landing on the wrong note: The price we paid for *Brown. Educational Researcher, 33*(7), 3-13.

Lewin, K. (1952). *Field theory in social science: Selected theoretical papers by Kurt Lewin* (p. 169). London: Tavistock.

Lott, B. (2002). Cognitive and behavioral distancing from the poor. *American Psychologist, 57,* 100-110.

Lott, B., & Bullock, H. E. (2007). *Psychology and economic injustice: Personal, professional, and political intersections.* Washington, DC: American Psychological Association.

Lox, C. L., Martin Ginis, K. A., & Petruzzello, S. J. (2010). *The psychology of exercise: Integrating theory and practice* (3rd ed.). Scottsdale, AZ: Holcomb-Hathaway.

Norman, L. (2010). Feeling second best: Elite women's coaching experiences. *Sociology of Sport Journal, 27,* 89-104.

Rhoden, W. C. (2006). *$40 million slaves: The rise, fall, and redemption of the Black athlete.* New York: Three Rivers Press.

Sage, G. H. (1998). *Power and ideology in American sport: A critical perspective* (2nd ed.). Champaign, IL: Human Kinetics.

Sallis, J. F., Cervero, R. B., Ascher, W., Henderson, K. A. Kraft, M. K., & Kerr, J. (2006). An ecological approach to creating active living communities. *Annual Review of Public Health, 27,* 297-322.

Sartore, M. & Sagas, M. (2007). A trend analysis of the proportion of women in coaching positions. *International Journal of Sport Management, 8,* 226-244.

Sartore, M. L., & Cunningham, G. B. (2007). Explaining the under-representation of women in leadership positions of sport organizations: A symbolic interactionist perspective. *Quest, 59,* 244-265

Schulte, L. J., & Battle, J. (2004). The relative importance of ethnicity and religion in predicting attitudes towards gays and lesbians. *Journal of Homosexuality, 47,* 127-142.

Shaw, S. (2006). Scratching the back of "Mr. X": Analyzing gendered social processes in sport organizations. *Journal of Sport Management, 20,* 510-534.

Sutton, R. I. & Staw, B. M. (1995) What theory is not. *Administrative Science Quarterly, 40,* 371-384.

Tajfel, H., & Turner, J.C. (1979). An integrative theory of intergroup conflict. In W.G. Austin & S. Worchel (Eds.), *The social psychology of intergroup relations* (pp. 33–47). Monterey, CA: Brooks/Cole.

Turner, J., Hogg, M.A., Oakes, P.J., Reicher, S.D., & Wetherell, M.S. (1987). *Rediscovering the social group: A self-categorization theory.* Oxford, UK: B. Blackwell.

Van de Ven, A. H. (1989). Nothing is quite so practical as a good theory. *Academy of Management Review, 14,* 486-489.

van Knippenberg, D. (2011). Advancing theory in organizational psychology. *Organizational Psychology Review, 1,* 3-8.

# CHAPTER 3

## ETHICS

## John N. Singer

\*\*\*

**Learning Objectives**

After reading this chapter you should be able to:

1.  Articulate why there is a need to study ethics in sport.
2.  Define major concepts and theories associated with the study of ethics in sport and society.
3.  Describe the multi-level factors that influence the (un)ethical behaviors of different stakeholder groups in sport and society.
4.  Discuss some of the ethical issues and problems in various segments of the sport industry.


## INTRODUCTION

"Because sport is a pervasive force in modern society and is viewed with such awe, whatever happens in sport may be considered legitimate and right, at least by impressionable young people who pursue careers in sport and/or sport management"
  -*DeSensi and Rosenburg (2003, p. vii)*

As a college professor who for several years now has taught a graduate and undergraduate level class focusing on the intersection between ethical and legal issues in sport, one of the first things I have done at the beginning of each semester is pose the following questions: Should sport management programs offer and require students to take a course that focuses on ethics in sport? Can ethics be taught and learned in a university or college classroom setting? The typical response to the first question is "yes;" such a class could help students to better understand, reflect upon, and ultimately, deal with the myriad of ethical issues and dilemmas they might face as current and future participants, consumers, and professionals engaging in various levels of sport and physical activity. Indeed, given that sport has become a significant and integral part of people's lives (i.e., in terms of work, business, leisure, health, and fitness) it is important to offer a class that challenges students to engage in critical reflection and dialogue concerning ethics and its application to the social institution and cultural practice of sport.

On the other hand, the second question from above does not usually generate a simple "yes" or "no" answer. Instead, students typically respond by suggesting that students cannot necessarily be "taught" how to be ethical in a classroom setting; however, their exposure to the literature and a body of knowledge related to the topic, engagement in discussions about the topic, completion of various assignments and exercises, and the opportunity to hear about and glean insight from the experiences and perspectives of their instructor and peers could help students develop into more critical thinkers and conscientious individuals. Furthermore, the classroom setting has the potential to help bring about a critical consciousness, which could assist students as they reflect upon, evaluate, and if need be, refine their ethical profile and moral compass (i.e., values, attitudes, beliefs, and behaviors). In this regard, the classroom experience certainly could make a valuable contribution to students' ethical reasoning ability and moral development as they participate in sport and physical activity, consume it, and/or pursue professional careers in the sport and other industries.

Although the above-mentioned course I have taught during my time in the academy has emphasized the natural link and inherent relationship between ethics and legal issues in the sport industry, the focus of this chapter will be on the former. That is, I will specifically center the discussion and analysis on the study of ethics. This is not to negate the importance of legal issues or diminish its relevance to our analysis and discussion of ethical issues. To the contrary, I acknowledge that some of the issues to be addressed in this chapter will have both ethical and legal overtones, and when appropriate, reference will be made to this. For example, the respective labor disputes between owners and players in the National Football League (NFL) and National Basketball Association (NBA) in 2011 were filled with various ethical (e.g., distributive justice issues concerning how to split the financial pie) as well as legal issues (e.g., antitrust lawsuits against the owners related to the collective bargaining process) (see Munson, 2011; Zillgitt, 2011). And certainly, the sex-abuse allegations and scandals that made headlines in 2011 involving two prominent assistant coaches at Penn State University and Syracuse University, respectively, are demonstrative of the intertwined nature of ethical and legal issues in the sport context (see Brady & Garcia, 2011; Weiberg, 2011).

In thinking about these and other issues in society in general and the social context of sport in particular, it is important to note that just because something is (il)legal does not mean it is (un)ethical, and vice versa (De-Sensi & Rosenburg, 2003). For example, it is no secret that immoral laws—aimed at discrimination against Black people in particular—have been created throughout American history (i.e., Jim Crow Laws) and conscientious individuals (e.g., Dr. Martin Luther King, Jr.) engaged in illegal, but arguably, ethical behavior (i.e., civil disobedience) in defiance of these unjust, immoral laws. Moreover, because it could reasonably be argued that laws (moral or immoral) and legal systems of societies emanate from and are rooted in the minds and hearts of individuals (particularly those with power and privilege) who espouse certain ideals and moral positions, a specific examination of ethics in various social contexts is warranted. In that vein, this chapter is an attempt to contribute to the important dialogue that several authors and scholars have already started concerning the study of ethics in the social context of sport and physical activity (cf., Appenzeller, 2011; Branvold, 2005; Crosset & Hums, 2005; DeSensi & Rosenburg, 2003; Eitzen, 1988; Hums & Mac-Lean, 2004; Lumpkin et al., 2003; Malloy et al., 2003; Morgan et al., 2001; Walsh & Giulianotti, 2007).

I specifically and intentionally adopt a critical social perspective in my analysis of ethics in various sport and physical activity contexts and settings. This is important because as Sage (1998) stated, a critical approach allows "us to step back from thinking about sport as merely a place of personal achievement and entertainment and study sport as a cultural practice embedded in political, economic, and ideological formations" (p. 11). The critical approach offers a necessary departure from the functionalist perspective, which tends to stress the virtues of sport participation and organized sport in terms of bringing people together, socializing the youth, and serving as a model for success and achievement; functionalism also emphasizes the maintenance of the status quo (see Coakley, 2007; Cunningham, 2011). It embraces the idea that the relationship between sport and society is harmonious, and the current structure of sport in American society has positive benefits for the various stakeholders involved with this social institution. For example, functionalist believe organized sport participation helps with building character, increasing social mobility, and teaching valuable life lessons (e.g., teamwork, work ethic, perseverance) to athletes; they also suggest that sport helps to facilitate positive race relations, by allowing members of particular racial groups that have historically had troubled relationships with one another (e.g., Blacks and Whites) to put aside their differences and past circumstances as they pursue a common goal (e.g., winning), as members or fans of a particular team (see Brown et al., 2003).

Given its emphasis on the potentially positive aspects of sports in society, the functionalist approach might be a popular and attractive lens for many people — particularly students seeking careers in the industry — to analyze ethical issues in sport. However, in this chapter, I take the position that the weaknesses of functionalism makes it of limited utility in studying ethics in the world of sport and play. More specifically, its failure to acknowledge sport is a social construction (i.e., it is something to which people create and assign meanings), overestimation of the positive benefits of sport, and assumption that the needs of all groups within society are the same does not allow one to move beyond a focus on societal needs and how sports are related to the satisfaction of those needs. Functionalism focuses on sports in society from the top down, not bottom up, and ignores the complexities of everyday social life. That is, as opposed to critical theories, it fails to "tell us about sports in everyday life or the ways that people are active agents who participate in the processes through which sports and society are organized and changed" (Coakley, 2007, p.40). As a broad perspective that comes in a variety of forms, the critical approach is based on the following assumptions: (a) groups and societies are characterized by shared values and conflicts of interest, (b) social life involves continuous processes of negotiation, compromise, and coercion because agreements about values and social organization are never permanent, and (c) values and social organization change over time and from one situation to another as there are shifts in the power balance between groups of people in society (Coakley, 2007).

With these assumptions in mind, I examine the nature of ethics and ethical dilemmas in sport and physical activity contexts. In doing so, I challenge readers to critically reflect upon the various relationships between and among groups and individuals in various sport contexts, and how these relationships might impact these various stakeholders' ethical choices and behaviors.

## THE STUDY OF ETHICS IN SPORT

Volkwein's (1995) attempt to clarify the terms "ethics" and "morality" in her discussion of ethics and top-level sport provides a starting point for defining ethics and related concepts, applying them to the study of the various levels of sport (see Chapter 1 in this book for definitions of sport;

see also Eitzen & Sage, 2003 for a discussion of the different levels of sport, i.e., corporate, organized, and informal). Volkwein differentiates between the terms by suggesting that moral behavior or *morality* involves actions that are based on certain basic values and norms of society, while *ethics* represent the reflection of such behavior. From another vantage point, DeSensi and Rosenburg (2003) offered a helpful definition of and demarcation between the terms. According to these authors, morality is observed on the level of practice (it is our behavior) and refers to the expression of values, attitudes, and lifestyles by specific social groups and individuals, with a focus on the "do's" and "don'ts" in life. Ethics, on the other hand, refers to principles of right or wrong conduct and decisions (how individuals ought to or should act), and is on the level of theory.

We base our ethics and morality on our value structure and moral standards. *Values* are deeply held views that motivate and guide a person's behavior. A value is an enduring belief that a particular way of behaving and living is personally and socially preferable to other ways of behaving and living (Malloy et al., 2003, p. 56). Although people can value (i.e., assign worth to) many different things (e.g., belief or opinion, way of life, type of individual or character, particular action, physical object, material possession), *morals* are those fundamental baseline values that ultimately dictate our behavior (Crosset & Hums, 2005). *Ethical reasoning* is a cognitive process that is explicitly and implicitly learned through others, is employed to help people arrive at a sound decision on some issue, and is dependent on personal values and morals, and perhaps, the values of the organizational settings (e.g., codes of ethics or personal conduct policies) and broader society in which we find ourselves. This process helps individuals to deal with ethical dilemmas they might face as decision-makers. An *ethical dilemma* occurs when people are presented with a circumstance that potentially challenges their beliefs and might force them to act one way or another to resolve some conflict (Lumpkin et al., 2003). It is a situation where the course of action might be unclear, or where reasonable people cannot agree on what should or should not be done (Hums & MacLean, 2004).

The social institution of sport offers a myriad of ethical dilemmas that various stakeholder groups must grapple with on a regular basis. As mentioned earlier, this is especially the case in corporate and organized sport settings where the stakes are high, and in many instances, the interests of different groups and individuals are at odds. Volkwein (1995) discussed the "crisis" in top-level sport where moral values have been confused with dollar values, and this has led to an ethical or moral dilemma in sport that must be situated within the social structures underlying top-level sport in modern societies. She attributed this crisis to the socio-structural context of top-level sport and stressed how it is based on the following notions: (a) winning at all costs, (b) the overemphasis on success, and (c) the body as an element of uncertainty (Volkwein, 1995). In her view, there is a strong link between these unwritten rules/laws of top-level sport and the actions (in many cases, unethical behaviors) taken by various stakeholders of sport (e.g., athletes, coaches, administrators, trainers, fans).

Volkwein (1995) discussed how the task of *ethics in sport* (i.e., theory of moral behavior in sport) is to critically reflect on the phenomenon of sport within its social and cultural setting, because sport derives much of its meaning from the society of which it is a part. In other words, in applying ethics to the study of sport one must place it within the ethics and moral values of society in general. A discussion of the cultural significance of college sport in the American higher education system helps illustrate this point. Beyer and Hannah (2000) discussed how intercollegiate athletics in American society is a phenomenon unlike that seen in other societies or cultures. In other countries it is not taken nearly as seriously, afforded such large operating budgets, or so embedded within the structure of universities. These authors focused on how certain cultural ideologies expressed in the larger American society — particularly the protestant ethic, capitalism, and the bureaucratic mentality — are also reflected in college sport. Critics of American college sport have argued that serious reform efforts are needed because the heavy emphasis on winning and competition, and commercial development and success has usurped the focus on student development, academic performance, and other educational values in these institutions of higher education.

Indeed, the above example pertaining to college sport demonstrates the importance of understanding how ethical issues manifest themselves in specific social and cultural contexts. What is considered to be an ethical issue in American college sport is probably not so much of an issue in college sport in most other societies throughout the world. In the next section, I build upon this section on the study of sport ethics by focusing on some of the societal, organizational, and individual level forces that help to shape the ethical choices and behaviors of individuals in American society and sport.

# FORCES THAT SHAPE ETHICAL BEHAVIOR
# IN SPORT AND SOCIETY

Forces at the macro (i.e., societal), meso (i.e., organizational), and micro (i.e., individual) levels have a great impact on the ethical decision-making and behaviors of various stakeholders in sport and physical activity. Although each level is discussed separately, it is important to note that these various levels are not necessarily mutually exclusive (i.e., they do not operate in isolation); they can indeed influence and be influenced by one another.

## Societal Level

From a macro perspective, the culture of a particular society, as well as its legal system, governmental regulations, and laws, could greatly influence and shape the ethical thinking and conduct of sport participants, consumers, and professionals. Coakley (2007) described a *culture* as consisting of "the ways of life that people create as they participate in a group or society" (p. 5). He defined a *society* as "a collection of people living in a defined geographic territory and united by a political system and a shared sense of self-identification that distinguishes them from other people" (Coakley, 2007, p. 5). Therefore, discussion of American culture, for example, refers to a society that encompasses traditions, ideals, customs, beliefs, values, arts, and innovations developed both domestically and imported via the immigration of various groups of people. In particular, prevalent ideas and ideals from the European continent such as democracy, capitalism, various forms of monotheism, and civil liberties are present; further, other aspects of American culture and society, such as important national holidays (e.g., Independence Day, Halloween, Thanksgiving, Christmas), a strong military tradition, innovations in the arts and entertainment (e.g., Hip Hop music), and uniquely American sports (e.g., college and professional football), evolved domestically as the United States developed over the course of time.

The individual-collectivism binary is a major dimension of cultural variability (see Gudykunst & Ting-Toomey, 1988) that nicely illustrates how the culture of a society can impact the ethical choices of individuals in sport and physical activity contexts. According to Gudykunst and Ting-Toomey, the emphasis in individualistic cultures is placed on the individual's goals, while in collectivistic cultures, group goals take precedence. People in individualistic cultures (e.g., United States of America) emphasize individual success and achievements in jobs and careers, and they tend to approach interpersonal relationships with their own self-interests in mind. Conversely, instead of thinking of themselves in terms of "I," people in collectivists cultures (e.g., China) value the well-being of the group and think more in terms of "we," harmony and loyalty within organizations is the goal, and avoidance of conflict is emphasized. Eitzen (1988) attributed the ethical problems in American sport to the culture and structural conditions of the broader society. More specifically, he discussed the political economy of the United States and how this capitalistic society is dominated by massification and commodification, which helps explain how individualism operates and why individuals make unethical choices in all areas of social life including sport.

Eitzen (1988) described *massification* as the "transformed social relations in society resulting from a more specialized division of labor, large-scale commodity production and consumption, the widespread use of technology to increase industrial and administrative efficiency, and an increasingly authoritarian state" (p. 25). It is the consequence of society's increased bureaucratization, rationalization, and routinization (Desensi & Rosenburg, 2003; Eitzen, 1988). According to DeSensi and Rosenburg, sport mirrors the massification in society at large by being displayed as work, spectacle, power politics, and big business. Eitzen spoke of how the increasing complexity and specialization of tasks in sport leads to a circumstance where anonymity, even in team sports, increases.

To illustrate this point, Eitzen (1988) considered the structure and specialized functions of football teams (e.g., head coach, offensive coordinator, defensive coordinator, special teams coach, and so on). In many instances, these specialized units in football meet and practice separately from the larger group, and individuals have limited social interactions with others because they are focused almost exclusively on their respective tasks and specific roles as coaches and players. Even though football is a "team" sport, this type of structure could lead to superficial or disingenuous relationships between and among players and coaches where they fail to see each other as whole persons (Eitzen, 1988). Further, because sport can be an internally and externally competitive endeavor (DeSensi & Rosenburg, 2003), such an environment could lead to the promotion of an "I got to get mine" or a "me-first" attitude or type of behavior, which is typically reflected in individualistic cultures such as the USA. Perhaps this helps explain why many American college head football coaches choose to leave a university, abandoning their players, fan base, and co-workers in pursuit of higher salaries, greater prestige, and social status (e.g., Lane Kiffin leaving the University of Tennessee in

2010 after only one year to take head coaching job at the University of Southern California; see Schrager, 2010).

Closely related to massification in the sport industry is the issue of *commodification*, which scholars define as the social, psychological, and cultural uses of social structures for the commercial needs of monopolies (DeSensi & Rosenburg, 2003; Eitzen, 1988). Commodification is a process that involves viewing and treating human beings as objects to be manipulated, bought, and sold. Individuals, who are fixated on profit maximization, money, winning, power, prestige, social status, and the like, sometimes become oblivious to the human qualities of other members of the sport community as they pursue success and individual accolades. A prime example of commodification in American sport is how the NFL treats and deals with its primary labor force (i.e., the players). My experiences working for an NFL team allowed me to see firsthand how players are, first and foremost, viewed as commodities to be manipulated, bought, and sold. In most cases, once a player depreciates in value (e.g., due to injuries or aging) they are jettisoned from the team (at any given point in time) to make room for the next young, physically gifted athlete. Executives, coaches, and scouts are constantly looking for the next crop of players to replace the current crop. This process of commodification typically unfolds via (a) the NFL scouting combine, where college players are evaluated and put through a battery of physical and mental tests to assess their "fit" and capabilities; (b) the NFL draft, where college players are selected to play for specific teams in the league; (c) free agency, where players are allowed to negotiate with different teams for their services; and (d) trades, where teams send players to other teams in exchange for players, and sometimes, cash considerations.

Many people might view this current structure of the NFL as being the "nature of the beast" or just part of how the business of professional sport should be operated and run, especially since many professional athletes in the NFL and other professional leagues are paid six and seven figure salaries for their athletic services. However, this argument fails to acknowledge that "the hierarchy of the organization in power and performance sports features the athletes at the bottom of the structure who are trained, manipulated, and humiliated, in some cases, to produce a winning team worthy of sponsorships and monetary rewards" (DeSensi & Rosenburg, 2003, p. 248). Given this reality, it should come as no surprise that players often "hold out" (i.e., refusing to come to training camp or mandatory workouts) or refuse to play games and participate in team activities during seasons and off seasons while demanding bigger and more favorable contracts. Many of these athletes feel the team is only using them as a means to an end, and therefore, chose to embrace egoism or a "what's in it for me" attitude (DeSensi & Rosenburg, 2003) in their dealings with the team.

The second major societal force that impacts ethical behavior in sport settings is the legal system, laws, and governmental regulations within a particular society. The U.S. Constitution is the foundation of the government and American legal system; however, the various social movements (e.g., slave revolts, Women's Rights Movement, African American Civil Rights Movement) that have taken place in American society and the major court cases and decisions, legislation, mandates, and laws that resulted from these movements have certainly had an impact on the attitudes, decision-making, and behavior of people within the sport industry. For example, the passage of civil rights legislation (e.g., Civil Rights Act of 1964) and gender equity mandates (e.g., Title IX of the Education Amendments of 1972) have had implications for those decision-makers in college sport who are charged with hiring personnel (e.g., coaches, administrators) and providing participation opportunities for athletes. It has also had an effect on the expectations as to how athletes, coaches, and other employees (particularly women and racial minorities) are to be treated as members of these sport organizations. There are several examples of instances where females and racial minorities have filed lawsuits against these sport organizations claiming access or treatment discrimination (see Cunningham, 2011). Indeed, the issues of access discrimination and treatment discrimination have become ethical as well as legal issues with which stakeholders in sport have had to deal.

As another example of the implications governmental regulations and law can have for ethical decision-making in sport, the issue of illicit drug use at different levels of sport has garnered considerable attention. According to the Office of National Drug Control Policy website (see www.whitehousedrugpolicy.gov), the USA Federal Government has made attempts to combat the criminal trafficking and the use of performance enhancing drugs (e.g., anabolic steroids, human growth hormone, counterfeit prescription drugs). Federal and State law enforcement agencies have worked with sports authorities and foreign governments to address this issue. For example, USA law enforcement officials created Operation Raw Deal, led by the Drug Enforcement Administration (DEA) in conjunction with enforcement agencies in several other countries, to take action against the global underground trade of steroids and other performance enhancing drugs. Moreover, concerns over the growing illicit market and prevalence of abuse combined with the possibility of harmful long-term effects of steroid use caused Congress to place anabolic steroids into Schedule III of the Controlled Substances Act in 1991. Doing so made it illegal to possess or sell them without a valid prescription. In addition, some States have implemented additional fines and penalties for the illegal use of steroids.

This governmental intervention and legislation has certainly had an impact on how leadership and other stakeholders in various sport contexts have had to deal with this legal and ethical issue. Several sport governing bodies, such as the International Olympic Committee (IOC), NCAA, NFL, NBA, National Hockey League (NHL), and Major League Baseball (MLB), have banned the use of steroids by athletes due to their potentially dangerous side effects and because they could give the user an unfair advantage over the competition. Others suggest that the use of steroids and other performance-enhancing drugs by players severely compromises the integrity of the game; therefore, this is an issue these sport organizations continue to deal with on a continual basis. In particular, MLB has continued to grapple with the issue in the aftermath of the historic Mark McGwire and Sammy Sosa home run chase of the late 1990s. The death of 1996 National League MVP, Ken Caminiti, an admitted steroid user, has further illuminated the potentially dangerous effects of steroid and drug use and abuse (Associated Press, 2004; Sheinin, 2004). Moreover, since the early 2000s, several players have been called to testify before Congress, and some high profile players have tested positive for and/or admitted to steroid and other drug use since that time (e.g., Mark McGwire, Alex Rodriguez). Clearly, the presence of steroids and performance-enhancing drugs in sport has become and is an ethical issue that has been greatly impacted by the law.

**Organizational Level**

From a meso perspective, factors such as the organizational culture and organizational systems help to shape the ethical choices and behaviors of various stakeholder groups in sport. Schein (1985) defined *organizational culture*, as "a pattern of basic assumptions — invented, discovered, or developed by a given group as it learns to cope with its problems of external adaptation and internal integration — that has worked well enough to be considered valid and therefore, to be taught to new members as the correct way to perceive, think, and feel in relation to those problems" (p. 9). As an example, given the increasing diversity in American society, and thus, the workforce, the manner in which diversity is managed (or not) has become an ethical issue in various organizational contexts, including sport organizations. Doherty and Chelladurai (1999) argued that managing diversity in an organization is a function of the culture of the organization. In differentiating between an organizational culture of diversity and an organizational culture of similarity, they suggested that sport organizations should embrace an organizational culture that values diversity because it is a *social responsibility* (i.e., legal and moral responsibility people have to themselves and others; see DeSensi & Rosenburg, 2003) and a contributing factor to organizational performance.

In contrast to an organizational culture of similarity, an organizational culture of diversity is born out of a social responsibility to treat all organizational members fairly, and is characterized by an underlying respect for differences, as well as flexibility, innovation, risk acceptance, tolerance of ambiguity, conflict acceptance, people orientation, and future orientation. Moreover, this culture places value on reaching desired outcomes via multiple means, views differences as a source of strength, and assumes that there is a range of right or good behavior. The values and assumptions of this type of culture are manifested in the form of open, two-way, and inclusive communication, performance appraisals based on outcomes or substance rather than style, and a flexible reward and promotion system providing equitable opportunities and career development. Finally, there is multiple decision-making, with power distributed throughout the organization among diverse members, and group dynamics are characterized by open membership, mutual respect, a shared influence (Doherty & Chelladurai, 1999).

Conversely, organizational cultures of similarity are based on the value system, perspectives, and cultural symbols of the homogenous dominant group (typically, heterosexual, white, able-bodied males). This type of culture compels individuals who do not fit the mold of the dominant group to relinquish their unique values, attitudes, and symbols in the workplace, and the focus is on the reduction of ambiguity and promotion of a particular person-organization fit. Further, this culture values the dominant group's mentality that "our way is the only or best way" to do things (Doherty & Chelladurai, 1999, p. 288). There is a narrow view of right or good behavior, and "difference" is viewed as a deficit. Rigidity, risk avoidance, intolerance of ambiguity, conflict avoidance, task orientation, and an orientation to the present characterizes a culture of similarity. This culture is manifested in such processes as a one-way, closed, and exclusive communication network, performance appraisals based on style and culturally biased criteria (e.g., aggression), and an inflexible reward and promotion system in which opportunity and career development perpetuate the dominant group. Finally, there is also unilateral decision-making by a few in the dominant group who hold power, and group dynamics are characterized by relatively closed membership and a status hierarchy that restricts members who are different from the dominant group (Doherty & Chelladurai, 1999).

Doherty and Chelladurai (1999) argued that sport organizations have historically had cultures of similarity. For evidence, consider intercollegiate athletics and the lack of diversity in this setting. Many scholars and critics suggest that the dearth of racial minorities (particularly African Americans) in major decision-making positions of power (e.g., head football coaches, athletic directors, conference commissioners) in these programs is an ethical issue that needs to be addressed (Brooks & Althouse, 2007; Lapchick et al., 2009; Shropshire, 1996). They have further argued this lack of diversity in these upper level positions is due to an organizational culture of similarity that is comprised of an "old boys' network" (i.e., a system of social networking among White males in the sport business industry that limits and inhibits the ability of racial minorities and women to gain access to those positions of power that have been predominantly held by White males). Some might view this old boys' network as troubling, especially when considering that a large percentage of the primary labor force (i.e., athletes) in big-time college sport or revenue-generating sports (i.e., football and basketball) are racial minorities (see Lapchick et al., 2009). This begs the ethical question, "Why does it appear that diversity is embraced at the entry level, but not so much at the upper management levels within many of these organizational settings"?

In addition to the culture of an organization, organizational systems serve as formal devices to reinforce ethical values. More specifically, the structure, policies, procedures, and rules within various types of sport organizations can all impact the decisions and actions of individuals in these settings. An organizational structure serves as a formal and informal framework of polices and rules within which an organization arranges its lines of authority and communications, and allocates rights and duties. Organizations are characterized by divisions of labor, power, and communication responsibilities through which regularities such as task allocation, supervision, and coordination are developed (Jackson, 1987). Typically, the structure of an organization is revealed through its organizational chart, where the hierarchy and reporting structure within that organization becomes evident.

Within the American sport context, there are several sport governing bodies responsible for the governance of college sport. However, the NCAA is by far the most predominant one of them all. According to Hums and MacLean (2004), the NCAA is a voluntary association of colleges and universities, run by a President and staffed by several hundred employees. The NCAA national office works with the various athletic conference (e.g., Southeastern Conference, Big Ten) offices and member institutions (i.e., colleges and universities) in efforts to provide programming and deliver national championships for intercollegiate athletes.

Hums and MacLean (2004) included an organizational chart in their chapter on college sport that provides a helpful illustration of the governance structure of the NCAA. At the top is the Executive Committee, which is charged with the responsibility of ensuring that each division operates consistently with the basic purposes, fundamental policies and general principles of the NCAA. The President of the NCAA is typically a member of this committee. Beneath this level is the Division I (Board of Directors), Division II (Presidents Council), and Division III (Presidents Council) members, and this includes the institutional CEOs or college and university presidents. The Division I, II, and III management council members are next, and this includes athletics administrators (e.g., athletic directors, associate and assistant athletic directors, executives) and faculty athletic representatives. The three different division committees are below this, and the sport and rules committees are at the bottom of this organizational chart (see Hums & MacLean, 2004, p. 190).

The *Sports Business Journal* (SBJ) provided a breakdown of the NCAA's organizational structure, with a specific focus on the Association-wide committees at the Division I level. These are committees that deal with issues that affect all members of the NCAA, and perform duties necessary to the ongoing operation of the association (Sport Business Journal, 2006). As indicated by the name and function of these various committees, they provide insight into some of the policy areas and rules the NCAA deems to be important and appropriate to the governance of college sport. The following committees were highlighted by the SBJ: executive committee subcommittee on gender and diversity issues; competitive safeguards and medical aspects sports committee; honors committee; minority opportunities and interests committee; Olympic sports liaison committee; playing rules oversight panel; postgraduate scholarship committee; research committee; sportsmanship and ethical conduct committee; Walter Byers scholarship committee; committee on women's athletics; student-athlete advisory committees.

These various committees and their functions are indicative of what the NCAA has deemed to be important to the operations of college sport organizations. This emphasis could certainly impact the ethical choices of various stakeholders of college sport. For example, the sportsmanship and ethical conduct committee is charged with developing and promoting strategies that foster a collegial atmosphere and a greater acceptance of the values of respect, caring, fairness, civility, honesty, integrity and responsibility among athletes, coaches, officials, fans and other stakeholder groups. The strategies implemented by such a committee could ultimately have an effect on the behavior of various stakeholders of college sport. Certain policies, rules, and codes of ethics could emerge from such a committee's work. In fact, several member institutions of the NCAA have created codes of ethics or written guidelines for its stakeholders groups to help them conduct their actions in accordance with the values and ethical standards of the organization.

The NCAA and its various committees also exist to create rules, regulations, and guidelines for how its member institutions and people within them should conduct its affairs. The NCAA rules govern specific games, the conditions for institutional participation in the NCAA and its sanctioned leagues and championships, the recruitment and participation of individual athletes, consequences for breaching NCAA rules, and so forth. The NCAA manual is a major document that encompasses hundreds of pages of rules for which member institutions and individuals are accountable. This explains why athletic departments at these institutions have compliance offices (or officers). Compliance officers work with the NCAA, the conference the athletic department belongs to, and the coaches, athletes, and administrators in the athletic department to ensure they are in compliance with NCAA rules. Despite this, there have been cases where individuals have intentionally or unintentionally breached NCAA rules and been punished as a result. Moreover, sometimes ethical questions have arisen as to whether or not some of these rules created by the NCAA are even right, fair, or just (e.g., rules related to athlete benefits and compensation; see Gardiner, 2011; Weiberg, 2011).

### Individual Level

From a micro perspective, individuals' personal ethics could have a powerful impact on their decision-making and behavior in sport and physical activity settings. *Personal ethics* are a set of morals and values that an individual brings into an organization, workplace, or social setting. People's personal ethics could originate from their family background, upbringing, and life experiences, the society and culture into which they were born and socialized, religious beliefs or spiritual background, formal and informal education, work experiences in various organizational settings, and overall moral development, among other things.

In many instances, an individual's personal ethics are grounded in one or more ethical frameworks. Malloy et al. (2003) outlined and discussed three ethical bases, theories, or orientations grounded in philosophy that could be helpful for describing, analyzing, and understanding how people approach ethical issues in sport. First, deontology is a rules-based approach that focuses on obligation and duty, which is similar to the orientation found in the Bible (e.g., The Golden Rule). Deontological theories have been termed, "ethics of duty", because they stress that one's moral obligation does not involve consideration of the outcomes of action—the focus should be on the act itself and doing what is "right" (De-Sensi & Rosenburg, 2003). For example, as a high school basketball official for the Texas Association of Sports Officials and the University Inter-scholastic League I take a deontological approach to officiating because I feel officials have an absolute duty (i.e., Kantian ethics) to remove all bias and make the proper call at all times, regardless of how it might impact the outcome of the game. The concern is not for protecting the interests of the "best" team or players on the court; rather, the concern should be with protecting the integrity of the game. This continues to be my mentality as I strive to move up the ranks of basketball officiating at the high school and college levels.

Second, teleology is the antithesis of deontology in that the focus is on the consequences of one's actions, and whether or not the behavior brings about "good," particularly for the greatest number of people (i.e., Utilitarianism). Teleological theories are not necessarily concerned with character or intentions as long as the outcomes of our behaviors and decision-making are good and desirable. In staying with the basketball officiating example, if an NBA official were to embrace the mentality that the calls he or she chooses to make (or not make) should ultimately be predicated upon how the outcomes of the games might impact the overall "success" of the league that would be an example of taking a utilitarian approach to ethical decision-making. Some commentators have suggested that this is indeed the mentality some NBA officials have taken in recent years (e.g., the first decade of the 2000s) during playoffs games so that the NBA's marquee teams (in big media markets) and star players could continue to play, and consequently, help boost fan interest, television ratings, and financial outcomes for the league (see Taylor, 2009). The well-documented story of former NBA official, Tim Donaghy, who pleaded guilty to and served time in prison for conspiracy to engage in wire fraud and transmitting betting information through interstate commerce in the tips-for-payoffs scheme (Alipour, 2009; Shulman & Branigin, 2007), is indicative of an NBA referee who took a teleological approach, particularly egoism or a "what's in it for me" attitude, in the (un)ethical choices he made as an official. Donaghy, a self-admitted gambling addict who was looking out for his own personal financial interests, also accused the NBA and some of the other referees in the league of working together to intentionally manipulate the outcome of certain games so that marquee teams could win, which would boost ratings and increase financial benefits for the league (Beck, 2009).

Third, existentialism, also known as virtue ethics (see DeSensi & Rosenburg, 2003), focuses on the character and authenticity of the individual and how people's decision-making affects them and their personal relationships with others. The belief is that achieving good character is like developing good sport skills, in that it requires personal (moral) training and practice. People's character is always being tested in the face of new ethical challenges and dilemmas, and when faced with these dilemmas they must be honest and true to themselves and all others who might be affected by their decisions and actions. Consider again a basketball official at any level of sport, from youth to professional: that official would have to examine her conscience to decide whether or not ethical choices and decisions made (i.e., the calls made or not made) are instances of authentic behavior. "Am I being true to myself, others, and the game of basketball" is a question that the official might ask when contemplating his or her decision-making. And this might be a question the official continues to interrogate throughout her career in officiating.

## ETHICAL DILEMMAS IN THE SPORT INDUSTRY

Sport is a multi-billion dollar, diverse industry that consists of several different segments. As such, there is a need to focus on some ethical issues and dilemmas unique to various industry segments. Hums et al. (1999) discussed the tremendous growth of the industry and the shift toward a profit-oriented approach to doing business in the various segments of the industry. This has led to many new and varied ethical dilemmas for managers and other stakeholder groups to consider. Some of the major segments of the industry, according to these authors, include professional sport, college sport, recreational sport, health and fitness club sport, and facility management. Although I recognize ethical issues abound in industry segments (e.g., high school and youth sport) and support segments (e.g., sport media, sporting goods and licensed products) that were not mentioned by these authors, I focus on the first four segments highlighted by these authors as a way to provide a critical analysis of some pertinent ethical dilemmas that have been well-documented in the popular press and academic literature. However, readers are encouraged to consider other segments of the sport industry, and some of the ethical issues that exist in those sport contexts.

**Professional Sport**

The professional sport segment creates sport spectacles in which consumers (i.e., fans, sponsors, and the media) pay fees to consume or affiliate themselves with these events and exhibitions and the athletes or participants are paid for their performance and services. It includes major league sport leagues and teams, minor league teams, individual sports, and other major sporting events in the USA and other parts of the world. This segment is a major international business grossing billions of dollars each year (Masteralexis et al., 2005). Given that the purpose of professional sport is mainly entertainment and profits, it has some ethical issues that other industry segments might not have, or that are not as pronounced in those other segments.

Some of these issues were mentioned earlier in this chapter, and also extend to other segments of the sport industry, perhaps to a lesser extent (e.g., massification and commodification). Hums et al, (1999) discussed the following issues: (a) the local communities which support teams (ticket prices and franchise relocation), (b) the players, and (c) the front office personnel (diversity of personnel). Although all these ethical issues and others are worthy of discussion and critical reflection, the focus here will be on the second issue highlighted by these authors because the players are the primary labor force and "core product" of professional sport.

In particular, athlete pay and benefits, athlete health and participation, and athlete conduct and behavior have commanded a great deal of attention in recent years. Each of these issues could be examined with a critical lens. In terms of athlete pay and benefits, as mentioned in the introduction to this chapter, the labor disputes in 2011 between owners and players in the NFL and NBA, arguably the two most popular American sport leagues, raise some important questions about the nature of the relationship between management and labor in professional sport. Though these individuals (i.e., owners/upper level managers and athletes) are highly paid individuals (in comparison to the average member of the workforce), issues of distributive justice (i.e., fairness in the distribution of resources; see Mahony et al., 2010) are important considerations. For example, as an agreement between management and employees of an organization regarding the rights and duties of each party, the collective bargaining agreement in the NFL, arguably the most dangerous and violent of the major team sports in American society, is much more restrictive toward players and tends to favor the interests of management. NFL player contracts are not guaranteed, and management is able to terminate contracts with players with minimal financial loss. This is why players' unions (e.g., NFLPA) have become important for the players as they negotiate with the team owners and executives and the leagues offices. Indeed, ethical questions pertaining to distributive justice should be raised in examining these labor issues in professional sport (see DeSensi & Rosenburg, 2003 for an overview of ethical theories of justice).

In terms of athlete health and participation, ethical questions surrounding whether or not players should play when they are "hurt" or "injured" are common. What role do the coaching staff, team trainer, team doctor, and the athletes play in deciding if and when athletes should participate? In particular, the perceived increase in head concussion injuries among NFL players (as well as football players at lower levels) has become a major issue, so much so that it made the cover of *Time Magazine* (see Vol. 175, No. 5, February 8, 2010) and Congress called NFL commissioner, Roger Goodell, to testify and discuss his plans for addressing the issue. Equally important, Hums et al, (1999) discussed the issue of athletes with diseases (e.g., HIV or AIDS). Although medical advances have certainly been made over the years, the potential for transmission of certain diseases from player to player is at the heart of this ethical issue. Additionally, the dilemma of whether or not to allow athletes with certain health issues (e.g., heart problems) to participate has been and continues to be an ethical and legal issue. The tragic death of former basketball player (e.g., Reggie Lewis of the Boston Celtics) during actual games or practice sessions illuminated this issue, and raises further questions about who has the responsibility to ensure the safety and well-being of these sport participants.

Finally, athlete behavior and conduct, particularly issues related to players' personal and professional lives is important to consider. Upon taking over as NFL commissioner in 2006, Roger Goodell created a code of ethics or personal conduct policy aimed at addressing issues related to the lawful and ethical conduct of all NFL employees, including players under contract and those in negotiations for potential contracts with teams. This personal conduct policy places a heavy emphasis on the ethical and legal issues surrounding the behavior of players and other NFL employees. Goodell has been bold in his enforcement of this code of conduct. There are several examples of players who violated this code, and subsequently, were punished with fines and/or suspension from the league. This raises questions regarding procedural justice (i.e., fairness of procedures and processes used to make decisions; see Mahony et al, 2010) and the consistency with which the personal conduct policy is enforced, among other things.

## College Sport

As mentioned earlier, the college sport industry segment is particularly unique to American society (Beyer & Hannah, 2000). As alluded to earlier, there are several sport governing bodies charged with the responsibility for the governance of college sport; however, the most recognizable sport governing body is the NCAA, with roughly 1000 member institutions (i.e., colleges and universities), including three divisions, with division membership being determined by the number of sports offered, and the amount of scholarship money offered to participants. Since its humble beginnings in the latter half of the nineteenth century, college sport, particularly at the Division I level, has taken on a professional sport model. It has received more exposure in the media (e.g., ESPN U), television rights fees have increased dramatically (e.g., NCAA multibillion dollar deal with CBS sports to air men's basketball tournament), and corporate sponsorship opportunities and coaches salaries have escalated (see Brady et al., 2011). It has taken on a business model as athletics administrators and coaches at all levels have become more involved in budgeting, fund raising and revenue generation, and controlling expenses. Moreover, the increase in rules and regulations that have been created by sport governing bodies has led to more paperwork in areas such as recruiting and academics (Masteralexis et al., 2005).

The popularity and growing commercialization of college sport in the USA, its connection to higher education, and the dominant belief or ideology that college athletes are amateurs has created many ethical issues worthy of discussion and critical reflection. Hums et al. (1999) discussed five salient ethical issues in American college sport: (a) athlete pay or compensation, (b) athlete relationships with player agents, (c) gender equity, (d) diversity, and (e) improprieties by coaches and administrators. Each of these ethical issues as well as others related to college sport are worthy of critical reflection and dialogue. For our purposes here, the focus will be only on the first ethical dilemma: should athletes be paid?

Briefly, the "pay for play" debate raises several important ethical questions that could be contemplated from a critical perspective. NCAA rules and guidelines prohibit athletes on an athletic scholarship from receiving anything more than the monetary equivalent of tuition, room, board, books, and fees plus Pell Grant money up to the athlete's full cost of attendance. These guidelines also now include a provision which allows athletes to work a limited number of hours to supplement their athletic grant-in-aid. Further, as of 2011, the NCAA has enacted a rule change that increases the duration and raises the value of the athletic scholarship (see Gardiner, 2011). However, given the continued growing commercialism of college sport, and the tremendous amounts of revenue generated from this enterprise, several questions should still be considered. What is meant by "paid"? What do athletes, the primary labor force, deserve? Is the athletic scholarship appropriate and sufficient compensation for athletes' services? Are current NCAA rules or bylaws on athlete compensation ethical? Should coaches and administrators be able to earn six and seven figure salaries annually for their services? If athletes were to receive additional compensation, in what form should it come? Which athletes should be paid? How much should they be paid? These questions, and perhaps others, are at the heart of this ethical debate.

### Recreational Sport

The recreational sport industry segment has been integral to most American's lives from childhood through adulthood (Masteralexis et al., 2005). Whether it is a summer camp, little league baseball, swim class at the local YMCA, a church sponsored basketball league, whitewater rafting, social running groups, or a family trip to Yellow Stone National Park, these indoor and outdoor physical and leisure activities have provided fun, excitement, relaxation, social interaction, challenge, and lifestyle enhancement for participants. The operation of private camps and public campgrounds as well as local, state, provincial, and national park management fall into this segment of the industry (Hums et al., 1999). Further, therapeutic recreation and campus recreation are included in this segment. According to Hums et al. (1999), this industry segment has grown from a loose collection of fledgling organizations to professional associations, which continue to define and refine standards in programming and professionalism.

Hums et al. (1999) highlighted some ethical issues facing this industry segment that are worthy of critical reflection and discussion. First, responsibly incorporating risk into activities was discussed because the use of adventure in recreation (e.g., rock climbing wall at student recreation center) has raised serious issues of client trust and informed consent to participate in programming. This is both a legal and ethical issue with which service provides must be concerned. Second, the cost of programming has been viewed as a barrier for low-income participants, and this has limited the diversity among customers in many activities. This speaks to the issue of corporate social responsibility that is directly related to the social contract (i.e., obligation or duty) that exists between the business of sport and society (DeSensi and Rosenburg, 2003). Wendy Frisby and colleagues' (see Frisby et al., 1997; Frisby et al., 2005) participatory action research with low-income women in a Canadian province illuminated this issue from a critical perspective.

**Health and Fitness Club Sport**

The health and fitness club sport industry segment has experienced tremendous growth since the 1970s (Masteralexis et al., 2005). This industry segment includes many different types of organizations. Some are small, individually owned and operated, and others are franchises of international chains (e.g., Gold's Gym, Bally's Fitness Centers; Hums et al., 1999). The aim and purpose of this industry segment is to offer various club memberships to meet the wide variety of exercise and fitness goals for members. These clubs provide different types of equipment and services for their clientele. According to Hums et al. (1999), the International Health and Racquet Sportsclub Association (IHRSA) is an organization that acts as an information center for the health fitness segment of the industry, providing information on industry programming, membership, and financial trends.

Hums et al. (1999) highlighted some ethical issues that are worthy of our critical reflection and discussion. First, high pressure sales have been viewed as a major issue because it has the potential to lead to the abuse of customers. The sales orientation as opposed to service orientation mentality that many sales representatives embrace causes customers to sign contracts sometimes before they fully understand them. Second, lifetime contracts or contracts which are misleading should be of concern. Hums et al. raised some important ethical questions related to this topic: are there clauses concerning if the club moves or if a member becomes disabled and cannot use the club services? Does the club retain the right to change hours or discontinue certain services? These questions and others are important to the discussion of ethical issues in this industry segment. Third and related to the first two issues, abrupt club closings has been a concern. Hums et al. (1999) discussed how health clubs have been notorious for switching locations, reducing hours, and changing their names to confuse creditors. All of these ethical issues have potentially negative effects for the consumers in this particular industry segment.

## CHAPTER SUMMARY

This chapter attempted to take a critical approach to the study and analysis of ethics in sport. In doing so, concepts and theories relevant to the discussion of ethics in sport were discussed. A major portion of this chapter emphasized the societal, organizational, and individual level factors or forces that help to shape or impact the ethical choices and behaviors of various stakeholder groups in sport and physical activity, particularly at the highly commercialized, institutionalized level of sport. The chapter ended with an attempt to briefly highlight some of the ethical issues or dilemmas that have been and continue to be present, and have emerged in various segments of the sport industry.

## DISCUSSION QUESTIONS

1. What is the relationship between ethics, morality, and law/legal issues?
2. In thinking about your experiences as a sport participant, consumer, and/or professional at the various levels of sport (i.e., informal, organized, and corporate), what are some examples of ethical dilemmas you have faced, and how did you deal with them?
3. Which sport industry segment has the most challenging ethical issues, and why?

# RECOMMENDED READINGS

Bell, D. (2002). *Ethical ambition: Living a life of meaning and worth.* New York: Bloomsbury. (This book uses the author's professional and personal life as an example of how a person can be "successful" in a chosen career while still living by their core values and ethical convictions)

Walsh, A., & Giulianotti, R. (2007). *Ethics, money and sport: This sporting mammon.* London: Routledge. (This book combines sociological evidence with analytical tools of philosophy to explore the way money has changed our experience in sport throughout the world. It poses the question, "Is sport 'fair game' for commodification, or are business values destroying sport?").

# REFERENCES

Alipour, S. (2009, October 28). Donaghy book canceled over liability. Retrieved on March 20, 2010 from www.espn.com

Appenzeller, H. (2011). *Ethical behavior in sport.* Durham, NC: Carolina Academic Press.

Associated Press. (2004, November 2). Drugs ruled as cause of death for Caminiti. Retrieved on March 21, 2010 from www.nbcsport.com

Beck, H. (2009, October 30). Tim Donaghy again forces an NBA investigation of referees. Retrieved on March 10, 2010 from www.nytimes.com

Beyer, J.M., & Hannah, D.R. (2000). The cultural significance of athletics in U.S. higher education. *Journal of Sport Management, 14,* 105-132.

Brady, E., & Garcia, M. (2011, November 29). Is Syracuse the next Penn State? Scandals at two schools offer contrasts as well as similarities. *USA Today,* 1A, 2A.

Brady, E., Upton, J., & Berkowitz, S. (2011, November 17). Coaches' pay soars again: Average salary at top schools top $1.47 million. *USA Today,* 1A, 2A.

Branvold, S. (2005). Ethics in sport management (4th ed.). In B. L. Parkhouse (Ed.), *The management of sport: Its foundation and application,* pp. 31-46, Boston: McGraw Hill.

Brooks, D. & Althouse, R. (Eds.) (2007). *Diversity and social justice in college sports: Sport management and the student athlete.* Morgantown, WV: Fitness Information Technology.

Brown, T. N., Jackson, J. S., Brown, K. T., Sellers, R. M., Keiper, S., & Manuel, W. J. (2003). "There's no race on the playing field: Perceptions of racial discrimination among athletes." *Journal of Sport and Social Issues, 27,* 162-183.

Coakley, J. (2007). *Sports in society: Issues and controversies* (9th ed.). Boston: McGraw Hill.

Crosset, T.W. & Hums, M.A. (2005). Ethical principles applied to sport management. In L.P. Masteralexis, C.A. Barr, & M.A. Hums (Eds.), *Principles and practice of sport management* (2nd ed.), pp. 107-123, Boston: Jones and Bartlett.

Cunningham, G.B. (2011). *Diversity in sport organizations* (2nd ed.). Scottsdale, AZ: Holcomb Hathaway.

DeSensi, J.T., & Rosenberg, D. (2003). *Ethics and morality in sport management.* Morgantown, WV: Fitness Information Technology.

Doherty, A. J., & Chelladurai, P. (1999). Managing cultural diversity in sport organizations: A theoretical perspective. *Journal of Sport Management, 13,* 280-297.

Eitzen, D.S. (1988). Ethical problems in American sport. *Journal of Sport and Social Issues,* 12(1), 17-30.

Eitzen, D.S., & Sage, G.H. (2003). *Sociology of North American sport* (7th ed.). Boston: McGraw Hill.

Frisby, W., Crawford, S., & Dorer, T. (1997). Reflections on participatory action research: The case of low income women assessing local physical activity services. *Journal of Sport Management, 11,* 8-28.

Frisby, W., Reid, C.J., Millar, S., & Hoeber, L. (2005). Putting "participatory" into participatory forms of action research. *Journal of Sport Management, 19,* 367-386.

Gardiner, A. (2011, October 28). NCAA enacts rule changes: Scholarship value, duration raised.*USA Today,* 7C.

Gudykunst, W.B., Ting-Toomey, S., & Chua, E. (1988). *Culture and interpersonal communication.* Newbury Park, CA: Sage.

Hums, M.A., & MacLean, J.C. (2004). *Governance and policy in sport organizations.* Scottsdale, AZ: Holcomb Hathaway.

Hums, M.A., Barr, C.A., & Gullion, L. (1999). The ethical issues confronting managers in the sport industry. *Journal of Business Ethics, 20*(1), 51-66.

Jackson, J. J. (1987). Organizational structure. *Journal of Sport Management, 1,* 74-81.

Lapchick, R., Little, E., Lerner, C., & Matthew, R. (2009). *Racial and gender report card: College Sport.* The Institute for Diversity and Ethics in Sport, University of Central Florida: Orlando, Florida.

Lumpkin, A., Stoll, S.K., & Beller, J.M. (2003). *Sport ethics: Applications for fair play* (3rd ed.). Boston: McGraw Hill.

Mahony, D., Hums, M.A., Andrew, D.P.S., & Dittmore, S.W. (2010). Organizational justice in sport. *Sport Management Review, 13,* 91-105.

Malloy, D.C., Ross, S., & Zakus, D.H. (2003). *Sport ethics: Concepts and cases in sport and recreation* (2nd ed.). Canada: Thompson Educational Publishing, Inc.

Masteralexis, L.P., Barr, C.A., & Hums, M.A. (Eds.). (2005). *Principles and practices of sport management* (2nd Ed.). Boston: Jones and Bartlett Publishers.

Munson, L. (2011, July 9). NFL lockout ruling raises timing issues. Retrieved on November 30, 2011 from http://espn.go.com

Morgan, W.J., Meier, K.V., & Schneider, A.J. (Eds.). (2001). *Ethics in sport.* Champaign, IL: Human Kinetics.

Sage, G.H. (1998). *Power and ideology in American sport* (2nd ed.). Champaign, IL: Human Kinetics.

Schein, E.H. (1985). *Organizational culture and leadership.* San Francisco: Jossey-Bass.

Schrager, P. (2010, January 13). Kiffin weasels out at Tennessee, lands in Holly-wood. Retrieved on February 22, 2010 from http://msn.foxsports.com

Sheinin, D. (2004, October 12). Caminiti's death met with sadness, but not shock. Retrieved on March 21, 2010 from www.washingtonpost.com

Shropshire, K. (1996). *In Black and White: Race and sports in America.* Albany, NY: New York University Press.

Shulman, R., & Branigin, W. (2007, August 16). Donaghy pleads guilty in scandal. Retrieved on March 20, 2010 from www.washingtonpost.com

Sports Business Journal. (2006, January 9). How the NCAA works: Breaking down the organizational structure. Retrieved on March 21, 2010 from www.sportsbusinessjournal.com

Taylor, P. (2009, December 8). Why is the NBA getting a pass in Donaghy, referee scandal? Retrieved on March 20, 2010 from http://si.printthis.clickability.com

Volkwein, K.A.E. (1995). Ethics and top-level sport—A paradox? *International Review for the Sociology of Sport, 30,* 311-321.

Walsh, A., & Giulianotti, R. (2007). *Ethics, money and sport: This sporting mammon.* London: Routledge.

Weiberg, S. (2011a, March 30). This shot was worth $1.4 million to Arizona and the Pac-10: Should players get some of it? *USA Today,* 1A, 2A.

Weiberg, S. (2011b, November 29). AD backs background checks for coaches. *USA Today,* 1C.

Zillgitt, J. (2011, November 17). Boies runs point for players: Lawyer has plan to end lockout. *USA Today,* 7C.

# CHAPTER 4

# SPORT AND HEALTH

## Michael B. Edwards and Jonathan M. Casper

\*\*\*

**Learning Objectives**

After reading this chapter, you should be able to:

1. Understand different sociological perspectives of the study of sport and health.
2. Discuss the complex and often-contradictory relationship between sport and health outcomes.
3. Comprehend the ways in which different socialization processes and constraints in adolescence restrict access to many of sport's health promoting benefits for some social groups across the lifespan.
4. Articulate strategies for organizing and promoting sport to develop positive health outcomes.

## INTRODUCTION

Of the many suggested individual and societal benefits attributed to sport, one has been its ability to promote health. The World Health Organization (WHO) defines health as "a state of complete physical, mental, and social well-being and not merely the absence of disease and infirmity"(World Health Organization, 1946, p. 2). Physical health refers to the overall functioning of the human body. Mental health includes self-efficacy and self-esteem, coping with stress, and the ability to think clearly, reason, and function in society (World Health Organization, 2005). Social health has been conceptualized from many different perspectives, but largely it relates to how individuals interact with others and function as members of a community (Durkheim, 1966; Renne, 1974). An individual's health status is theorized as a continuum, with death at one end and maximum well-being on the other (Patrick et al., 1973). Rather than being an objective set of measures, health represents an ideal state where individuals make judgments about their functional status as informed by social and cultural norms.

In a 2004 poll, Americans rated cancer, obesity, heart disease, and diabetes as the biggest health concerns in the US (Trust for America's Health, 2004). A 2001 poll by the Mayo Clinic added stroke and respiratory diseases to that list (Kulas, 2011). In terms of global health, the World Health Organization has identified ischemic heart disease (i.e., disease that restricts normal blood supply) as the leading cause of death worldwide (World Health Organization, 2009). They also suggested that eight risk factors (alcohol use, tobacco use, high blood pressure, high body mass index, low fruit and vegetable intake, and physical inactivity) account for over three-quarters of the likelihood of developing heart disease. What is notable about the WHO's report for the study of sport is that they suggested physical inactivity is as important of a risk factor as smoking. The question is what is the efficacy of sport to promote physical, mental, and social health and to mitigate some of the risk factors associated with health concerns?

To examine this question, we take a sociological perspective to examine the relationship between sport and health. Sociologists attempt to understand how different social institutions and social interactions affect health behaviors (Hyman, 1967). Many sociologists are also interested in understanding how social structures and social problems create inequality in health benefits and access to health promoting resources and, relatedly, what socio-economic groups benefit and suffer in this process (Hyman). The influence of community and social environments on individual health and well-being has been a common theme in sociology since Durkheim's (1966) analysis in the late 19th century of the roles of social structures to influence differences in suicide rates (Lee & Ferraro, 2007). More recently, scholars have utilized social ecological views of health and social behavior to examine how individuals interact with their multiple environments (e.g., social, physical, natural) and how these environments either facilitate or constrain healthy behaviors (McLeroy et al., 1988). This movement reflects an overall trend in the social sciences to move beyond individualistic perspectives that suggest, for example, that poor health is a result of individual choices and behaviors, to an orientation that examines the influences of structural environments on shaping those choices and behaviors (Edwards et al., 2011; Macintyre et al., 2002).

In this chapter, our approach to examining the efficacy of sport to promote health blends multiple sociological approaches (see Table 4.1). First, we use the functionalist approach to health advocated by Parsons (1951), which emphasizes illness and poor health is dysfunctional to society. In this sense, sport is positioned as a beneficial part of the social system. It should be noted, however, that criticisms related to functionalist approaches to health suggest this perspective fails to critically examine the role of legitimate institutions of health and issues related to power and social inequality. In this sense, definitions of health and the status of "acceptable" institutions that determine treatment and prevention strategies are socially constructed and may exclude marginalized perspectives. Even the WHO's definition of health comes under criticism in this way (Callahan, 1973). Therefore, we also incorporate an examination of sport from a conflict perspective advocated by Starr (1982) and Sage (1998), among others. From this perspective, social institutions like sport are seen primarily as serving as a mechanism for social control and reproduction where benefits and dominance of some groups come at the expense of others (Starr). Rather than being universally positive, sport may instead be a site of exploitation and coercion that undermines its assumed benefits (Eitzen, 2003). It should be noted that while we address sport in different ways, based on the relative low rates of sport participation among adults, the emphasis on sport participation in this chapter will often focus on youth sport.

## HISTORY OF SPORT AS A HEALTH REFORM TOOL

The perception of sport's ability to provide positive health outcomes has provided the primary justification for the subsidization of sport by governmental authorities as well as the continual promotion of sport as a societal good (Eitzen, 2003; Gratton, 2006). This perception traces its roots back to the ancient Greeks and the writings of Plato (Plato) in particular. Plato believed that participation in sport and physical activity was necessary for building healthy bodies and the development of moral character in Athenian elites. While historical sport served other utilitarian roles as well, particularly in military-related skills (e.g., archery, jousting), proponents of the *Muscular Christianity* movement in 19th Century Britain and the US were important in the promotion of sport as a health tool (Dunning, 1971). This movement rejected the anti-leisure narrative of Puritanism to advocate for constructive use of leisure time. Leaders of the *Muscular Christianity* movement argued that sport participation was important to develop a balance of physical and spiritual harmony (Putney, 2001). Their ideology resonated with Industrial Revolution-era social reformers who argued sport participation would help improve the quality of life for the urban poor by making them stronger and more physically healthy (Dunning, 1971). Sport was also seen as an important mechanism to help assimilate immigrants to US cities and to promote

Table 4.1. Comparison of Functionalist and Conflict Perspectives of Sport and Health

|  | Functionalist Perspective | Conflict Perspective |
|---|---|---|
| Origins | Based on assumptions about society formed by shared values and social systems that hold society together; social structures exist to contribute to positive social interaction and maintain social order. | Based on assumptions about society formed in use of economic and social power to exploit and oppress lower socio-economic classes; social structures are used as tools of social control to maintain interests of those with power. |
| Conclusions about Sport and Health | Sport transcends social issues and therefore all members of society can receive health benefits from playing sports; sport provides positive health outcomes that benefit individuals and society by reducing illness and poor health; sport programs should be expanded to ensure maximum contribution to social order. | Sport reflects society and therefore sport's health benefits are more likely to be obtained by more privileged socio-economic groups; sport promotes performance and entertainment spectacle, exploiting working class and minority participants who are encouraged to sacrifice bodies for economic gain rather than acquiring health benefits. |
| Criticisms of Approach | Overstates positive health benefits directly attributable to sport participation; assumes all types of sport participation experiences are similar and positive; ignores inability of some groups (e.g., low income, women, minorities, disabled) to fully access sport programs. | Overstates role of socio-economic structures on influencing individual choices in type and style of sport participation; assumes all types of socio-economic groups have similar experiences with sport participation; ignores ability of sport to challenge power relations. |

community interaction (Riess, 1991). These arguments provided the cata-lyst for public space to be set aside for parks and the creation of public and private recreational sport programs (Riess, 1991).

Critics of the health promotion legacy of sport argue that sport during the industrial-era reform period was used more as a means of social con-trol and for promotion of capitalist ideology than to improve the popula-tion's well-being. Social reformers of this era were concerned about pro-moting sport to maintain order by providing a constructive alternative to perceived deviant and unsupervised leisure activities among working class urban dwellers that supposedly threatened moral values and civic political structures (Riess, 1991). Coakley (2004) also points out that the promotion of sport to improve fitness and physical abilities was largely related to increasing economic productivity. In addition to increasing the ability of workers to handle their often poor working conditions, some argued that particular sports (often the ones promoted for public partici-pation) could teach workers the production-oriented values of obedi-ence, punctuality, dependability, self-sacrifice, and the value of hard work as the means to success (Miracle & Rees, 1994).

It is also important to note that sport was organized exclusively as a masculine domain. Females were excluded from full participation in or-ganized sport. Physicians warned that sport participation could reduce women's abilities to conceive and bear healthy children (Coakley, 2004). Luther Gulick, a physician regarded as one of the pioneers in the recrea-tion movement, believed sport was harmful to women's minds and bod-ies, saying, "Athletics do not test womanliness as they test manliness" (cited in Riess, 1991, p. 160). While occasional sporting opportunities ex-isted for women, critics are right to point out that the historical marginal-ization of women continues to affect the inclusion of females in sport and the beliefs about physical benefits of sport for women, even after the passage of Title IX.

## HEALTH AND SPORT

### Benefits of Sport and Physical Activity

Physical activity is defined as "bodily movement produced by skeletal muscles that results in energy expenditure" (Caspersen et al., 1985, p. 126). The enduring popularity of sport's promotion for health benefits is largely based on the increased levels of physical activity realized by its participants. The promotion of sport participation as a central means of increasing physical activity has intensified since growing global concerns about population health and the economic costs of public health issues have increased awareness of the importance of physical activity to maintaining health (Coakley, 2004; World Health Organization, 2003). One important health concern related to levels of physical activity has been increasing obesity rates, particularly among children and adolescents, which tripled between 1979 and 2004 (Hedley et al., 2004). With significant decreases in occupational physical activity (i.e., physical activity on the job) in developed nations occurring with increases in workforce automation and service sector careers, increased attention has been placed on increasing leisure-time physical activity in these countries (Kaczynski & Henderson, 2007).

Lack of leisure-time physical activity is a direct antecedent to obesity (Cawley et al., 2007), and strong associations exist between obesity rates and rates of physical inactivity (Brock et al., 2009). However, physical activity serves to combat public health issues beyond obesity (Floyd et al., 2008). While obesity itself is a risk factor for most identified health concerns, increased physical activity has been shown to decrease health risks independent of weight status (Blair & Brodney, 1999; World Health Organization, 2003). A report by the United Kingdom's Department of Health (2001) suggested that regular physical activity has been shown to decrease cardiovascular mortality; reduce high blood pressure; improve bone health; increase cognitive functioning; reduce risk of cancers; reduce risk of depression; and provide positive benefits for mental health, including reducing anxiety and enhancing self-esteem. Sport is not only believed to increase physical activity in participants, but it is regarded as a more enjoyable, satisfying, and motivating way to be physically active (Right to Play International, 2008). Based on this position, organized sport programs remain an important mechanism to promote physical activity worldwide (Moore & Werch, 2005). In fact, the World Health Organization (2003) suggests that participation in sport programs is an essential part of a healthy lifestyle. This proposition has received support in research showing individuals who participate in sport average more weekly physical activity than those who do not participate in sports (Phillips & Young, 2009). Additionally, evidence suggests that physically active children grow up to be physically active adults (Green et al., 2005). Getting involved in sports in childhood is important to staying involved as a teenager and pursuing physical activity as an adult. Researchers have found that joining youth sports at an early age and continuing through adolescence increases the likelihood of being physically active later in life (Perkins et al., 2004). For example, women who participated in team sports in their youth are more likely to be physically active later in life; as a result, they have decreased risk factors for heart disease, as well as maintaining healthier weight and body mass index (BMI) (Alfano et al., 2002).

Physical activity is the primary direct health benefit associated with sport participation. Beyond the suggested increased physical activity, sport may provide multiple secondary health benefits based on participation, as well as using sport as a communication platform to promote health. Sport participation is connected with improved social, emotional, and mental health, as well as decreased risks of engaging in presumed risky health behaviors. Most frequently, this association has been examined with youth sport participants. Compared to non-participants, adolescent sport participants consume higher levels of fruits and vegetables (Pate et al., 2000) and report lower use of cigarettes (Escobedo et al., 1993) and hard drugs (Pate et al., 2000). Adolescent girls who participate in sport are also less likely to engage in risky sexual behavior or have an unwanted pregnancy (Kulig et al., 2003; Miller et al., 2005). Sport participation is also associated with lower anxiety and depression and higher levels of self-esteem and social competence (Babiss & Gangwich, 2009; McHale et al., 2005; Vilhjalmsson & Thorlindsson, 1998).

In terms of increasing social health, sport is portrayed as a source of social connectivity that creates opportunities for individuals and communities to come together (Right to Play International, 2008). Regular participation in organized sport provides opportunities for social interaction and is associated with increased social connectivity among co-participants (Putnam, 2000). Youth sports also allow families to not only bond with each other through their different roles in playing, spectating, and organizing teams and leagues, but also families can develop relationships with other sports families (Trussell, 2009). Finally, spectator sports are perceived to increase collective experiences among fans that lead to more social cohesion across communities, ethnic groups, and economic classes (with the notable exceptions created through racism, hooliganism, and sectarian violence) (Smith, 1988).

Although less studied, some have argued that sports provide indirect health benefits through the entertainment appeal of elite athletes and sport organizations as a mechanism to deliver health education information and support health initiatives (Right to Play International, 2008). For example, the National Football League in the US has launched a campaign, "Play 60," to promote youth physical activity and play (Bamesberger, 2011). While the connections between football and physical activity may be more obvious, leveraging the popularity of high performance sport to promote other health behaviors is increasing. For example, the Roll Back Malaria Partnership in Africa uses global soccer stars in a series of television commercials to educate the public about malaria prevention, and Major League Baseball teams wear pink uniforms on Mother's Day to promote breast cancer awareness (Feinsand, 2011; Right to Play International). The demonstration of sport's effectiveness as a health awareness tool was also seen in the prominent role of basketball star Earvin "Magic" Johnson to change public perceptions about HIV/AIDS and push for increased research for the disease following his HIV-positive diagnosis (Casey et al., 2003). This aspect of sport's role in promoting positive health outcomes may be worth exploring in the future, although sport seems to deliver its main health benefits through direct participation.

## Criticisms of Sport's Efficacy to Promote Positive Health Outcomes

The benefits of regular engagement in leisure-time physical activity are obvious. This relationship has been central to arguments made by advocates for increased expenditures on and promotion of recreational sport since antiquity. However, this advocacy approach often fails to distinguish between the benefits of broader physical activities and sport more specifically (Robson, 2001). Sport, of course, is a specialized form of leisure-time physical activity, but not all leisure-time physical activity is sport. Particularly in the US, sport is organized to emphasize competition, specialization, and rule structures (Coakley, 2004). While, to a point, the physical activity and training required of sport participation is beneficial, this may not be an intentional outcome of participation in competitive sport (Eitzen, 2003). Indeed, even Plato insisted that competitive sport was not a suitable source for health-promoting physical activity, citing that its focus on winning encouraged training regimes that were ill-designed to foster comprehensive physical fitness. This position has also received increased attention in research. For example, Walters et al. (2007) found that while former youth sport participants remained more physically active than non-participants in adulthood, physical activity levels dropped more significantly among youth sports participants in adulthood. In their longitudinal study, these researchers also suggested that socio-economic status and gender were important moderators of the retention of physical activity levels into adulthood among youth athletes, with lower SES male youth sport participants showing the most significant declines in physical activity. Additionally, the US childhood obesity crisis has occurred despite dramatic increases in youth sport participation (Louv, 2005). Thus, organized, competitive sport may not deliver recommended levels of physical activity to enough participants in comparison to unstructured sport or non-competitive physical activities (Kanters et al., 2011). Critics also point out that some popular organized sports encourage healthy physical activity more so than others do. For example, to maximize performance at some positions, American football players may be encouraged by coaches to become overweight or obese (Kaplan et al., 1995). Bat and ball sports may also provide fewer opportunities for physical activity than other sports (Floyd et al., 2008), perhaps due to the games' requirements for more sedentary time (e.g., sitting in the dugout waiting to bat or standing in the field). Conversely, Ainsworth et al. (2000) found that participants in sports, which encourage more continuous play (e.g., handball, martial arts, rugby, soccer, racquet sports, and swimming) recorded higher levels of physical activity.

In addition to questions about the efficacy of sport to universally deliver recommended levels of physical activity, many scholars have argued that sport may be as likely to provide poorer health outcomes as positive health outcomes. Injuries are common to sport participants. Many former athletes are able to quickly point out nagging aches and pains that remain from their playing days. For example, many retired players from the National Football League report living with chronic pain and musculoskeletal disabilities due to the extreme physical contact endured in that sport (Schwenk et al., 2007). Some have suggested that injuries are so common to sport that they have been normalized as an accepted part of playing games (Curry & Strauss, 1994). Athletes are even celebrated for "playing hurt" or returning to games too quickly after a serious injury, even if the decision to continue participation increases the likelihood of more permanent disability (Nixon, 1993). Additionally, the nature of many sports encourages violence that is both legitimate (i.e., within the rule of the game, like hard hits in football or body checks in hockey) and illegitimate (i.e., outside the rules of the game, like fighting). These acts heighten the risk of injuries to participants. Coaches and sport leagues encourage much of this violence and aggressive behavior as ways of intimidating opponents and increasing the excitement of the sport performance, respectively. Some research has even suggested that when coaches encourage aggression and violent behavior, athletes have an increased likelihood of being aggressive or violent off the field (Wagmiller et al., 2006).

There have also been dramatic increases in sport injuries to children. Nearly half (48%) of all youth sport participants have experienced injuries due to their participation (Patel & Nelson, 2000). What may be most troubling is that the most common injuries to youth sport participants are musculoskeletal overuse injuries due to increased and specialized training regimens designed to assist these young athletes reach elite status (Hawkins & Metheny, 2001). Intense training routines for sport are also responsible for another condition described as the "female athlete triad" (Birch, 2005). This condition refers to three prominent risks to female athletes who exceed healthy levels of physical activity in their training programs: Amenorrhea (i.e., premature cessation or delay of menstruation), anorexia athletica (i.e., eating disorders associated with weight control for training and sport performance), and osteoporosis (i.e., loss of bone mineral density).

There have also been questions raised about sport's ability to promote mental and emotional health, particularly high performance sport. Too often the focus on winning and getting to elite levels changes the meaning of sport and discourages participation. Many individuals stop playing sport due to low self-competence (Hedstrom & Gould, 2004). Instead of being a place to encourage self-esteem and promote self-confidence, sport often has the opposite effect for less skilled athletes. Additionally, one of the most common negative outcomes of high performance sports is increased stress resulting in burnout. Competitive sport places excessive levels of stress on athletes, particularly children, who often burnout as a result. Some of the most common factors associated with sport burnout include: high expectations, a win at all cost attitude, parental pressure, long repetitive practices with little variety, inconsistent coaching practices, overuse injuries, excessive practices and time demands, social support displayed on the basis of winning and losing, and perfectionism (Weinberg & Gould, 2003). These factors suggest that sport has the potential to also negatively impact socio-emotional and mental development.

Finally, critics have examined sport's ability to promote healthy social interactions among participants and spectators. Dyreson (2001) argues that trash talking, which is often racist, misogynistic, and homophobic in nature, frequently permeates interactions on the court or playing field, calling "in-your-face rather than face-to-face communication" (p. 23). Far from Putnam's ideal of sport as a fountain of bridging social capital, Dyreson argues that playing sport often fosters an "us" versus "them" mentality (see also Chapter 1). This sentiment, frequently fueled by media glamorization, has elevated many groups of players and spectators to violent acts against each other. Sometimes, this violence transcends sport such as in the case of religious sectarianism that underlies some soccer rivalries. For example, supporters of the biggest soccer clubs in Glasgow, Scotland, have experienced numerous high profile violent clashes rooted in their historical religious, economic, and cultural animosity (the city's Protestants have historically associated with Rangers Football Club and Catholics with The Celtic Football Club) (Roadburg, 1980). Other times however, the sports rivalry itself can fuel fan violence leading to severe injury and death. For example, in August 2011, 70 fans were ejected from an exhibition game between the National Football League rivals San Francisco Forty-Niners and Oakland Raiders for violent acts against opposing fans; 12 fans were arrested, two were shot in the parking lot, and one was assaulted and beaten in a stadium restroom (Klemko, 2011). This type of behavior, historically absent from North American sport, is on the rise. Additionally, while research on youth sport violence is limited, it is easy to find numerous instances in the media about confrontational and even violent behaviors at youth sporting events, including acts of aggression by parents toward coaches, officials, and even youth sport participants (Heinzmann, 2002). When the stakes of winning and losing and the performance ethic in sports get high, emotional stress and anxiety may interfere with healthy social functioning. It is also important to note that the stress of high performance sport may affect spectators in other unhealthy ways too. For example, a 2008 study in the *New England Journal of Medicine* found that watching World Cup soccer matches more than doubled the risk of acute cardiovascular events (e.g., heart attacks) among Germans during the 2006 World Cup (Wilbert-Lampen et al., 2008).

Overall, the ability of sport to provide expected levels of healthy physical activity and promote mental and social health may be contextual to how specific sports are organized and delivered. The current way many sports are managed and marketed in our society may inhibit sport's direct contribution to health promotion (Chalip, 2006). Sport's efficacy to promote positive health outcomes may only be realized if sport is organized in a way that deemphasizes competitive performance and intentionally promotes health, positive social interaction, and inclusive participation across all population groups (Coakley, 2004).

# ACCESSIBILITY OF "HEALTHY" SPORT ACROSS THE LIFESPAN

As indicated earlier, one important aim of sociological approaches to health is to understand inequalities associated with differential access to health promoting resources based on wealth or social status (Hyman, 1967). It has been well established that the risk of poor health is not distributed equally across the social hierarchy of populations. For example, disadvantaged socio-economic groups such as the poor, racial/ethnic minorities, women, people with disabilities, and senior citizens are more likely to have poorer health outcomes than advantaged socio-economic groups (Braveman, 2006). Not surprisingly, these disadvantaged groups are also more likely to be physically inactive both in childhood and as adults (Coakley, 2004; Day, 2006; Floyd et al., 2008; Richmond et al., 2006; Young et al., 2007).

Table 4.2 shows differences in youth sport participation by race and gender, and Table 4.3 shows group differences in participating in recommended levels of leisure-time physical activity.

Table 4.2: United States Youth Sport Participation Rates by Race and Gender

| Race | Gender | Sport Participation |
|------|--------|---------------------|
| White, Non-Hispanic | Male | 64% |
| | Female | 58% |
| Black, Non-Hispanic | Male | 67% |
| | Female | 47% |
| Hispanic | Male | 62% |
| | Female | 44% |

*Source*: CDC HS YRBS 2009

As indicated, some groups, particularly racial and ethnic minority females, are more at risk for physical inactivity than others. Sociologists and health researchers have sought to determine how differences in access to supportive environmental resources (e.g., programs, facilities, safe neighborhoods), and differences in social and cultural practices function to either reduce or maintain these health disparities. As an important social and cultural institution, sport has also been examined from this perspective. As we have suggested, sport's health benefits are not necessarily universal and must be intentional to the organization and management of specific sport activities. Therefore, we should examine

80

the ways in which some groups may have better access to par
in the types of sport that promotes health.

As mentioned previously, playing sports across the lifespan may lead to
many desirable physical, mental, and social health outcomes. Therefore,
continued sport participation across a lifespan is important. Sport participation rates peak around age 13 and then decline for older age cohorts.

Table 4.3: United States Adults Meeting Recommended Levels of LTPA by Race
and Gender

| Race | Gender | Recommended LTPA |
|------|--------|------------------|
| White, Non-Hispanic | Male | 53% |
| | Female | 50% |
| Black, Non-Hispanic | Male | 45% |
| | Female | 36% |
| Hispanic | Male | 42% |
| | Female | 41% |

Source: CDC BRFSS 2007

The most noticeable decline in sport participation is the older adolescent
age group. Researchers have suggested that participation in sport at exactly this stage of adolescence is a critical mediator for keeping young
people physically active into adulthood (Curtis et al., 1999; MacPhail &
Kirk, 2006). Therefore, the likelihood of maintaining healthy levels of
physical activity through sport participation becomes much lower if
youth are discontinuing sport at this period in their lives.

In addition to age discrepancies with respect to physical activity, the fact
that rates of participation in sport and attrition from sport are not the
same across socio-economic groups is troubling. For example, girls, particularly those from racial and ethnic minority groups, drop out of sport
at higher rates than boys do during the adolescent years (Phillips &
Young, 2009; Young et al., 2007). Sport participation over time is often
directly linked to economic status because of significant barriers faced by
low income youth (Day, 2006). Youth with physical and mental disabilities also have increasing difficulty participating in sport (Kozub & Porretta, 1996). Additionally, the universal negative effects of aging on preventing participation in sport increases for minorities, members of lower
socio-economic classes, and persons with disabilities (Adler & Rehkopf,

2008). To better understand how social inequality may prevent many people from accessing the positive health benefits sport may offer, we need to examine the process by which different groups become socialized into sport as well as understand the constraints different groups experience to participating in "healthy" sport.

## Mechanisms for Socializing Youth into Sport

Socialization is fundamental to understanding sport participation across the lifespan. The basic premise is that understanding sport participation requires a social element, arguing that people can learn new information and behaviors by watching other people. Socialization is the process of learning to live in and understand a culture or subculture by internalizing its values, beliefs, attitudes, and norms (Long & Hadden, 1985). It is an active process of learning and social development that occurs as we interact with others.

Socialization is the cornerstone of the functionalist approach to sociology. Social order is maintained through the process of learning and development that transmits central values and culture of a society to individuals (Rojek, 2005; Ruddell & Shinew, 2006). Socialization involves the formation of ideas about who we are and what is important in our lives. In sport, socialization occurs through contact with socialization agents (e.g., family, peers, and media) from which individuals interpret what is societally approved behavior. Parents serve as the dominant socialization agent for children in these formative years prior to adolescence (Dotson & Hyatt, 2005; Moschis, 1987). Parents are also most likely to introduce their children to sport (Green & Chalip, 1998; Greendorfer et al., 2002), and children are likely to adopt their parents' beliefs and motivations toward sport (Eccles, 1993). Siblings may also provide an "intragenerational" influence that becomes stronger in the transition from childhood to adolescence (Cotte & Wood, 2004; Pechmann & Knight, 2002). Because children have indicated that their desire for affiliation, and social recognition is a primary motive for their involvement in sport programs (Weiss & Petlichkoff, 1989), peer influence is likely to be integral in a child's sport behavior. In addition to peers and siblings, teachers and school-specific peer groups also affect the socialization of youth (Moschis, 1987). Lastly, the influence of the mass media may also be especially important in the development of attitudes about participating in sport because of the significant presence of sports on television and video games. For example, the portrayal of athletes as celebrities and actions of athletes promoted in these media may encourage some children to participate in certain sports (Bailey & Sage, 1988).

Another way in which researchers have approached socialization is to examine the sociological factors that encourage participation across parts of the lifespan. In particular, sociologists are interested in social inequality and its reproduction based on three prominent socially constructed contexts for inequality: gender, race, and social class. This research focuses on why some social groups maintain sport and physical activity participation from childhood and adolescence into adulthood, and why other groups are more likely to withdraw from these activities at different transitional points in their lifespan. This approach suggests adults learn their role as a sport participant based upon the opportunities they had to participate during childhood and adolescence. As individuals age, they will seek to maintain some level of continuity in their lifestyle (Atchley, 1989). In order to encourage people to participate in recreational sport throughout their lifespan, they must be provided with the opportunity to participate in a broad range of activities in childhood and adolescence that can be realistically maintained in adulthood (Green et al., 2005). Throughout the lifespan, it is expected that participation in many of these activities will cease, but having a wider pool from which to choose may encourage the continuation of participation in some activities (Green et al., 2005). Therefore, youth sports that are considered "lifetime" in nature, that is they can be played across the lifespan, are especially important in facilitating physical activity into adulthood. Thus, the Centers for Disease Control and Prevention (CDC) guidelines indicates that community sports and recreation program coordinators can help increase physical activity among youth in a variety of ways, including providing a mix of competitive team and non-competitive teams, lifelong fitness, and recreational activities.

In addition to exploring the process by which youth engage in sport participation and then maintain participation into adulthood, research has also examined why youth do not engage in sport. Understanding constraints to sport participation could help explain the decline in youth sport participation across different social groups (Casper et al., 2011). Constraints theory suggests that individuals perceive various intrapersonal, interpersonal, and structural barriers that inhibit or prohibit participation and enjoyment in leisure activities (Crawford et al., 1991). Sallis et al. (2000) showed that perceived constraints were the most consistent negative psychological correlate of physical activity among children. The most salient constraints that limit or prevent sport participation include a lack of time, partners, facilities and equipment, and a perceived lack of skill or confidence. While the types of constraints that often prevent youth from continuing sport participation are similar across groups, socio-economic disadvantage seems to intensify the strength of constraints to prevent participation (Cunningham, 2008). Constraints have been found to be especially prevalent in predicting decreased sport participation for girls, Latinos, lower SES youth.

## Socialization and Disparities in Sport's Health Benefits

We have provided some understanding of the ways sport can be organized to increase the likelihood of providing desired health outcomes. Additionally, we have discussed the process that encourages or constrains some individuals from participating in sport from childhood into adulthood. Now, we will use these concepts to better understand how the organization and delivery of sport in our society may serve to reproduce health disparities. In particular, why are many socio-economically disadvantaged groups less likely to engage in some lifetime sports and more likely to abandon sport participation after adolescence and become mere sports spectators (Bourdieu, 1978)? Some authors have suggested that the organizational system in the US promotes participation for elite athletes as age increases and consequently benefiting already advantaged groups while simultaneously discriminating against the disadvantaged (Barr-Anderson et al., 2007; Edwards, 1986). In the long term, the exclusion of certain groups from participation in sports may lead to less leisure time physical activity and more health risks in adulthood. In this case, sport practices may serve to reproduce health inequality among marginalized groups in society.

In addition to requiring a high level of skill, competitive sports participation generally demands a greater commitment of time for practices and traveling to competitions. Kimm et al. (2006) discovered that lack of time was the primary reason girls in this age group dropped out of sport. Adolescent girls also seek out a broader range of cooperative physical activities than are offered in traditional recreational sports programs. For example, Barr-Anderson et al. (2007) found that adolescent girls favored participation in swimming, dance, cheerleading, and gymnastics rather than traditional competitive team sports. Traditional programs of competitive sports may also emphasize socially constructed masculine values, such as violence and aggression (Hanson & Kraus, 1999). In communities that promote more traditional gender ideologies, sport and physical activity may be viewed as a male domain. In these contexts, athletic ability and participation in sport and physical activity should only be celebrated among men, and women who participate in physical activities beyond a certain age may be labeled as "masculine" (Shakib & Dunbar, 2004, p. 286). Adolescent girls also often model their mother's physical activity behavior (Shakib & Dunbar, 2004) and may not perceive adult women as being physically active in sport environments. These characteristics may discourage interest in sport by girls who might view playing sport solely within the context of masculine values historically promoted in sports (Coakley, 2004).

Members of higher socio-economic classes participate in sport, particularly lifetime sports, more and longer than do members of lower socio-economic classes. It is understood that certain economic and structural constraints (e.g., available spare time, transportation, money for equipment) are heightened for members of lower socio-economic classes. Parents' level of education, one of the key markers of social class, continues to be the most significant factor in predicting sport participation (Young et al., 2007), particularly in females (Hasbrook, 1987). Additionally, public and private opportunities that support sports participation (e.g., parks, recreation programs) are less likely to be found in low income and minority communities and neighborhoods (Edwards et al., 2011; Smoyer-Tomic et al., 2004). While in Europe, some of the social class differences in participation have diminished (Scheerder et al., 2005), community resources for these activities in the US are often distributed unequally based upon social class (Eitzen, 1996). Education budgets have also been cut dramatically across the US. Increasing emphasis is being placed on academic achievement measured through standardized testing leading to a significant reduction in financial resources for physical education and co-curricular physical activities. While reduced school-based activities, and its negative effects on health across the lifespan, has been experienced across our society, the most severe cuts have occurred in socio-economically disadvantaged schools with high populations of low-income and minority populations, in inner cities, and rural areas (Edwards et al., 2011; Outley & Floyd, 2002). Thus, socio-economically disadvantaged youth are increasingly becoming the least likely to have access to the resources necessary to provide support for public opportunities for physical activity (Sallis et al., 2001).

Some researchers have also attempted to explain social class disparities in sport participation through both structural and cultural conditions using the theoretical framework of Bourdieu (1978) (see also Chapter 16). Bourdieu argues that the meaning we attach to socially constructed institutions and leisure activities, like sport, and the appropriateness of how we participate in these activities is shaped by historical and cultural structures. From this perspective, sport may be viewed in the more practical terms of social and financial mobility for members of lower socio-economic classes, rather than for health and fitness outcomes. In this case, sport becomes seen as a setting to sacrifice the physical health of the body for extrinsic gain, rather than a health promoting mechanism. According to Bourdieu, sport participation therefore becomes limited for lower socio-economic classes beyond adolescence based on their concentration in intensive contact team sports (e.g., football) that pay off in status attainment and possible social mobility. Conversely, the upper class tends to participate in sports that offer more health benefits and participation opportunities long into adulthood. These sports, "practiced for their functions of physical maintenance and for the social profit they bring, have in common the fact that their age-limit lies far beyond youth" (Bourdieu, p. 837).

The reasons for racial differences in participation in sport are complex (Philipp, 1998). Philipp argues that race becomes central to peer group approval of leisure activities. The interpersonal influences of friends, family members, and other adult role models are critical for getting children to participate in sport (Crossman et al., 2006). Children of racial and ethnic minority groups are therefore often socialized to participate in activities that are culturally appropriate and discouraged from participating in sports which are not. For many racial and ethnic minorities, sport is seen in the utilitarian terms described by Bourdieu, offering faint hope of a college football or basketball scholarship and social mobility (Eitle & Eitle, 2002). Additionally, sport participation is often considered suitable for males but not necessarily for females within the cultural traditions of many racial and ethnic minority populations. Therefore, culture may explain why racial and ethnic variations in physical activity participation are often found among girls, but not boys (Phillips & Young, 2009). In contrast, other differences in participation are a result of poverty, historic discrimination of minority groups, and neighborhood locations (Washburne, 1978). For example, African Americans have historically been excluded from public spaces for swimming and therefore may be less likely to develop the skills necessary or the interest in participating in swimming activities (Hastings et al., 2006). Additionally, soccer gained popularity in the United States as a middle class suburban sport, and therefore middle class children are more likely to play it (Goldsmith, 2003). Based on their family's SES or residence within less-deprived neighborhoods, White children have earlier access to swimming and soccer and may be more likely to develop the skills and attitudes toward the sport required to continue their participation.

Overall, sport's ability to provide health-promoting benefits across the lifespan requires accessibility to sport programs and facilities, as well as to specific lifetime sports that provide participants with recommended levels of physical activity from adolescence into adulthood. The inclusion of all socio-economic groups into these sport experiences is vital to reducing health disparities and promoting population health. Unfortunately, divergent socialization patterns and cultural constructions of the meaning of sport participation may prevent all socio-economic groups from accessing and being included in sport participation.

## CONCLUSIONS AND RECOMMENDATIONS

The relationship between sport and health is complex. Rather than promoting universal physical, mental, and social health benefits as advocated in the functionalist perspective, sport can also heighten risks of injury, produce emotional stress and anxiety, and encourage violence and social conflict. However, rather than focusing on the negative aspects of sport, as often becomes the case in the conflict perspective, it is more constructive to acknowledge the potential for sport as a site to promote lifetime physical activity and reduce health disparities to seek strategies to improve sport's efficacy in this regard. Sport must be organized and delivered in a way that reduces the emphasis on high performance and competition. To ensure sport provides maximum health benefits, the ultimate focus of sport programs needs to be promotion of physical activity, positive social and mental health outcomes, and the encouragement of healthy lifestyles across the lifespan. Policy and practices related to sport programs would also need to ensure the reduction of cultural and structural constraints that have traditionally prevented the full inclusion of all socio-economic groups from sport participation.

Given these findings, we offer nine recommendations to increase sport's efficacy to promote maximum health benefits and reduce health risks and disparities.

1.  Recreation and school extracurricular programs must increasingly offer and encourage a broad range of competitive sport and non-competitive physical activities that appeal to all interests and abilities and can be continued across the lifespan.

2. Youth sport specialization must be limited, and children and adolescents should be encouraged to participate in many different sports.
3. To reduce some barriers to entry that have developed as youth sport became more competitive and selective, education programs should be implemented to teach youth sport skills and build competence to engage in new sports.
4. Sport programs should also be developed and supported to allow participation across all skill levels, physical abilities, and commitment levels.
5. Financial barriers (e.g., entry fees, cost of equipment and uniforms, and travel) should be reduced at all competitive levels.
6. Within sport programs, opportunities to move and be physically active should be increased, and time spent sitting on the sidelines or standing around should be reduced.
7. Excessive violent contact and physicality should be discouraged at all levels of competitive sport.
8. Sport programs should intentionally encourage positive interaction between opposing players and fans to build a culture of ethics and good sporting behaviors.
9. Continuous youth coaching certification and education programs should be developed and implemented to ensure best practices are promoted and encouraged.

While these recommendations are not comprehensive, they present clear strategies to improve sport's ability to promote positive physical, mental, and social health. As with any imbedded social institution, attempts to change sport in this way will likely be met with some resistance, most notably from those individuals and groups who have a vested interest in maintaining the status quo. Sport has become a powerful cultural and economic phenomenon that prioritizes the performance ethic and commercialization of the entertainment experience of spectator sports. Additionally, myths related to sport's role in society overstate sport's positive health outcomes and ignores many of the negative aspects of sport. However, sport is socially constructed and therefore can be changed for the better. This chapter has provided an outline of sport's potential for delivering positive health outcomes, and suggested how sport can be intentionally transformed to promote health to individuals and society.

## CHAPTER SUMMARY

The purpose of this chapter was to examine the relationship between sport and positive health outcomes from a sociological perspective. First, we defined health and discussed two primary sociological approaches, functionalism and conflict, that frame different perspectives about sport and health. We then discussed many of the health benefits of sport participation found in the research, including increased physical activity, reduced risk behaviors, lower anxiety and depression, higher levels of self-esteem, social competence, and social connectivity. Next, we presented criticisms of sport's health efficacy that suggested sport can also lead to increased injuries, higher emotional distress, and violence, particularly when it focuses on elite performance and competition. We then described different health disparities related to socio-economic status and described how levels of sport participation across the lifespan, particularly in sports more likely to encourage healthy lifestyles, are higher for individuals from more privileged socio-economic status groups. These group differences are based on differences in socialization methods and social, cultural, and economic barriers to participation in adolescence. We ended the chapter by presenting some potential strategies for organizing sport programs in ways that may maximize sport's health efficacy and promote inclusion across all socio-economic groups.

## DISCUSSION QUESTIONS

1. Think back to your own participation or non-participation in youth sport. How were you socialized into specific types of sport participation? What were some of the significant facilitators or constraints to your sport participation as you entered adulthood?
2. Considerable attention has been focused on suggested increases in violence in sport. Do you think violence is an issue in sports today? Why or why not?
3. Some critics of Title IX argue that it has only helped increase sport and physical activity participation for White girls. Is this criticism justified? How can we increase opportunities for girls of color to engage in healthy sport and physical activity across the lifespan?
4. Examine the sport programs in your community (from youth sports up to college and professional sports) from both a functionalist and conflict perspective. Describe the relationship of these programs to promote physical, mental and social health based on each of these perspectives.

5.  We presented some strategies to improve the efficacy of sport to promote positive health outcomes across the population. What other strategies can you suggest to improve the ability of sport to promote health?

## RECOMMENDED READINGS

Right to Play International. (2008). *Harnessing the power of sport for development and peace: Recommendations to governments.* Toronto, ON: Sport for Development and Peace International Working Group. (A United Nations working group report that comprehensively discusses global health and social issues and the ways in which sport can be used to alleviate these issues. It is a very comprehensive examination of sport in this context and provides excellent examples.)

Eitzen, D. S. (2003). *Fair and Foul: Beyond the Myths and Paradoxes of Sport.* New York: Rowman & Littlefield. (One of the best and most direct critical examinations of sport, Eitzen lays out the paradoxes of sports and its dual benefits and issues across numerous topics.)

Riess, S. A. (1991). *City Games: The Evolution of American Urban Society and the Rise of Sports.* Urbana, IL: University of Illinois Press. (Although 20 years old, this book still provides one of the best comprehensive descriptions of the rise of sport as a health and social reform tool during the industrial-era urbanization period.)

## REFERENCES

Adler, N. E., & Rehkopf, D. H. (2008). US Disparities in Health: Descriptions, Causes, and Mechanisms. *Annual Review of Public Health, 29,* 235-252.

Ainsworth, B. E., Haskell, W. L., Whitt, M. C., Irwin, M. L., Swartz, A. M., Strath, S. J. et al. (2000). Compendium of Physical Activities: an update of activity codes and MET intensities. *Medicine & Science in Sports & Exercise, 32*(9), S498-S516.

Alfano, C. M., Klesges, R. C., Murray, D. M., Beech, B. M., & McClanahan, B. S. (2002). History of sport participation in relation to obesity and related health behaviors in women. *Preventive Medicine, 34*(1), 82-89.

Atchley, R. (1989). The continuity theory of normal aging. *The Gerontologist, 29,* 183-190.

Babiss, L. A., & Gangwich, J. E. (2009). Sports participation as a protective factor against depression and suicidal idealation in adolescents as mediated by self-esteem and social support. *Journal of Developmental and Behavioral Pediatrics, 30,* 376-384.

Bailey, C. I., & Sage, G. H. (1988). Values communicated by a sports event: The case of the Super Bowl. *Journal of Sport Behavior, 11*, 126-143.

Bamesberger, M. (2011, December 3). 'Fuel up to Play 60' Puts Focus on Food and Fitness, *Omaha World-Herald*. Retrieved from www.omaha.com.

Barr-Anderson, D. J., Young, D. R., Sallis, J. F., Neumark-Sztainer, D. R., Gittel-sohn, J., Webber, L. et al. (2007). Structured physical activity and psychosocial correlates in middle-school girls. *Preventive Medicine, 44*, 404-409.

Birch, K. (2005). Female athlete triad. *BMJ, 330*(7485), 244-246.

Blair, S. N., & Brodney, S. (1999). Effects of physical inactivity and obesity on morbidity and mortality: Current evidence and research issues. *Medicine & Science in Sports & Exercise, 31*(11), S646-S662.

Bourdieu, P. (1978). Sport and Social Class. *Social Science Information, 17*, 819-840.

Braveman, P. (2006). Health disparities and health equity: Concepts and Measurement. *Annual Review of Public Health, 27*, 167-194.

Brock, D. W., Thomas, O., Cowan, C. D., Allison, D. B., Gaesser, G. A., & Hunter, G. R. (2009). Association between insufficiently physically active and the prevalence of obesity in the United States. *Journal of Physical Activity and Health, 6*(1), 1-5.

Callahan, D. (1973). The WHO definition of 'health'. *The Hastings Center Studies, 1*(3), 77-87.

Casey, M. K., Allen, M., Emmers-Sommer, T., Sahlstein, E., Degooyer, D. A. N., Winters, A. M. et al. (2003). When a celebrity contracts a disease: The example of Earvin "Magic" Johnson's announcement that he was HIV positive. *Journal of Health Communication, 8*, 249-265.

Casper, J., Bocarro, J. N., Kanters, M. A., & Floyd, M. F. (2011). "Just let me play!" Understanding constraints that limit adolescent sport participation. *Journal of Physical Activity and Health, 8*, S32-39.

Caspersen, C. J., Powell, K. E., & Christenson, G. M. (1985). Physical activity, exercise, and physical fitness: Definitions and distinctions for health-related research. *Public Health Reports, 100*(2), 126-131.

Cawley, J., Meyerhoefer, C., & Newhouse, D. (2007). The correlation of youth physical activity with state policies. *Contemporary Economic Policy, 25*, 506-517.

Chalip, L. (2006). Toward a distinctive sport management discipline. *Journal of Sport Management, 20*, 1-21.

Coakley, J. J. (2004). *Sport in society: issues & controversies* (8th ed.). Boston: McGraw-Hill.

Cotte, J., & Wood, S. L. (2004). Families and innovative consumer behavior: A triadic analysis of sibling and parental influence. *Journal of Consumer Research, 31*, 78-86.

Crawford, D. W., Jackson, E. L., & Godbey, G. C. (1991). A hierarchical model of leisure constraints. *Leisure Sciences, 13*, 309-320.

Crossman, A., Sullivan, D. A., & Benin, M. (2006). The family environment and American adolescents' risk of obesity as young adults. *Social Science & Medicine, 63*, 2255-2267.

Cunningham, G. B. (2008). The influence of race on barriers to physical activity. *Applied Research in Coaching and Athletics Annual, 23,* 175-193.

Curry, T. J., & Strauss, R. H. (1994). A little pain never hurt anybody; a photoessay on the normalization of sport injuries. *Sociology of Sport Journal, 11,* 195-208.

Curtis, J., McTeer, W., & White, P. (1999). Exploring effects of school sport experiences on sport participation in later life. *Sociology of Sport Journal, 16,* 348-365.

Day, K. (2006). Active living and social justice - Planning for physical activity in low-income, black and Latino communities. *Journal of the American Planning Association, 72*(1), 88-99.

Department of Health. (2001). *Exercise referral systems: A national quality assurance framework.* London, UK: Department of Health.

Dotson, M. J., & Hyatt, E. M. (2005). Major influence factors in children's consumer socialization. *Journal of Consumer Marketing, 22*(1), 35-42.

Dunning, E. (1971). The development of modern football. In E. Dunning (Ed.), *The sociology of sport* (pp. 133-151). London: Frank Cass Publishing.

Durkheim, É. (1966). *Suicide: a study in sociology* (J. A. Spaulding & G. Simpson, Trans.). New York: Free Press.

Dyreson, M. (2001). Maybe it's better to bowl alone: Sport, community and democracy in American thought. *Culture, Sport, Society, 4*(1), 19-30.

Eccles, J. S. (1993). School and family effects on the ontogeny of children's interests self perceptions, and activity choices. In J. Jacobs (Ed.), *Developmental perspectives on motivation: Vol. 40 of the Nebraska symposium on motivation* (pp. 145-208). Lincoln, NE: University of Nebraska Press.

Edwards, H. (1986). The collegiate arms race. In R. A. Lapchick (Ed.), *Fractured Focus.* Lexington, MA: Lexington Books.

Edwards, M. B., Jilcott, S. B., Floyd, M. F., & Moore, J. B. (2011). County-level disparities in access to recreational resources and associations with adult obesity. *Journal of Park & Recreation Administration, 29*(2), 39-54.

Edwards, M. B., Kanters, M. A., & Bocarro, J. N. (2011). Opportunities for extracurricular physical activity in North Carolina middle schools. *Journal of Physical Activity and Health, 8*(5), 597-605.

Eitle, T. M., & Eitle, D. J. (2002). Just don't do it: High school sports participation and young female adult sexual behavior. *Sociology of Sport Journal, 19,* 403-418.

Eitzen, D. S. (1996). Classism in sport: the powerless bear the burden. *Journal of Sport & Social Issues, 20*(1), 95-105.

Eitzen, D. S. (2003). *Fair and foul: Beyond the myths and paradoxes of sport.* New York: Rowman & Littlefield.

Escobedo, L. G., Marcus, S. E., Holtzman, D., & Giovino, G. A. (1993). Sports participation, age at smoking initiation, and the risk of smoking among United States high-school-students. *Journal of the American Medical Association, 269,* 1391-1395.

Feinsand, M. (2011). Nick Swisher thrilled about MLB Breast Cancer awareness initiative featuring Mother's Day pink gear, *New York Daily News*. Retrieved from www.nydailynews.com

Floyd, M. F., Bocarro, J. N., & Thompson, T. D. (2008). Research on race and ethnicity in leisure studies: A review of five major journals. *Journal of Leisure Research, 40*(1), 1-22.

Floyd, M. F., Spengler, J. O., Maddock, J. E., Gobster, P. H., & Suau, L. (2008). Environmental and social correlates of physical activity in neighborhood parks: An observational study in Tampa and Chicago. *Leisure Sciences, 30,* 360 - 375.

Goldsmith, P. A. (2003). Race relations and racial patterns in school sports participation. *Sociology of Sport Journal, 20,* 147-171.

Gratton, C. (2006). Health. In R. M. Bartlett, C. Gratton & C. Rolf (Eds.), *Encyclopedia of International Sports Studies* (Vol. 2). New York: Routledge.

Green, B. C., & Chalip, L. (1998). Antecedents and consequences of parental purchase decision involvement in youth sport. *Leisure Sciences, 20,* 95-109.

Green, K., Smith, A., & Roberts, K. (2005). Young people and lifelong participation in sport and physical activity: a sociological perspective on contemporary physical education programmes in England and Wales. *Leisure Studies, 24*(1), 27-43.

Greendorfer, S. L., Lewko, J. H., & Rosengren, K. S. (2002). Family and gender-based influences in sport socialization of children and adolescents. In F. L. Smoll & R. E. Smith (Eds.), *Children and youth in sport: A biopsychosocial perspective* (2nd ed., pp. 153-186). Dubuque, IA: Kendall-Hunt Publishing.

Hanson, S. L., & Kraus, R. S. (1999). Women in male domains: Sport and science. *Sociology of Sport Journal, 16,* 92-110.

Hasbrook, C. A. (1987). The sport participation-social class relationship among a selected sample of female adolescents. *Sociology of Sport Journal, 4,* 37-47.

Hastings, D. W., Zahran, S., & Cable, S. (2006). Drowning in inequalities: Swimming and Social Justice. *Journal of Black Studies, 36,* 894-917.

Hawkins, D., & Metheny, J. (2001). Overuse injuries in youth sports: biomechanical considerations. *Medicine & Science in Sports & Exercise, 33,* 1701-1707.

Hedley, A. A., Ogden, C. L., Johnson, C. L., Carroll, M. D., Curtin, L. R., & Flegal, K. M. (2004). Prevalence of overweight and obesity among US children, adolescents, and adults, 1999-2002. *Journal of the American Medical Association, 291,* 2847-2850.

Hedstrom, R., & Gould, D. (2004). *Research in youth sports: Critical issues status.* Retrieved January 28, 2009, from www.educ.msu.edu

Heinzmann, G. S. (2002). Parental violence in youth sports: Facts, myths, and videotape. *Parks & Recreation, 37,* 66-75.

Hyman, M. D. (1967). Medicine. In P. F. Lazarsfeld, W. H. Sewell & H. L. Wilensky (Eds.), *The uses of sociology* (pp. 119-155). New York: Basic Books, Inc.

Kaczynski, A. T., & Henderson, K. A. (2007). Environmental correlates of physical activity: A review of evidence about parks and recreation. *Leisure Sciences, 29*(4), 315-354.

Kanters, M. A., Bocarro, J. N., & Edwards, M. B. (2011). *School sport policy analysis: Examining policy changes to increase the impact of after-school sports and facilities on physical activity*. Raleigh, NC: North Carolina State University: IPARC: Investigating Places for Active Recreation in Communities.

Kaplan, T. A., Digel, S. L., Scavo, V. A., & Arellana, S. B. (1995). Effect of obesity on injury risk in high school football players. *Clinical Journal of Sport Medicine, 5*(1), 43-47.

Kimm, S. Y. S., Glynn, N. W., McMahon, R. P., Vorhees, C. C., Striegel-Moore, R. H., & Daniels, S. R. (2006). Self-perceived barriers to activity participation among sedentary adolescent girls. *Medicine & Science in Sports & Exercise, 38*, 534-540.

Klemko, R. (2011, August 29). Leagues, clubs deal with perception of rise in fan violence, *USA Today*. Retrieved from www.usatoday.com.

Kozub, F. M., & Porretta, D. (1996). Including athletes with disabilities: Interscholastic athletic benefits for all. *The Journal of Physical Education, Recreation, and Dance, 67*, 19-24.

Kulas, M. (2011). Top 10 Health Problems in America. Retrieved November 1, 2011, from www.livestrong.com.

Kulig, K., Brener, N., & McManus, T. (2003). Sexual activity and substance abuse among adolescents by category of physical activity plus team sports participation. *Archives of Pediatric and Adolescent Medicine, 157*, 905-912.

Lee, M.-A., & Ferraro, K. F. (2007). Neighborhood residential segregation and physical health among Hispanic Americans: Good, bad, or benign? *Journal of Health & Social Behavior, 48*(2), 131-148.

Long, T. E., & Hadden, J. K. (1985). A reconception of socialization. *Sociological Theory, 3*(1), 39-49.

Louv, R. (2005). *Last child in the woods: Saving our children from nature deficit disorder*. Chapel Hill, NC: Algonquin Books.

Macintyre, S., Ellaway, A., & Cummins, S. (2002). Place effects on health: how can we conceptualise, operationalise and measure them? *Social Science & Medicine, 55*(1), 125-139.

MacPhail, A., & Kirk, D. (2006). Young people's socialisation into sport: Experiencing the specialising phase. *Leisure Studies, 25*(1), 57-74.

McHale, J. P., Vinden, P. G., Bush, L., Richer, D., Shaw, D., & Smith, B. (2005). Patterns of personal and social adjustment among sport-involved and non-involved urban middle-school children. *Sociology of Sport Journal, 22*, 119-136.

McLeroy, K. R., Bibeau, D., Steckler, A., & Glanz, K. (1988). An ecological perspective on health promotion programs. *Health Education Quarterly, 15*, 351-377.

Miller, K. E., Melnick, M. J., Barnes, G. M., Farrell, M. P., & Sabo, D. (2005). Untangling the links among athletic involvement, gender, race, and adolescent academic outcomes. *Sociology of Sport Journal, 22*, 178-193.

Miracle, A. W., & Rees, C. R. (1994). *Lessons of the locker room: The myth of school sports*. Amherst, NY: Prometheus Books.

Moore, M. J., & Werch, C. E. C. (2005). Sport and physical activity participation and substance use among adolescents. *Journal of Adolescent Health, 36*, 486-493.

Moschis, G. P. (1987). *Consumer socialization.* Lexington, MA: Heath and Company.

Nixon, H. L. (1993). Accepting the risks of pain and injury in sport: mediated cultural influences on playing hurt. *Sociology of Sport Journal, 10*, 183-196.

Outley, C. W., & Floyd, M. F. (2002). The home they live in: Inner city children's views on the influence of parenting strategies on their leisure behavior. *Leisure Sciences, 24*, 161-179.

Parsons, T. (1951). *The social system.* New York: Free Press.

Pate, R. R., Trost, S. G., Levin, S., & Dowda, M. (2000). Sports participation and health-related behaviors among US youth. *Archives of Pediatric and Adolescent Medicine, 154*, 904-911.

Patel, D. R., & Nelson, T. L. (2000). Sports injuries in adolescents. *Medical Clinics of North America, 84*, 983-1007.

Patrick, D. L., Bush, J. W., & Milton, M. C. (1973). Toward an operational definition of health. *Journal of Health and Social Behavior, 14*(1), 6-23.

Pechmann, C., & Knight, S. J. (2002). An experimental investigation of the joint effects of advertising and peers on adolescents' beliefs and intentions about cigarette consumption. *Journal of Consumer Research, 29*(1), 5-19.

Perkins, D. F., Jacobs, J. E., Barber, B. L., & Eccles, J. S. (2004). Childhood and adolescent sports participation as predictors of participation in sports and physical fitness activities during young adulthood. *Youth & Society, 35*, 495-520.

Philipp, S. F. (1998). Race and gender differences in adolescent peer group approval of leisure activities. *Journal of Leisure Research, 30*, 214-232.

Phillips, J. A., & Young, D. R. (2009). Past-year sports participation, current physical activity and fitness in urban adolescent girls. *Journal of Physical Activity and Health, 6*(1), 105-111.

Plato. (1902). *The Republic* (J. Adam, Trans.). In J. Adam (Ed.). Cambridge, U.K.: The University Press.

Putnam, R. D. (2000). *Bowling alone: The collapse and revival of American community.* New York: Simon & Schuster.

Putney, C. (2001). *Muscular Christianity: Manhood and sports in Protestant America 1880-1920.* Cambridge, MA: Harvard University Press.

Renne, K. S. (1974). Measurement of social health in a general population survey. *Social Sciences Research, 3*, 25-44.

Richmond, T. K., Hayward, R. A., Gahagan, S., Field, A. E., & Heisler, M. (2006). Can school income and racial/ethnic composition explain the racial/ethnic disparity in adolescent physical activity participation? *Pediatrics, 117*, 2158-2166.

Riess, S. A. (1991). *City games: The evolution of American urban society and the rise of sports.* Urbana, IL: University of Illinois Press.

Right to Play International. (2008). *Harnessing the power of sport for development and peace: Recommendations to governments.* Toronto, ON: Sport for Development and Peace International Working Group.

Roadburg, A. (1980). Factors precipitating fan violence: A comparison of professional soccer in Britain and North America. *The British Journal of Sociology, 31,* 265-276.

Robson, S. (2001). Sport and health. In K. Hylton, P. Bramham, D. Jackson & M. Nesti (Eds.), *Sports Development: Policy, Process and Practice* (pp. 126-147). New York: Routledge.

Rojek, C. (2005). *Leisure theory: Principles and practices.* New York: Palgrave Macmillan.

Ruddell, J. L., & Shinew, K. J. (2006). The socialization process for women with physical disabilities: The impact of agents and agencies in the introduction to an elite sport. *Journal of Leisure Research, 38,* 421-444.

Sage, G. H. (1998). *Power and ideology in American sport* (2nd ed.). Champaign, IL: Human Kinetics.

Sallis, J. F., Prochaska, J. J., & Taylor, W. C. (2000). A review of the correlates of physical activity of children and adolescents. *Medicine and Science in Sports and Exercise, 32,* 963-975.

Sallis, J. F., Conway, T. L., Prochaska, J. J., McKenzie, T. L., Marshall, S. J., & Brown, M. (2001). The association of school environments with youth physical activity. *American Journal of Public Health, 91,* 618-620.

Scheerder, J., Vanreusel, B., Taks, M., & Renson, R. (2005). social stratification patterns in adolescents' active sports participation behaviour: A time trend analysis 1969-1999. *European Physical Education Review, 11*(1), 5-27.

Schwenk, T. L., Gorenflo, D. W., Dopp, R. R., & Hipple, E. (2007). Depression and pain in retired professional football players. *Medicine & Science in Sports & Exercise, 39,* 599-605.

Shakib, S., & Dunbar, M. D. (2004). How high school athletes talk about maternal and paternal sporting experiences: Identifying modifiable social processes for gender equity physical activity interventions. *International Review for the Sociology of Sport, 39,* 275-299.

Smith, G. J. (1988). The noble sports fan. *Journal of Sport & Social Issues, 12,* 54-65.

Smoyer-Tomic, K. E., Hewko, J. N., & Hodgson, M. J. (2004). Spatial accessibility and equity of playgrounds in Edmonton, Canada. *Canadian Geographer-Geographe Canadien, 48,* 287-302.

Starr, P. (1982). *The social transformation of American medicine.* New York: Basic Books.

Trussell, D. E. (2009). *Organized youth sport, parenthood ideologies and gender relations: Parents' and children's experience and the construction of "Team family".* Doctoral Dissertation. University of Waterloo. Waterloo, ON.

Trust for America's Health. (2004). *Poll on America's top health concerns from the American Cancer Society and Trust for America's Health.* Washington, D.C.: Trust for America's Health.

Vilhjalmsson, R., & Thorlindsson, T. (1998). Factors related to physical activity: a study of adolescents. *Social Science & Medicine, 47,* 665-675.

Wagmiller Jr, R. L., Kuang, L., Aber, J. L., Lennon, M. C., & Alberti, P. M. (2006). The dynamics of economic disadvantage and children's life chances. *American Sociological Review, 71*, 847-866.

Walters, S., Barr-Anderson, D. J., Wall, M., & Neumark-Sztainer, D. (2009). does participation in organized sports predict future physical activity for adolescents from diverse economic backgrounds? *Journal of Adolescent Health, 44*, 268-274.

Washburne, R. F. (1978). Black underparticipation in wildland recreation: Alternative explanations. *Leisure Sciences, 1*, 175-189.

Weinberg, R.S., & Gould, D. (2003). *Foundations of sport and exercise psychology (3rd ed.)*. Champaign, IL: Human Kinetics.

Weiss, M. R., & Petlichkoff, L. M. (1989). Children's motivation for participation in and withdrawal from sport: Identifying the missing links. *Pediatric Exercise Science, 1*, 195-211.

Wilbert-Lampen, U., Leistner, D., Greven, S., Pohl, T., Sper, S., Völker, C. et al. (2008). Cardiovascular Events during World Cup Soccer. *New England Journal of Medicine, 358*, 475-483.

World Health Organization. (1946). *Preamble to the Constitution of the World Health Organization*. Paper presented at the International Health Conference, New York.

World Health Organization. (2003). *Health and development through physical activity and sport*. Geneva, Switzerland: WHO Document Production Services.

World Health Organization. (2005). *Promoting mental health: Concepts, emerging evidence, practice*. Geneva, Switzerland: World Health Organization, Department of Mental Health and Substance Abuse.

World Health Organization. (2009). *Global health risks: Mortality and burden of disease attributable to selected major risks*. Geneva, Switzerland: World Health Organization.

Young, D. R., Felton, G. M., Grieser, M., Elder, J. P., Johnson, C., Lee, J. S. et al. (2007). Policies and opportunities for physical activity in middle school environments. *Journal of School Health, 77*(1), 41-47.

# CHAPTER 5

## SPORT AND THE ECONOMY

### Emily Sparvero

***

### Learning Objectives

After reading this chapter, students will be able to:

1. Differentiate between the leisure and laboring classes.
2. Apply the relationship between the proletariat and bourgeoisie to labor issues in sport.
3. Explain the commodification of sport and provide examples.
4. Critique the use of public funds for sport stadiums.


### INTRODUCTION

Consumer spending on sport and recreation represents a significant part of the domestic and global economy. In 2005, the final consumer expenditures for products and services related to sport and physical activity in the US, or the *gross domestic sport product*, ranged from $168.469 billion to $207.503 billion (Milano & Chelladurai, 2011). Specific elements of the industry, such as media rights deals, athlete salaries, and recreational sport expenditures provide additional support for the significant role of sport and recreation in the economy. There has been dramatic growth in the value of media rights fees paid to sports properties. In 1970, television networks paid $50 million to broadcast the NFL. By 2010, the three major network stations (ABC, CBS, NBC) and one cable station (ESPN) paid a combined $2.9 billion annually to broadcast NFL games (Ourand, 2011). When we adjust these amounts for inflation, the value of the initial NFL rights deal is approximately $281 million, and the value of the MLB deal is approximately $49.4 million. As of 2011, the NFL deal is worth a staggering 932% more than the deal in 1970. Examples of broadcast rights deals for other sport properties involve less dramatic but still substantial sums: CBS/Turner Broadcasting Network pays approximately $771.4 million per year for the right to broadcast the NCAA men's basketball tournament; CBS and NBC pay $491.7 million for rights to broadcast PGA tour events; and ESPN and Univision pay $17.9 million for the rights to MLS games (Ourand, 2011). There has been a significant increase in the value that media place on the rights to sport events, and that the increase in media rights deals cannot be explained by inflation.

Athlete salaries in the professional sport leagues have also skyrocketed in recent years. Data collected from the US Census Bureau 2012 Statistical Abstract illustrates as much. In 1990, the average salary for an NFL player was $354,000 and the median base salary was $275,000. By 2010, the average NFL salary was $2 million and the median base salary was $906,000. In MLB, the average salary in 1990 was $598,000, which increased to over $3 million by 2010. Similar trends are seen in niche sports like professional rodeo. In the last 20 years, the number of professional rodeos has decreased, but the total prize money has more than doubled, from $18.2 million in 1990 to $39.9 million in 2010. The economic significance of sport is not limited to professional or spectator sport. In 2009, sales of sporting goods (including athletic clothing, athletic footwear, sport equipment, and recreational transport) totaled over $70 billion.

The figures presented here do not represent the entirety of sport consumption in the economy, but rather they indicate the magnitude of sport-related spending in recent years. It is clear that sport is an important economic institution. Yet, sport is also an important social institution. Sport consumption and sport participation both affect and are affected by the social systems in which they are embedded. In this chapter, I examine the relationship between sport and the economy, and in doing so, present three sociological approaches: the theory of the leisure class, commodification and Marxist critiques of sport, and political economy/growth coalition theory. These theoretical and conceptual approaches provide the foundation for understanding the decisions made at an individual level (i.e., sport consumption and participation) and at the community level (i.e., public subsidization for private sport).

## THEORY OF THE LEISURE CLASS

Consider the following: you are a sport management student and golf enthusiast who is working at the pro shop of a neighborhood country club to earn money to help pay your tuition. While taking a short break during your shift, you see a man get out of his Mercedes and remove his Louis Vuitton Damier Geante golf bag (retail price $8400). He is a regular customer of yours, and you know that his golf bag includes top-of-the-line Majesty Prestigio clubs (retail price over $10,000) and Maxfli

BlackMAX balls (retail price $50 a dozen). As he walks by, you notice his custom-made John Lobb golf shoes (retail price $5000), his Oakley sunglasses (retail price $375), and his J. Lindeberg golf shirt (retail price $165).

So, what conclusions can you draw about the individual you just observed? Maybe you felt a bit of jealousy, as you thought about the high-end equipment and accessories your customer had. Could you make a reasonable guess about his annual income? Net worth? Social class? Family background? Based on his possessions (and your mental tally of what those possessions cost), you might assume that he is someone who is either wealthy himself, or that he is someone who comes from a wealthy family. In addition to his possessions, the fact that he is a member of the country club and is able to spend time playing tennis in the middle of a workday provides clues to his social class and status. People communicate their social status to others by their possessions and the ways in which they spend time. This example illustrates the basic idea behind the theory of the leisure class.

At the turn of the 20th century, Thorsten Veblen published *The Theory of the Leisure Class: An Economic Study of Institutions*. Veblen was trained as an economist, but he believed that economics did not allow for an understanding of the social causes and effects of economic change. Prior to the publication of *The Theory of the Leisure Class*, consumption was viewed in the context of neoclassical economic theory. Individuals were seen as rational actors who would act in a way to maximize their utility (i.e., satisfaction received from the consumption of a good or service). Veblen's theory of the leisure class was one of the earliest attempts to understand economic behavior in the context of social relations and social class rather than strictly through the lens of normative economic science.

In order to understand the theory of the leisure class and how it applies to sport consumption and participation, a definition of leisure is required. *Leisure* is the non-productive consumption of time. Individuals have a finite amount of time available during the day, and they will allocate their time to either leisure or labor. The way in which individuals choose to allocate their time determines the status of individuals, and as a result, two distinct classes emerge – the leisure class, which is the superior pecuniary class, and the laboring class, which is the inferior pecuniary class. In the golfer example described above, we saw two individuals. The first was an employee of the pro shop and needed to work in order to earn money that could then be used to cover expenses. The second individual was seemingly free from this pressure to work.

This highlights the key characteristic that distinguishes the leisure class from the laboring class. Members of the leisure class are exempt from employment necessary for the accumulation of goods (i.e., useful employment). Historically, members of the leisure class pursued occupations including public/government service, the military, the priesthood, and in some cases, sport. These occupations were distinctly non-industrial and were considered honorable and worthy. Unlike the leisure class, the laboring classes cannot avoid productive employment, and laboring is the accepted mode of existence for lower classes. In order for the laboring classes to accumulate goods, they must engage in productive labor, which provides the means for such accumulation.

The accumulation of goods is important as evidence of an individual's social class. Return to the example at the pro shop for a moment, and imagine that you saw your customer at a thrift store, without the pricey sunglasses and clothes. In this case, there would be little to signal his status. In order to establish leisure class bona fides, individuals have to be able to display their wealth and power, which can be done through conspicuous consumption and conspicuous leisure.

*Conspicuous consumption* is lavish expenditure on consumer goods or services. Luxury goods belong to the leisure class, and consumption of luxury goods (e.g., cars) is evidence of the leisure class's pecuniary or economic superiority. According to Veblen, "it becomes indispensable to accumulate, to acquire property, in order to retain one's good name." (1899 [1994], p. 29). Whereas conspicuous consumption refers to the possessions that an individual acquires, conspicuous leisure refers to how an individual spends her or his time. *Conspicuous leisure* is participation in extensive and visible leisure activities to display social status. Conspicuous consumption and conspicuous leisure demonstrate that individuals in the leisure class are able to "waste" their money on inessential goods and "waste" their time on inessential activities. The luxury of being wasteful provides evidence of the wealth and status of the leisure class (Trigg, 2001).

The ability of members of the leisure class to accumulate belongings and spend time engaged in nonproductive activities (e.g., golf) confers an honorable status on these individuals. As a result, members of the lower classes want to imitate the consumption behaviors and activities of the members of the leisure class, a condition that Veblen calls *pecun lation*. If individuals accumulated possessions for the purpos filling basic needs, there would eventually be an end to the at tion. However, because individuals strive to increase possessions in order to obtain the status of the leisure class, the pressure to "keep up with the Joneses" continues ad nausea.

## Sport Participation as Conspicuous Leisure/Consumption

Members of lower socio-economic groups are less physically active than members of higher socio-economic groups. The *2005 Behavioral Risk Factor Surveillance System* (BRFSS) conducted by the Centers for Disease Control (CDC) provides data on various health-related behaviors, including exercise and physical activity, for individuals in the US. When asked whether or not they had exercised in the last 30 days, 75.4% of respondents indicated that they had exercised in the last 30 days. If the responses to this question are viewed by income level, it becomes apparent that individuals with lower socioeconomic status exercise less than individuals with higher socioeconomic status. Only 55.9% of individuals who earn less than $10,000 reported exercising in the last 30 days, whereas 87.2% of individuals earning more than $75,000 reported exercising. The BRFSS also asked adults whether they met the recommendation of 30 minutes or more of moderate physical activity five or more days per week, or vigorous physical activity for 20 minutes or more three or more days per week. The responses to this question provide additional support that more individuals with higher socioeconomic status meet the national guidelines for physical activity than those with lower socioeconomic status. For the national sample, over half of the individuals earning $75,000 or more met the guidelines, whereas only 38.1% of those making less than $10,000 met the guidelines. Table 5.1 provides a complete breakdown of physical activity by socioeconomic status.

This pattern is not unique to the US. Sport England, the organization that is charged with the promotion and provision of grassroots sport in England, found similar results in its nation-wide Active People Survey. The sports participation measure counted the number of adults who participate in at least 30 minutes of moderate intensity sport at least three times per week. From October 2010 to October 2011, 19.1% of individuals employed in managerial and professional occupations indicated sport participation. Only 12.5% of individuals who were employed in low supervisory/technical occupations, semi-routine and routine occupations, students, and the unemployed indicated sport participation at the recommended level. This finding, in particular the inclusion of the unemployed, provides support for the theory of the leisure class and suggests that the decision to participate in sport is not solely a function of having time available to participate.

Table 5.1: Adults Meeting Physical Activity Guidelines by Income

| Income | Meets Physical Activity Recommendation | Not Enough Physical Activity | No Physical Activity |
|---|---|---|---|
| < $10,000 | 38.1 | 34.1 | 27.8 |
| $10,000-$14,999 | 37.2 | 36.2 | 26.6. |
| $15,000-$19,999 | 39.7 | 37.3 | 23.0 |
| $20,000-$24,999 | 44.2 | 37.3 | 18.5 |
| $25,000-$34,999 | 46.1 | 39.4 | 14.4 |
| $35,000-$49,999 | 49.0 | 39.7 | 11.4 |
| $50,000-$74,999 | 52.2 | 39.3 | 8.5 |
| > $75,000 | 55.9 | 37.4 | 6.7 |

*Source.* Centers for Disease Control

The theory of the leisure class has application beyond participation numbers. There are certain sports (e.g., skiing, golf) that confer greater status benefits than others because of the wealth necessary for participation (Edensor & Richards, 2007). Skiing takes the form of both conspicuous leisure and conspicuous consumption. In order to participate, an individual must be able to afford all of the equipment (e.g., skis, boots, lift tickets) that constituted a $533 million segment of the sporting goods industry in 2010. For most adults, skiing also requires travel to a ski resort, which requires the means to afford the cost of travel and the time engaged in unproductive employment. Not surprisingly, individuals who earn more than $75,000 per year accounted for more than three-quarters of all skiers in 2010. In golf and tennis, high-earning individuals ($75,000 or more) accounted for over half of the participants.

Similar status gains can be observed through the simultaneous conspicuous consumption and conspicuous leisure associated with youth sport. However, in youth sport, the participation and consumption of children reflects the status of the parents. For children, sailing, surfing, and skiing are classified as glide sports, which are practiced in specific environments and are commonly provided through profit-oriented businesses (Taks & Scheerder, 2006). In order for a child to participate in these glide sports, the parents must have the means to provide participation opportunities. In the case of aspiring elite figure skaters, parents can spend as much as $40,000 a year on skates, coaching, costumes, and ice rental, in addition to dedicating their time to their children's daily practice sessions (Grenfell & Rinehart, 2003).

So, all sport participation is not equal. While participation in the expensive sports listed above do confer status on their participants, other sports have become the province of lower classes. These sports that are associated with lower classes include boxing, rugby, bodybuilding, and football (Bourdieu, 1978). The association of sports with either the upper class or the lower class can be explained by economic capital, cultural capital, or a combination of the two. According to Bourdieu (1978), cultural consumption requires appropriate preferences and tastes as well as skills and knowledge. He calls this concept *cultural capital*. Cultural capital varies by social class, so individuals in the leisure class would develop appreciation for certain activities, including sport, and individuals in lower classes would develop appreciation for other activities, depending on the norms of the class. *Economic capital* also plays a role, as sports that are preferred by the lower classes tend to be inexpensive.

**Sport Team Ownership as Conspicuous Consumption/Leisure**

The ownership of professional sport teams can also be viewed as a form of conspicuous consumption and leisure. In 2010, the value of professional sport franchises in North America ranged from $1.81 billion (the Dallas Cowboys) to $134 million (the Phoenix Coyotes). For many team owners, ownership of a sports team is a very visible form of conspicuous consumption and leisure. The escalating values of sport teams make the purchase of a franchise a possibility for only the very rich. A 2010 list of the richest Americans includes several individuals with ownership stakes in sport. Larry Ellison is the co-founder of Oracle and has a net worth of $33 billion. An elite yachtsman in his own right, he purchased the BNP Paribus Open and the Indian Wells Tennis Garden facility. Paul Allen, the founder of Microsoft with a net worth of $13.2 billion, owns the Portland Trailblazers and the Seattle Seahawks and is part owner of the Seattle Sounders.

Given that an individual must already be wealthy in order to purchase the team, team owners do not rely on the financial success of their team to continue their accumulation of wealth. Many sport team owners have either inherited their fortunes or made their fortunes in non-sport enterprises. Because of this, their role as owners of a sport team is a form of conspicuous consumption. Consider the example of Mark Cuban, the owner of the 2011 World Champion Dallas Mavericks. Cuban made his fortune when he sold Broadcast.com to Yahoo for $5.7 billion in 1999. Cuban's management of the Mavericks suggests that he is not motivated by a desire to maximize profit; rather, he has shown a willingness to spend whatever is necessary to produce a winning team. As a member of the leisure class, Cuban is willing to spend in a way that reflects conspicuous consumption. During the championship celebration in Miami, Cuban reportedly bought a bottle of champagne worth $90,000 *and* paid for a celebratory parade when the city of Dallas cited budget pressures as a reason they would not be able to do so.

Socioeconomic status can serve as a proxy for one's social class, but annual income or net worth does not automatically determine whether an individual is a member of the leisure class. Recall that leisure is the nonproductive use of time. For members of the leisure class, their wealth allows them to dedicate their time to unproductive activities. Consequently, while many professional athletes are rich, their sport participation is not reflective of their status as a member of the leisure class. Rather, in this context, there has been a fundamental transformation of elite sport into productive employment. Whereas athletes previously engaged in sport without expectation of pecuniary gain, sport today is seen as a productive occupation (rather than conspicuous leisure).

*Forbes* magazine compiles a list of the most powerful individuals in the entertainment business each year. The individuals on this list are evaluated based on their entertainment-related earnings, among other variables. In 2011, this list included 19 athletes, with combined annual entertainment-related earnings of $647 million. This list includes professional golfers, tennis players, international soccer stars, racecar drivers, as well as representatives from the five major professional sports leagues in North America. A complete list is provided in Table 5.2. While these athletes' earnings (and their celebrity lifestyles) put them in the highest socio-economic groups, their sport participation is quite different from the concept of sport as conspicuous leisure advanced by Veblen.

Table 5.2: Professional Athletes on Forbes Celebrity 100 List

| Rank | Athlete | Sport | Earnings |
|------|---------|-------|----------|
| 6 | Tiger Woods | PGA | $75 million |
| 10 | LeBron James | NBA | $48 million |
| 14 | Kobe Bryant | NBA | $53 million |
| 25 | Roger Federer | ATP | $47 million |
| 35 | David Beckham | MLS | $40 million |
| 35 | Phil Mickelson | PGA | $47 million |
| 43 | Cristiano Ronaldo | La Liga (soccer) | $38 million |
| 46 | Rafael Nadal | ATP | $31 million |
| 49 | Alex Rodriguez | MLB | $35 million |
| 55 | Tom Brady | NFL | $31 million |
| 57 | Dwyane Wade | NBA | $26 million |
| 59 | Dwight Howard | NBA | $28 million |
| 62 | Lionel Messi | La Liga (soccer) | $32 million |
| 69 | Derek Jeter | MLB | $29 million |
| 72 | Peyton Manning | NFL | $26 million |
| 80 | Maria Sharapova | WTA | $24 million |
| 84 | Serena Williams | WTA | $12 million |
| 86 | Venus Williams | WTA | $13 million |
| 96 | Danica Patrick | Auto racing | $12 million |

*Source. Forbes* magazine.

## COMMODIFICATION OF SPORT/MARXIST CRITIQUES

Take a moment and make a list of all of the goods and services you have consumed in the past month that are related to sport and recreation. Did your list include any of the following: fantasy sport teams, gambling, tickets to spectator sports, all-league broadcast packages, gym memberships, donations to your college athletic department, internet sport sites? Were you surprised by how many ways you can spend money on sport? As sport and recreation become increasingly commercialized, there are more and more opportunities to spend money to enjoy sport as a leisure activity.

Whereas Veblen believed that the relationship between the labor and leisure class was one characterized by emulation, Marxist theory views the relationship between the two classes as inherently antagonistic. The *bourgeoisie* is the ruling capitalist class that controls the factors of production. The *proletariat* comprises the workers who provide labor for the bourgeoisie. These two classes are engaged in constant struggle as the ruling class exploits the laborers to maximize surplus value (i.e., profit). In *The Communist Manifesto*, Marx and Engels offer the following criticism of the bourgeoisie who control the factors of production:

> The bourgeoisie, wherever it has got the upper hand…has left no other nexus between people than naked self-interest, than callous "cash payment". It has drowned out the most heavenly ecstasies of religious fervor, of chivalrous enthusiasm, of philistine sentimentalism, in the icy water of egotistical calculation. It has resolved personal worth into exchange value, and in place of the numberless indefeasible chartered freedoms, has set up that single, unconscionable freedom -- Free Trade" (1848 [1992], p. 5).

The goal of the bourgeoisie is capitalist accumulation. In order to continue capitalist expansion, new markets have to be created and goods and service distributed within them. Within these new markets, the laborer exchanges labor for wages and then exchanges wages for goods and services that meet his or her leisure needs. This expansion of markets is enabled by commodification. *Commodification* is the transformation of goods, services, or relationships into commodities that are bought and sold in market-oriented exchange.

As commodities produced for exchange become the dominant objects in a leisure activity, the leisure activity itself is transformed (Butsch, 1984). We see this in the transformation of play into sport. According to Frey and Eitzen (1991), play is:

> an activity where entry and exit are free and voluntary, rules are emergent and temporary, fantasy is permitted, utility of action is irrelevant, and the result is uncertain. Play has no formal history nor organization; motivation

and satisfaction are intrinsic; and the outcome does not have serious impact beyond the context of the activity. (p. 508)

Play is explicitly unproductive, which is consistent with Veblen's description of leisure class occupations. Over time, the commodification of play and games resulted in the organization of sport that we have today. The consequences of commodification are revealed in the changes made to games to make them more media-friendly and more appealing to consumers. Examples include the introduction of the shootout by the NHL and the shot clock and 3-point shot by the NBA. At the college level, we see fans' passion for their team turned into a commodity. Students are encouraged to join supporter groups as evidence of commitment to the team and the university. At Temple University, the Wild Cherry Owl Club "encompasses all students who desire a closer connection to Temple's athletic programs." Students can purchase this "closer connection" for $70 per year. Finally, Olympic sport and its associated ideals (peace, excellence, skill, friendship) are turned into commodities that are sold to sponsoring corporations.

As sport organizations are commercialized and commodified, we see the conflict between the proletariat and the bourgeoisie exhibited in issues related to the distribution of profits between the two classes. While the term proletariat is associated with the working class, we see the conflict over profits even when the laborers are not impoverished. Because of their economic significance, the NCAA and professional sport leagues provide recent examples of this conflict.

## NCAA

The primary purpose of the NCAA is "to initiate, stimulate and improve intercollegiate athletics programs for student-athletes and to promote and develop educational leadership, physical fitness, athletics excellence and athletics participation as a recreational pursuit" (NCAA, 2011). The cornerstone of the NCAA is the idea of amateurism, which prohibits an athlete from receiving any pecuniary reward in relation to his or her athletic participation.

The NCAA is a nonprofit organization, and nowhere in the organization's mission statement or expression of core values is there any indication of extent to which college sport has been commodified or the financial status of the organization. According to the organization's tax filings, e NCAA generated total revenues of over $740 million, includ-ing $645 million from television rights fees. As a nonprofit organization, the NCAA is prohibited from generating "profit." There are no "owners" to whom profits would be paid, yet the president of the NCAA received compensation totaling $1.76 million. The NCAA's total reported surplus was over $38 million in 2009. This surplus was not out of the ordinary; from 2005 to 2009, the average surplus reported by the NCAA was $40,924,902.

The NCAA has frequently been criticized for the commodification of college sport. The NCAA's response is that the amateur ideal pertains only to the athlete, not the "enterprise" ("Commercialism," n.d.). In a March 2011 column, a syndicated sports columnist wrote, "smart people need to figure out a way to financially compensate the football and basketball players who generate the cash...this is America. The people who produce the profits are supposed to benefit from those profits" (Whitlock, 2011). If this comment were viewed through a Marxist lens, one could argue that the capitalist system of America is what contributes to the perceived inequalities and unfairness of the system. The NCAA exercises complete control of the college athlete and college athletics, and the surplus accrue to those who control the sport system.

The exploitation of the labor of college athletes also generates surplus value for universities and their athletic departments, as illustrated by the case of the University of Texas at Austin. In 2008, the football team generated $63.8 million in revenue, which resulted in a surplus of $46.3 million. This includes the sale of $8 million of Longhorns merchandise, which accrued to the athletic department (Gwynne, March 2010). In this case, the athletic department has commodified the athlete-laborer by selling a jersey with the athlete's name on the back, and the athlete is expressly prohibited by the NCAA and its amateur ideal from reaping any of the financial gains made possible by the athlete's performance and success.

## Professional Sport

The situation in professional sports is influenced by the same sense of exploitation and alienation of labor. The league establishes the rules, the owners control the means of production, and athletes generate substantial profits for the professional sport ruling class. The fact that professional athletes are paid for their services does not change the fundamental relationship between the athletes and the league and team owners; it only changes the magnitude of the financial profit involved. The perceived exploitation of professional athletes is revealed in recent comments made by host Bryant Gumbel (2011) during an episode of HBO's "Real Sports": "[Stern's] comments were typical of a commissioner who has always seemed eager to be viewed as some kind of modern plantation overseer treating NBA men as if they were his boys...his moves are intended to do little more than show how he's the one keeping the hired hands in their place."

In both the 2011 NFL and the NBA lockouts, one of the contentious issues was the distribution of league revenues. In the NFL, both sides eventually agreed to a deal in which players would get 48% of league revenues, and the owners would keep 52%. In the NBA, the owners and players also had to determine how $4 billion in league revenue would be split. In both cases, several other issues in the CBA were in dispute, but the split of revenue highlights the conflict between owners and labor – a conflict that is created and maintained by the dominant capital accumulation logic.

**Sport as an Opiate of the People**

While professional sport provides the medium for the conflict between those who control capital and those who provide labor, sport can also be used to stabilize the dominant capitalist system and reinforce the social hierarchy. In his Critique of Hegel's *Philosophy of the Right*, Marx suggested that religion created illusory happiness for the masses. As "the opium of the people," religion prevented the people from seeking true happiness, which would be possible only through the abolition of the capitalist system. It has been suggested that sport has replaced religion, as it can be seen as an "ideological tool, misleading the masses to sustain bourgeois control" (Giulianotti, 2005, p. 32).

In the early industrial period, factory owners encouraged their workers to form sport teams in order to build loyalty and create a norm of teamwork (Budd, 2001). Several of today's professional teams have roots in the factory teams of the late nineteenth and early twentieth centuries. Workers at the Royal Arsenal, an armaments manufacturer, originally formed the British soccer team Arsenal. The modern day Chicago Bears were originally located in Decatur, Illinois, where the team was known as the Decatur Staleys and consisted of employees of the A.E. Staley food starch company. As employers provided organized sport for laborers, the laborers could be distracted from the ongoing class struggle. In addition to providing a distraction or amusement, sport reallocates resources (e.g., time, money, critical thought) away from the class struggle to sport. This is the case for sport spectators as well as sport participants. As early as ancient Rome, entertainment was used to placate and distract residents from the unpleasant realities of their condition, and the result was citizens who longed for only "bread and circuses." Today, spectator sports function as the "circuses" that reinforce the cultural and social order.

## SPORT STADIUMS AND POLITICAL ECONOMY

A Marxist interpretation suggests that sport is organized to maximize the gains that accrue to those who control the mode of production. Thus far in this chapter, the commodification of sport and the struggle between those who own the mode of production and those who labor for others' benefit have been discussed. The struggle between classes is also relevant to the political economy of sport. Political economy "interrogates economic doctrines to disclose their sociological and political premises" (Maier, 1987, p. 3). An issue that is particularly relevant to the political economy of sport is the way in which gains are privatized but costs are socialized. The increasing commercialization and commodification of sport has created a condition in which many sport products and services are monetized in the capitalist system. In spite of the fact that the bourgeoisie at all levels of sport realize the profits from the production and exchange of goods and services, the associated costs are socialized in various ways. For example, when someone purchases a professional sport team franchise, she or he may be able to deduct the cost of the team from their income taxes. The team owner realizes profits from the team, but the taxpayer bears an implicit cost of foregone income tax receipts from the team owner. Similarly, because the NCAA is incorporated as a nonprofit organization (as mentioned earlier in this chapter), it is exempt from federal, state, and local income taxes, state and local property taxes, and state and local sales taxes. This is another form of implicit subsidy provided by taxpayers.

The development of a new sport stadium provides a more explicit example of socialized costs and privatized benefits. During the period between 1990 and 2006, 82 new professional sport facilities were built, at an average cost of $250 million. The cost of state-of-the-art sport facilities continues to rise, and in recent years we have seen the advent of the billion-dollar stadium (e.g., New York Yankees stadium in Brooklyn, Dallas Cowboys stadium in Arlington). This sport facility trend is not limited to major league facilities in major urban centers. According to *Street and Smith's Sports Business Journal*, 39 minor league sport markets had completed construction on at least one new or substantially renovated facility between 2007 and 2011.

If these facilities were built with private funds, their sociological importance would be as evidence of (a) conspicuous consumption by team owners, or (b) the increasing commodification of spaces for sport. However, because these new stadiums are rarely financed entirely by the team owners, the decision to undertake a sport facility project is a reflection of how these projects socialize costs while privatizing benefits.

With few exceptions (e.g., Minneapolis's Target Center, Milwaukee's Bradley Center, Boston's Fleet Center), new sport facilities are financed through a public-private partnership. In a public-private partnership, the sport team provides part of the funding for the project and the government provides the rest. An estimated $12 to 15 billion of public (i.e. taxpayer) funds have been spent on these sport projects since 1990 (Humphreys, 2006; Long, 2006). While the cost of the facility is typically shared between the public and private sectors, the same is not true of the facility's revenues. New stadiums are designed to maximize revenues by transforming food and drink, socialization, entertainment, and the relationship with the team into commodities. Team owners almost exclusively capture the revenues derived from these facility enhancements.

Historically, sport stadiums were completely private ventures. In the early twentieth century, team owners constructed eponymous stadiums with their own money or resources (e.g., Comiskey Park, Ebbetts Field). Through this commodification of the game and the sporting space, team owners were able to increase their own profits by excluding any potential spectators who were unwilling to pay the entrance fee. By the 1970s, the public provided nearly all of the funding for new sport facilities. Eighteen of the 22 sport facilities built between 1970 and 1984 were completely financed by local governments, and two other facilities received public funds that covered 90% of facility costs (Crompton et al., 2003). In the ensuing decades, the public's share of facility financing has decreased, but because of the increasing cost of construction, taxpayers are paying more real dollars than at any other time in history.

The first issue to address is why the public would become involved in the finance of a private enterprise. Elected officials face pressure to deliver economic growth and revitalization in the areas that they serve.

Stadium supporters claim that economic benefits such as job creation, increases in resident income, and area redevelopment would result from the presence of a sport stadium. Academic research on the economic impacts of sport stadiums has overwhelmingly found that sport facilities have either a negligible or negative impact on employment and income in host communities (Siegfried & Zimbalist, 2000). Additionally, public opposition to subsidization of sport stadiums has grown as citizens become more knowledgeable about supporters' claims. Public funding of stadiums is commonly viewed as a form of corporate welfare. In fact, a primary argument against providing public subsidies to finance sport projects is that team owners are millionaires or billionaires with access to well-developed capital markets. Still, in spite of this, public subsidization of sport facilities persists.

If a rational economic approach were used to make decisions about public subsidization, a cost-benefit analysis would be conducted at the community level. A project would only be pursued if it produced net benefits for the community (i.e., the total societal benefits were greater than the total societal cost). Few sport facility projects would be able to demonstrate net benefits, and it would be unlikely that a community would provide the funds for construction – if that was the only basis for the decision. However, economic decisions are subject to social and political influences and are not determined only by economic factors. Thus, economic reasoning provides a normative analysis of public subsidization that does not reflect what actually happens.

A return to Marx and Engels provides a theoretical context for understanding this issue. They wrote in *The Communist Manifesto*, "the executive of the modern state is but a committee for managing the common affairs of the whole bourgeoisie" (1848 [1992], p.9). This means that government officials are a tool of the bourgeoisie and will make decisions that maintain the capitalist system. While the Marxist interpretation is consistent with the issue of the class struggle already discussed, this issue can also be considered within the American urban context. There are various interests and agendas among community elites in American cities. However, these stakeholders share a common goal of economic growth, and in order to achieve this goal, they are willing to come together to develop pro-growth strategies (Molotch, 1976). Such a growth coalition may include any citizen who is dedicated to the growth agenda and has resources to contribute. Typically, though, growth coalitions that mobilize behind sport projects include the community elite—business owners and executives, land developers, politicians, representatives of non-governmental organizations including chambers of commerce and convention and visitor bureaus, sports team executives, and local media. These members of the coalition are able to influence political decisions, and they are incentivized to do so because of the social, economic, and cultural benefits that they expect. Growth coalitions often have different priorities than the general population, and they are able to use their power and access to the community elite to produce their favored outcomes (Delaney & Eckstein, 2007).

Having provided an explanation of the process, we can now turn our attention to the social consequences of public subsidization. As governments allocate public funds to sport facilities, they may neglect other community concerns. Governments have limited resources to invest in public projects and services, and expenditure in one area typically means that there is less money available for other areas. Concerns over *opportunity cost*, or the value of the next best alternative, are amplified when governments have to make budgetary choices that negatively impact the lower classes. In Hamilton County, Ohio, elected leaders spent an estimated $454 million on a new stadium for the Cincinnati Bengals. At the same time, one in seven people live beneath the poverty line and there were county-level cuts to schools and emergency services. Delaware County, Pennsylvania provided $10 million for the Philadelphia Union's new soccer stadium. The weekend before the stadium opened, the mayor of Chester – the host city so economically depressed that it lacks a grocery store – declared a state of emergency after four murders were committed in one week. A more detailed description of one community's experience with public subsidization of professional sport is provided in the case of Corpus Christi, Texas, in the following case study. This case illustrates how a growth coalition can play a major role in securing support for the baseball team. Additionally, the case provides evidence of the unintended social costs that can result from a project intended to encourage economic development.

---

Case Study: Corpus Christi, Texas

Corpus Christi, Texas, is the eighth largest city in Texas, with a population of approximately 280,000. The city is located halfway between Houston and the US/Mexico border and prides itself on its natural beauty and location on the Corpus Christi Bay. Like most large cities, the city faces challenges related to economic development and "smart growth," education, and retention of the workforce. In particular, the city has struggled economically. The Port of Corpus Christi is the sixth largest port in the United States and its operations involve agricultural and petrochemical products. In the late 1990s, the Port began to ex-

---

plore ways to expand into tourism and recreation projects.

In 2000, a group of community leaders formed "Forward Corpus Christi," a growth coalition that was formed with the intention of promoting economic growth and improving the quality of life for residents of Corpus Christi. Forward Corpus Christi included representatives typical of an urban growth coalition: the Port of Corpus Christi, the Corpus Christi Regional Economic Development Council (CCREDC), the Convention and Visitors Bureau (CVB), business executives, and local media. This coalition represents the community elite, which created the impression that the community was being run by a handful of powerful residents.

Forward Corpus Christi experienced its first pro-growth victory in November 2000. Prior to that time, Corpus Christi residents had not held a bond election (i.e., referendum in which residents approve a bond issue for public projects) in 14 years. This means that the city went over a decade without additional public money for capital improvements, which resulted in failing infrastructure, education, and other public services. In 2000, however, Forward Corpus Christi mobilized the support necessary to pass the bond issue, which would provide funds for improvements to the seawall, streets, parks, and *a new sports arena* to replace Memorial Coliseum, a multipurpose arena built in 1953.

Encouraged by its success with the 2000 bond issue, Forward Corpus Christi set its sights on a bigger prize – an affiliate minor league baseball stadium. In May of 2002, Hall of Fame pitcher Nolan Ryan announced his intention to bring a minor-league baseball team to the city. In order to bring a team to Corpus Christi, the city would need to provide a stadium. It was then up to the growth coalition to get the issue on the ballot and communicate its pro-growth message to the voters. Forward Corpus Christi raised over $170,000 from community leaders and had a substantial funding advantage over stadium opponents. The only significant opposition to the project was Forward ALL Corpus Christi, who managed to raise only $10,000 to be used to defeat the ballpark proposition. The stadium bond issue was passed by a 55-45 margin, with high voter turnout in the wealthier precincts. To emphasize the funding advantage of Forward Corpus Christi -- they spent $5.19 for each pro-stadium vote, and Forward ALL Corpus Christi spent only $0.37. The monetary advantages of the growth coalition are consistent with the status of its members.

The justification for spending over $32 million on a sport stadium was primarily economic, which is to be expected from a growth coalition. Ultimately, the stadium did little to change the economic conditions of the community. The team began play in 2005, and according to a 2006 survey, only 2% of visitors to Corpus Christi reported attending *any* sporting event. Macro-level economic data also provides support that the presence of the team did not help the community's economic problems. When the stadium opened in 2005, unemployment was 5.3% and reached its zenith in January of 2011 at 8.7%. It was unlikely that the sport stadium (with fewer than 35 full time employees) would have a significant effect on the economy of a large city, despite what the growth coalition would have voters believe. The more profound consequence is that Corpus Christi continues to pay a significant amount toward debt service on a stadium that is delivering little economic benefit to residents. Meanwhile, the owners of the team are able to keep the revenues from the team and facility operations.

Because the city was committed to providing funds for the stadium, there was less money available when other public needs arose. This situation became worse in the recession of 2008, when cities were seeing fewer local tax dollars and less financial support from the federal government. Local residents questioned the priorities of city leaders, as evidenced by the following Letter to the Editor in the *Corpus Christi Caller Times*:

> "How come we have all this money for Whataburger Field and there's no money for poor employees? There's no money on the budget for this, none for that. But there's money for the field. How come? Everything else is forgotten because of the field. Let's get real. This is our money."

While public funds were indeed the people's money, government officials – largely influenced by the local growth coalition made the decisions about how that money was spent.

The stadium also intensified class conflict. The stadium was located on the Port land near the Northside neighborhood. This area was a historically low socioeconomic area, and the presence of the stadium resulted in the closure of a neighborhood school. One resident noted the inconsistencies of claiming the stadium as a growth engine while changing the institutions of the neighborhood:

> "[Closing the school] was the last straw. It's a historical place. They are tearing [the Northside] down slowly. They say closing [the school] was for the better, but it's not. It's better for the economy, it's better for the tourism. We have a right to be here, just as much as that baseball field. Every event they have, we have to listen because we're neighbors. We've got kids that would like to go, but we can't afford it."

The growth coalition successfully passed a ballot initiative that enabled Corpus Christi to attract a minor league baseball team. However, the expected economic growth did not materialize. Instead, the decision to invest in the stadium (at the expense of other public priorities) served to reinforce social class divisions.

## CHAPTER SUMMARY

In this chapter, we provide a sociological context for issues related to sport and the economy. The theory of the leisure class helps us to understand the association between social class and sport participation and the consumption of sport/recreation goods and services. Marxist critiques of the commodification of sport provide context for the role the sport industry plays in capital accumulation and the conflict between those who control the mode of production and those who provide labor. Finally, the public subsidization of sport is examined in the context of American political economy. The examples presented in this chapter provide evidence of the interrelatedness of sport, social relations and norms, and the economy.

## DISCUSSION QUESTIONS

1.  What factors influence an individual's choices regarding sport participation? Select a sport or recreation activity not mentioned in this chapter and explain what effect social class has on participation in your selected sport.
2.  How do fantasy sport leagues represent the commodification of sport? Explain your answer and specify what is being commodified.
3.  Do you agree with the idea that sport acts as the opiate of the people? Explain your answer using specific examples from either recreational or spectator sport.
4.  How does a growth coalition affect a community's decision to subsidize a sport project? What is the value of a growth coalition? What problems do you see with the influence of growth coalitions?

## RECOMMENDED READINGS

Horne, J. (2006). *Sport in consumer culture.* New York, NY: Palgrave Macmillan. (This book explores how the consumer culture affects the provision of sport and leisure and the degree of control consumers of sport-related goods and services have in this culture. Specific issues related to consumerism include (a) globalization, (b) the commodification of sport through advertising and sponsorship, and (c) social class divisions and sport consumption.)

Delaney, K. J., & Eckstein, R. (2003). *Public dollars, private stadiums: the battle over building sport stadiums.* New Brunswick, NJ: Rutgers University

Press. (Delaney and Eckstein present a growth-coalition framework that is used to examine the efforts of several American cities to obtain public funding for professional sport stadia. The authors discuss the creation and maintenance of growth coalitions generally and use case studies to identify conditions necessary to gain approval for public subsidization of facilities.)

Clotfelter, C. T. (2011). *Big-time sports in American universities.* New York, NY: Cambridge University Press. (This book provides an overview of the economic importance and priorities of the collegiate athletic system in the United States. Clotfelter examines the exploitation of athletes in revenue-producing sports and the exploitation of university's tax-exempt status – two issues which are appropriate for consideration from a Marxist lens.)

## REFERENCES

Bourdieu, P. (1978). Sport and social class. *Social Science Information, 17,* 819-840.
Budd, A. (2001). Capitalism, sport and resistance: Reflections. *Sport in Society, 4,* 1-18.
Butsch, R. (1984). The commodification of leisure: The case of the model airplane hobby industry. *Qualitative Sociology, 7,* 217-235.
Centers for Disease Control (2005). *Behavioral risk factor surveillance system.* http://www.cdc.gov/brfss/.
Crompton, J.L., Howard, D.R., & Var, T. (2003). Financing major league facilities: Status, evolution, and conflicting forces. *Journal of Sport Management, 17,* 156-184.
Delaney, K.J., & Eckstein, R. (2007). Urban power structures and publicly financed stadiums. *Sociological Forum, 22,* 331-353.
Edensor, T., & Richards, S. (2007). Snowboarders vs skiers: Contested choreographies of the slopes. *Leisure Studies, 26,* 97-114.
Frey, J.H., & Eitzen, D.S. (1991). Sport and society. *Annual Review of Sociology, 17,* 503-522.
Giulianotti, R. (2005). *Sport: A critical sociology.* Cambridge, MA: Polity Press.
Grenfell, C.C., & Rinehart, R.E. (2003). Skating on thin ice: Human rights in youth figure skating. *International Review for the Sociology of Sport, 38,* 79-97.
Gwynne, S.C. (2010, March). Come early. Be loud. Cash in. *Texas Monthly, 36,* 142-243.
Gumbel, B. (2011, October 18). *Real Sports.* HBO.
Maier, C.S. (1987). *In Search of Stability: Explorations in Historical Political Economy.* Melbourne, Australia: Cambridge University Press.

Marx, K., & Engels, F. (1992). *The Communist Manifesto*. Oxford: Oxford University Press. Originally published in 1848.

Milano, M., & Chelladurai, P. (2011). Gross domestic sport product: The size of the sport industry in the United States. *Journal of Sport Management, 25*, 24-35.

Molotch, H. (1976). The city as a growth machine: Toward a political economy of place. *American Journal of Sociology, 82*, 309-332.

National Collegiate Athletic Association (n.d.).

National Collegiate Athletic Association (2011). *2011-12 NCAA Division I Manual*. Indianapolis: NCAA.

Ourand, J. (2011, June 6). How high can rights fees go? *Street & Smith's Sports Business Journal, 1*.

Siegfried, J., & Zimbalist, A. (2000). The economics of sport facilities and their communities. *Journal of Economic Perspectives, 14*, 95-114.

Sport England (2011). Active People Survey 5. Retrieved from www.sportengland.org.

Taks, M., & Scheerder, J. (2006). Youth sports participation styles and market segmentation profiles: Evidence and applications. *European Sport Management Quarterly, 6*, 85-121.

US Census Bureau (2011). 2012 Statistical Abstract. Retrieved from www.census.org.

Veblen, T. (1994). *The theory of the leisure class*. In *The collected works of Thorstein Veblen*. Originally published 1899. Reprint, London: Routledge.

Trigg, A.B. (2001). Veblen, Bourdieu, and conspicuous consumption. *Journal of Economic Issues, 35*, 99-115.

Whitlock, J. (2011). Greedy NCAA still exploiting athletes. Retrieved from www.foxsports.com.

# CHAPTER 6

# INTERNATIONAL SPORT

Brandon Brown, Chanho Kang, & Woojun Lee

\*\*\*

**Learning Objectives**

After reading this chapter, you should be able to:

1. Explain key changes that occurred in international sport from 1900 to the present time.
2. Discuss how the history of international sport has influenced present day sport.
3. Discuss the current state of international sport business.
4. Describe how international sport events are developed and established.

## INTRODUCTION

In 2005, celebrated author Thomas Friedman released his international best-selling book, *The World is Flat*, a work concentrating on the unification of the world's political and technological capabilities and how businesses have seen an increase in international trade, capital flow, technology, and more. Friedman asserts an increase in unification, technology, and communication have led to a reduction of barriers from one country to another, thus enabling the global business world to be without obstruction, or, as Friedman would have it, a world that is flat. The notion of the world being "flat" has suggested to entrepreneurs that an investment in global business affairs may be worth merit. It is no surprise, therefore, that the sport industry has followed suit in international commerce.

Those in the sports world have reiterated Friedman's (2005) sentiments toward international exchange. Over the last few decades, sports have seen an increase in the creation of leagues, the attendance of spectators, and the amount of business conducted globally (Allison, 2005; Bairner, 2005). Not only have individuals migrated to distant countries to play sports, but sport organizations have gone overseas to conduct business with foreign conglomerates. But how did this start, and where does international sport stand today? What were the major causes of such a transition to international sport business? In this chapter, we will address these issues, as well as detail the current state of international sport business and the development of international sporting events.

## THE HISTORY OF GLOBALIZING SPORT

The aforementioned concept of countries collectively conducting business can be amalgamated to define *globalization*, or the consolidation of the world into a whole space (Robertson, 1992). It includes the movement of labor, knowledge, and technology across borders. At its core, the history of sport globalization was not derived from a desire to introduce other countries to new sports; rather, it originates from a desire to impose culture upon other countries. The notion of establishing dominance by imposing one's culture upon another country is known as *imperialism* (Brain, 2006). In the past, imperialism was a main contributor to new sports' introduction to foreign countries. For example, in the 1700s the British Empire sought to achieve colonial expansion (Fletcher, 2011). In doing so, they were able to apprehend colonies across the world, displace their systems of rule, and replace them with new British systems (Fletcher, 2011). In the process of such take over, the new inhabitants were able to impose their culture, and in particular, their likings. Because cricket was widely respected and treasured by Britain, the sport was therefore imposed upon the newly subjugated colonies (Sandiford, 1983). Such was the case in South Africa, the West Indies, and other territories, where Britain was able to impose their British culture upon these territories. Today, in such places as South Africa and the West Indies, cricket is widely regarded as a national pastime.

In 1888–1889, Albert Spalding took a group of professional baseball players on a "tour" around the world to promote Spalding sporting goods and baseball (which at the time was widely popular in America). The tour visited Hawaii, New Zealand, Australia, Ceylon, Egypt, Italy, France, and England, and became known as the "Spalding Tour" (Zeiler, 2006b). On the surface, the tour may have seemed as a mere plug for the Spalding product or the sport of baseball; however, many scholars see Spalding's expeditions as an attempt to compel other countries to accept an American culture that was prime for expansion (Zeiler, 2006a). Spalding was not simply promoting sporting goods and baseball, but was publicizing the features that enabled America to thrive – free enterprise, progress, racial hierarchy, and cultural virtue. As Zeiler (2006a) stated, "Albert Spalding linked baseball to a U.S. presence overseas, viewing the world as a market ripe for the infusion of American ideas, products, and energy" (p. xi).

These examples showcase the notion of imperialism as a main contributor toward the growth of sports overseas. Baseball and other American sports such as basketball and football were expanded overseas not simply because the world needed new sports, but because of America's desire to introduce other countries to the dynamics which characterize the sports, and therefore the dynamics which characterize the country itself (Zeiler, 2006b). Such was the case for most countries until the majority of territories were established with their own identity, at which point international sport began to flourish.

According to Bennett (2008), the growth and evolution of modern international sport took place during three generations: the Monopoly Generation (1900-1949), the Television Generation (1950-1989), and the Highlight Generation (1990-present). We outline each in the following space.

**The Monopoly Generation (1900-1949)**

The Monopoly Generation of international sport took place during 1900 through 1949. Prior to this period, sporting events were largely unstructured, with many organizers simply creating ticket prices and advertisements without justification or reason. It was not until around 1900 when entrepreneurs took notice of the demand for sport and started creating business plans in accordance to the demand (Bonde, 2009). The generation is aptly named the Monopoly Generation because of its exclusive limitations. This was a generation in which there were a small number of sports, very few means for spectators, and a limited number of individuals who were in charge of these businesses. Owners and league officials held the majority of power over most leagues and therefore left the players with very little input (Bonde, 2009).

During this period spectators were limited to live events, radio, newspaper, or magazines. Furthermore, many nations were seeing a rapid population growth that caused a corresponding demand for sports (Coakley, 2007). Because demand was high, and entrepreneurs were starting to take notice, more structure was invoked in both the marketing aspect of sport and in the formation of policies. The Monopoly Generation saw an increase in the amount of stadiums that were built and an influx in the amount of formal leagues that were created.

As early as 1901, the "American League" entered into Major League status for baseball, thus laying the foundation for Major League Baseball ("MLB History," 2011). In 1916 the Professional Golfers Association (PGA) was created, and in October of the same year, the first PGA Championship was held with a total purse of $2,500 ("PGA of America History," 2011). The American Professional Football Association was created in 1920, and eventually changed its name to the National Football League (NFL) in 1922 ("NFL: History," 2011). The Basketball Association of America was founded in 1946, and went on to adopt the name the National Basketball Association (NBA) in 1949 after merging with the National Basketball League ("NBA History," 2011).

The creation of these leagues represents a period of growth and structure for the international sports world. Nevertheless, one sports league more than others truly exemplifies an international conglomeration of different countries: the Fédération Internationale de Football Association (FIFA). Founded in Paris in 1904 ("FIFA History of Football," 2011), this international soccer league originally consisted of only European associations up until 1909, when South Africa joined the Federation. In the years following, Argentina, Chile, and the United States joined the league to make it the first of its kind (Bennett, 2008). FIFA is an important aspect of international sport not only because of its success, but because of its ability to foster social harmony across borders. More than any other league, FIFA has become a league that brings together different regions, people, and nations.

The expansion and formation of these leagues became harmonious with the growth of sport business. Accordingly, in 1950 a famous quote surrounded the sport business world: "Baseball is too much of a sport to be a business and too much of a business to be a sport" (Seymour, 1960, p. 4). It was clear that at the dawn of the 1940s, sport was not simply a business, but a profitable one at that. It was a perfect time therefore to have advancement, leading to a new stream of sport business.

### The Television Generation (1950-1989)

The time frame from 1950 through 1989 is aptly named the Television Generation due to international sport becoming popular through a means of television. Though television was invented in the early 1900s, it was not until the mid 1900s when television became a commodity, and the majority of households owned a television set (Hilmes & Jacobs, 2008). Due to a vast increase in the amount of television being watched, the world's culture started to change. For many, watching television served as the first time a household could sit down and watch events that were taking place in another country. Whereas in previous years individuals would read or hear about the happenings in foreign countries, the infiltration of television marked the first time in history where these individuals could actually see what was happening.

Society was changing, and sport organizations now had to cater to a new consumer. Consequently, sport organizations would have to redefine how they would market their products towards a new audience. Sports that were reliant upon live spectatorship, such as horseracing, boxing, and traditional wrestling, were now replaced by sports that were aesthetically pleasing and could be seen on television (Hughson, 2009). During 1950-1989, the popularity of sports such as basketball and football increased greatly (Hughson, 2009). Sport programs became specialized and saw an increase in marketing, communication, and advertising.

Newspapers and magazines now had to change their styles in order to compete with television. This process eventually led to a sequence of patterns that concluded by seeing a shift in the power structure between owners and players. As newspapers and magazines began changing their approach to reach a different type of audience, they began to emphasize personal story lines for players instead of focusing on in-game action. The campaign brought success to the newspaper and magazine industry, but also brought an increased amount of attention towards the players themselves (Lambie, 2010). Players, realizing their significance, sought representation to capitalize on their newly discovered star power. This led to an increase in the amount of players seeking personal representation, and thus led to the creation of player management groups or agencies. In 1960, Mark McCormack signed American golfer Arnold Palmer and created one of the first sport agencies which eventually expanded globally, the International Management Group (IMG; "IMG World", 2011).

Agencies such as IMG were able to promote players and events to worldwide audiences, emphasizing their abilities. Such emphasis on player abilities enabled fans to become accustomed to high skill levels, and cleared a path for the next generation of international sport – the Highlight Generation.

## The Highlight Generation (1990-Present)

As technology increased, so too did the world's attraction to sports. Starting in the 1990s, the world had evolved into an ever-changing information society. The Highlight Generation features traditional sports, but reconfigures the sports so that they are heavily reliant upon highlights and individuals. During the 1990s, the world was taking full advantage of the Internet, and countries were able to obtain more information about other countries than ever before (Friedman, 2005). Leagues witnessed an increase in the amount of players coming from overseas, and even non-native individuals filled national coaching positions (Thibault, 2009).

The passing of the Civil Rights era enabled cultures around the world to increase their efforts towards equality, and as a result individuals throughout various countries became more independent. This echoed throughout the sports world as highlights of individuals were (and still are) at an all-time high. Individual sports, such as extreme sports, started to gain momentum in the 1990s, and in 1995 the first X-Games tournament was held in Rhode Island (Pickert, 2009). The X-Games featured athletes from around the world, and once again exemplified international companionship.

As even more attention was being given to individuals, many sports players found themselves with a unique opportunity. Whereas owners and league officials once had the majority of power over sports, players could now make demands because of their highly-touted star power. For the first time, the Highlight Generation showed that athletes were no longer considered to be mere laborers. Instead, the athletes were widely recognized and were able to have significant influences on society.

International sports history relies on its ability to be influenced by culture and society. While the history of sport becoming globalized has been filled with various events and happenings, one topic greatly influential toward international sports history is the Olympics. In the following section, we detail the fundamental aspects of the Olympics and their impact on international sport today.

### The Olympic Games

As many know, the Olympic Games are a worldwide event featuring summer and winter sports. Both the Summer and Winter Games take place every four years, and host thousands of athletes from various parts of the world. Athletes represent their country as a testament to the ability of sports fostering togetherness (Torres, 2006). The Olympic Games have come to be known as the world's primary sports competition involving the competition of multiple countries (Torres, 2006). While the first modern Olympic Games were held in 1896 in Athens, Greece with 14 nations and 241 athletes, much has changed. While the Olympic Games characterize the very meaning of international competition, they also serve as precursors for change inside and outside of the sports world. The Olympics have impacted the way sport business is conducted, and has impacted society in itself. We provide examples of how the Olympics have accomplished such feats.

## The Olympics Impacting Sport Business

The Olympics have impacted sport business several times throughout history. The 1984 Olympics provide an example as to how these events can have an impact on everyday sport business. The 1984 Summer Olympic Games were preceded by the 1980 Olympics, which saw the United States and other countries boycott the Games in protest against the Soviet War in Afghanistan (Crossman & Lappage, 1992). The boycott caused the Olympics to lose a vast amount of money, and thus, concerned the city hosting the 1984 Olympics: Los Angeles, California. The Organizing Committee was therefore determined to ensure that the Olympic Games would bring in revenue. Olympic coordinator Peter Ueberroth conducted a plan to not only use existing venues from around the area, but to also have these venues sponsored by widely known corporations (Dyreson & Llewellyn, 2008). This resulted in the Levi Corporation giving ten million dollars in cash and in-kind sponsorships to the Games and to the participating athletes. The corporation Seven-Eleven built the Velodrome, and the McDonalds Corporation built a swimming pool. Both were specifically created for the Olympics. These sponsor partnerships, along with other business dealings, brought in hundreds of millions of dollars in revenue (Dyreson & Llewellyn, 2008). The success of the Games served as a blueprint for sport organizations. In the 1980s, sponsor partnerships with sport organizations were at an all-time high and are still a main source of revenue for sport businesses today (Dyreson & Llewellyn, 2008).

## The Olympics Impacting Society

On more than one occasion, the Olympic Games have been used as a platform to promote societal issues. In 1968, during the Mexico City Olympic Games, track and field athletes Tommie Smith and John Carlos won first and third place in the 200-meter dash. While on the victory stand, accepting their medals, both athletes wore black gloves, and raised their fists representing a symbolic Black Power salute (Parks et al., 2002). The athletes did so to bring attention to America's civil rights movement, which had not gone far enough to eliminate the injustices that Black Americans were facing. Though they faced considerable criticism for their actions, Smith and Carlos' salute had a lasting effect on racial equality in sport. It was not long after that in 1976 African nations boycotted the Montreal Games over South Africa's policies towards Apartheid.

Though these demonstrations were for a positive outcome, there have been other instances where negative events during the Olympic Games have impacted society. In 1972, spectators of the Munich Olympics witnessed a horrible act, as 11 Israeli Olympic athletes and coaches were murdered by Palestinian terrorists. The incident was over 20 hours and was watched by over 900 million viewers (Parks et al., 2002). The catastrophe permanently changed security procedures for the Olympics, and left an everlasting memory which has since tarnished Munich's reputation for hosting the Olympics (Parks et al., 2002).

Such examples serve as illustrations as to how powerful sport can be on an international scale. These events, which have taken place in the past, lead to an ever-growing present. In the following section, we will discuss the current state of international sport from a business perspective.

## INTRODUCTION OF INTERNATIONAL SPORT BUSINESS

According to Parks and Quarterman (2003), "The international sport industry in the beginning of the 21st century has shifted from being perceived as a niche in the sport marketplace to representing the foundation of the sport enterprise" (p. 376). The term *internationalism* refers to having an influence on more than one nation (Masteralexis et al., 2005). As sport leagues continue to grow, there are more restrictions involving professional athletes playing internationally, sport fans watching sporting events held in other nations, and individuals purchasing licensed sport products from other nations (Masteralexis et al. 2005). With the current circumstances, sport marketers increasingly embrace diverse opportunities to sell their sport products in global markets. For example, English Premier League Association Football is televised in 152 nations (Falcous & Maguire, 2006). In 2002-2003 season, the NBA was broadcast in 212 nations and territories in 42 different languages, capturing a global audience of 750 million households (Falcous & Maguire, 2006). Furthermore, the International Olympic Committee (IOC) reported that approximately 3.9 billion people in 220 nations and territories watched the 2004 Athens Olympics (Falcous & Maguire, 2006).

## Environment of International Sport Business

In the environment of global sport business, market share and investment in a given sport product are currently measured on a worldwide basis rather than national basis (Parks & Quarterman, 2003). Although there are some attempts to confine and defend industry segments based on national bias, Parks and Quarterman illustrate that "the future in the early decades of the 21st century portends an almost seamless integration and movement of goods, services, and personnel on a grand global scale" (p. 376).

As most sports have strengthened the exchange of internationally talented people or sport programs at all levels, major international trade agreements have begun to directly influence the industry (Parks & Quarterman, 2003). For example, international trades and exchanges in a wide-ranging cross section of sports at youth levels will continue to become more commonplace (Parks & Quaterman, 2003; Pitts & Stotlar, 2002). According to Barrand (2001), national and international sport federations have challenged professional sports leagues and franchises for the global market share of their revenues and profits from the licensing of trademarks, merchandise, and broadcasting rights. Furthermore, these sport federations and their major sporting events will profit from growing broadcasting rights (Parks & Quarterman, 2003). The revenues and profits made from these rights come from several sources, including deregulation of worldwide cable, expanded Internet access agreements, and stretched access through satellite broadcasting (Parks & Quarterman, 2003). Moreover, sport teams, celebrities, superstars, and branded sport products are globally recognized. Parks and Quarterman (2003) argue that the conglomeration of these aspects will bring new challenges to the global sport industry, which will be compounded by cultural differences, national laws, and traditions.

## The Globalization of Sport

These days, more than ever, sport governing bodies, corporations, and sport franchises have attempted to increase popularity and revenue in the global sport market (Masteralexis et al., 2005). Technology, particularly with respect to the broadcasting of visual images, significantly enhances the ease with which sport marketers or practitioners can introduce and sell their products to foreign markets (Masteralexis et al., 2005). Corporations have attempted to benefit from this trend by sponsoring international sporting events in an effort to increase the distribution tools for their products and services (Parent & Slack, 2007; Jozsa, 2009). Moreover, major professional franchises have also endeavored to utilize the shrinking global market to increase exposure for their sport leagues in an effort to increase their profits (Jozsa, 2009; Pitts & Stotlar, 2002). Masteralexis et al. (2005) argue that both professional sport leagues and corporations have attempted to improve the global market share for their products.

### Corporate Involvement with International Sport

With technological advances, such as satellite broadcasting technology and high-speed Internet service, sport fans have access to a variety of major international sporting events. Corporations are therefore utilizing sport to sell their products to customers in other nations (Masteralexis et al., 2005). Such activities can be categorized into two aspects: (a) efforts by sport manufacturers to distribute their products overseas, and (b) efforts by companies to utilize sponsorship to sell their products in global markets (Masteralexis et al., 2005).

Similar to other corporations in the world, sport related manufacturers have attempted to capitalize on potential markets (Masteralexis et al., 2005). The reason behind the trends is simple: the North American markets are saturated. Although North Americans are sport oriented, sport related manufacturers have reached a point where the corporations can no longer dramatically increase their sales to consumers in the national market. As a result, sport-related corporations have expanded their product distribution overseas (Masteralexis et al., 2005).

Non-sport-related corporations have attempted to utilize sport to introduce and sell their products internationally (Masteralexis et al., 2005). Primarily, Masteralexis et al. (2005) argue that this is done through the sponsorship of international sport teams and individual athletes. In gen-

eral, such efforts are geared toward increasing brand aware-
ness/recognition, brand loyalty, and sales in global markets. Shank (2005)
argues, "one of the most basic objectives of any sponsor is to generate
awareness or raise levels of awareness of its products and services,
product lines, or corporate name" (p. 333). Reaching a new global target
market is another objective of sponsorship programs. For example, given
the importance of global markets, Budweiser and its parent company,
Anheuser-Busch, were interested in using sports sponsorship as a vehicle for increasing brand awareness and sales in global markets. In 1986,
the beer company became the title sponsor of an American football
league in the United Kingdom (Wilcox, 1995). Researchers found that
consumers in the United Kingdom did not consume Budweiser because
individuals considered that Budweiser's taste was weak and unattractive
when compared to its English competitors (Wilcox, 1995). Therefore,
Anheuser-Busch tried to overcome Budweiser's image as a weak beer by
sponsoring a sport league with a strong brand image (Wilcox, 1995).

By sponsoring prominent international sport leagues, corporations can
increase benefits from the sponsorship. Through international sport
event sponsorship efforts, global corporations have not only attempted
to develop new distribution channels but have also tried to increase their
popularity worldwide (Shank, 2005). For example, Coca-Cola has sponsored some of the NBA's international events in order to increase sales
and expand distribution of Sprite abroad (Masteralexis et al., 2005). In
conjunction with exhibition Games played in Mexico City, Coca-Cola
produced over 1 million NBA logoed cans of Sprite in an effort to increase sales in Mexico (Masteralexis et al., 2005; "National Basketball Association", 1997).

### The Involvement of Professional Sport
### Franchises with International Sport

North American professional sport leagues are aggressively trying to
increase the reputation of their leagues worldwide (Masteralexis et al.,
2005). For example, the NFL's Super Bowl XLV was televised in more
than 230 countries around the world ("NFL International", 2012). An
increase in technology has enabled sport fans around the world to watch
North American professional sporting events. With this in mind, each of
the major sport leagues has created an international division to attempt
to spread the international popularity of their leagues. For example, Major League Baseball International Partners has an office in some countries,
such as Sydney and Australia, concentrating on increasing the populari-

ty of baseball through merchandise sales, game broadcasting, and grass-roots programs (Masteralexis et al., 2005).

These divisions and international offices have focused on improving the popularity of North American professional sport, employing the following techniques and strategies: (a) broadcasting sporting events around the world; (b) licensing and merchandising of sport products; and (c) playing exhibition and regular season games in other nations and territories (Masteralexis et al., 2005). We outline each in the following space.

In an effort to introduce their sports to other nations, professional sport leagues rely on broadcasting their sports to foreign territories. During the 1996-1997 seasons, the NBA attracted over 550 million households in 188 nations ("National Basketball Association," 1997). Such broadcasts have begun to produce significant revenue for the NBA. The NBA received $200,000 from a cable company in France to broadcast NBA games in French (Wilcox, 1995). The NFL is also aggressively expanding distribution of American football games abroad. From 1989 to 1996, the number of countries carrying NFL games increased from 35 to 175 ("NFL International," 2011). By the 2002 season, 226 nations were able to receive NFL programming, again displaying a dramatic increase ("NFL International," 2011). In addition, for a half an hour once a week, the NBA broadcasts a show entitled NBA *Jam* to more than 15 countries. Masteralexis et al. (2005) argue that the Internet has also played a major role in leagues increasing their popularity. For example, all the professional leagues have developed websites presenting up-to-date information about their respective leagues accessible to everyone on the Internet base.

Another strategy commonly used to expand the global markets for a sport is to sell licensed merchandise (Masteralexis et al., 2005). Merchandise displaying a team logo allows fans to identify with their favorite teams. Through the sales of logoed merchandise as a promotional vehicle, professional leagues may increase the popularity of their sport leagues. For example, people purchasing and wearing Manchester United T-shirts and hats in Seoul, Korea, serve to increase brand awareness of both the English premier leagues and Manchester United in Korea. Moreover, holding games in other countries is a practical way for a team to export its product (Masteralexis et al., 2005). In this way, foreign sport fans have the opportunity to watch their favorite sporting events in person. The NBA started to play their foreign exhibition games in 1988, when an NBA team (the Atlanta Hawks) traveled to the former Soviet

Union for exhibition games (Masteralexis et al., 2005). Since then, NBA exhibition games have been played worldwide in countries, such as Spain, Mexico, France, Germany, the United Kingdom, Japan, and Korea. Through these efforts, professional sport franchises can increase their brand awareness in foreign countries.

Looking into how major sporting events are developed and established can further enhance the current examination of international sport organizations. The following section details the development of major international sport events.

## THE DEVELOPMENT OF MAJOR
## INTERNATIONAL SPORTING EVENTS

Major sporting events have become prominent and significant in recent years (Roche, 2000). Their prominence originates in part from a greater degree of commercialization. This has caused the amount of private capital associated with said events to increase dramatically. Recently, large-scale sporting events have become prominent due to local and national governments concentrating on planning and development. Very frequently, committees in charge of local or national development plans consider sporting events as viable catalysts for both short and long-term economic growth. The reasons for this are threefold. To begin, major sporting events are often noted for their perceived ability to encourage and attract a greater amount of foreign and domestic investment. Second, hosting an international sporting event such as the Olympics or the World Cup means that the national infrastructure, such as roads and public transportation, will be improved. Finally, individual events can cause a surge in hospitality and tourism because of the influx of spectators and athletes into the hosting nation (Bale & Moen, 1995; Hall, 1992; Baade & Matheson, 2002).

The impact of hosting an international sporting event is quite complex. Advocates and opponents often wage heated debates about whether such events will help or hinder the economy. Naturally, most arguments, both pro and con, center on economic dimensions and financial gains. A number of scholars and researchers have recently begun to look beyond dollar signs, and instead have chosen to investigate such aspects as the socio-cultural dimensions of events (Chalip, 2006; Hall & Hodges, 1996; Owen, 2002; Valera & Guardia, 2002). This is an area lacking official discussions between authorities and the consultants they employ (Waitt, 2001). Due to the fact that socio-cultural dimensions are often overlooked in the planning stages of events, the debates of their impact are often unbalanced. In addition, discussions of how these impacts articulate with broader processes of development towards their host cities or countries are lacking a holistic outlook (Smith & Fox, 2007). The very concept of development (i.e., tangible and sustainable improvement in the life situation of a given population) may be thought of as being largely undocumented in the body of research, which has grown substantially (Horne & Manzenreiter, 2006).

Literature on development has recently demonstrated a very noticeable shift where there has been an attempt to analyze the effects of these events, and how the events influence the development of a hosting city/country. Within the realm of the Olympic Movement, there have been more concerted efforts at improving sustainability standards. Such was the case when, in 1999, the International Olympic Committee (IOC) adopted a resolution that would have members promote sustainable development through sport. Nevertheless, there has not been a consensus on which particular benefits are gained from hosting sporting events (Jones, 2001). However, this has done nothing to diminish the fact that promoters will sometimes fabricate the potential benefits that come along with hosting a major event (Hall, 2006). The claims that are in existence seem to have originated in the Global North, represented by the economically developed societies of Europe, North America, Australia, Israel, and South Africa amongst others (Odeh, 2010). In more recent decades however, the Global South, which represents the still-economically developing countries of Africa, India, China, Brazil, and Mexico, among others, has been making strong attempts to host these major events. There are slightly different reasons as to why the Global South is seeking to host international events. While both the North and South are eager to attract foreign capital and investment, Southern hosts (more so than the Northern hosts) want to showcase their accomplishments and display to the world their modernization (Van der Westuize, 2007; Cornelissen, 2008).

**Economic Impact of International Sporting Events**

As has been discussed, hosting a major international sporting event is a goal many countries strive for, yet it is not without economic impact. There have been numerous studies suggesting that the money spent on preparing the infrastructure of the country for the event (such as repairing roads, building stadiums and improving public transport) may actually outweigh the financial gains the nation may receive. While this may be true, the global auditors of Klynveld Peat Marwick Goerdeler (KPMG) reported that the 2010 World Cup held in South Africa had a very positive effect on that nation's economy (Prinsloo, 2010). They estimated that the World Cup contributed to approximately 5% of the quarterly GDP growth in South Africa for 2010. Tourism increased 20% higher than it normally is in July, which led to a positive impact on employment (Prinsloo, 2010). When surveyed, 95% of the visitors to South Africa during the World Cup stated that they might visit the country again and would recommend it to a friend as a travel destination. Furthermore, KPMG claims that by hosting the World Cup, South Africa was cushioned from the effects of the global economic crisis (Prinsloo, 2010).

## Social Impact of International Sporting Events

Though global sport events have been known to help a country's economy, these events have also been known to have a social impact. Another prominent effect of the 2010 World Cup was that it inspired young South Africans to become international players and induced much needed investments in youth soccer and training facilities in South Africa. This led to a surge in soccer academies in South Africa.

Social impacts have been observed in Korea, as well. In 1961, Park Chung-hee seized the reins of power in the budding Korean democracy through a military coup, and maintained an authoritarian regime until his assassination in 1979. Although he is credited with enabling the nation to industrialize and strengthen its economy, he severely restricted personal and social freedoms. His successor, President Chun Doo-hwan, continued that repressive regime. Doo-hwan cracked down on any hint of true democracy. This was exemplified in the infamous Gwangju Massacre that occurred when students rose up to protest the manner in which Chun had gained power resulting in the President turning the army on its own citizens.

When Korea was selected by the Olympic committee to host the 1988 Summer Olympic Games, many Koreans were not pleased. It was widely viewed to be a plot instigated by President Chun Doo-hwan to legitimize his rule of the nation (Kuide, 2007). The people of Korea once again began widespread protests directed at President Chun when, in 1987, he handpicked his successor. Chun could once again turn the military on the protestors to stop the demonstrations in a decisive manner as he had in 1980. The eyes of the world were on Korea and such a move on the part of the President could forfeit the chances of the nation to host the

Games. Instead, Chun chose to give in to the will of the people and held democratic elections. This paved the way for true democracy and massive reforms in the nation.

These same Games had another positive effect on Korea outside of the obvious economic effects. The Olympics enabled Korea to begin diplomatic relations with China and the USSR. Presidents Park and Chun were strongly anti-communist and refused to consider dialogue with its communist neighbors. However, because of the Olympics, not only dialogue, but also avenues of trade, opened between the nations. Today, China is one of the largest importers of Korean goods and is essential to the health and growth of the Korean economy (Chung, 1988).

Large-scale sport events have thus demonstrated in a decisive manner that they can impact local and national development in ways that are both sustainable and long lasting. Major sporting events may assist in the socio-cultural development of a nation as a side effect of hosting a major event.

## CHAPTER SUMMARY

International sport has many facets that influence its very nature. The history of international sport shows that an introduction of sports to other nations did not come from a want to introduce other countries to their sports; rather, the notion of imperialism allowed countries to take in foreign culture, and therefore foreign sports. International sport came across three distinct, yet important phases throughout its history: The Monopoly Generation which took place during 1900-1949, the Television Generation which took place during 1950-1989, and the Highlight Generation which took place during 1990-present time. International sport business is currently expanding, and sees corporations across the globe flocking towards sport for a source of revenue. Manufacturers are seeing North American markets become saturated and are expanding their businesses globally. Moreover, broadcasting, licensing, exhibition games, and marketing foreign athletes are all aspects, which have seen an increase in popularity overseas. As countries are seeking to host major international sporting events, they are realizing the risks and benefits for doing so. International sport has showcased a conglomeration of countries, regions, and people. In doing so, it has echoed a society, which is ripe for expansion, growth, and harmony.

## DISCUSSION QUESTIONS

1.  Name the three major time periods of modern international sport, and briefly describe each.
2.  Describe how the Olympic Games have had an impact on modern day business and society.
3.  In what two ways has the sport product been globalized?
4.  How have international offices focused on increasing the popularity of sport across the globe?
5.  Why have economies been interested in developing international sporting events?

## RECOMMENDED READINGS

Thibault, L. (2009). Globalization of sport: An inconvenient truth. *Journal of Sport Management, 23*, 1-20. (Thibault concentrates on the various implications of international sport and discusses issues such as labor development, the increasing amount of athletes migrating to foreign countries, and the global media.)

Houlihan, B. (2003). *Sport & Society: A student introduction.* London: Sage Publications. (This book presents the relations between sport, social policy and the social context.)

## REFERENCES

Allison, L. (Ed.) (2005). *The global politics of sport. The role of global institutions in sport.* London: Routledge.

Baade, R. A. & Matheson, V. A. (2002). Bidding for the Olympics: Fools' gold? In C. Barros, M. Ibrahim and S. Szymanski (Eds.) *Transatlantic Sport: The Comparative Economics of North American and European Sport* (pp. 127-151). London: Edward Elgar Publishing.

Bairner, A. (2005). Sport and the nation in the global era. In L. Allison (Ed.), *The global politics of sport. The role of global institutions in sport* (p. 87–100). London: Routledge.

Bale, J. & Moen, O. (1995). *The Stadium and the City.* Keele: Keele University Press.

Barrand, D. (2001). Building for a long-term future. *Sports Business International,* 20-22.

Bennett, G. (September, 2008). *They did all that without the Internet? Historical foundations of sport as an international commodity.* Lecture conducted from Texas A&M University, College Station, Texas.

Bonde, H. (2009). The time and speed ideology: 19th century industrialization and sport. *The International Journal of the History of Sport, 26*, 1315-1334.

Brain, S. (2006). Sport, cultural imperialism and colonial response in the British empire. *Sport in Society, 9*, 809-835.

Chalip, L. (2006). Toward a distinctive sport management discipline. *Journal of Sport Management, 20*, 1-21.

Chung, J. H. (1988). South Korea-China economic relations. *Asian Survey, 28*, 1031-1048.

Coakley, J. (2007). *Sports in society* (9th ed.). Thousand Oaks, CA: Sage Publications.

Cornelissen, S. (2008). Scripting the nation: sport, mega-events and foreign policy in post-apartheid South Africa. *Sport in Society, 11*, 481-493.

Crossman, J. & Lappage, R. (1992). Canadian athletes' perceptions of the 1980 Olympic boycott. *Sociology of Sport, 9*, 354-371.

Dyreson, M., & Llewellyn, M. (2008). Los Angeles is the Olympic city: Legacies of the 1932 and 1984 Olympic Games. *International Journal of the History of Sport, 25*, 1991-2018.

Falcous, M., & Maguire. J. (2006). Imagining 'America': The NBA and local-global mediascapes. *International Review for The Sociology of Sport, 41*, 59-78.

FIFA History of Football. (2011). *FIFA.com*. Retrieved from www.fifa.com.

Fletcher, T. (2011). The making of English cricket cultures: empire, globalization and (post) colonialism. *Sport in Society, 14*, 17-36.

Friedman, T. (2005). *The world is flat*. New York, NY: Farrar, Straus and Giroux.

Hall, C. M. (1992). *Hallmark tourist events*. London: Belhaven Press.

Hall, C. M. (2006). Urban entrepreneurship, corporate interests and sports mega-events: the thin policies of competitiveness within the hard outcomes of neoliberalism. In J. Horne & W. Manzenreiter (Eds.) *Sports mega-events: Social scientific analyses of a global phenomenon* (pp. 59-70). Oxford: Blackwell.

Hall, C. M. & Hodges, J. (1996). The party's great, but what about the hangover? The housing and social impacts of mega-events with special reference to the 2000 Sydney Olympics, *Festival management and Event Tourism, 4*, 13-20.

Hilmes, M., Jacobs, J. (2008). *The television history book*. London, England: British Film Institute.

Horn, J. & Manzenreiter, W. (2006). An introduction to the sociology of sports mega-events. In J. Horne and W. Manzenreiter (Eds). *Sports mega-events: Social scientific analyses of a global phenomenon* (pp. 1-24). Oxford: Blackwell Publishing.

Hughson, J. (2009). Sport and history on the ground: documentary and the feature film. *Sport in Society, 12*, 118-133.

IMG World: About us. (2011). *IMG World*. Retrieved from www.imgworld.com.

Jones, C. (2001). Mega events and host region impacts: determining the true worth of the 1999 Rugby World Cup. *International Journal of Tourism Research, 3*, 117-133.

Jozsa, F. P. (2009). *Global sports cultures, markets and organizations*. Hackensack, NJ: World Scientific Publishing.

Kuide, C. (2007). Two Historical Turning Points: The Seoul and Beijing Olympics. *China Rights Forum, 3*, 36-40.

Lambie, J. (2010). *The story of your life: A history of the sporting life newspaper.* England: Troubador Publishing.

Major League Baseball. (1997). MLB International. Retrieved from www.majorleaguebase.ball.com.

Masteralexis, L. P., Barr, C. A., & Hums, M. A. (2005). *Principles and practice of sport management* (2nd ed.). Sudbury, MA: Jones and Bartlett Publishers.

MLB History. (2011). *MLB.com.* Retrieved from www.mlb.mlb.com.

National Basketball Association. (1997). Global game. Retrived Nov 1, 2011, from http://www.nba.com.

NBA History. (2011). *NBA.com.* Retrieved from www.nba.com.

NFL International. (2011). NFL international. Retrieved from www.nfl.com.

NFL:History. (2011). NFL.com. Retrieved from www.nfl.com.

Odeh, L. E. (2010). A comparative analysis of Global North and Global South economies. *Journal of Sustainable Development in Africa, 12,* 338-348.

Owen, K. (2002). The Sydney 2000 Olympics and urban entrepreneurialism: local variations in urban governance. *Australian Geographical Studies, 40,* 563-600.

Parent, M. M., & Slack, T. (2007). *International perspectives on the management of sport.* Burlington, MA: Elsevier Academic Press.

Parks, J. B., & Quarterman, J. (2003). *Contemporary sport management* (2nd ed.). Champaign, IL: Human Kinetics.

Parks, J. B., Quarterman, J., & Thibault, L. (2002). *Contemporary Sport Management* (3rd ed.). Champaign, IL: Human Kinetics.

PGA of America History. (2011). *PGA.com.* Retrieved from www.pga.com.

Pickert, K. (2009, January 22). A brief history of the X-Games. *Time Magazine,* Retrieved from www.time.com.

Pitts, G. G., & Stotlar, D. K. (2002). *Fundamentals of sport marketing* (2nd.). Morgantown, WV: Fitness Information Technology

Prinsloo, L. (2010). SA's hosting of FIFA World Cup brought economic benefits. *Engineering New Online.* Retrieved July 30, 2010, from www.engineeringnews.co.za.

Robertson, R. (1992). *Globalization: Social theory and global culture.* New York: Russell Sage.

Roche, M. (2000). *Mega-events and Modernity: Olympics and Expos in the Growth of Global Culture.* London: Routledge.

Sandiford, K. A. P. (1983). Cricket and the Victorian society. *Journal of Social History 17,* 303–317.

Seymour, H. (1960). *Baseball: The early years.* New York, NY: Oxford University.

Shank, M. D. (2005). *Sport marketing: A Strategic perspective* (4th ed.). NJ: Pearson Education, Inc.

Smith, A & Fox, T. (2007). From 'event-led' to 'event-themed' regeneration: the 2002 commonwealth Games Legacy Programme. *Urban Studies,* 44, 5, 1125-1143.

Thibault, L. (2009). Globalization of sport: An inconvenient truth. *Journal of Sport Management, 23,* 1-20.

Torres, C.R. (2006). Results or participation: Reconsidering Olympism's approach to competition. *Quest, 58,* 242-254.

Valera, S. & Guardia, J. (2002). Urban social identity and sustainability: Barcelona's Olympic Village. *Environment and Behavior*, 34, 54-66.

Van der Westhuizen, J. (2007). Glitz, glamour and the Gautrain: Mega-projects as political symbols. *Politkon: South African Journal of Political Studies*, 34, 335-352.

Waitt, G. (2003). The social impacts of the Sydney Olympic. *Annals of Tourism Research*, 30, 194-215.

Wilcox, R. C. (1995). The American sporting enterprise in contemporary Europe: Capitalist imperialism or cultural homogenization? *Proceedings of the Third European Congress on Sport Management*, Budapest, Hungary.

Zeiler, T. (2006). *Ambassadors in pinstripes: The Spalding world baseball tour and the birth of the American Empire*. Lanham, MD: The Rowman & Littlefield Publishing Group.

Zeiler, T. (2006). A night at Delmonico's: The Spalding baseball tour and the imagination of empire. *International Journal of the History of Sport, 23*, 28-45.

# CHAPTER 7

# SPORT AND THE MEDIA

## E. Nicole Melton

***

Learning Objectives

After reading this chapter, you should be able to:

1. Define sports media and articulate its basic functions.
2. Explain the various ways media has influenced sport, and how sports impacts media operations.
3. Discuss the different ideologies and themes communicated in sports media.
4. Identify new and emerging trends in sports media.

## INTRODUCTION

By many accounts, the sports media devotes little attention to women's sport or female athletes when compared to the coverage of men's sport or male athletes. Those who have the power to decide who and what is covered generally contend the disproportional coverage is due to the public's lack of interest in women's sport. However, this assumption may not be the reality. For instance, the US women's soccer team captivated American audiences during their quest for the 2010 World Cup in Germany. The televised coverage of the games garnered the largest TV ratings in Women's World Cup history, and fans wrote over 7,000 tweets per second during the final match between the US and Japan. This interest primarily stemmed from the overall success of the US women's team and a few late-game heroics from key players.

Indeed, fans witnessed many exciting moments during the tournament; however, the epic quarterfinal comeback against Brazil, in which Abby Wambach scored a header goal in the 120th minute of stoppage time, was perhaps the most memorable. This goal allowed the team to prevail in penalty kicks and advance to the semifinals. In the semifinal match, Wambach was again the hero when, in the 79th minute of regulation, she scored another dramatic header to give the US a 2-1 lead over France —

propelling the team into the championship game. Similar to previous matches, the championship game was a highly competitive, suspense-filled contest, with the US losing in penalty kicks. Despite being one win short of capturing the 2010 World Cup, American's enthusiasm for women's soccer was at an all-time high following the tournament.

Given the team's success, all of the players received warm receptions when they returned to the states; however, some players received more media attention than others. For instance, Hope Solo's popularity increased considerably after the championship. In fact, despite having a relatively unexceptional World Cup performance, the keeper was offered numerous endorsement deals, appeared on several talk shows, was a contestant on ABC's "Dancing with the Stars," and appeared on the cover of ESPN's "The Body" issue. Meanwhile, Abby Wambach, who was the standout and team leader during the tournament, received relatively little media attention compared to Solo.

Brandt James, a writer for ESPN.com and ESPNW.com, attempted to explain why the women received dissimilar media attention and endorsement opportunities. James argues the women's personalities and career choices were the reasons for the difference: Solo has an infectious personality, exudes confidence, is attractive, and makes a concerted effort to put herself in the public eye; on the other hand, Wambach shares many of the same characteristics, but has no desire to market herself, instead only wishing to increase the popularity of soccer in the US. James concludes that the difference between the women represents "not only a contrast in personalities, but a study in how female athletes become stars, personalities and well-paid endorsers, and the choices that impact that aspect of their careers." Thus, Solo's go-getter attitude, compared to Wambach's laid-back approach to life, is why she received a number of lucrative endorsements and significant media coverage after the World Cup.

Although James' points may be valid, some who read the article were quick to challenge his conclusion and suggested other factors contributed to why these women ventured down different career paths. For example, one comment read, "the real issue here is that Wambach is an out lesbian who, in all likelihood, wasn't offered the same type of endorsement deals that were offered to Solo… It's a shame since Wambach is clearly a stellar athlete and role model." Other readers criticized ESPNW for not taking this opportunity to discuss how women are portrayed in the sports media. A popular writer for womentalksports.com—a sports blog with the mission of promoting and empowering female athleticism—posted a response to Brandt's article. In her blog, she echoes the sentiments made by other readers and discusses how, contrary to Brandt's assessment, the women share many qualities and characteristics—both are intense competitors, pump up their team during games, serve as role models in the community, and have very positive off-field personalities. She contends that Brandt failed to critically examine how the sports media portrays female athletes, and he neglected to mention that the sports media affords little space to "a strong, successful female athlete [who] is not heterosexual (or who does not pass as heterosexual)." In her opinion, Solo and Wambach had very similar personalities and on-field demeanors; however, one was a lesbian and one was not—thus forcing the women to follow divergent paths.

The dialogues presented here are significant to the current chapter for several reasons. First, the enthusiasm surrounding the Women's World Cup contradicts the taken-for-granted assumption that people are simply not interested in women's sport. Unfortunately, many executives, producers, and journalists in sports media still abide by this belief and continue to neglect women's sport—thus perpetuating the notion that women's sport is uninteresting or not important in the sports world. Second, the comments made in response to the ESPNW article highlight how women who present themselves in an ultra-feminine and heterosexual manner (termed heterosexy; Griffin, 1998), oftentimes receive considerably more attention from the sports media than equally-skilled athletes who fail to convey such an image (e.g., Abby Wambach). Later in the chapter, we will discuss why the sports media values heterosexy images, and how this impacts female athletes, spectators of women's sport, and society as a whole.

Finally, the counter narratives offered by individuals who read Brandt's article point to the new way in which sports media can empower fans. Specifically, the Internet affords those working outside sports media the power to shape public perceptions relating to issues in sport. Before the Internet, there were few (if any) opportunities to challenge what the sports media presented; however, today's fan can easily comment directly below an article on ESPN.com, develop her or his own sports blog, or use new media (e.g., social media) to post opinions on Twitter or Facebook.

As the previous example illustrates, the messages and images the sports media produces can exert considerable influence in sport society; however, some may wonder how the sports media became such a powerful force. To answer this question, consider both the media and the sport industry (a) experienced enormous growth over the past few decades and (b) successfully use the other to achieve their respective goals. Media conglomerates reap financial rewards by capitalizing on the popularity and global appeal of sport, and the sport industry uses various forms of media to access immense segments of American and international culture. Recent sport events illustrate this mutually beneficial relationship. For instance, for the third consecutive year, the Super Bowl set the record for most-watched television show in US history, with an estimated 111.3 million viewers in 2012, 700 million people worldwide watched the World Cup Final in 2010, and the 2012 London Olympic Games will be the most-watched television event in world history (Roxborough & Jones, 2010).

Given the impact the media can have on society, researchers have devoted considerable attention to exploring the ways in which sports media enacts and depicts social stratification and inequity. Some contend sport (and media promoting it) contributes to and even intensifies divisions (based on race, ethnicity, gender, and so on), while others believe sport can enable social changes that alleviate inequities within society. The purpose of this chapter is to explore these and other, related issues. Specifically, I illustrate how sport and the media can influence society by outlining the basic elements of what sports media is and what it does. In addition, I examine the relationship between sport and the media, and ways in which sports media entities construct social realities. By doing so, it will become evident how these realities affect the lives and behaviors of the athletes and fans involved. Finally, I will touch on recent trends in the sports media.

## SPORTS MEDIA: THE BASICS

The mass media is composed of organizations with professional communicators who can, almost instantly and simultaneously, disperse messages to large audiences over large geographic areas. What makes the mass media so powerful and influential is its ability to transcend time and space limitations that are inherent in interpersonal and group social settings. In essence, the mass media is able to efficiently and effectively relay a specific message or image to a large group of people in a limited amount of time. When the mass media manifests in a sport context, it can be known as *sports media* (Jarvie, 2006).

The sports media generally produces a mediated account of the following: live sporting events; media promotion of the events; print, electronic, and digital news coverage of these events; print, electronic, and digital commentary concerning the participants, coaches, leagues, and governing bodies; the media promotion of athletes, team, and leagues; fan-to-fan discussions; digital simulations of games and leagues (fantasy leagues and video games); and fictional accounts of all of the above, which are depicted in motion pictures, television sitcoms, and made for TV movies (Coakley, 2009). These various sports media productions provide multiple avenues for sports media entities to achieve their primary objective of generating financial profits. In the process of reaching this goal, sports media performs the following three functions: convey information, provide entertainment, and promote cultural values.

The general information communicated refers to the statistical and factual accounts of the sport event. For instance, sports media lets the public know what sporting events will be taking place, where they will be, the specific time, and who will be competing. Also, the media relays final results, scores, and individual statistics. Simply providing the facts of an event in a mundane report will not capture the interest of sport consumers. Consequently, sports media has evolved into an entertainment industry, preventing boredom by captivating audiences with dramatic narratives, emotional storytelling, and action highlights (Coakley, 2009).

In order to transform a sport event into a memorable production, producers must first decide which events to broadcast, and then chose appealing narratives and images to complement the event. Doing so ensures the event will entertain consumers and satisfy corporate sponsors. This selection process gives sports media the ability to dictate what ideological themes and messages audiences will experience. Most viewers believe media's depiction of sport and physical activity is a true representation of sport. People embrace the narratives they hear and images they see as reality. In so doing, the realities that emerge in sports media become instrumental sources for learning and reinforcing cultural beliefs within a society. The sports media provides fans with significant insights into issues of race, ethnicity, gender, class, sexual orientation, physical and mental ability, and more. Later in the chapter, I discuss the issues in greater depth, and explain how the sports media implicitly and explicitly promotes various ideologies that inundate our culture. For now, we turn the discussion to the unique relationship between sport and the media.

ɔort and media (sports media) have developed an array of ɪ ⸺ ⸺ ᴜⱥat are particularly alluring to audiences. People are drawn to sports media's ideal combination of entertainment, excitement, and remarkable audio and visual appeal. Media, with its ability to reach large audiences all over the world in a limited amount of time, has had a tremendous impact on the sports industry, and the popularity of sport worldwide has greatly influenced how the media operates (Eitzen & Sage, 2003; Coakley, 2009). In the space below, we address the effects of the relationship between sport and the media.

## Media's Impact on Sport and Sport Consumers

In many respects, the media allows people from various backgrounds, from all over the world, to enjoy sport. On any day a fan can watch a variety of sporting events on a host of television channels, access an event on the Internet, stream live coverage on a mobile device, interact with fans on a sports blog, or view the reactions others have during a game via Twitter update. Sport at all levels—from little league baseball to profession football—can benefit by using media. Media allows sport organizations to disseminate important information, connect with loyal fans, and reach new consumers. And, while the benefits of using media can be immense, relying on the media can also create negative outcomes for sport and sport consumers. Thus, in the next section we address how the media impacts sport.

*Financial Rewards*

Financially speaking, the benefit of sport using the media is relatively overt. For instance, the NFL receives nearly $3.1 billion in television rights fees a year (Coakley, 2009). In addition, Businessinsider.com reported that during the 2009 MLB season, more than 400,000 signed up for live game products, including MLB.TV ($80-110/year) or Gameday Audio ($15/year). The MLB also gained a net profit of over $1.5 million for its "At Bat" iPhone app that same year (Frommer, 2009). The new ways media has been able to bring MLB to fans could contribute to why the 2009 World Series witnessed its largest viewership since 2004.

Sports media, specifically television, recently played a significant role in changing traditional college sports conferences. In 2010, ESPN, the leader in sport coverage, and the University of Texas athletic program, one of

146

the wealthiest athletic programs in the country, joined together to create the Longhorn Network. The lucrative contract allowed the university to launch a 24-hour channel, devoted entirely to covering events at the University of Texas—primarily athletic events. The contract is worth approximately $11 million a year with an annual 3% increase. Once ESPN reaches its initial $295 million investment, the University of Texas will then receive 70% of annual revenues.

The Longhorn Network is yet another example of media's influence on sport. A major consequence of this deal involves the break-up of one of the strongest conferences in the NCAA, the Big 12. Angered by the deal between Texas ESPN, two teams (i.e., the University of Nebraska and the University of Colorado) immediately left the Big 12 in an effort to reap greater media revenues in the PAC 10 conference. A year later, Texas A&M University and the University of Missouri decided to join the Southeastern Conference (SEC), so they too could increase their media revenues. After losing four schools in two year, the Big 12 added Texas Christian University (TCU) and West Virginia for the 2011-2012 season, giving the conference a total of 10 schools.

These changes will result in greater revenues; however, having a singular focus on financial return will significantly impact athletes who participate in non-revenue sports at these universities. Specifically, new travel schedules will undoubtedly increase athletes' time away from campus, which can negatively impact their academic success. Consider the following example, a typical conference schedule for women's college volleyball in the Big 12 involves each team playing a conference foe twice, once at home and once away. The schedule includes one mid-week conference game, typically Wednesday, and one weekend game. West Virginia is over 1,400 miles from new conference opponent Texas Tech. Both schools have volleyball programs. If a West Virginia vs. Texas Tech conference game happens to fall on a Wednesday, how does this affect a student-athlete's academic class schedule?

In addition to disrupting the student-athletes, how do conference realignments impact the sport consumers? As previously mentioned, the sports media frequently emphasize rivalries as a way to increase fan interest in a game. In fact, ESPN devotes two weeks in their football and basketball coverage to "Rivalry Week." The launch of the Longhorn Network ultimately ended the state of Texas's best rivalry—one that started in 1894. Unfortunately, the 2011 Thanksgiving game may be the last game between these two schools. A rivalry ended in one of America's most sports-crazed states because of money.

The BCS bowl game dilemma also sheds light on media's influence on sport. Traditionally non-BCS conference teams have been excluded from BCS bowl games and receive lower BCS rankings. The argument in the past has been that top schools from non-BCS conferences are not competitive with the top schools from the six 'power conferences' that make up the BCS. However, from 2005 to 2009, non-BCS teams that were allowed to play in the major bowls went 3-1 against their BCS competition. The 2010 season marked the first time two non-BCS schools qualified for BCS bowl. Coincidently the two schools played against one another, thus preventing any possibility for a BCS school to lose. This would not be consequential except that tens of millions of dollars are involved, money the six BCS conferences want to keep in order to continue to improve their athletic programs.

Many people frustrated with the BCS have suggested college football go to a play-off series to determine the national champion, rather than use the BCS ranking and bowl system. *Sentinel,* an Orlando based newspaper examined the argument more closely, and discovered that under the current conference revenue-sharing structure, the BCS conferences are able to dictate and reap how financial benefits are distributed among teams. BCS conferences now share revenue generated from the postseason BCS bowls 12 ways; however, under a play-off system, this money could be split among 120 parties. Most BCS conference schools seem to have a problem with this concept (Adelson, 2009). In 2008, another study, done at Brigham Young University, concluded that the BCS conference automatic qualifiers have earned $1.87 billion in bowl money since 1998, due to the tremendous media attention and sponsor revenue. Non-BCS conference members have earned a combined $196.4 million during that span, less than the total $218.85 million BCS automatic qualifiers received in 2008 alone (Pimeniel, 2009). Considering the fact ABC/ESPN has committed to pay BCS conferences over $4.3 billion in exchange for the television rights, and $125 million a year to broadcast all of the BCS bowl games, it is rational to assume ABC/ESPN might be influential in guaranteeing the BCS system stays in place.

*Modifications to Sport*

The media's influence on sport in not solely financial — the power of the media has also caused significant changes to numerous sports over the years. Some of these modifications include (a) games (particularly in college sport) being moved to awkward times of day to satisfy television schedules; (b) giant, expensive video screens installed in arenas and stadiums; (c) alteration of rules, as in the creation of the "TV time-out" for television commercials; (d) free agency for players and consequent moves to the "highest bidder;" (e) pro teams moving to better "markets," as was the case for the Oklahoma City Thunder (previously the Seattle Super Sonics); (f) wild-card games designed to increase playoff participants; (g) the 40-second play clock in the NFL and 24 second shot clock in the NBA; (h) the designated hitter in the American League; (i) over-expansion in the professional leagues; (j) salary caps; (k) recruiting abuses as college teams chasing television riches; (l) the playing of World Series games at night in freezing October weather; (m) electric lights in Wrigley Field; (n) players strikes and lock-outs; (o) stroke play rather than match play in golf; (p) shootouts in soccer and hockey; and (q) penalties assessed for what is deemed excessive celebration (Eitzen & Sage, 2003; Coakley, 2009).

*Sport Made Popular by the Media*

The media can also have a drastic impact on an entire sport, which is the case regarding the US speed skating team. In 2009 the team's primary sponsor (Dutch bank DSB) filed for bankruptcy months before the 2010 Winter Olympic Games. Fortunately, Stephen Colbert, the host of Comedy Central's "The Colbert Report," stepped in and became the main US speed skating sponsor. Colbert not only provided financial support for the team, by persuading his loyal viewers to donate over $300,000, but also created unprecedented publicity for the sport. Repeated features of the players and coaches on "The Colbert Report" largely contributed to the sports increased popularity, and helped make speed skating a high profile sport in the United States. In addition, Colbert posed in the US speed skating suit for the December, 2009, cover of *Sports Illustrated's* "Year in Sports Media" edition (Berkes, 2010).

*Media Created Sports and Events*

Noticing the growing popularity of action sports, ESPN executives believed it would be advantageous to devote significant resources to create an international stage for action sport athletes to compete. A team assembles to develop the concept, and in 1995 the first X Games (then called the Extreme games) took place in Rhode Island (History of the X Games, 2007).

1, the event has gained in popularity but still does not compete
tional commercial sport events. ESPN is driven to increase the
Λ Games visibility and ensure its success because they keep all revenue
generated by sponsors and merchandise. ESPN achieved worldwide exposure in 2007 when 18 overseas ESPN networks showed live coverage
of the first five minutes of ESPN's X Games to 145 countries (Hiestand,
2007). The intent was to give the world a glimpse into the X Games, and
hopefully viewers would want to see more. In addition, there were 14
hours of coverage on ESPN, ESPN2 and ABC, 40 hours of online coverage, and ESPN developed a mobile video channel devoted to the X
Games. Fans were also able to download iTunes podcasts of various X
Games athletes' favorite songs.

ESPN's complete control of the X games has allowed them the flexibility
to change the date of the games, add and drop events, and create the
Winter X Games. ESPN's global exposure of the X Games was a contributing factor in snowboarding becoming an Olympic sport, led to NBC's
Dew Action Sports Tour, and created the sport Skier X. This sport, now
named Skiercross, involves competitors elbowing each other while going
over moguls, and made its debut as an Olympic sport at the 2010 Winter
Games in Vancouver (Skiercross, 2009).

## Sport and Sports Fans influence on Media

Some media reap a substantial financial benefit from their relationship
with sport, particularly newspaper and television.

*Newspaper and Television*

Once relegated to the sports section, news stories involving sport and
sport celebrities are making the front page more frequently, and account
for 25% of the news content (Coakley, 2009). Featuring stories and images of the local team winning is one way for newspapers to sell more copies. It is also common to see special sections in the newspaper that coincide with various sporting events. Generally the NBA Championship or
Olympics will have their own section, as well as the normal sport section
where regional and local sports are covered. The increase in sports coverage is largely due to the substantial amount of advertising revenue
newspapers are able to garner from organizations wanting to attract
sport fans, specifically men.

The lure of advertising dollars has attracted television companies as well. The first Super Bowl, which was televised by both NBC and CBS, had a rate of $42,000 for a 30 second commercial. Similar airtime for the 2010 game cost sponsors $3.1 million (Seidman, 2009). Advertising on ESPN is sold out for months in advance, and major advertisers are continually buying airtime to reach the 15-35 year old male audience. ESPN's ad revenue averages $441.8 million with an ad rate of $9,446 per 30-second spot (ESPN, 2009). The tremendous amount of sponsor support has made it possible for ESPN to have multiple channels, websites, and radio stations.

In the past, media networks primarily used sport to fill low ratings days like Saturday or Sunday. This strategy is still used, but now it is not uncommon to miss your favorite primetime show because a popular sport event, such as a MLB World Series game, went longer than expected. One way for networks to gain exposure for one of their shows or guarantee high ratings is to air it right after the Super Bowl. Fox's animated comedy *The Family Guy* originally premiered after the Super Bowl and continues to be a top rated show for the network (Seidman, 2009).

Most televised commercial sports have been profitable venues for sponsors because they can attract male consumers (e.g., beer companies, auto makers), but the media has realized that other sports can attract other specific target markets. High-end or luxury products, such as Cadillac, have been advertised during golf and tennis events. Women have been targeted during figure skating and gymnastics, and companies wanting to reach young males advertise during the X Games.

Media have always used accomplished former athletes as commentators on sports news programs, but now they are using popular athletes to increase ratings on their regular programming (e.g., athletes starring on "Dancing with the Stars"). In addition, networks have combined sport and physical activity with reality TV in order to achieve maximum ratings. For instance, NBC's "Biggest Loser" premiered in 2004 and is now broadcasted in over 15 countries (The Biggest Loser, 2009). The show follows the workout challenges and successes of persons considered to be overweight as they attempt to lose the highest percentage of weight loss for a cash prize.

*The Coach Potato Culture*

Recent studies show that youth, adults, and the elderly all contribute to America's culture of inactivity. Today people are likely to watch TV or sit in front of the computer instead of exercising (Painter, 2008). Unfortunately, this trend contributes to American's growing health problems caused by obesity. However, fortunately for sports media, sedentary American's will consume traditional sports media at high levels, and are predicted to turn video gaming into a $65 billion industry by 2013 (Mitchell, 2010). One cannot deny the impact sport has on the video game industry when considering the top selling game in 2009 was Wii Fit. Others top revenue generators included: EA Active Sport, UFC (Ultimate Fight Championship) Undisputed, Wii Sports Resort, and Tiger Woods PGA Tour 10 (Best-selling, 2009).

*Reaching Global Markets*

NBA.com reported that the 2009-10 NBA season had 83 international players from 36 countries and territories on official rosters. The media has discovered a new revenue stream by broadcasting NBA games in the home countries of international players. For instance, Yao Ming, originally from Shanghai, China, became a member of NBA's Houston Rockets team in 2002. Due to his immense popularity among Chinese fans, NBA games are now aired on 51 television stations in China. ESPN.com also reported that NBA retail sales in China increased by 50 percent in 2007, and, in conjunction with Adidas, the league opened additional NBA stores in the country during 2008 (Kobe, 2007).

Both the increase of international players in American sports leagues and the general rise of sports popularity have allowed the media to permeate all parts of the world and benefit financially. The media's ubiquitous nature gives it the responsibility of selecting the narratives and images that showcase these various sports worldwide. This pervasive power enables the media to construct, reinforce, and perpetuate various ideologies and perceptions that will inevitably create more sport consumers.

## A MEDIATED REALITY

Symbolic interactionist theory (see Chapter 2) contends realities are constructed during social discourse (LaRosse & Reitzes, 1993); as such, sports presented by the media are symbolic constructions of reality. For instance, symbolic constructions during televised PGA tour events reinforce our ideas about the game of golf, personal values, social life, and the characteristics of the viewing audience. Though everyone may have slightly different interpretations of what they see and hear, the media's presentation will influence our thoughts about sports, society, and relationships (Coakley, 2009).

Drawing from symbolic interactionist theory, it is easy to see how sports media has modified the way sport is played and the meanings associated with sport. To explain, it might be best to think of a fish bowl. Most people watching sport believe they are watching the event through a transparent fish bowl and thus see an objective reality. However, what they are actually seeing is comparable to a 3D aquarium screen saver made by computer programmers. In the real fish bowl, you witness the average happenings of normal fish, but in the computer version, exotic fish are designed to move in pre-programmed patterns for your entertainment. We know that fish are not as exciting as the computer program makes them out to be, but in sport people forget that TV editing, camera angles, commentary and images are used to transform the game into an entertainment show. Sports events become eye-catching products sold in the marketplace, as a way to attract large audiences and secure lucrative endorsement deals.

Consumers are certainly within their power to reject the explicit and implicit messages the sports media displays; however, they rarely do so because sports media entities have carefully constructed an event that appeals to their unique interests, attitudes, and beliefs about sport. Before we examine various themes the sports media promotes during its productions, it is first necessary to discuss who produces these events, what techniques do they use to create these events, and who is the intended audience.

**Procedures**

Large media conglomerates now control the mass media, and the specific sports media industry is dominated by an even smaller number of multinational companies (Jarvie, 2006). Media companies earn most of their profits by selling advertisements and sponsorships to global corporations. In turn, the global corporations are able to use media's expansive reach to generate global brand awareness and disseminate values and ideologies that make them more profitable. Generally the ideologies that saturate the culture of business promote competition, accomplishment, and consumption (Coakley, 2009).

## Presentation Rules

Presentation rules reflect the various ways media showcase sport in an attempt to capture the interests of the audience. Sports producers and commentators transform ordinary sport into captivating entertainment by highlighting action and implementing personalization and story-telling techniques (Jarvie, 2006). Rivalry stories are particularly effective in creating an "us" versus "them" atmosphere in which people can identify with the athletes that symbolize their personal values. Competitions become wars, in which athletes are the soldiers and the games are won and lost on sacred battlegrounds. The heroes and heroines that emerge from these contests immediately receive celebrity status from the media, and fans are eager to learn more about these newly created idols. These dramatic narratives and images generate suspense and excitement before sport events, and ensure large audiences will be attracted.

## Audience Assessments

According to Eitzen and Sage (2003), men are usually drawn to these exciting sports media events. Studies also show that sports consumption gradually increases in relation to education level (Eitzen & Sage, 2003). However, people of all classes, genders, race, and ethnicities enjoy what sports media has to offer. Among those who consume sports, generally professional football and baseball are most popular, followed by college football, college basketball, and professional basketball. Estimates of who makes up the sport consumer market and what those individuals want to see usually dictates what and how sports are shown on television (Eitzen & Sage, 2003).

## IDEOLOGIES AND THEMES

Producing an entertaining sports media production that balances corporate interests and audience demands can be a difficult task, especially when you take into account most sport consumers want maximum action in a minimum amount of time. These constraints lend media to explicitly and implicitly convey certain ideological messages in their coverage. These ideologies and themes usually concern competition, achievement, instant gratification, gender, and race.

## Winning is Everything

Media's depiction of sport encourages people to believe that winning is everything. Americans admire winners who demonstrate competitiveness, determination, and can make the big plays under pressure. There are no Mr. or Ms. Congenialities on the playing field, only MVPs and tournament champions. Fans will even excuse violent behavior if they believe those actions are needed to win games. Winning championships has become so important that fans will view an athlete's career as incomplete if she or he does not have a national title on their resume. For instance, Dan Marino, retired quarterback for the Miami Dolphins, holds many NFL passing records, led his team to the Super Bowl, and had eight playoff wins. Yet many fans consider Marino's illustrious career incomplete because he never won a Super Bowl. To ensure their careers do not turn out like Marino's, many professional athletes now switch teams late in their career in hopes of capturing a championship before they retire, further solidifying the idea that championships are all that matter. The trend is also persistent at the college level. Many fans of top tier football programs consider the season a failure if they are not in the conference and national championship game (even when the team wins 10 games).

The media usually neglects sports and athletes who do not adopt a "win at all costs" attitude. Unlike commercial sport events, the Gay Games considers doing one's best the true determinate of success. All people are encouraged to participate, irrespective of sexual identity, age, or physical ability. Rather than focusing on athletic excellence, the Gay Games focus on bringing athletes and artists together from around the world in an effort to enhance the lives of GLBT people (Cunningham & Melton, 2011). Although this alternative approach to participation is a healthier perspective toward sport participation, because it does not mesh with the dominant ideals and norms of sport, the sports media oftentimes ignores the Gay Games.

Much like the previous example, the Paralympics were originally formed to give veterans with disabilities the opportunity to participate in sport. The Games evolved into a multi-sport event for athletes with visual and physical disabilities, and are now held every four years following the Olympics (Beijing, 2009). The Paralympics remained focused on athletic enjoyment rather than excellence until the International Paralympics Committee sought to gain media attention through corporate sponsors. Consequently, the Games were moved directly after the Olympics in

1996 to gain media attention, and began focusing on medal counts and athletes' athletic achievements. By mirroring Olympic themes of competition and success, the 2008 Beijing Games were the most watched in Paralympics history (Beijing, 2009), and similar consumption took place for the 2010 Winter Paralympics (Dowd, 2009).

## Consumption

Sport consumption and immediate gratification are dominant themes in commercial sports today. Global corporations allocate large amounts of their advertising budget to sports. Consequently, fans watch teams play in University of Phoenix Stadium during the Tostitos Fiesta Bowl, and are encouraged to stay tuned for the Dr. Pepper halftime report. It is estimated that 20% of televised sport is devoted to advertising, and an organization will spend anywhere from 75,000 to 100,000 for one full-page ad in *Sports Illustrated* (Coakley, 2009). Sponsors want their products prominently displayed in front of the consumer to gently remind them what they offer.

Social media outlets, like Twitter, are now used to give fans up to the minute news updates, and provide another opportunity to exhibit sponsors' names. The media has led fans to believe they must know what is going on with their favorite sport, team, or player every minute of the day. It has become such a part of culture that if fans are not constantly updated, they will seek out other sports media outlets to give them the information they want.

This desire for constant information has been the driving force behind mobile applications becoming so popular. College and professional teams can now ensure their fans know when events are held, how to buy tickets, and where they can purchase their official logo gear to wear to the game no matter where they are.

## Gender Issues

### Men's Sport and Male Athletes

Hegemonic Masculinity refers to various gendered practices that strengthen the dominant social position of men and the subordination of women within a society (Connell, 2005). Many sport sociologies contend the sport industry continues to produce and reproduce narratives and images of what it means to be a man. Sports media provides men the perfect opportunity to emphasize masculine ideals by provided viewing enjoyment for male spectators (Davis & Duncan, 2006).

Traditionally, scholars have pointed to American football, ice hockey, and boxing as prime examples of how real men are physical, hard-hitting, aggressive, winners who are able to attract beautiful women (Eitzen & Sage, 2003). However, emerging media, such as the Internet, digital television, and mobile devices, are offering new sites for hegemonic masculinity to prosper. In particular, Fantasy Leagues perpetuate hegemonic ideologies of authority, sports knowledge, competition, male bonding, and traditional gender roles by allowing online users to act as owners, managers, and coaches of professional leagues (Davis & Duncan, 2006). It is interesting to note that fantasy sports enthusiasts are predominately White, male college graduates who earn more than $50,000 a year in income (Davis & Duncan, 2006).

*Women's Sport and Female Athletes*

In terms of media coverage, a number of scholarly investigations examine the differential treatment women's sport receives when compared to men's sport. For instance, male sport participants and men's events are given disproportionally more attention than female athletes and women's athletic competitions. The media portrays men's sport as an exciting, fast-paced event played by men with superior athleticism—themes that rarely appear when women's sport is shown. Rather, when women are in the media, they are often depicted in sexualized ways or shown in supportive roles, such as the girlfriend or wife of a male athlete. These representations reinforce the notion that sport is a male domain and women are only permitted to enter if they conform to traditional gender roles.

Generally, only attractive (tan, unblemished skin, slender, toned, and long blonde hair) female athletes will be used in the media and attract corporate sponsorships (Duncan, 1990). When they are not available, print media will use models instead. These images perpetuate the idea that women must be beautiful and successful in order to receive media attention. This imagery downplays the achievements made by serious female athletes and reinforces the erroneous belief that women's sport is noncompetitive and should be relegated to sex-appropriate sport (e.g., gymnastics, tennis, and figure skating).

According to Kane and Maxwell (2011), the sports media and sports marketers generally depict female athletes in one of six ways:

- **Athletic Competence:** sportswoman portrayed in uniform, on court, in action.
- **Ambivalence**: some indication of athleticism is present, but the primary image features a non-athletic, off the court, feminine portrayal.
- **All-American "Girl Next Door":** "wholesome" representation with minimal or no indication of athleticism.
- **Hyper-Heterosexual:** image of well-known female athlete explicitly linked to traditional heterosexual role such as girlfriend, wife, or mother.
- **Sexy Babe**: image of "hot" female athlete, falling just short of soft pornography.
- **Soft Pornography:** representation that reinforces sexual objectification such as Olympic sportswomen appearing semi-nude in men's magazines.

Oftentimes, sport organizations contend they must present female athletes in a sexualized or hyper-heterosexual way in order to attract male fans to women's sport. However, results from Kane and Maxwell's study reveal "sex sells" approaches created a backlash effect among both male and female sport consumers—whereas images emphasizing athletic competence were the most effective in garnering interest in women's sport. Thus, in order to increase interest in women's sport, sports media needs to implement strategies that are similar to how they promote men's sport—focus on skill, athleticism, and competition.

### Sexual Orientation

Except for the rare 'coming-out' story of a professional athlete, one's sexual orientation is only mentioned in regards to heterosexual relationships. Wives or girlfriends are usually shown supporting their athletic men on and off the field. PGA Tour commentators frequently mention the wives and families who travel with players on tour. During the 1999 US Open, on almost every golf hole, the commentator found it necessary to remind spectators that Phil Michelson's wife was expecting their first child.

In women's sports, where a lesbian stigma persists (Sartore & Cunningham, 2009), it is sometimes overtly obvious that the media tries to reinforce the norm of heterosexuality. During the 2008 College Softball World Series Championship, color commentator (and US Team member) Jenny Finch announced the entire game with her children by her side. Each camera shot made sure to capture the little ones for the audience to see. As another illustrative example, consider the commentary during the 2011 Women's World Cup in Germany. Every time US defender Christie Rampone touched the ball, the announcers reminded the audience that she was formally Christie Pearce and was now the mother of two children. Perhaps they felt the need to repeat this fact over and over again because Rampone was actually the only mother on the 2011 team (Wahl, 2011). Though no derogatory remarks were made in regards to lesbianism, it was evident that being married to man and having children was the valued norm—there was no mention of Abby Wambach's (a notable lesbian player on the team) partner or family.

Fortunately, the advent of various forms of social media has given female athletes a way to avert mass media outlets, and gives them the opportunity to present themselves to public in a manner they deem appropriate. Now female athletes can post their own YouTube videos, comment on Facebook or twitter, or create their own blog without having to answer to gatekeepers in the mass media. Given the infancy of social media, it will be interesting to see if and how this type of communication can help reduce the lesbian stigma in sport.

**Race**

Over the past few decades more and more Black athletes have been able to participate in commercialized sport, leaving many to believe that racial barriers have collapsed, and the sport industry sees no color. By emphasizing teamwork and camaraderie, sport causes racial tensions to disappear as White and Black athletes work together to succeed. However, this belief is beginning to fade as commentators continue to use racial stereotypes during their broadcasts.

White athletes have been described as intellectual, whereas Black athletes have natural instincts. Commentators would remark how Black athletes were blessed with "god-given" ability, contrasting White athletes who depended on their tenacious work ethic to succeed. Research now suggests these types of comments have subsided, and people and the media are more sensitive to racial stereotypes (Coakley, 2009; Eitzen & Sage, 2003; Leonard, 2007). Then again, Jerry Jones' statement that the new Dallas Cowboys Stadium appeals to Hispanic fans because it offers frozen margaritas leaves one wondering if things are actually getting better.

What appears to be a new trend in sports media is the casting of White athletes as upstanding young adults with impeccable moral character, and Black athletes as thuggish, sexually deviant, selfish, arrogant, and prone to violence (Eitzen & Sage, 2003). The media's coverage of the scandal involving Duke Lacrosse players in 2007 and the 2009 Heisman winner seem to illustrate these stereotypes. The first example refers to when members of the Duke lacrosse team (all White men) were accused of dragging a Black women into their bathroom during a party, at which time she reported being punched, kicked, and strangled, and then violently sexually assaulted. The media, online commentaries, and bloggers chose to respond to this story by portraying the accused males as model athletes who represented everything good about college athletics. They were merely the innocent victims of reverse discrimination and could not have done these horrible acts (Leonard, 2007).

On the other hand, the coverage of 2009 Heisman winner Mark Ingram paints a different picture. That year the SEC Championship game between No. 1 Florida and No. 2 Alabama would determine who played in the BCS Championship game. The games also featured two Heisman hopefuls (Tim Tebow for Florida and Ingram for Alabama). Midway through the second half it was evident that Ingram's stellar play was making him the front-runner for the Heisman. As one announcer remarked on his stellar performance, another announcer interjected and said it was a shame Ingram's father could not see his son because he was currently incarcerated. It was interesting that during one of Ingram's finest athletic moments, the commentator felt it necessary to bring up his father's personal life. Some may excuse this comment because it was on live TV, and it could have been an isolated incident. However, the Sunday after Ingram was awarded the Heisman, one *Dallas Morning News* reporter (Kate Hairopoulos) wrote two stories about Ingram, and devoted five paragraphs to discussing the details of his father's incarceration. In the article titled "Father is on Ingram's mind as he collects Heisman," she made a point to describe Colt McCoy (also a Heisman nominee) as a small town kid from Texas, whereas Mark Ingram grew up in Flint, Michigan (the city that gained a reputation for its high crime rate during the 1990s). These two examples question the perceived colorblindness of competitive sports, and force people to realize what messages the media is truly conveying.

# CURRENT TRENDS

In 2009 the demand for social media grew exponentially. According to Nielsen Online, Twitter grew 1,382% in February alone, registering a total of more than 7 million unique visitors in the US during the month. Meanwhile, Facebook continued to be the most popular social networking site as of 2010. This rapid increase probably means that social media will become more popular, more mobile, and more expansive. Certain trends in social media include: (a) Real-Time collaboration (where people are able to communicate with multiple people while using multiple forms of social media), (b) Real-Time search (the ability to locate people near you by using your cell phone), (c) digital niche marketing, (d) need for social media filters, and (e) the need for social media policies. Below are some examples of how social media is already impacting the sports industry.

## YouTube and Twitter Working Together

The 2009 rivalry football game between Florida and Georgia was relatively uneventful. Most fans changed the channel when Florida went up by three touchdowns, but a student at the University of Connecticut continued to watch. The spectator became enraged when CBS announcers failed to mention a Florida defender's attempt to eye-gouge a Georgia running back at the end of a play. The student reacted by recording the incident and sending it via Twitter to various sports reporters. One reporter for SI.com re-tweeted the message and video to over 6,000 of his followers, who in turn re-tweeted it to their tweeter followers. Within three hours, the video had received more than 1,000 views and was featured on Twitter's "Currently Popular Twitvids." The video, and 30 others like it, was then posted on YouTube, eventually garnering over 25,000 views. The attention generated by these two forms of social media helped bring national attention to a disturbing act that had gone undetected by the network sportscasters. Two weeks later the Florida defender was suspended (Van Grove, 2009).

Fans have become empowered like never before because of the popularity of social media outlets like Twitter, Facebook and YouTube. Millions of fans everywhere can now use their laptops and iPhones to expose player misconduct, officiating mistakes, and controversial comments that have gone unreported by traditional media in the past. Schools and conferences have widely embraced social media outlets, using them to promote events and achievements. College coaches have become Twitter regulars so they can update top recruits on what is happening with the team. Conferences use the site to highlight its teams' latest rankings and accolades. However, the greater involvement of fans can also create public relations nightmares and weakly controversies. Fans' ability to post and review clips on YouTube, then disperse and debate them on blogs and on Twitter, has helped turn such controversies into national stories over night. Social media has become the bigger and better version of instant replay. Schools and conferences can no longer believe something will not be noticed or they can handle an issue internally. Social media has made fan opinion so influential that entities must take their concerns into consideration. It will also be important for professional sports and teams to develop policies concerning how social media should be used by their athletes.

## Athlete's Using Social Media

Shaquille O'Neil is probably the best example of an athlete using social media to his advantage. He had been able to increase his fan base, enhance his brand name, and get people to generally like him by using Twitter as a way to connect to people everywhere. One reason for his instance Twitter fame comes from his "Random Acts of Shaqness," in which he plays a form of digital tag. For example, on O'Neil's Twitter page he tweeted, "random act of shaqness. 480 west under sign 17b Brooklyn heights nxt right pair of autograph lebron shoes, and bobble head I saw it myself." Upon reading this tweet, the first person who follows Shaq on Twitter, and is able to get to exit 17b, will be given the shoes and bobble head doll. Another time, O'Neil was with his teammate Lebron James at Barns & Nobles the same week the two appeared on *Sports Illustrated*. They both signed five copies of the magazine, and O'Neil tweeted that they would be available on first come first serve bases. The magazines were gone within five minutes, and the story was on the news in 30 minutes.

## The YouTube Effect

On Thursday, September 3, 2009, #14 Oregon played #12 Boise State in Boise, Idaho. After the game dejected Oregon tailback, LeGarrette Blount, was walking off the field with his head down. Boise State player, Byron Hout then grabbed Blount, and shouted something. Whatever Hout said caused Boise State coach, Chris Petersen to run over to Hout, restrain him and then yell at him. Suffice it to say, if Hout had merely said "good game," Peterson would not have reacted the way he did. As the Boise State coach moved to separate Hout from Blount, the Oregon senior threw a right cross that connected with Hout's right jaw. Hout went down and popped right back up. ESPN cameras and commentators following the entire incident even followed LeGarrette Blount all the way into the locker room. During the reply, one announcer reiterated how unconscionable and reprehensible the punch was. They painted the picture that the innocent Hout was simply standing on the field and got sucker punched by the Oregon player. The live broadcast showed that as Blount was walking off the field, one Boise State fan threw a chair at him and another punched him. However, if you were listing to the ESPN commentators they continued to emphasize how "out of control" Blount was, and how immediate sanctions should be enforced. To their credit, they did finally mention that there may have been a little taunting by Hout, but the punch was still inexcusable.

Various YouTube videos of the event, which combined for over half a million views, only highlighted the punch by itself, and then viewers were shown Blount being dragged off the field by Oregon players and staff. The videos rarely included the taunting done by Hout, and never showed the Boise State fans who hurled a chair or punched Blount. A few days after the incident, Blount was suspended for the rest of the season (though he was later allowed to return for the last few games of the season), whereas Hout received no punishment from the NCAA or his conference. One possible explanation why Hout escaped being reprimanded could be because YouTube videos, and the media in general, depicted him as the innocent victim, who had done nothing but win a football game.

## CHAPTER SUMMARY

Meanings, messages, and representations are brought to people during the process of producing sports media. The producers in these large media conglomerates are the ones selecting what images and narratives will be attached to sports and athletes. Informed by profit maximizing principles, this selection process encourages themes of success and individual achievement rather than ensuring equality. Consequently, the media oftentimes neglects various classes, racial minorities, and sexual minorities so more attention can be focused on the prime target market of White, Protestant, able-bodied, heterosexual males (Fink, Pastore, and Reimer, 2001). As social media becomes the technology of choice, it will be important to understand its implications. Primarily, the Internet, digital television, and mobile phones are not readily available to everyone.

Only those with the physical and financial means to acquire these emerging forms of media will enjoy the benefits. Also, while new forms of media enable people to communicate digitally all over the world from the privacy of their home, face-to-face interactions and physical activity are sacrificed. It is important that people become aware of media's power and understand how their lives and society are impacted.

## DISCUSSION QUESTIONS

1. How will the dependence of social media affect those in lower socio-economic classes?
2. As people become more cognizant of the ideologies that permeate through sports media, will coverage of sports continue to focus on sports performance, or will there by a rise in more critical coverage of the sporting world?
3. What ways can fans and athletes use new forms of media to create social change in sport?

## RECOMMENDED READINGS

Hundley, H. L., & Billings, A. C. (Eds.). (2009). *Examining identity in sports media*. Thousand Oaks, CA: Sage Publishing. (Explores a variety of issues related to identity, including gender, race, sexual orientation, and ability, as well as the effects related to the intersection of these various identities.)

Rowe, D. (2004). *Sport, culture, and the media: The unruly trinity*. Philadelphia, PA: Open University Press. (Examines how the sport media has firmly situated itself into everyday life. In doing so, Rowe outlines the rise of the sport media and explores how various media forms influence the way sport is performed and experienced in society.)

Sage, G. H. (2011). *Globalizing sport: How organizations, corporations, media, and politics are changing sport*. Boulder, CO: Paradigm Publishers. (This book provides a comprehensive, critical analysis of the globalization of sport. In particular, the author discusses how global corporations and the media influence these processes and shape the business and experience of sport.)

## REFERENCES

Adelson, A. (2009, June 17). Hatch steps up criticism of BCS calling it exclusionary and unfair. Retrieved from http://blogs.orlandosentinel.com.

Beijing 2008 Olympic Games: Mount Olympus Meets the Middle Kingdom. (2009). In *Encyclopedia Britannica*. Retrieved December 15, 2009, from Encyclopedia Britannica Online: www.britannica.com.

Berkes, H. (2010, January 19). U.S. *speedskating finds savior in Stephen Colbert*. Npr.org. Retrived January 25, 2010, from www.npr.org.

Coakley, J. (2009). *Sports in society: Issues and controversies*. New York: McGraw-Hill.

Connell, R.W. (2005). *Masculinities* (2nd ed). Berkeley, CA: University of California.

Cunningham, G. B., & Melton, E. N. (forthcoming, 2011). Gay Games. In L. E. Swayne & J. G. Golson (Eds.), *Encyclopedia of sports management and marketing*. Thousand Oaks, CA: Sage.

Davis, N. W., & Duncan, M. C. (2006). Sports knowledge is power: Reinforcing masculine privilege through fantasy sport league participation. *Journal of Sport & Social Issues, 30*, 244-264.

Dowd, A. (2009, March 16). Olympics-Paralympics sponsorship hopes dimmed by economy. [Web log message]. Retrieved from http://www.reuters.com.

Duncan, M. D. (1990). Sports photographs and sexual difference: Images of women and men in the 1984 and 1988 Olympic Games. *Sociology of Sport Journal* , 7, 22-43.

Eitzen, D. S., & Sage, G. H. (2003). *Sociology of North American Sport* (7th edition ed.). Boston, MA: McGraw-Hill.

ESPN, Inc. (2009). In *Encyclopedia Britannica*. Retrieved December 15, 2009, from www.britannica.com.

Fink, J. S., Pastore, D. L., & Riemer, H. A. (2001). Do differences make a difference? Managing diversity in Division IA intercollegiate athletics. *Journal of Sport Management, 15*, 10-50.

Frommer, D. (2009, July 29). More live baseball video on MLB's iphone app. Retrieved from www.businessinsider.com.

Griffin, T. (2009, July 28). Beebe hopes to expand big12 tv. Retrieved from www.espn.go.com.

Hiestand, M. (2007, July 31). X games stills tries to hip, gain new viewers. [Web log message]. Retrived from www.usatoday.com.

Jarvie, Grant. 2006 *Sport, culture and society. An introduction*, London: Routledge.

Kane, M. J., & Maxwell, H. D. (2011). Expanding the boundaries of sport media research: Using critical theory to explore consumer responses to representations of women's sports. *Journal of Sport Management, 25*, 202-216.

Kobe has top selling jersey in china. (2007). Retrieved from www.nba.com.

Krangle, Eric. (2009, August 9). CBS scores 75% spike in March madness streams. Retrieved from www.businessinsider.com.

LaRossa, R. and Reitzes, D.C. (1993) Symbolic interactionism and family studies. In P. G. Boss, W. J. Doherty, R. LaRossa, W. R. Schumm, & S. K. Steinmetz (Eds.), *Sourcebook of family theories and methods: A contextual approach* (pp. 135-163). New York: Plenum Press.

Leonard, D.J. (2007). Innocent until proven innocent: In defense of duke lacrosse and white power (and against menacing black student-athletes, a black stripper, activists, and the Jewish media. *Journal of Sport & Social Issues, 31,* 25-44.

Mitchell, R. (2010, February 19). Report: Games industry to $65 billion by 2013. Joystiq.com. Retrieved February, 25, 2010 from www.joystiq.com.

Painter, A. (2008, June 15). Your health. [Web log message]. Retrieved from www.usatoday.com.

Pimentel, R. (2009, July 10). The BCS on trial: Understanding the implications. Retrieved from http://howtowatchsports.com.

Roxborough, S., & Jones, B. (2010). World Cup finale draws 700 million viewers. Retrieved from www.reuters.com.

Sartore, M.L., & Cunningham, G.B. (2009). The lesbian stigma in the sport context: Implications for women of every sexual orientation. *Quest, 61,* 289-305.

Skiercross named official sport in 2010 winter Olympics. (2009). Retrieved December 15, 2009, from www.active.com.

Seidman, R. (2009, January 26). The Nielsen company's guide to Superbowl XLIII Retrieved from www.tvbythenumbers.com.

Southwest Conference. (2009, December 10). In *Wikipedia, the free encyclopedia.* Retrieved October 10, 2009, from http://en.wikipedia.org.

The history of the X Games. (2007). Retrieved from www.skateboard.com.

The biggest loser. (2009, December 15). In *Wikipedia, the free encyclopedia.* Retrieved from http://en.wikipedia.org.

Top-sellers. (2009). Retrieved from www.newsweek.com.

Wahl, G. (2011, July). Rampone adds a special story to US women's World Cup Quest. Retrieved from www.si.com.

Van Grove, J. (2009, November 2) Brandon Spikes eye gouging: Bad behavior caught on video. Retrieved from http://mashable.com.

# CHAPTER 8

# SPORT, PHYSICAL ACTIVITY, AND
# THE ENVIRONMENT

## Brian P. McCullough

*** 

## Learning Objectives

After reading this chapter, you should be able to:

1.  Define environmental sociology and explain the tenets differentiating it from sociology.
2.  Identify the relationship between environmental movements and sport.
3.  Discuss the various threats sport poses to the environment.
4.  Explain the evolution of environmental initiatives in sport.
5.  Provide examples of measures sport organizations are taking to reduce their environmental impact.


## INTRODUCTION

> There, Mother Nature designed the links – grasses on sandy stretches were fertilized by the droppings of breeding seabirds and cut short by grazing rabbits. Bunkers were allegedly formed by sheep and other animals burrowing into the turf. The result: wide open playing areas with random clumps of razed grass, the perfect terrain for thumping a small, hard ball across the countryside. (Keast, 2001, p 37)

Golf is perhaps one of the most exclusive and expansive individual sports across the globe. With the popularity and success of Tiger Woods, interest in golf has exploded to include more diverse participants. Additionally, it is common to see municipal, semiprivate, and private golf courses in large metropolitan to rural areas. But despite the popularity of golf, there are environmental effects of designing, constructing, maintaining and participating on the various courses.

Environmentalists have voiced concerns over the detrimental impact of golf courses since the 1960s. Part of these concerns surrounds the fact that the average 18-hole golf course requires 75 to 150 acres to build. In America alone, U.S. golf courses amass the size of Delaware and Rhode Island combined (Adams, 1995). Because of the expansiveness of these courses, natural populations of wildlife are oftentimes displaced or perish. After the natural environment is demolished and often times customized to meet the designs of the course developer, nonnative plants are introduced into the landscape. As a result of these nonnative plants being planted, extreme amounts of water are used to sustain them.

Additionally, toxic and environmentally damaging pesticides and fertilizers are used to maintain the pristine expectations that golfers have come to expect as a result of watching PGA events on television (Wheeler & Nauright, 2006). However, golf courses did not first start as artificial wonders of landscape architecture. As the opening quotation exemplifies, golf courses started by embracing the natural environment. Links courses are commonly seen in Scotland, the birthplace of golf. These courses embrace the natural environmental features of rolling hills, thick brush, and oftentimes-sandy costal conditions—they were not formed as the oasis-resembling courses of today are.

New courses are frequently designed with the golfer in mind instead of the environment and natural landscape. The focus on golfers and their high expectations has caused golf course managers to take these extreme measures to sustain their profits. All the while, the environment suffers. Wildlife populations are threatened. Local water tables are infiltrated with toxic chemicals from pesticides and fertilizers (Wheeler & Nauright, 2006). Natural landscapes are destroyed in order to make room for another golf course without concern for compromising the health of the environment. These threats on the environment happen to simply meet the expectations of their customers and members.

However, there are ways to maintain these high levels of quality on the course. Audubon International has partnered with golf courses around the United States and Canada to promote more environmentally friendly course management. These programs include education on the necessity of using fertilizers and pesticides and responsible watering techniques. Additionally, Audubon promotes responsibility to the surrounding and displaced wildlife. This firm also offers a certification program for the various course management and wildlife management practices that golf courses should embody to become more environmentally friendly (Audubon, 2010).

As with the management of golf courses, the business practices of other organizations, including sport organizations, have the potential to negatively impact the surrounding environment. An organization's environmental impact will differ from industry to industry and even from organization to organization. Like with the golf courses, business organizations and human activity impact the environment. As seen in the opening example, the decision to make customized courses by changing the landscape and the continual use of chemicals in pesticides and fertilizers has a detrimental impact on the environment. Likewise among other organizations across the industry, the environmental consequences resulting from business decisions should be considered among organizational managers. Considering this, examination of the organization's impact on the environment can be quite revealing. These examinations commonly focus on the product life cycle but can also include organizational internal operations as well. Considering the environmental impact of organizational processes can reduce the organization's carbon footprint.

It is unreasonable and naive to believe that changes can be made to completely eliminate an organization's environmental impact. However, just because an organization cannot altogether eliminate its impact on the environment does not mean that these considerations should be neglected or ignored. This perspective (i.e., the stance to ignore and neglect an organization's impact on the environment) has fueled a backlash from environmental groups to community stakeholders. These inspired stakeholders encourage organizations to minimize their impact on the environment and move towards more environmentally sustainable business practices and procedures. Reducing an organization's environmental impact is an ongoing process. It cannot be limited to a one time evaluation and modification. The process of becoming environmentally friendly needs to continually adapt to new technologies and be introduced into all aspects of the organization.

The purpose of this chapter is to demonstrate the impact that sport has on the natural environment. Specifically, I will provide an operational definition of sustainability and environmental sociology. I will then offer an overview of the environmental impacts of various aspects of the business of sport and the various levels of sport. Additionally, I will provide background into the social movements that lead to the greening of the sporting world. Lastly, I will discuss various green initiatives in sport, as well as future opportunities for sport organizations to engage in the green movement.

## KEY CONSTRUCTS

### Sustainability

In order to understand sustainability, it is important to first define the term. The following are similar, yet distinct, definitions of sustainability as cited from Gatto (1995, p. 1181):

- Applied biologist definition – "sustained yield of resources that derive from the exploitation of populations and ecosystems"
- Ecologist definition – "sustained abundance and genotypic diversity of individual species in ecosystems subject to human exploitation or, more generally, intervention"
- Economist definition – "sustained economic development, without compromising the existing resources for future generations"

There are several key points that can be demonstrated through these definitions. First, sustainability focuses on the exploitation and the overconsumption of natural resources. Second, the exploitation of these recourses comes as a result of human activity. For example, the use of natural resources such as timber can have negative effects on the environment, if clear cutting techniques are used. Third, the overconsumption of natural resources can have detrimental effects on future generations. Damaging ecosystems due to human activity does not necessarily have a quick fix to recover and reestablish environmental responsibility. That said, actions are needed to evaluate the degree of environmental damage human activity might cause.

The concept of sustainability extends from the need for the natural environment to provide for future generations. But as personkind and business organizations recklessly consume natural resources, the overall wellbeing of the environment is threatened. People have oftentimes ignored this threat. Discussion over how to neutralize and even reverse our effect on the environment has commonly been avoided or underestimated. It may be simple to see the effects people's activity has on the environment. Simply looking at the skylines of major metropolitan areas to see the smog hovering over these cities can demonstrate these effects. Landfills filling up with post consumption waste cover our country and the globe. Raw and untreated sewage is oftentimes dumped offshore into the ocean, threatening the health of water sources. Pollution and other results of our insensitivity to the environment show the impact that we have on the environment through our behavior and current ways of life. These behaviors impact the world and its future generations.

There is considerable debate surrounding the issues of global warming and climate change. One side of the argument tries to establish that climate change has been caused by fossil fuels and human activity, which have been exacerbated by the Earth's increasing population. Conversely, others suggest that the Earth is naturally warming itself with little to no effect from people. Positions in these debates oftentimes appear to align with political ties or personal interests. Despite one's political affiliation, it would be difficult to demonstrate that the amount of waste produced, the energy/fossil fuels consumed, and the expansion of personkind into vulnerable ecosystems does not have an impact on the environment and its ability to sustain itself.

For years these debates have resulted in calls for environmental reform. New lines of scientific, political, and academic inquiry have been formed. Environmental groups have conveyed the importance of environmental consideration. Conversely, other groups, backed by large environmentally threatening organizations, have formed to defend the actions of corporations that potentially could be deemed environmentally damaging.

The issue of conservation and environmentalism has caused clashes from these perspectives over the wellbeing of an important yet inanimate perspective, the environment. Environmental groups and organizations provide a voice for the environment. This voice conveys the damages that have been apparent and visible to the signs that have often gone unnoticed by the general population. From this perspective, interaction between personkind and the environment has formed into a new branch of sociology called environmental sociology.

**Environmental Sociology**

From a sociological perspective, environmental sociology recognizes "the fact that physical environments can influence (and in turn be influenced by) human societies and behavior" (Dunlap & Catton, 1979 p. 244). From this perspective, environmental sociologists refrain from the typical sociological "insistence that social facts can only be explained by other social facts" (p. 244). Sociologists have typically distinguished differences among the social and cultural environment from the natural and physical environment (Bernard, 1925). However, traditional sociologists ignore the influences that the natural environment can have on the social and cultural environment. Thus, the effects and consideration of environmental variables distinguish environmental sociology from its parent field (i.e., sociology) and its preexisting theories.

Just as there are different categories to classify people into religious backgrounds or ethnicities, there are similar ways to classify the environmental movements within the United States. Understanding these different groups provides insight into the environmental movement within a sport context and into environmental sociology. Robert Brulle (2009) provides a summary of different environmental groups that manifested through the environmental movements in American history. That is, these groups have different perspectives on the definition of sustainability and what it means to be environmentally responsible. More specifically, these classifications correspond to their response to environmental issues. Referring to the previous example, when asking someone to define their concept of God or of faith, responses will vary: depending on one's spiritual background or religious denomination, responses will have different foci than from others. The same is true with environmental issues: individuals might classify themselves as being environmentally friendly, but their idea of what consists of being environmentally friendly may differ.

From the groups that Brulle (2009) describes, wildlife management, conservation, and reform environmentalism are of considerable interest with relation to sport and the environment. Wildlife management was the first environmental movement to form over concern for the natural environment. This movement actually started in the mid 1800s by wealthy sportsmen who wanted to protect the wild game they hunted. From this perspective, excess wildlife is seen as "a crop that can be sustainably harvested" (Brulle, 2009, p. 213).

Later, one of the most politically influential movements began. The conservation movement looked at the ecosystem as a machine or parts of a body that are necessary to function properly. Conservationists take a utilitarian perspective striving to "realize the greatest good for the greatest number of people over the longest period of time" (Brulle, 2009, p. 213).

Lastly, one of the longest sustaining environmental movements, reform environmentalism, spurred off conservationism in the mid-1960s. Reform environmentalists were motivated by the constant pollution of humankind and depicted the environment as an interconnected system with delicate relationships. This movement depicts nature as the basis for all existence.

## ENVIRONMENTAL IMPACTS

Just as with business organizations and their daily practices, sport organizations of all sizes have an impact on the environment. However, unlike many other businesses, sport organizations rely on attracting thousands of customers and fans to consume an intangible product. Because sport organizations typically provide a service rather than a tangible good, the environmental impact of sport organizations is different than non-sport organizations. The following section outlines various aspects to consider when evaluating the environmental impact of a sport organization.

### Facility Construction and Management

As the opening example to the chapter demonstrated, the construction of sport facilities and venues can have a considerable impact on the natural environment. Also, construction is inevitable when older facilities are replaced. Substantial consideration should be given to the construction of new facilities because of the financial investment in construction and the lifespan of sport venues. Investing in environmentally friendly construction practices can increase the building costs roughly 1% for major projects. These aspects can include energy saving lights, low flow water features, and updated HVAC (heating and air condition) systems. This small investment into energy efficient aspects and other environmentally friendly features can have substantial long-term benefits, cutting organizational operational expenses.

Much like Audubon's certification process for golf course and wildlife management, there is a certification for buildings and sport venues as well. The Leadership in Energy and Environmental Design, or LEED program, is a renowned program developed through the US Green Buildings Council. Through this certification, various environmental aspects are considered. Most importantly building strategies, materials, energy saving, water usage, carbon emissions and consumption of additional resources are evaluated. There are multiple levels of certification ranging from being simply certified to higher levels of compliance including silver to platinum, which is the highest level of accreditation.

Achieving LEED certification is becoming quite popular among sport facilities. The Washington Nationals were one of the first Major League Baseball teams to achieve this distinction (MLB Advanced Media, 2009). Additionally, many higher education institutions are mandating that new sport and non-sport facilities achieve at a minimum silver certification under the LEED guidelines. However, due to the construction materials needed to build sport facilities (e.g., massive amounts of concrete and steel), these facilities are limited to only attaining Silver LEED Certification.

Examining the environmental impact of the construction of a sport facility has been given the most attention by sport organizations. This attention is understandable considering the financial investment of such construction projects. For instance, the Cowboys Stadium in Arlington, Texas, cost nearly $1.2 billion to construct. However, environmental considerations were made throughout the construction of this facility, thus increasing the success of environmental programs. The new Cowboys Stadium includes:

> State-of-the-art bio composting reactor from Totally Green, a retractable roof that allows a lot of events to be held in natural lighting, retractable end zone doors that allow for natural ventilation, permeable pavement that helps with water drainage and pollution, a comprehensive recycling program, and more. Overall, it has reduced solid waste, energy use, and water consumption considerably due to its green initiatives (Shahan, 2011).

As noted by Shahan, the initiatives that were implemented have been recognized as being one of the most environmentally friendly sport facilities in the country as well as the first facility to be certified by the US EPA's National Environmental Performance Track Program. The EPA's certification program has since been dissolved but, the initial planning to include environmentally friendly aspects in the construction of the facility helped the facility not only reduce its impact on the environment during, but more importantly, after construction where environmental impacts may be less recognized.

## Transportation

One of the major considerations with any event is dealing with an increase in spectators. Sport venues are used throughout the year and can attract more than 200,000 people per event. Obviously, the more people that attend an event, the more money can be made off an event. However, considerations are needed to manage the increase in spectators and the impact that those people have on the surrounding area. More people attending events mean more cars and eventually more pollution. Transportation to and from an event has a tremendous impact on the overall carbon footprint of a particular event. As discussed later, transportation can contribute about 30% to an event's carbon emissions.

Public education campaigns are commonly used and recommended. These programs can educate the public on transportation alternatives. However, these alternatives are only used if they are efficient and are seen as an easier alternative to using private transportation. It is inevitable that a number of spectators will choose private transportation. Considering this, facility managers are encouraged to have transportation procedures for entering and exiting vehicles.

Additionally, infrastructures are commonly redesigned and adapted to accommodate new sporting venues. Public railways and extensions of freeways and highways are used to ease traffic congestion at new facilities. Improvements to a city's infrastructure are more commonly seen in metropolitan areas. However, for smaller cities that host mega events, parking programs to ease traffic are used to facilitate traffic congestion. For example, programs offered at Texas A&M University during football games are called "Get to the Grid." This program allows fans to park away from the stadium but close to the highway. Public transportation brings fans from the offsite location to the stadium before and after the game and offers a quick and easy way to get home, all the while decreasing traffic and the impact on the environment.

## Foot Traffic

Professional sport facilities and venues, like football and baseball stadiums, are designed to accommodate spectators and increased traffic. However, some facilities are designed for participatory sports, like golf and skiing. That is to say, these facilities are designed to accommodate the people who will be using the facilities for recreational use. When being designed, these facilities may not be considered for hosting a larger event, such as a golf tournament or ski competition. Hosting such events attracts more spectators than the venue may have been designed to accommodate. Increased foot traffic from spectators can ruin the natural landscape and integrity of the surrounding environment.

During ski competitions and golf tournaments, spectators are sometimes granted unlimited access to their respective venues. This free access can threaten the surrounding environment as a result of meandering spectators. Major PGA Tour golf tournaments, like the Masters, can attract upwards of estimated 35,000 spectators per round (Harig, 2008). The influx of people on the course at major golf tournaments can cause tremendous harm to the already altered landscape. Because of this increased traffic of spectators, these golf courses are normally closed for three months after a major event.

### Solid Waste Trash & Recycling

Along with increased foot traffic, a large sporting event generally draws an enormous amount of tailgating spectators, and where spectators congregate trash and recyclables are sure to follow. Tailgating before and after a game can increase the trash produced. Oftentimes, sport organizations and events are charged for every dumpster of solid waste (i.e., landfill waste). This charge covers the transportation fee and the actual dumping fee the waste management company pays to empty the bin or truck in the local landfill. However, waste management companies do not charge to dispose of recyclable materials because the waste management company can subsequently sell the recyclable materials on the secondary market. Thus, a focus on reducing solid waste and recovering recyclable materials can help sport organizations' bottom line.

As an example, Penn State made $40,000 (Lease, 2000) by selling recycled cardboard on the secondary market. Additionally, the San Francisco Giants saved $200,000 during the 2005 season by implementing a stadium wide recycling and composting program at AT&T Ballpark (Williams & Sherman, 2005). The San Francisco Giants extended their savings by diverting foot waste from local landfills and in turn reduced the amount of waste going into solid waste dumpsters. In 2011, with a $50,000 grant from the Office of the University President, Ohio State implemented a zero waste campaign at their football stadium. Ohio State defines zero waste "as a 90 percent diversion rate of waste material such as food, paper products and plastics away from landfills" (Ricchiuto, 2011). To help in this goal, Ohio State redefined their procurement, or purchasing, behaviors, and Ohio Stadium facility officials ensured that everything sold inside the stadium was either compostable, recyclable, or biodegradable (i.e., destined for landfill but would decompose quickly).

Researchers have also started to examine the recycling behaviors of sport spectators (McCullough & Cunningham, 2011). This research indicated the influence of social pressures to engage sport spectators to recycle; as such, athletic departments can take advantage of their spectator's fan identification levels and encourage attending spectators to recycle their waste. They can do so by taking several small steps, including: better signage informing spectators what can and cannot be recycled, public address announcements encouraging spectators to recycle, and creative advertisements and public service announcements to appear on the jumbo-tron before specific time in the game where spectators will congregate on the concourse (McCullough, 2011). Implementing such programs can improve the environmental standing of the athletic department and can increase the fan identification of moderately identified fans of the university (McCullough & Cunningham, 2010).

## SPORT AND THE ENVIRONMENT

Researchers have previously examined the effects sports have on the environment from the various forms of pollution. I will cover these aspects and also outline the response that sport organizations, leagues, and individuals have taken to decrease their environmental impact. As previously mentioned, organizational behavior and human actions will have an inevitable impact on the environment. It is important to realize these impacts to effectively change or modify behaviors. Before modification can happen, awareness is critical. As part of a social movement, environmentalism and environmental awareness hit mainstream media during the 1960s (Dunlap & Marshall, 2007). All industries, including the sport industry, were criticized for their environmental impacts. The following sections outline various aspects within the sport industry from mega events to individual participation sports like golf and alpine skiing.

### Mega-Events

Mega-events are large social or sporting events that are designed to attract large amounts of people and media attention, like the Summer or Winter Olympics and FIFA's World Cup. There is a tremendous amount of research surrounding these events and the economic impact that the participants, fans, and tourists can inject into the local economy (Hotchkiss et al., 2003; Porter & Fletcher, 2008; Preuss, 2004, 2006). It was not until recently that environmental impacts were estimated before or after such events. These impacts are only increased with the size of the events. Events like the Olympic Games can attract more than 11,000 athletes and sell in excess of 7 million tickets (like the 2008 Games in Beijing; Eimer, 2008). With this many fans and the construction of new facilities, these events have a tremendous environmental impact.

*Olympics Takes Charge*

The Olympic Games have exploded in terms of the number of athletes who participate and fans who attend each Olympiad. As a result of the increased popularity and a heightened awareness to environmental issues, the International Olympic Committee (IOC) has come under fire to improve their environmental reputation. Preliminary studies commonly focus on the economic benefits for the host city and country, but before the 1990s the cost to the environment for hosting such events was not common practice among bidding or host cities. The same is not the case today. In the following sections, I provide an overview of the changes that resulted in a more eco-conscious Olympics.

*Pressures to Go Green.* Protests developed in North America against Olympic bids in both Canada and the United States, with concerns regarding the environmental implications of hosting the Games. The Olympics began to grow exponentially from one Olympiad to the next, thus increasing the environmental implications for the host community. The first Olympic bid lost because of an environmental protest was in 1966 during the bidding process for the 1972 Winter Games. Banff, in the Canadian providence of Alberta, was figured to be the running favorite as Calgary finished second for the 1968 Winter Games. However, the Canadian Wildlife Association actively protested Canada's bid to host the 1972 Winter Games, mainly because of the relation of Olympic venues in proximity to Lake Louise in Banff National Park (Chappelet, 2008).

Instead, Sapporo, Japan, received the winning Olympic bid for the 1972 Winter Games. The Japanese bid did not win solely because it did not face the resistance that the Canadian bid did. On the contrary, the Japanese bid included many environmental considerations that were typically unseen in Olympic bids. The Japanese town of Sapporo supported and promoted its newly developed infrastructure. This was much stronger than Banff could offer. This infrastructure included "metro, a railway station, new roads, and improved urban heating systems, water supplies, and sewage treatment facilities" (Chappelet, 2008 pp. 1889). Another feature that the Japanese bid promoted was the proximity of venues. All venues were within a 35-kilometer (22 miles) radius, a relative close proximity for Olympic host site standards especially considering the terrain needed for the Winter Games. The close proximity of all the facilities reduced the need for transportation, thereby lessening traffic congestion and increasing usage of public transportation. Interestingly, the one site that was located outside of the 35 kilometer radius, the downhill run for skiing, had to be relocated to The Mount Eniwa in Shikotsu National Park because of necessary gradient of the mountain. After the completion of the 1976 Winter Games, the slopes were removed and trees were replanted on the ski runs developed for the Olympiad.

Within the United States, the Citizens for Colorado's Future was one of the first social groups that successfully politicized the environmental impact of the Olympic Games (Chappelet, 2008). After Denver had been granted to host the 1976 Winter Games, this collective group of Colorado residents protested over concerns regarding the impact that the Winter Games would have on over development of Denver and impact on Colorado's natural environment. There was much debate over the benefits of hosting the Games versus the tangible and intangible costs. As a result, the State of Colorado put a ballot measure to vote on whether the State would accept the Olympic bid. In 1973, 93% of voters overwhelmingly turned out to vote on the measure to keep the Games or reject the offer for the Games. The voters rejected the Olympic bid by a three to two margin. Denver then withdrew their acceptance to be the host city of the 1976 Games. On such short notice, the IOC awarded the Games to Innsbruck, Austria, because they previously hosted the Winter Games.

Further protests surrounded the 1980 Winter Games in Lake Placid with regards to the conditions of the bobsled and luge run. These runs require enormous amounts of ammonia to refrigerate the ice. The use of ammonia is tremendously damaging to the surrounding environment, especially when the runoff from the course goes directly into the ground and into the natural water table. This became an issue as the Lake Placid Games approached. Lake Placid was eventually able to upgrade their facilities to address these concerns. Additional reservations surrounded the use of ski runs used for short and long distance jumping. These runs were located in a New York state park run by New York State Department of Environmental Conservation, thus leading to conflicts of interest. But, these protests were eventually dropped. One major problem surrounding the 1980 Games was that the infrastructure originally created for the Winter Games that were hosted there in 1932 and the subsequent tourism to the region did not keep pace with the necessities of the Winter Games. The increased traffic to the region could not withstand the increased traffic for the 1980 Games (Chappelet, 2008). That is, the development of Lake Placid did not match the growing popularity of the Winter Olympic Games. This further demonstrates that an increased number of spectators creates a larger environmental impact.

*Development of Environmental Policies.* Protests surrounding the environmental impact of the Olympics became commonplace since the Winter Olympic Games were hosted in Sapporo, Japan. These protests developed into losing bids by potential host cities based on their poor environmental management. Subsequent bids for the 1976 and 1988 Winter Games were rejected because of the lack of environmental considerations. But even the winning bid cities that hosted the Olympic Games in Sarajevo (1984) and Calgary (1988) did not follow through on environmental promises (Chappelett, 2008). As a result, the IOC decided to focus on developing an environmental aspect to the Olympic charter. As part of this development, the IOC wanted to focus on the legacy of the Olympic Games. This would be demonstrated in Lillehammer during the 1994 Winter Olympic Games. The IOC included the environment as the third pillar of the Olympic movement. This includes incorporating environmental aspects to sport federations, national Olympic committees, and all Olympic sponsored events. The IOC was able to further develop their environmental programs through a partnership with the United Nations. For more information, see Exhibit 8.1.

Exhibit 8.1: International Olympic Committee & Agenda 21

In keeping with their declaration of the environment being the third pillar of the Olympic Movement, in 1999 the IOC implemented Agenda 21 – Sport for sustainable development. This document has been used by future bidding countries as a guideline to host a sustainable mega-event. Agenda 21 outlines the responsibilities of "different members in implementing action, which respect the concept of sustainable development". The document also encourages the International Federation, National Olympic Committees, athletes, clubs, and sponsors to follow Agenda 21 as a reference for sustainable development (International Olympic Committee – Sport and the Environment Commission, 1992; Balderstone, 2001).

*1994 Lillehammer Winter Games.* One of the first Olympiads to incorporate environmental considerations was at the 1994 Winter Games in Lillehammer, an approach subsequent Games incorporated. However, based on the setting of the venues in Lillehammer, it was used as the example to exemplify the new face of the IOC with regards to the environment. The IOC's intentions were exemplified by Norway's Prime Minister saying that the Olympic Games were an opportunity to forward "an ethic of solidarity with our current and future generations, a responsibility to the global balance of nature and an understanding of our role within it" (Mathisen, 1993). These words embodied the purpose and spirit of the third pillar to protect the environment.

The Lillehammer Games were deemed an environmental success. The backdrop of the falling snow in Norway, combined with the early instituted environmental programs, subdued criticism from the media and environmental groups. The Norwegian government invested heavily into the incorporation of environmental aspects to the Games. Additionally, the government opened their doors to environmental groups and worked together to host the "greenest" Olympiad to that point.

*2000 Sydney Summer Games.* Though environmentalism was strong in the 1994 Winter Games, the 2000 Summer Games in Sydney were the first Olympic Games to incorporate the IOC's environmental pillar throughout the bidding process and through the completion of the Olympic Games. The Sydney Games featured many environmental considerations, such as cleanup of toxic sites, environmentally friendly construction of facilities, facilitating increased use of public transportation, and the introduction of recycling in Olympic facilities. Despite a partnership with Greenpeace international to formulate environmental considerations, programs and policies, the Sydney Games faced criticism. Critics from other environmental groups claimed that the Games were not truly environmentally friendly and accused the Games of green washing, or making false environmental friendly claims (Beder, 1999). Despite the challenges to the environmental programs and initiatives taken at the 2000 Olympic Games, there were considerable strides in hosting a more environmentally friendly event.

*Six Nations Rugby World Cup*

While the Olympics garner considerable attention, other mega events also have the potential to negatively impact the environment. Rugby's Six Nations tournament represents one example, as event organizers must consider not only the economic benefits but also the environmental costs of hosting such an event.

Researchers at Cardiff University (2007) examined the environmental impact of a 2006 Rugby match during Rugby's Six Nations Tournament. The researchers found that hosting the event required extreme amounts of energy and natural resources. In fact, hosting more than 85,000 fans for one rugby match consumed scores of natural resources and produced massive amounts of carbon emissions. To offset the resources that were consumed and CO2, it would take nearly 3,600 rugby pitches, meaning that the energy and resources consumed at one rugby pitch produced such a large carbon footprint it takes over 3,000 times the land to offset the environmental impact.

Cardiff University encouraged large sporting events like Six Nations to consider alternatives to decrease their environmental impact. Basic elements surrounding the event such as concessions and transportation had the largest impact on the event, totaling 60% and 31% of the carbon footprint, respectively. The study suggested simple solutions such as encouraging the use of mass public transit. If 50% of the spectators took a public or private bus or took the train to the event, the carbon footprint can decrease by as much as 15%. However, many solutions to decrease the environmental impact of sporting events have not been explored or possibly discovered.

Some sport organizations, such as the Welsh Rugby Union, have called upon their fans and followers to help decrease sport events' environmental impacts. Nonetheless, it is clear to see that even one sporting event can have a significant impact on the surrounding environment. Imagine the compounding effects of repeating sporting events of a collegiate football team with seven home games or a Major League Baseball team hosting 81 home games. The environmental impacts of these events are even more significant than a weekend rugby match.

**Participatory Sports**

Much has been written on the environmental impact of mega events and spectator sports, but little attention has been given to physical activity, or participatory sports. These sports include individual sports and recreation, like fishing and surfing. Participatory sports are important to investigate because they are not regulated as closely as organized sports. As a result of the lack of management, these activities can be considered a notable environmental threat. In fact, the environmental movement within the United States can be traced back to hunters in the mid 1800s.

The wildlife movement stands as one of the oldest environmental movements within the United States, initially forming in the mid 1800s. This classification consists of wealthy hunters who became concerned with the depletion of the particular game that was hunted. As a result, these hunters formed the country's first environmental groups, like the Boone and Crocket Club and the National Audubon Society, to institute bag limits while fishing and hunting wild game animals (Brulle, 2009). Eventually, restrictions further developed to include hunting and fishing seasons for specific species of wild game and fish.

Later, with populations of the United States growing combined with an ever-growing suburbanized America in the 1930s, habitats for these animals dwindled. As a result, wildlife management was created, establishing habitats and wildlife refuges for animals. This paved the way for population controls and the mindset that "wildlife populations can be seen as a crop from which excess populations can be sustainably harvested" (Brulle, 2009 pp. 213). From a sports perspective, environmental sporting groups are commonly seen today. Groups like Ducks Unlimited and Trout Unlimited actively preserved the natural wetlands and streams that waterfowl and trout inhabit. These two groups also work closely with the Department of the Interior shaping federal environmental policy (for more information, See Exhibit 8.2).

## OPPORTUNITIES FOR GREEN SPORT

Organizations face several challenges to legitimize their environmental credibility during the transformation into a "green" organization. The environmental movement has expanded into many industries, including sport and physical activity. More and more sport organizations are starting to implement environmental policies and programs as a result of social, functional and political pressures (McCullough & Cunningham, 2010). Public concern comes from the environmental impact of not only the construction of sport facilities (e.g. stadiums, arenas, practice facilities) but also regular use of those facilities that can attract thousands of people to the area. Although there are economic benefits for constant crowds, with these crowds come environmental impacts.

In some cases, environmental programs are implemented due to the overwhelming necessity to avoid criticism from public outlets for degrading the environment and to avoid governmental regulations mandating environmental initiatives. However, some organizations implement environmental or green programs. As these programs are implemented, some sport organizations are criticized for the lack of environmental integrity, a phenomenon commonly referred to as green washing (Hartman & Stafford, 1997). These "green washing" claims discredit not only the organization's environmental policies but also can hurt the overall image and brand that an organization has established.

Exhibit 8.2 – Republican Conservationists

Have you considered how politically conservative people might be environmentalists? Conservatives might not necessarily refer to themselves as environmentalists but possibly as conservationists. Much in the tradition of Conservationists, like President Theodore Roosevelt, in the early 1900s, members of one of the oldest sport environmental groups in the country, Ducks Unlimited members generally are politically conservative. Founded in 1937, Ducks Unlimited concentrates on the preservation of natural wetlands. This concern for the environment came as a result to protect the waterfowl that inhabited these wetlands. The preservation and repopulation efforts extend from the United States to Mexico and Canada. To date Ducks Unlimited has preserved over 12.6 million acres of wetlands and replenished the populations of wild waterfowl in those habitats. Additionally, the organization dedicates close to $174 million to further protecting the wetlands that are home to the desired waterfowl. Doing their part to decrease their environmental impact is best exemplified in their slogan of "Conservatism today, ducks tomorrow" (Ducks Unlimited, 2009). For more information, see Holsman (2000).

As a way to neutralize green washing claims, sport organizations have partnered with environmental groups, such as the Environmental Protection Agency, United Nations Environmental Program, Greenpeace, and other governmental or nonprofit environmental agencies (Hartman & Stafford, 1997). These partnerships, also referred to as alliances (Hartman & Stafford, 1997), have legitimized environmental programs and bring a certain level of expertise to initiatives taken by a sport organization. Also, through the alliances between the two organizations, image transfer is possible between the sport organization and environmental agency. These image transfers can create win-win situations that can further organizational objectives.

These alliances can also assist in market entry for both environmental agencies and sport organizations (Cornwell, 2008). Sport organizations can assist environmental agencies as certification programs expand into new industries. Likewise, environmental agencies can add legitimacy to a sport organization's efforts to establish environmentally friendly business practices and how to properly convey those changes to stakeholders. Despite the benefits from these partnerships, there are negative aspects that need to be considered by both the sport organization and environmental agency.

Much like the challenges marketers have with effectively conveying sponsorships to sport fans, sport organizations face the same problems with conveying their environmental responsibility partnerships with outside organizations. However there are some concerns regarding the depiction of alliances between an organization and an environmental group. One of the important perceptions to keep in mind is to ensure that the alliance is seen as a partnership rather than an economic tradeoff. Social aspects are important to convey to establish an effective association between a sponsor and host organization (Meenaghan, 2001). By establishing a strong alliance, goodwill can be created for both organizations. However, if the alliance is weak between the sport organization and environmental agency, both risk damage to their respective organizational reputations, image and legitimacy.

## FUTURE TRENDS OF ENVIRONMENTAL PROGRAMS

As the sport industry becomes more aware of environmental impacts, new opportunities will be presented for increased revenue and business ventures. Professional sport teams can look to new environmentally friendly companies as new avenues for sponsorships. Existing sponsors who want to promote their environmentally friendly products can have easy access to the sport market. New sporting goods organizations that offer environmentally friendly aspects or other responsible business practices can be tied together to gain market share. As sport organizations upgrade and build new facilities, environmentally friendly aspects can be incorporated to attract new customers and members (for an example, see Exhibit 8.3).

Exhibit 8.3: Philadelphia Eagles' Green Initiatives

Owners of the Philadelphia Eagles, Jeffery and Christina Lurie, made a leap before any other football team in the National Football League and before most other professional sport organizations. Because of their influence, the Philadelphia Eagles decided to green their organization and their business practices. The decision came in part as the Eagles plan "to create and sustain championship performance on the field and in the community through programs that promote the quality of life in our region, green the environment to improve our impact on the planet and enhance our profitability as a business" (Philadelphia Eagles, 2009). The Eagles have partnered with The Conservation Fund's program GO ZERO and created "Eagle Forest," home to over 5,000 trees to offset the carbon emissions from the Eagles' away game travels. The Eagles even go as far as to collect all the solid waste the team produces during road trips and bring it back and dispose of it properly in Philadelphia to minimize the team's carbon footprint.

As environmental management aspects become more prevalent and visible in sport various environmental behaviors should encourage fans and spectators to act more environmentally responsible. Smith and Westerbeek (2006) described sports as carrying a "green virus" that can promote social change across populations. The power of sport can inspire more people outside of the sport industry to incorporate environmentally friendly practices into their own lives. Sport has been promoted as the forum to provide social change.

## CHAPTER SUMMARY

Sport will be forever tied to the environment. As environmental issues become more profound and exposed, sport must respond to the long history of environmental impacts. Through the evolution of environmental sociology, new considerations are taken with regards to the health of the environment and its impact on human interaction. In response to the deterioration of the natural environment, sport has responded to protect its intimate relationship with nature. Modifications in the interactions between humans and sport organizations with the environment occur at all levels of sport, from international events like the Olympics to individual participation in sports like hunting. The future of sports' interaction with the environment is yet to be seen, but special considerations need to be taken to ensure the viability of the environment to sustain humankind and to support sport.

## DISCUSSION QUESTIONS

1. What are the differences between the perspectives of sociology and environmental sociology?
2. What are steps that sport organizations are taking to reduce their environmental impact?

3. Several organizations have provided guidelines for sport organizations to follow to become more environmentally friendly. From your perspective, do these programs have a positive or negative impact on the environment? Why or why not?
4. State and federal laws do not require sport organizations to be eco-friendly. Why would sport organizations go above and beyond the state and federal legal requirements?
5. What future opportunities does the "green" movement provide for sport organizations?

## RECOMMENDED READINGS

Balderstone, S. (2001). Agenda 21 and IOC Requirements. IOC: Lausanne. (An International Olympic Committee endorsed document that outlines the environmental considerations of subsequent Olympiads.)

Chernushenko, D. (2001). *Sustainable sport management: Running an environmentally, socially and economically responsible organisation.* UNEP: Kenya. (A book sponsored by United Nations Environmental Program written as a guide to change the managerial paradigm of running sport organizations to consider environmental impacts.)

Schmidt, C. (2006). Putting the earth in play: Environmental awareness and sports. *Environmental Health Perspectives, 114,* 286-295. (A journal article that focuses on various sectors of the sport industry to examine their impact on the environment and ways they have become more environmentally friendly.)

## REFERENCES

Adams, R. L. A. (1995). Golf. In Raitz, K. B. (Ed.), *The theater of sport* (pp. 231-269). Baltimore: Johns Hopkins University Press.
Audubon International. (2010). Golf and the environment. Retrieved from http://www.golfandenvironment.com.
Balderstone, S. (2001). Agenda 21 and IOC Requirements. Olympic Games and Architecture – The Future for Host Cities. Joint Conference IOC / IUA, May 2001.
Beder, S. (1999). Greenwashing an Olympic-sized toxic dump, *PR Watch, 6*(2), 1-6.
Bernard, L. L. (1925). A classification of environments. *American Journal of Sociology 31*, 8-22.
Brulle, R. J. (2009). U.S. environmental movements. In Gould, K. A. & Lewis, T. L. (Eds.), *Twenty lessons in environmental sociology* (pp. 211-227). New York: Oxford University Press.

Cantelon, H., & Letters, M. (2000). The making of the IOC environmental policy as the third dimension of the Olympic movement. *International Review for the Sociology of Sport, 35*, 294-308.

Centre for Business Relationships Accountability, Sustainability and Society. (2007, February 9). Rugby internationals leave large environmental footprint. Cardiff University. Retrieved from http://www.brass.cf.ac.uk/news.

Chappelet, J-L. (2008). Olympic environmental concerns as a legacy of the winter games. *The International Journal of the History of Sport, 25*, 1884-1902.

Collins, A., Jones, C. & Munday, M. (2008). Assessing the environmental impacts of mega sporting events: two options? *Tourism Management 30*, 828-837.

Cornwell, T. B. (2008). State of the art and science in sponsorship-liked marketing. *The Journal of Advertising, 37*(3), 41-55.

Ducks Unlimited. (n.d.). Ducks Unlimited. Retrieved from http://www.ducks.org.

Dunlap, R. E., & Catton, Jr., W. R. (1979). Environmental sociology. *Annual Review of Sociology 5*, 243-273.

Dunlap, R. E., & Marshall, B. K. (2007). Environmental sociology. In C. D. Bryant and D. L. Peck (Eds.), *21st Century Sociology: A Reference Handbook, Vol. 2* (pp. 329-340). Thousands Oaks, CA: Sage.

Eimer, D. (2008, August 2). Beijing Olympics: By the numbers. *The Telegraph*, Retrieved from http://www.telegraph.co.uk.

Gatto, M. (1995). Sustainability: It is a well defined concept? *Ecological Applications, 5*, 1181-1183.

Greenpeace. (2000) Greenpeace Olympic environmental guidelines: A guide to sustainable events. Retrieved from http://www.greenpeace.org.

Harig, B. (2008, April 7). Unlike most practice rounds, the Masters' brings plenty of passion. Retrieved from http://sports.espn.go.com.

Hartman, C. L. & Stafford, E. R. (1997). Green alliances: Building new business with environmental groups. *Long Range Planning 30*, 184 – 196.

Holsman, R. H. (2000). Goodwill hunting? Exploring the role of hunters as eco-system stewards. *Wildlife Society Bulletin 28*, 808 – 816.

Hotchkiss, J. L., Moore, R. E., & Zobay, S. M. (2003). Impact of the 1996 Summer Olympic Games on employment and wages in Georgia *Southern Economic Journal, 69*, 691-704.

International Olympic Committee – Sport and Environment Commission. (1992). Olympic movement's Agenda 21: sport for sustainable development.

Keast, M. (2001, Spring). Going for the Green. Canadian Wildlife.

King, B. (2008). Finding growth in green: Seeds of opportunity. *Sports Business Journal*. November 10, 2008.

Lease, K. (2000, June). Where the crowds gather, recyclables are sure to follow. *BioCycle Magazine*. Retrieved from http://www.jgpress.com/BCArticles/2000/060037.html

Mathisen, O. M. (1993). Are we using this golden opportunity? Oslo: Norwegian Ministry of Foreign Affairs.

McCullough, B. P. (2011). *The recycling intentions of sport spectators: A theory of planned behavior approach.* (Unpublished doctoral dissertation). Texas A&M University, College Station, TX.

McCullough, B. P., & Cunningham, G. B. (2010). A conceptual model to understand the impetus to engage in and the expected organizational outcomes of green initiatives. *Quest, 62,* 348-363.

McCullough, B. P., & Cunningham, G. B. (2011). Theory of planned behavior, recycling intentions, and youth baseball. *International Journal of Sport Management and Marketing, 10*(1/2), 104-120.

Meenaghan, T. (2001). Understanding sponsorship effects. *Psychology & Marketing, 18*(2), 95-122.

MLB Advanced Media. (2009). Green ballpark. Retrieved from http://washington.nationals.mlb.com.

Philadelphia Eagles. (n.d.). Forest – Philadelphia Eagles. Retrieved from http://www.philadelphiaeagles.com/gogreen/Forest.asp.

Porter, P. K., & Fletcher, D. (2008). The economic impact of the Olympic Games: Ex ante predictions and ex post reality. *Journal of Sports Management, 22*(4), 470- 486.

Preuss, H. (2004). Calculating of the regional impact of the Olympic Games. *European Sport Management Quarterly, 4*(4), 234-253.

Preuss, H. (2006). The Olympics. In W. Andreff & Szymanski (Eds.), Handbook on the economics of sport (pp. 183-196). Northampton: MA: Edward Elgar.

Ricchiuto, K. (2011, May 18). Ohio Stadium goes zero waste. *On Campus.* Retrieved from http://oncampus.osu.edu.

Schmidt, C. (2006). Putting the earth in play: Environmental awareness and sports. *Environmental Health Perspectives, 114,* 286-295.

Shahan, Z. (2011, February 6). Cowboys Stadium 5th greenest stadium in U.S. (top ten list). *Planetsave.* Retrieved from http://planetsave.com.

Smith, A., & Westerbeek, H. M. (2004). *The sport business future.* London: Palgrave Macmillan.

Wheeler, K., & Nauright, J. (2006). A global perspective on the environmental impact of golf. *Sport in Society, 9,* 427-443.

Williams, C. & Sherman, S. (2005, February). Baseball stadium hits home run for recycling and composting. *BioCycle, 46*(2), 56.

# CHAPTER 9

# SPORT FOR SOCIAL CHANGE AND DEVELOPMENT

## Jon Welty Peachey and Adam Cohen

***

## Learning Objectives

After reading this chapter, you should be able to:

1. Articulate a definition of sport for development and briefly explain its historical significance.
2. Provide examples of individuals, non-profit, and professional sport organizations that have used or are using sport in an attempt to affect positive social change.
3. Explain the challenges facing the field of sport for social change and development and its opportunities for future growth.

## INTRODUCTION

When many people think about the nature of the sport industry, they are likely drawn to professional sport with its multi-million dollar contracts and larger-than-life personalities, or to the frenzy and excitement of big-time intercollegiate athletics. For many, sport is considered a business industry and not an agent for social change. People grow up spending time watching professional and college sports, and money on tickets, merchandise, equipment, and other related products. Often, lives are dedicated to following and supporting these massive billion-dollar sports teams and industries. However, a little-known backwater in the industry that has gained a foothold is the proliferation of hundreds of organizations around the globe that strive to use sport to make a positive difference in society. Even professional sport franchises and other traditional elements of the sport industry have launched programs to give back to the community and attempt to create positive social change. Furthermore, there has been a growing social movement towards the use of non-traditional sport practices as a vehicle for social change, reaching communities with messages in ways traditional sport practices cannot.

Sport for social change — the focus of this chapter — is the use of sport as a vehicle or platform for transforming the social structure of a social group or society (i.e., a change in the nature, social institutions, social behaviors, or social relations of a society). Sport for social change can constitute a program or initiative aimed at effecting change (i.e., sport for development) or it can be instances where sport is used as a platform to advocate for a social cause or issue. Within the domain of sport for social change lies the field of sport for development (SFD). We can broadly define SFD as the use of sport to exert a positive influence on public health, the socialization of children, youth and adults, the social inclusion of the disadvantaged, the economic development of regions and states, and the fostering of intercultural exchange and conflict resolution (Lyras & Welty Peachey, 2011; Sugden, 1991, 2006, 2008). Generally, organizations or groups involved in SFD design and implement a sport-related program or initiative for the purpose of effecting social change.

While the social environment shapes members of a society, people also have the human agency to shape social life by changing its social structures (Eitzen & Sage, 2009). Researchers have acknowledged that sport and its value systems have the potential to influence society for both good and ill (Brevik, 1998), and that sport can serve as a platform to point towards the need for societal change (Woods, 2007). SFD programs, then, actively work at social change through a variety of mediums, such as using sport to target at-risk populations (e.g., HIV in Africa; peace and conflict in Israel, Ireland, and Cyprus; poverty in India), and developing initiatives to help resolve challenges of "the north" (U.S., European Union) that could potentially transform the focus of traditional sport practices to more human-oriented programs, governance and functions (Lyras & Welty Peachey, 2011).

Consider, for example, the case of the World Scholar-Athlete Games (WSAG). Held every four years, the WSAG bring together thousands of high school scholar-athletes from as many as 175 countries to take part in sport competitions and participate in cultural and educational activities. Its mission is to bring together the future leaders of the world to break down stereotypes, foster peace and understanding, and affect personal development and social change (Lyras & Welty Peachey, 2011). However, in contrast to most international sporting events, there are no national teams at the WSAG; rather, participants from diverse countries and cultures are placed on the same teams or cultural activity groups, using the team environment to help teach understanding and acceptance. Thus, the mandate of the WSAG is to use sport as an avenue for social change.

Given this backdrop, we next provide an overview of the philosophy of SFD, followed by a discussion of sport for social change and development's historical significance, SFD's global influences, and the application of sport for social change and development in the U.S. Throughout, we showcase and provide examples of how various individuals, non-profit and professional sport organizations are embracing sport for social change and development. Finally, we examine the challenges facing the field of sport for social change and development and discuss future growth opportunities.

## OVERVIEW OF THE PHILOSOPHY OF SPORT FOR DEVELOPMENT

Historically, the potential of sport lies not with the values promoted by global sport or particular forms of capitalism for these are invariably unjust and uneven. The possibilities that exist within sport are those that can help with radically different views of the world perhaps based upon opportunities to foster trust, obligations, redistribution and respect for sport in a more socially oriented humane world (Jarvie, 2007, p. 422).

Jarvie's statement provides an excellent summary of the philosophy of SFD. He suggests that the true value of sport goes far deeper than the economic impact and that its value lies in the influence that can be had on social and interpersonal levels. Sport has been shown to have numerous impacts upon its participants, including fitness, bonding, structure, and social development (Darling et al., 2005; Eccles & Barber, 1999; Marsh & Kleitman, 2002; Sabo et al., 1993; Silliker & Quirk, 1997). For example, researchers have shown that high school athletes receive better grades (Darling et al., 2005; Silliker & Quirk, 1997), have higher educational and occupational aspirations (Darling et al., 2005; Marsh & Kleitman, 2002; Sabo et al., 1993), spend more time doing homework (Marsh & Kleitman, 2002), and have more positive attitudes towards school (Darling et al., 2005; Eccles & Barber, 1999) than do non-athletes.

Coalter (2007) also articulates five major benefits of sport participation: (a) physical fitness and improved health, (b) improved mental health and well being, (c) personality development, (d) socio-psychological benefits, and (e) social capital. The last benefit has received considerable attention among SFD scholars. Drawing from Putnam (1995), social capital is defined as the "features of social organization such as networks, norms, and social trust that can facilitate coordination and cooperation for mutual benefit" (p. 66). It can allow members of the community to act together more effectively to pursue shared objectives (DeGraaf & Jordan, 2003), something that might occur through 'bonding' and 'bridging' individuals into a larger united group. Bonding social capital occurs when individuals from similar social strata are linked together, whereas bridging social capital refers to linking together individuals from different social strata (e.g., linking together marginalized participants in a SFD program with their volunteer coaches). These bridging relationships allow disadvantaged persons the opportunity to access other society resources to change their life situations.

Sport programs, especially in a team atmosphere, have the ability to maximize social capital, as they build cohesion, bonding and capacity (Burnett, 2006; Shilbury et al., 2008). Sport also has the capability to provide connections between diverse groups, which potentially would not exist without the medium of sport. Also, Burnett (2006) linked social capital to health, life satisfaction, and trust, among other benefits (Burnett, 2006). Finally, sport can facilitate social capital by developing social inclusion, as it creates an opportunity to make friends and form relationships that can minimize social isolation and solitude (Jarvie, 2003; Sherry, 2010; Spaaij, 2009a).

As previously noted, beyond benefits on a personal level, sport has been influential within various social justice initiatives across the globe. SFD initiatives include: using sport to create dialogue between different cultures to bridge divides (Lyras, 2007; Sugden, 2008); building social capital among urban youth and in underprivileged communities (Skinner, Zakus, & Cowell, 2008; Spaaij, 2009a); using sport to diminish crime and promote awareness and activism (Burnett, 2006; Crabbe, 2000); and utilizing soccer to help homeless participants make positive changes in their lives (Sherry, 2010). We describe examples of initiatives such as these in more detail throughout this chapter.

## SPORT FOR SOCIAL CHANGE AND DEVELOPMENT'S HISTORICAL SIGNIFICANCE

The impact of sport and the notion of sport for social change and development can be traced to ancient times when the Olympic Games caused wars to cease and truces to form. In modern society, the Olympics have continued to serve as a platform for athletes to advocate for social causes and social change. For example, Jesse Owens won four gold medals during the 1936 Berlin Olympics, which featured strong Nazi propaganda that touted White supremacy. During a time in America when many African-Americans were denied equal rights, Owens' athletic feats rose above racism and served as an inspiration for people around the country. During the 1968 Olympics in Mexico City, sprinters Tommie Smith and John Carlos made their prominent political statement on the podium by wearing black gloves and raising their fists to represent Black Power. During the 2000 Games in Sydney, Cathy Freeman served as an advocate for Aboriginals, whom had long been victims of racism in Australia, by receiving the honor of lighting the Olympic flame.

Beyond the Olympic movement, sport for social change and development is grounded in the idea that sport speaks a simple, common language that can unite divergent peoples irrespective of religion, race, gender, social background, and nationality (Schwery, 2003). The interest in the field stemmed out of a response to communities in need (Green, 2008), and from the belief that meaningful social change could be enacted through sport in people's daily lives. While SFD initiatives have their roots in events such as the Olympics mentioned above or programs designed to help wounded veterans in World War I (Burnett, 2001), they have become more formalized in the past two decades. Many countries (United Kingdom, Australia, Canada, Ireland, Finland, South Africa, U.S.) have utilized sport and recreation based programs for social outreach intervention, often combined with additional philanthropic efforts to enhance efficacy (Coalter, 2007; Hartmann, 2003). Harris (1998) asserted that sport and physical activity play an important role in "fostering self-esteem, human agency and social equity . . . an important step toward strengthening and expanding civil society" (p. 1 45).

While it is impossible to list the thousands of moments in sports history that had a direct impact on society, there have been several prominent occurrences in the last 100 years that deserve mention. One of the most memorable social justice moments in sport happened in 1947 when Jackie Robinson broke the color barrier for the Brooklyn Dodgers. This event transcended far beyond sport and had a direct impact on racial segregation in the United States. Another one of the most recognizable athletes in history, Muhammad Ali, served as a civil rights activist in his opposition to the Vietnam War. This protest cost him his heavyweight title and four years of his career. In defense of his decision to boycott the war, Ali stated in 1966:

> Why should they ask me to put on a uniform and go ten
> thousand miles from home and drop bombs and bullets
> on brown people in Vietnam while so-called Negro peo-

ple in Louisville are treated like dogs and denied simple human rights? (Zirin, 2008, p. 147)

Another relevant sport moment that impacted racial equality was the 1995 Rugby World Cup. This was the first major sporting event in South Africa that took place following the end of its apartheid. Nelson Mandela, who became the first Black president of South Africa after serving 27 years in prison, stepped onto the field wearing the team jersey and presented the championship trophy to the captain of the Springboks (South Africa's national team), who was a famous White athlete in the country. The symbolism of this event was much larger than the South African rugby team's victory on the field, as this moment signified a prominent step toward reconciliation and the unification of White and Black South Africans. The events that transpired over the 1995 Rugby World Cup inspired books, movies and documentaries.

Billie Jean King, a female tennis player who defeated Bobby Riggs in a "Battle of the Sexes" match in 1973 while an estimated 90 million viewers watched, has been considered one of the leaders in women's rights. In 1974 she founded the Women's Sports Foundation, with a mission dedicated to promoting athletic opportunities for women. King stated "in the '70s we had to make it acceptable for people to accept girls and women as athletes. We had to make it okay for them to be active. Those were much scarier times for females in sports" (Schwartz, no date).

The above examples illustrate a handful of ways in which famous sports athletes, teams or moments have had an influence on society beyond the playing field, using sport as a medium to advocate for some type of societal change. Although NBA great Charles Barkley stated, "I am not a role model" in a Nike commercial, athletes will always inspire emotions and reactions from the fans they touch. Because of this passion they arouse, they have the capability to serve as change agents simply through their actions on and off the field.

## SPORT FOR DEVELOPMENT'S GLOBAL INFLUENCE

As previously mentioned, SFD falls within the broader concept of sport for social change. Within the last decade, SFD has received support from many prominent organizations and affiliations. One of the most impactful endorsements recently came from the United Nations (Kidd, 2007). In 2003, the United Nations (UN) published an article entitled "Sport for development and peace: Towards achieving the Millennium Development Goals" (UN, 2003), which was the first step towards the global promotion of sport as a tool for social justice initiatives. Representing 192 member states, the UN is one organization that encompasses the entire planet and can have a global impact. The UN followed up the 2003 report with an announcement declaring 2005 to be the International Year of Sport and Physical Education (IYSPE) (UN, 2005a). This announcement only furthered the UN's dedication and promise to use SFD as part of its long-term development agenda.

Kofi Annan, who served as Secretary General of the UN at the time, offered further support for the role of sport in working for social change at the Olympic Aid Roundtable in Salt Lake City:

> Sport can play a role in improving the lives of individuals, not only individuals, I might add, but whole communities. I am convinced that the time is right to build on that understanding, to encourage governments, development agencies and communities to think how sport can be included more systematically in the plans to help children, particularly those living in the midst of poverty, disease and conflict. (UN, 2005a, p. 1)

According to the International Platform on Sport and Development (IPSD, 2011), there are currently 341 registered sports-related organizations that contribute to SFD in one facet or another. Others have suggested that there are well over 1,000 SFD organizations scattered throughout the world (Lyras & Welty Peachey, 2011). Despite recent progress, SFD is still in its early stages as many individuals and policymakers need further convincing of its potential impact on society and the role sport can play in international, regional, and local development.

Attempts to investigate the impacts and effects that these organizations have on their target audiences have only scratched the surface. Some researchers have examined the impact of sport in countries that have suffered through war-time tragedy and violence. For instance, Armstrong (2002, 2004) examined football's (soccer) impact in Liberia, where it has been used as a tool for reconstruction and child protection, demonstrating how the game can be used to build social cohesion. Gasser and Levinsen (2004) looked at an organization in Bosnia, and Herzegovina examined the Open Fun Football Schools that use soccer to promote social cohesion between otherwise hostile groups. Another organization that uses sport to reach out to different ethnic communities is the Asian-

German Sport Exchange Programme (AGSEP). This organization attempts to contribute to overcoming intergroup rivalry and minimizing ethnic boundaries on a community level (Schulenkorf, 2010).

The social movement of sport for development and peace has also had a positive impact in some marginalized societies (Kidd, 2008). A program founded in the slums of Kenya, the Mathare Youth Sports Association (MYSA), uses soccer as a method of inclusion in an attempt to create safe space for females and to assist with school retention. The girls wear the MYSA jerseys with a sense of pride, creating a noticeable sign of group affiliation and belonging (Brady, 2005). The Ishraq program, an initiative in Egypt directed at girls aged 13-15, provides a safe atmosphere for girls to be active and play games such as table tennis or handball (Brady, 2005). This organization has the goal of providing a protective learning environment for girls in an area that normally would not be secure for younger girls. In India, an organization called Magic Bus has an annual positive impact on 200,000 impoverished children in slum communities. It uses sport and recreation to provide "five pillars": (a) safe environment, (b) 100% participation, (c) fun with responsibility, (d) mentoring, and (e) experiential learning (Magic Bus, 2011).

Olympic Aid and Right to Play are two organizations that reach out to impoverished countries. Established and funded by Olympians around the world, these groups provide coaching and mentoring in African, Asian and Middle Eastern nations along with attempting to promote healthy child and community development. Another organization that began in 2003 out of Nambia, Physically Active Youth (PAY), addresses the high dropout rate (as high as 50%) that occurs after grade 10 in that country. The initial pilot program, which combined daily sport activity with academic counseling and sex education, resulted in 75% of the students passing the 10th grade.

Sherry et al., (2011) evaluated the impact of the Homeless World Cup in 2008 and 2009, a soccer initiative aimed at helping homeless individuals make positive changes in their lives. In this study, the authors determined that a fan's perspective towards marginalized groups (in this case homeless individuals) could be shifted and changed to a more positive light by attendance at the event. Sherry (2010) also interviewed participants of a homeless soccer team in Australia and determined that homeless players increased their social capital and reengaged with society through the intervention. This work built on previous studies suggesting that social bonding through sport can have an impact on marginalized groups (Collins, 2004; Jarvie, 2003).

Street Soccer USA (SSUSA) is also using soccer to combat homelessness in 22 cities in the U.S. SSUSA attempts to achieve three major goals for participants: (a) building community and trust through sports; (b) requiring participants to set 3-, 6-, and 12- month life goals; and (c) empowering individuals by marrying clinical services to sport programming and providing access to educational and employment opportunities (SSUSA, 2010). Research has shown that SSUSA has not only had a prominent impact on the clients they attempt to serve, but also on the volunteers who donate their time and energy towards the program (Welty Peachey, Cohen, Borland, & Lyras, in press).

Another initiative in Israel, Football 4 Peace (F4P), has a mission that includes: (a) providing opportunities for social contact across community boundaries, (b) promoting mutual understanding, (c) engendering in participants a desire for and commitment to peaceful coexistence, and (d) enhancing soccer skills and technical knowledge (Sugden, 2008). The goals are part of an overarching effort aimed to bridge the divide between Israeli and Arab cultures in Israel that have been constantly teetering on the prospect of war. Through the use of soccer, F4P currently reaches out to over 1,000 children of both cultures and is located within 24 mixed communities. The F4P program has been operating in Arab and Jewish towns and villages since 2001 (Football 4 Peace Mission Statement, 2011).

It is efforts like F4P which highlight the value of sport on a global level in facilitating social change. There are other initiatives which are attempting to fulfill similar missions as F4P. One example is Peaceplayers International, whose mission is to unite, educate, and inspire young people in divided communities through basketball (Peaceplayers, 2011). This nonprofit reaches out through basketball in efforts to unite communities such as the Irish and Protestants in Ireland, the Turkish and Greek Cypriots in Cyprus, and Whites and Blacks in South Africa. In a similar vein, the Doves Olympic Movement project has a mission of incorporating the UN Millennium Development Goals into a sport intervention platform in an effort to educate Turkish and Greek Cypriot youth in Cyprus about cultural acceptance.

As can be seen in these examples, SFD initiatives have the ability to allow sport to transcend poverty, bigotry, and racism (Coalter, 2007; Kidd, 2007). Burnett and Hollander (2003) suggest it is human instinct to want to play, roughhouse, run, catch, jump, and so on. Kids will be kids, no matter the culture or environment that surrounds them, and in turn, their participation in sports and the desire to be active will also translate nearly anywhere. The goal in SFD is to take these natural desires and instincts and harness them into scenarios that "can foster peace and development and can contribute to an atmosphere of tolerance and understanding" (UN, 2005b, p. 1).

## CURRENT SPORT FOR SOCIAL CHANGE AND DEVELOPMENT APPLICATIONS IN THE UNITED STATES

> Whether a transnational corporation committed to corporate social responsibility, an international aid organization pursuing the Millennium Development Goals or a grassroots non-governmental organization (NGO) seeking to meet the everyday needs of disadvantaged communities in the Global South, it is increasingly common to herald sport as a new engine of development and social development through sport as a new social movement. (Spaaij, 2009b, p. 1109)

Even though SFD is not yet recognized as a well-known area within the sport industry, it is relevant and becoming more widespread in the U.S. and globally. While many aspects of the sport industry focus on financial and marketing issues, the social aspect of the industry and developing a human connection are as important in promoting and selling a product to consumers (Richelieu & Boulaire, 2005). Social justice initiatives may commonly be implemented in an effort to engage in corporate social responsibility (CSR), which as Spaaij (2009b) indicates in the above quote, can be considered an aspect of SFD. CSR can be defined as activities aimed at promoting some type of social good, going beyond the economic interests of the organization and its legal requirements (McWilliams & Siegel, 2001). Babiak and Wolfe (2009) suggest that "nearly all professional sport teams have established charitable foundations over the last decade and a half" (p. 720) mainly in an effort to build relationships and good will amongst local stakeholders. However, often SFD initiatives are designed and implemented by sport businesses for reasons beyond pure altruistic intentions. For instance, Levermore (2008a) mentions, "sport-in-development corporate partners may use the schemes primarily to further their own concerns" (p. 63).

Criticisms aside, beyond the social justice and philanthropic benefits that can result from CSR, these endeavors help promote and endorse the sport industry to the general public and consumers. Sports teams develop social links and create emotional associations based around the product. Within this vein, many professional sports leagues in America are embracing a philanthropic philosophy in an effort to immerse themselves in the local community and use sport to help address various social issues. For example, Major League Baseball's (MLB) Reviving Baseball in Inner Cities initiative focuses on introducing baseball to low income areas around the U.S.

MLB designed and implemented this program to engage in CSR and to achieve a positive outreach amongst potential future fans of the sport. This initiative has also produced some famous athletes that have come from urban environments, such as CC Sabathia and Justin Upton, whom were featured in nationwide commercials endorsing the endeavor. One of the National Football League's (NFL) programs, Play 60, has centered on the activity levels and fitness of young Americans and even aired commercials that featured President Obama playing football with NFL players Drew Brees and Troy Polamalu. In addition, the NBA Cares initiative was successful in countering the bad will that was created from the Ron Artest melee (where an NBA player, after first being assaulted by fans, ran into the stands and attacked a fan), as the program profoundly influenced fans' perceptions of players in the league (Giannoulakis & Drayer, 2009).

However, SFD initiatives in the U.S. go far beyond the professional sports leagues and the individual players. Nearly every professional sports franchise has a foundation or initiative in which they make efforts to give back to the local community. The same can be said for minor league teams and niche sport organizations. Ranging from the sport of squash (e.g., Squashbusters, a non-profit that uses squash to reach urban youth in Massachusetts) to lacrosse (e.g., Lacrosse the Nations, a nonprofit that uses lacrosse to promote education and healthy living), and everything in between, SFD can be found almost anywhere that sport exists. Simply put, the concept of using sport to improve the lives of others encompasses a wide spectrum of endeavors. SFD can vary from as small as a local college soccer team volunteering time to play soccer with under-privileged urban youth at a neighborhood YMCA, to as large as a global Olympic movement which aims to use sport to foster peace and understanding between cultures and countries.

By harnessing people's excitement towards the sport industry, and combining that with philanthropic education and life experience, there is an excellent opportunity to reach out to those who could potentially spend their future working, improving and advancing SFD programs. Showing people a feel-good story, like a veteran losing a leg and continuing on in competitive sports or a homeless person using soccer to get off drugs and off the street, captures their attention and enhances their desire to become involved in SFD in some capacity. This cyclical nature of SFD is one of the major reasons so many initiatives are able to succeed. Not only are people around the world being helped through the use of sport, but the employees, donors, and volunteers of SFD initiatives are also impacted in positive ways.

Like most non-profit organizations, SFD programs involve a painstaking process to become established and effective. It takes far more than simply tossing a ball out onto a field or throwing money at a group of disadvantaged children to achieve positive impact. There is a significant amount of work that goes into creating an organization that can have an impact and be sustainable over time. In a growing field such as this, there needs to be constant innovation and research to assess what is successful and what needs improvement. Burnett and Uys (2000) discuss methods to evaluate the impact of SFD programs, focusing on three major themes: (a) demographics of the area targeted, (b) program delivery and management, and (c) individual and social aspects such as community involvement. The need for diligent research and efficient program implementation is even more critical than ever in today's strained economic climate.

## CHALLENGES

Thus, myriad and varied sport organizations around the globe have begun to implement sport-based initiatives with a social change mandate. As a relatively new field, however, SFD and sport for social change present a number of key challenges that must be addressed by policy makers, researchers and practitioners in order to move the field forward: (a) program efficacy, (b) limitations of SFD initiatives, (c) lack of theoretical frameworks, and (d) fragmentation of SFD organizations.

### Program Efficacy

The first challenge is that the efficacy of these programs in achieving impact and long-term, sustainable social change remains in question. While many SFD programs claim significant impact on participants (e.g., enhanced self-esteem, intergroup acceptance) and broader society (e.g., enhanced social capital, active citizenship), in many cases, the sport programs are poorly planned and do not provide scientific evidence about their effectiveness (Coalter, 2010; Kidd, 2007; Levermore, 2008b; Lyras & Welty Peachey, 2011). Many SFD programs do not have the internal capacity to carry out effective monitoring and evaluation, and thus this essential element is often neglected. In addition, there is a poor understanding of the conditions and mechanisms needed for achieving positive outcomes in specific settings (Coalter, 2007; Jarvie, 2003). For instance, effective mechanisms and organizational structures for a sport intervention in Ghana could vary greatly from the mechanisms and structure required to achieve the same positive outcomes in Norway. In addition, the strategies used to aid children suffering from malnourishment could vary from SFD techniques that target peace initiatives in war-torn countries. More longitudinal research is needed on both the outcomes of sport-based interventions and on the most effective structures, mechanisms, and processes for achieving these outcomes in specific contexts.

## Limitations of SFD Initiatives

Coalter (2010) outlines a second challenge for the field: the recent proliferation of SFD organizations could represent a form of neo-colonialism, with the main strategies for these programs being formulated in the West and then exported to other less-developed nations, promoting new forms of dependency. He cautions those involved in SFD work to avoid forming "overly romanticized, communitarian generalizations about the 'power' of sport for development" (p.1386). In other words, while sport can be an effective intervention tool in certain settings and under certain conditions, it is not the "cure all" that can solve every society's problems all of the time. SFD scholars are challenged to recognize this limitation and look for ways to package sport with other forms of interventions (e.g., arts, music, and education) to most effectively realize the power of sport for social change and development.

## Lack of Theoretical Frameworks

Third, there is a lack of theoretical frameworks undergirding sport interventions, which subsequently constrains effective monitoring and evaluation. Ziegler (2007) notes that sport management scholars should strive to develop tenable theory that is encompassing of "sport and physical activity involvement for people of all ages, be they normal, accelerated or special in status" (p. 298). Furthermore, Coalter (2007) explains that SFD scholars should strive to advance theory to understand the conditions, structures, and processes that can promote social change through sport. Recently, several scholars have provided conceptual frameworks that may be useful in advancing SFD and sport for social change theory. In Social Leverage Theory, Chalip (2006) positions sport events as having the ability to build social capital and strengthen the social fabric through two interrelated themes of liminality and communitas. Liminality is the concept that something more important than sport is taking place at an event, and that there is a collective energy and vitality that makes social rules and distinctions less important and which transcends sport. This liminality enables discourse and brings together divergent groups that might not otherwise interact, thereby facilitating the formation of new networks that can have both cognitive and affective impacts. Sport thus creates a safe space for sensitive issues to be explored, symbolized, and considered. The sense of community that is engendered through liminality is then labeled communitas.

To enable and facilitate the development of liminality and communitas, Chalip (2006) recommends that event organizers can foster social interaction and evoke a feeling of celebration by employing several structural and process elements. Organizers should enable sociability among event visitors, and create event-related social events, such as parades and concerts, to produce a celebratory atmosphere. Organizers should also facilitate informal social opportunities and incorporate ancillary events, such as arts and music activities, as a complement to the sport programming. Finally, organizers should theme widely, using symbols, colors, decorations, rituals, narratives, and stories to "make a visual statement that something special is happening" (Chalip, 2006, p. 117). Chalip then suggests that the celebratory nature of sport events creates the link between liminality and communitas, which facilitates the development of social capital and which can be leveraged to address social issues, build networks, and bring community action leading to social change.

As another example of a theoretically grounded framework, Lyras and Welty Peachey (2011) developed Sport-for-Development Theory (SFDT) to help understand the structures and processes of SFD initiatives that can facilitate impact, produce liminality and communitas, and develop social capital. Using grounded theory methodology, SFDT was developed out of the Doves Project in Cyprus, a SFD initiative aimed at addressing issues of social exclusion among Greek and Turkish Cypriots. SFDT proposes that blending sport with cultural enrichment (e.g., arts, dance, and music) and educational activities (e.g., life skills, goal setting, global issues awareness, and human rights) can provide a platform to help address various social issues and challenges. Much like Social Leverage Theory (Chalip, 2006), SFDT holds that the blend of sport with educational, festive, and cultural dimensions creates conditions of belonging, fosters a creative sense of community, and promotes peak experiences, all of which are essential for personal development and well being. When individuals interact in such conditions, participants' psychological needs are fulfilled—a phenomenon that transcends individual thoughts, emotions and behaviors to a more outward focus and perspective, and allows individuals to think, care and act beyond self, creating conditions for social change (Bandura, 1989; Lyras, in press).

**Fragmentation of SFD Organizations**

Finally, a last challenge is the current fragmentation of organizations involved in SFD and sport for social change work. Many of these small organizations operate in a vacuum in disparate regions of the world, with little opportunity to interact and share best practices with other SFD organizations to create a mutual learning community. This fragmentation has hampered the growth of the field, as many well-intentioned organizations and programs are not able to connect with similar organizations to learn from each other. However, strides are being made to build these bridges and reduce the isolation of organizations within the field. Several international conferences are now offered each year that bring together SFD practitioners, policy makers, and researchers to share ideas and formulate action steps. For instance, the 2011 Next Steps Conference held in Trinidad and Tobago brought together key stakeholders in SFD to discuss common struggles, learn from each other's best practices, and develop action steps to help build a global SFD network to serve as a resource for all stakeholders.

## FUTURE GROWTH OPPORTUNITIES

Despite the challenges facing the SFD field, there remains a number of exciting future growth opportunities. Many governments around the globe are beginning to recognize the power of sport to effect social change and that sport can serve as another engine of development in the 21st century. Furthermore, the UN has established the Office on Sport for Development and Peace, with a global mandate to support and encourage SFD efforts in all countries. While SFD is typically associated with sport programs and interventions taking place in the global South or developing nations, there is a growing recognition and proliferation of programs using sport as a vehicle for social change in the North and more developed countries. The U.K. and Australia, in particular, have embraced sport within policy circles as a necessary ingredient for a development mandate. Within the U.S., there are organizations such as SSSUSA and the Boys and Girls Clubs of America beginning to launch sport interventions in the inner cities and rural America. Despite the White House's establishment of the Office of Olympic, Paralympic and Youth Sport in 2009, an initiative meant to promote the values of the Olympic Movement and support youth participation in sports, the U.S. as a whole has been slow to embrace a SFD mandate. Thus, there is need and a future opportunity in the U.S. and abroad for many more organizations to initiate programs using sport to help address societal ills.

Another future growth opportunity is to develop academic/practitioner partnerships to advance the rigor of monitoring and evaluation of SFD programs and organizations. As mentioned previously in this chapter, a challenge for many SFD organizations is conducting effective monitoring and evaluation due to insufficient resources and capacity. Thus, there is tremendous opportunity for academicians, both within sport disciplines and without, to partner with practitioners to construct and implement monitoring and evaluation strategies. Currently, these partnerships are being formulated in a number of countries and with several programs. For example, Sherry (2010) formed a partnership with the Australian Street Soccer team, and assessed the long-term impact of team member's participation in the Homeless World Cup. Many additional organizations, such as the MYSA and PAY discussed earlier, have reached out to academic researchers in an effort to begin ascertaining their impact on the communities they aim to serve. In the U.S., in addition to faculty at institutions of higher education becoming involved in monitoring and evaluation of SFD programs, a number of think tanks have become interested in SFD and sport for social change. For example, the Aspen Institute, a think tank in Washington, DC, dedicated to fostering open-minded dialogue on contemporary issues, has added a sports and society component to its organization, with a mission to "convene leaders, foster dialogue, and inspire solutions that help sport serve the public interest, with a focus on the health needs of children and communities" (Aspen Institute, no date).

Finally, a future growth opportunity for SFD is to cultivate student engagement within higher education institutions. SFD and sport for social change is an area that few college students know much about, and therefore, there is opportunity to educate students about SFD through classes and service learning opportunities. For example, at the University of Louisville, undergraduate and graduate students in sport management can take a seminar class in SFD. Through this class, they are required to design and implement SFD projects in the city of Louisville that can have a positive impact on community life. One recent project entailed students creating a local SSUSA team. The students partnered with a local social service provider to offer the programming and began practicing and playing soccer with homeless youth several times a week. Within the same classroom setting, several students had the opportunity to volunteer at the Muhammad Ali Center. The projects have continued each semester, with new students taking over leadership and administrative roles. Based upon this example, there would be benefit to other higher education institutions designing courses in SFD and sport for social change where students can actively work in the local communities to translate classroom learning into practical application. Finally, in addition to the need for classes in SFD, another growth opportunity is for students to volunteer and seek employment with SFD organizations. These organizations offer a rich opportunity for students to apply management, coaching, human relations, finance, marketing, and other skills in an environment working for the greater social good, which can be a rewarding and inspiring career track.

## CHAPTER SUMMARY

The purpose of this chapter was to acquaint students with the field of sport for social change and development, and to highlight examples across the globe as to how sport is being used to better society. We began by providing an overview of SFD, which was followed by a discussion of sport for social change and development's historical significance and important milestones in its development. We then highlighted a number of individuals, organizations, and initiatives around the world and within the U.S. that have used or are using sport in some capacity to address social problems. Finally, we concluded the chapter by examining some of the challenges facing the SFD field that may hinder its growth, as well as opportunities for future growth and development of the field, including ways that students can become actively involved. It is our hope that students have been challenged in this chapter to rethink their concept of sport and to consider how they may embrace and actively promote the power of sport to affect social change.

## DISCUSSION QUESTIONS

1. How do you define sport for development?
2. Explain the origins of sport for development and sport for social change, and describe three key moments of historical significance.
3. Describe two sport-for-development initiatives working at a global level and two that are working within the U.S.
4. What are some of the key challenges to the field of sport for development?
5. Where are growth opportunities for the use of sport for development and social change?

## RECOMMENDED READINGS

Coalter, F. (2007). A wider social role for sport: Who's keeping the score? London: Routledge. (Examines the role of sport in development and social change and presents challenges and criticisms on the efficacy of using sport for social change).

Nicholson, M., & Hoye, R. (2008). Sport and social capital. Oxford: Elsevier. (Provides an excellent overview of how sport can be used to increase social capital and effect social change).

Tygiel, J. (2008). Baseball's great experiment: Jackie Robinson and his legacy, 25th anniversary ed. Oxford University Press, USA. (Tygiel tells the story of Robinson and other African-American players and how their actions impacted baseball and American desegregation).

## REFERENCES

Armstrong, G. (2002). Talking up the game: Football and the reconstruction of Liberia, West Africa. *Identities: Global Studies in Culture and Power, 9*, 471-494.

Armstrong, G. (2004). The lords of misrule: Football and the rights of the child in Liberia, West Africa. *Sport in Society, 7*, 473-502.

Aspen Institute (no date). Sport & society program mission. Retrieved from http://www.aspeninstitute.org/policy-work/sports-society.

Bandura, A. (1989). Human agency in social cognitive theory. *American Psychologist, 44*, 1175-1186.

Burnett, C. (2001). Social impact assessment and sport development. *International Review for the Sociology of Sport, 36*, 41-52.

Burnett, C. (2006). Building social capital through an `active community club'.

*International Review for the Sociology of Sport, 41*, 283-294.

Burnett, C., & Hollander, W. (2003). *An impact study on Australia Africa AA 2006. Sport development programme's active community clubs' initiative.* Report prepared for the Australian Sports Commission, Department of Sport and Movement Studies, Rand Afrikaans University, Johannesburg.

Burnett, C., & Uys, T. (2000). Sport development impact assessment: Towards a rationale and tool. *Journal for Research in Sport, Physical Education and Recreation, 22*(1), 27-40.

Chalip, L. (2006). Towards social leverage of sport events. *Journal of Sport & Tourism, 11*, 109-127.

Coalter, F. (2007). *A wider social role for sport: Who's keeping the score?* London: Routledge.

Coalter, F. (2010). The politics of sport-for-development: Limited focus programs and broad gauge problems? *International Review for the Sociology of Sport, 45*, 295-314.

Collins, M. (2004). Sport, physical activity and social exclusion. *Journal of Sports Sciences, 22*, 727-740.

Crabbe, T. (2000). A sporting chance? Using sport to tackle drug use and crime. *Drugs: Education, Prevention, and Policy, 7*, 381- 391.

Darling, N., Caldwell, L. L., & Smith, R. (2005). Participation in school-based extracurricular activities and adolescent adjustment. *Journal of Leisure Research, 37*(1), 51-76.

Eccles, J. S., & Barber, B. L. (1999). Student council, volunteering, basketball, or marching band. *Journal of Adolescent Research, 14*(1), 10-43.

Foer, F. (2004). Soccer vs. McWorld. *Foreign Policy* (January/February), 32-40.

Football 4 Peace (2011). *Football 4 Peace mission statement.* Retrieved from http://www.football4peace.eu/.

Giannoulakis, C., & Drayer, J. (2009). "Thugs" versus "good guys": The impact of NBA Cares on player image. *European Sport Management Quarterly, 9*, 453-468.

Glasser, P., & Levinsen, A. (2004). Breaking post-war ice: Open Fun Football Schools in Bosnia and Herzegovina. *Sport in Society, 7*, 457-472.

Green, B. C. (2008). Sport as an agent for social and personal change. In V. Girginov (Ed.), *Management of sports development* (pp. 129-147). Oxford: Butterworth-Heinemann.

Harris, J. (1998). Civil society, physical activity and the involvement of sport sociologists in the preparation of physical activity professionals. *Sociology of Sport, 15*, 138-153.

Hartmann, D. (2003). Theorizing sport as social intervention: A view from the grassroots. *Quest, 55*, 118-140.

International Platform on Sport and Development (2011). Organisation list. Retrieved from http://www.sportanddev.org.

Jarvie, G. (2003). Communitarianism, sport and social capital. *International Review for the Sociology of Sport, 38*, 139-153.

Jarvie, G. (2007). Sport, social change and the public intellectual. *International Review for the Sociology of Sport, 42*, 411-424.

Kidd, B. (2008). A new social movement: Sport for development and peace. *Sport in Society, 11*, 370-380.

Kidd, S. A. (2007). Youth homelessness and social stigma. *Journal of Youth and Adolescence, 36*, 291-299.

Levermore, R. (2008a). Sport in international development: Time to treat it seriously? *The Brown Journal of World Affairs, 14*, 55-66.

Levermore, R. (2008b). Sport: A new engine of development? *Progress in Development Studies, 8*, 183-190.

Lyras, A. (in press). The Doves Olympic Movement Project: Integrating Olympism, development, and peace. In S. J. Hanrahan, & R. Schinke (Eds.), *Development through sport*. Morgantown, West Virginia: Fitness Information Technology.

Lyras, A. (2007). *Characteristics and psycho-social impacts of an inter-ethnic educational sport initiative on Greek and Turkish Cypriot youth.* Unpublished Dissertation, University of Connecticut.

Lyras, A., & Welty Peachey, J. (2011). Integrating sport-for-development theory and praxis. *Sport Management Review, 14*, 311-326.

Magic Bus (2011). Mission statement. Retrieved from http://www.magicbus.org.

Marsh, H. W., & Kleitman, S. (2002). Extracurricular school activities: The good, the bad, and the nonlinear. *Harvard Educational Review, 72*, 464-515.

McWilliams, A., & Siegel, D. (2001). Corporate social responsibility: A theory of the firm perspective. *Academy of Management Review, 26*, 117-127.

Peaceplayers (2011). Mission statement. Retrieved from http://www.peaceplayersintl.org.

Putnam, R. D. (1995). Bowling alone: America's declining social capital. *Journal of Democracy, 6*, 65-78.

Richelieu, A., & Boulaire, C. (2005). A post modern conception of the product and its applications to professional sports. *International Journal of Sports Marketing and Sponsorship, 7*, 23-34.

Sabo, D., Melnick, M. J., & Vanfossen, B. E. (1993). High school athletic participation and postsecondary educational and occupational mobility: A focus on race and gender. *Sociology of Sport Journal, 10*, 44-56.

Schulenkorf, N. (2010). Sport events and ethnic reconciliation: Attempting to create social change between Sinhalese, Tamil and Muslim sportspeople in war-torn Sri Lanka. *International Review for the Sociology of Sport, 45*, 273-294.

Schwartz, L. (no date). Billie Jean won for all women. Retrieved from http://espn.go.com.

Schwery, R. (2003). The potential of sport for development and peace. Bulletin no. 39. Available at Swiss Academy for Development (SAD), Switzerland: www.icsspe.org.

Sherry, E. (2010). (Re) engaging marginalized groups through sport: The Homeless World Cup. *International Review for the Sociology of Sport, 45*, 59-71.

Sherry, E., Karg, A., & O'May, F. (2011). Social capital and sport events: Spectator attitudinal change and the Homeless World Cup. *Sport in Society, 14*, 111-125.

Shilbury, D., Sotiriadou, K., & Green, B.C. (2008). Sport development systems, policies and pathways: An introduction to the special issue. *Sport Management Review, 11*, 217-223.

Silliker, S. A., & Quirk, J. T. (1997). The effect of extracurricular activity participation on the academic performance of male and female high school students. *School Counselor, 44*, 288-293.

Skinner, J., Zakus, D. H., & Cowell, J. (2008). Development through sport: Building social capital in disadvantaged communities. *Sport Management Review, 11*, 253-275.

Spaaij, R. (2009a). Sport as a vehicle for social mobility and regulation of disadvantaged urban youth. *International Review for the Sociology of Sport, 44*, 247-264.

Spaaij, R. (2009b). The social impact of sport: Diversities, complexities and contexts. *Sport in Society, 12*, 1109-1117.

Street Soccer USA (2011). Street Soccer USA Mission. Retrieved from http://www.streetsoccerusa.org.

Sugden, J. (1991). Belfast United: Encouraging cross-community relations through sport in Northern Ireland. *Journal of Sport & Social Issues, 15*, 59-80.

Sugden, J. (2006). Teaching and playing sport for conflict resolution and co-existence in Israel. *International Review for the Sociology of Sport, 41*, 221-240.

Sugden, J. (2008). Anyone for football for peace? The challenges of using sport in the service of co-existence in Israel. *Soccer & Society, 9*, 405-415.

United Nations (2003). *Sport for development and peace: Towards achieving the millennium development goals.* Report from the United Nations inter-agency task force on sport for development and peace, United Nations, Geneva.

United Nations (2005a). *International year for sport and physical education.* Retrieved from http://www.un.org.

United Nations (2005b). *International day for tolerance.* Retrieved from http://www.un.org/events/tolerance/tolerance05.pdf.

Welty Peachey, J., Cohen, A., Borland, J., & Lyras, A. (in press). Building social capital: Examining the impact of Street Soccer USA on its volunteers. *International Review for the Sociology of Sport.*

Ziegler, E. (2007). Sport management must show social concern as it develops tenable theory. *Journal of Sport Management, 21*, 297-318.

Zirin, D. (2008). *A people's history of sports in the United States.* New York: The New Press.

# CHAPTER 10

# DEVIANT BEHAVIOR AND SPORT

## D. Scott Waltemyer

***

**Learning Objectives:**

After reading this chapter, you should be able to:

1. Define and discuss different forms of deviant behavior.
2. Understand deviant-related issues in sport, such as cheating and violence.
3. Discuss the consequences of deviant behavior, and formulate possible ways of controlling it.

## INTRODUCTION

> "To play this game you have to have that fire within you, and nothing stokes that fire like hate." – *Vince Lombardi, Hall of Fame NFL coach*

> "Serious sport has nothing to do with fair play. It is bound up with hatred, jealousy, boastfulness, disregard for all the rules and sadistic pleasure in witnessing violence; in other words, it is war minus the shooting." – *George Orwell, author*

American society places a great deal of importance on values such as competition and success, as portrayed in the aforementioned quotes. In fact, some of the most famous quotes from Green Bay Packers legendary coach Vince Lombardi reference, in some way, success and winning. Sports that emphasize these values receive considerable attention from both the media and the public, and play an important role in defining what are acceptable and unacceptable behaviors in sport. People within society, and specific social groups (e.g., sports teams), are expected to conform to and obey rules and norms related to what is acceptable behavior. The actions of those involved in sport, whether good or bad, receive generous amounts of media coverage, and those behaviors reflect back, not only on the individual, but also on the group or organization with which the individual belongs. And as the pressure to win is put on athletes and coaches, the pressure to perform to elite standards dramatically influences their actions and behaviors. The use of performance-enhancing substances, unsportspersonlike penalties, fines, recruiting violations, and improper relationships are among the many news stories covered by the media. These are the images and messages with which society is presented on a daily basis, and because many people believe that sports build character, every case of deviance in sports leads them to be disappointed (Coakley, 2007). Athletes and coaches engage in outrageous behaviors, searching for ways to gain a competitive advantage; all the while the media and fans glorify these behaviors (Eitzen, 2009).

## DEFINING DEVIANCE

People who do not conform to social norms, or unquestionably accept them (often to extreme levels), may be labeled as deviant. *Deviant behavior* refers to actions "departing from an accepted social norm" (Woods, 2011, p. 318). Coakley notes that, "Deviance involves a departure from cultural ideals: the greater the departure, the more disruptive the action, the greater the deviance. Deviance always involves violating a norm" (p. 155). In other words, deviant behavior occurs when individuals, knowingly or not, act in ways that go against, are different from, or involve extreme adherence to, generally accepted appropriate behavior within a group or society.

### Underconformity and Overconformity to Social Norms

Although most actions fall into a normally accepted range of behaviors, deviance can occur in two different forms: overconformity and underconformity. *Underconformity* occurs when social norms are ignored or rejected (Coakley, 2007). Typically, researchers study deviant behavior from the perspective of actions and behaviors that do not conform to normal societal standards (Woods, 2011). Actions that break the law (e.g., assault, stealing, speeding) or break other societal norms and policies (e.g., cutting in line at the store, using employer resources for personal benefit) are considered deviant underconformity. Examples of deviant underconformity in sport include breaking official rules, an illegal hit on an opponent, and taking banned performance-enhancing substances. On the other end of the spectrum is deviant *overconformity*, or extreme, unquestioned acceptance of social norms (Coakley, 2007). Examples of deviant overconformity in sport include an athlete following a coach's orders even if they are against the rules, coaches and managers spending every waking hour watching film on their opponents, athletes playing through pain, and athletes going through extreme measures to lose weight for competition.

Coaches and teammates often encourage elite athletes to overconform to norms and high standards of training and competition (Donnelly, 1996; Howe, 2004; Waldron & Krane, 2005). In a study of competitive body-building and distance running, Ewald and Jiobu (1985) found that men showed many of the extreme characteristics of unquestioned overcon-formity. Other research has revealed that many elite athletes, including cyclists, gymnasts, and wrestlers, have also shown characteristics of overconformity, such as self-injurious overtraining, unhealthy eating habits, and training and playing sports with serious pain and injury (Coakley, 2007).

Athletes and coaches who underconform to sport norms are typically punished or reprimanded for their actions. However, when athletes and coaches overconform to sport norms, they are often praised and treated as heroes. Most elite and performance sports encourage extreme actions among athletes. The old saying, "no pain, no gain," is a wonderful ex-ample of this, in which coaches and trainers motivate athletes to go above and beyond normal limits. The excessive conforming by athletes and coaches, due to placing such a high priority on competition and winning, can put considerable pressure on other social relationships out-side of sport (e.g., friends and family), which may result in the uninten-tional sacrifice of these relationships and other responsibilities.

### Issues with Studying Deviant Behavior in Sport

One problem in the analysis of deviance is that so many different actions and behaviors can be defined as deviant, no single sociological theory can explain them all (Coakley, 2007). When sociologists study issues in sport, such as athletes using performance-enhancing substances, off-field violence involving athletes, or coaches violating recruiting rules, they can be examined by a number of different approaches and perspectives, with no clear right or wrong answer.

Another problem is that some actions and behaviors that are acceptable within the realm of sport would be considered deviant in other social realms, and some actions and behaviors that are acceptable outside of sport may be considered deviant within sport. What is normal in sport is often different than what is normal in other social realms. The same type of fights which occur in an ice hockey arena would not be acceptable in a bar or restaurant. Athletes are often labeled as heroes and tough when they put their physical health on the line during competitions, or play through pain, but teachers who go to work sick are instructed to go home. However, when athletes and coaches break rules or engage in other deviant behaviors because of an extreme acceptance of sporting norms, the line between underconformity and overconformity can be blurred. Because deviance in sports often involves an unquestioned acceptance of norms, this can lead to a rejection of the same norms.

## EXPLANATIONS FOR DEVIANT BEHAVIOR

Hughes and Coakley's (1991) research found four norms that were especially important to elite athletes, which they call the "sport ethic." These include: (a) extreme sacrifice and dedication to the game, (b) striving for distinction, (c) risk taking and playing through pain, and (d) challenging personal limits in the pursuit of possibilities. With a mindset like this, many athletes are motivated to do whatever it takes to be successful in competition. As Freeman (1998) notes, "You have to be selfish, getting ready for a game that only a handful of people understand. It's tough on the people around you. It's the most unspoken, but powerful, part of the game, that deep seated desire to be better at all costs, even if it means alienating your family and friends" (p. 1).

Legendary NFL head coach Vince Lombardi once said, "Winning isn't everything, it's the only thing." For many involved in sport, especially elite sports, the ultimate goal is to win, and as the value of winning increases, the temptation to put moral thoughts aside becomes very seductive (Woods, 2011). As the importance of winning increases among athletes and coaches, due to public praise, status and promotion, and great financial rewards, violence and other deviant behaviors will ultimately ensue in an effort to gain an advantage over the opponent. Lombardi is also credited with making the statement, "Second place is the first loser," and if this is true, and all of the praise and rewards go to the winner, then some in sports will do whatever it takes to be first. Athletes may take performance-enhancing drugs, coaches may illegally scout or recruit athletes, and administrators may alter transcripts so a student-athlete is eligible (Eitzen, 2009). Winning demands commitment and loyalty to goals, and an attitude of "by any means necessary."

This emphasis on competition and success can lead those involved to do whatever it takes to be successful. Lumpkin et al. (2003) suggest, "Often people defend violent and ethically questionable conduct on the premise that 'everyone else does it.' That is, an athlete may believe a violent behavior is justified if opponents are engaged in violent behaviors or cheating" (p. 70). A good example of this mindset can be found in a quote from former Major League Baseball (MLB) player Ken Caminiti, who once said, "It's no secret what's going on in baseball. At least half the guys are using steroids. They talk about it. They joke about it with each other....At first I felt like a cheater. But I looked around, and everybody was doing it" (Verducci, 2002). With such a heavy emphasis on winning in the sporting realm, many athletes (especially elite athletes) struggle with the choice of winning at all costs and demonstrating good sportsmanship (Woods, 2011). Coaches of elite sports, at both the college and professional level, are rewarded handsomely for winning, and because of that, the temptation to break the rules is constantly present (Eitzen, 2009). When national television coverage, conference championships, all-star selections, and million dollar contracts and endorsement deals are on the line athletes, coaches and administrators are often tempted to do whatever it takes to succeed. And many administrators and managers simply ignore, or overlook, overconformity and rules violations because they benefit from these deviant behaviors.

Coaches place such an emphasis on winning, that many times they will push their athletes to the edge physically, take them out of classes to focus on their sport, and even encourage the use of performance-enhancing substances (Eitzen, 2009). Coaches will also use both verbal and physical abuse to motivate and push players. Also, because of their authoritative position, coaches can intimidate players, just as many supervisors may be intimidating to their employees (Lumpkin et al., 2003). Playing through pain or injury is often seen as heroic and a badge of honor within competitive athletics. Eitzen (2009) suggests five reasons why athletes may insist on playing with pain: (a) athletes are socialized to accept pain and injury as part of the game; (b) fear of losing a starting position, or even a spot on the team; (c) wanting to prolong their career as long as possible; (d) pressure from coaches and teammates to play; and (e) wanting to sacrifice themselves for the good of the team.

Administrators, coaches, parents, and elite athletes who engage in deviant behavior are poor role models for young athletes. Whether they choose to be or not, professional and other elite athletes are role models for young athletes, and when kids see behaviors such as trash talking and cheating by their favorite players, it is only natural for them to try and emulate them when they play sports.

# TYPES OF DEVIANT BEHAVIOR IN SPORT

## Cheating and Rule Breaking as a Competitive Strategy

On-field deviant behavior can take many different forms, but primarily occurs when players and coaches break the rules of the game. Some examples of on-field deviance include corking a bat in baseball, a goalie using illegal pads in hockey, faking an injury, and holding in football. Players and fans view many of these occurrences as strategies rather than cheating (Eitzen, 2009). Rather than attempt to match opponents' skill and strategy, coaches and players spend time and effort on seeking ways to "bend the rules" in order to gain an advantage without being penalized (Lumpkin et al., 2003). Whether motivated by external rewards, or laziness, many athletes and coaches will look for ways around the rules to gain a competitive advantage. Shields and Bredemeier (1995) noted that many athletes and coaches interpret rules very loosely during competitions and create their own informal norms or rationalizations, which often bend or break official rules. As athletes reach more elite levels of sport, they have typically been playing for several years, honing their skills and learning the rules, and as they move up the competitive ladder, the action is faster, players are more skilled, and some rules become looser (Woods, 2011). There is evidence that on-field deviance occurs more often in power and performance sports, such as "good fouls" and "cheating when you can get away with it," because these athletes and coaches use cheating and on-field violence as a strategy during competition (Pilz, 1996; Shields et al., 1995).

In sport, there are written and "unwritten" rules. The written rules are the officially published rules for a sport, while the unwritten rules are informal norms that are generally known by athletes and coaches. For example, an unwritten rule in baseball is that if the opposing pitcher hits a team's star player with a pitch, the star player on the other team should expect to be hit his next at-bat. In hockey, a skater should never intentionally spray ice into the face of the opposing goalie. Athletes will often adapt to what the officials are calling and what they are allowing during the course of a competition, incorporating deviant behavior as a calculated strategy. This might include a player using her hockey stick to slow down an opponent, an offensive lineman in football subtly holding a rushing linebacker, or a basketball player using her hands or physical contact to disrupt an opponent.

One unwritten rule that seems to be broken on a regular basis is faking an injury as a strategy to gain an advantage. In soccer, players fall down holding their head or leg in agony, even if the opposing player did not touch them. Watch the World Cup or Major League Soccer game, and you will see players "acting," and one can observe similar instances in football, basketball, tennis, and the like. There are written rules against this type of behavior (e.g., delay of game, poor conduct), but if "acting" is not absolutely clear, the referees have no choice but to rule on the side of caution, because they do not know if the player is really injured or not. Most players would say that this form of cheating and rule breaking to gain an advantage goes against the integrity of the game, yet if in the same position, many seemingly choose the advantage.

As an illustrative example, in a 2010 game against the Tampa Bay Rays, New York Yankee star Derek Jeter was awarded first base by the umpire because the umpire thought the pitch had hit Jeter. Replay clearly showed that the ball actually hit the bat, it rolled into fair territory, and Jeter was thrown out. But because of Jeter's acting (waving his hand and holding it like it was hurt), which also involved the trainer for the Yankees to come out onto the field and evaluate Jeter, the umpire gave Jeter the free base. Jeter went on to score; however, the Yankees lost the game. After the game, Jeter made the following comment, "he (referring to the umpire) told me to go to first base. I'm not going to tell him, 'I'm not going to first base.' It's my job to get on base" (Smith, 2010). If players are rewarded, and rarely punished, for cheating behaviors in an attempt to gain an advantage, many will continue to do so.

## On-Field Violence within Competition

Violence was practically nonexistent in early sport, when sport was played informally for fun and recreational purposes, but as sport has become more competitive and structured, deviant behavior by coaches and players rose dramatically. As sport became more competitive, and an emphasis was placed on winning, violence became a tool that could be used to intimidate opponents. Athletes use intimidation in an attempt to scare the opponent in an effort to gain an advantage, and it can be a strong motivator for engaging in deviant behavior. Violence in sport is also often praised in the sport media. As a hit in football that knocks another player off his feet (often referred to as a "de-cleater") can be replayed over and over. Violent behaviors are often learned, and imitated, by athletes based on what they view in the media (Lumpkin et al., 2003).

They may not do this with the intent to cause a serious injury, but in an effort to gain a physical or psychological advantage over the opponent.

In non-contact sports, players are rarely rewarded for violent actions; however, this does not mean that violence is not used as a strategy. A tennis player might slam her racquet or yell at an opponent in an attempt to intimidate them. A baseball pitcher might use a "brush back" pitch to scare a batter from standing too close to home plate. However, the use of violence was taken to an extreme level when figure skater Tonya Harding was implicated in an off-ice attack against rival Nancy Kerrigan, during the 1994 U.S. Figure Skating Championships. Kerrigan was unable to continue in that particular competition, but was given a spot on the Olympic team, and came home with a silver medal.

In many contact and collision sports (e.g., boxing, football, ice hockey, lacrosse), players have used violence as deviant overconformity for years. Many performance sports like these demand aggressive and violence actions, such as body checking, blocking, and tackling (Eitzen, 2009). Violence in many of the contact and collision sports is often highly visible, and even celebrated. The media replays hard hits in football and hockey, a bench-clearing brawl in baseball, and other aggressive and violent plays over and over. Violent on-field behavior can also validate the self-worth of an athlete or reaffirm an athlete's identity. Hard and violent hits (whether within, or outside, the rules of play) can also be used as a form of intimidation against an opponent. However, the place of violence in sport becomes unclear when actions go beyond the rules of play, but are generally accepted by the players (Woods, 2011). Athletes like Baltimore Ravens' Ray Lewis are renowned for their aggressive on-field play. In many cases, aggression and violence are used to intimidate an opponent. Hines Ward, wide receiver for the Pittsburgh Steelers, known for his physical play and hard hitting blocks against defenders, was voted by his peers as the NFL's "Dirtiest Player" in 2009. Ward took this as a compliment, but responded to being called "dirty" by commenting, "When I go over the middle, those guys aren't going to tackle me softly and lay me down to the ground. That's not football. I find it ironic that now you see a receiver delivering blows, and it's an issue" (Deitsch, 2009).

Injuries and pain are part of sport. In fact, sprains, strains, broken bones, and concussions are a regular occurrence in heavy contact and collision sports. This constant physical abuse can have long-term consequences. Athletes participating in contact and collision sports not only risk their current health, but often the outcome of years of physical abuse to one's body results in lifelong injuries and disabilities. A 1990 survey of 870 retired NFL players found that nearly two-thirds had a permanent disability from playing football (Nack, 2001). In a another study of nearly 200 NCAA student-athletes (both male and female from 18 varsity sports), over 75% of the student-athletes reported sustaining a significant injury from competition, and over 45% experienced long-term effects from those injuries (Nixon, 1993). Intensive training programs, and violent physical contact in sports, have detrimental effects for all athletes involved (Eitzen, 2009). In many cases, athletes playing football, hockey, and other heavy contact and collision sports risk their long-term health for short-term rewards.

Aggressive behaviors and violence in these sports is expected, and often encouraged. Defensive players in football are taught to make the opponent's offensive players "pay the price" for making a play. In 1997, a Kansas City Chiefs player said on live radio that head coach Marty Schottenheimer once offered to pay the fines any of his players incurred for injuring any Denver Broncos player (Schefter, 1997). Research has shown that athletes, particularly male athletes in high-performance contact sports, readily accept certain forms of aggression and violence, even if it results in rule-violating behaviors (Pilz, 1996; Shields & Bredemeier, 1995; White & Young, 1997). For example, in professional ice hockey, players known as "enforcers" are a regular part of the game. Almost every team has a player (or two) who act as the team "bodyguard," and if the star player on their team is physically harassed, the enforcer will go after the violating opponent. In fact, former NHL player Marty McSorley made his living as Wayne Gretzky's personal bodyguard, playing with Gretzky in Edmonton and then following him to Los Angeles when The Great One was traded in 1988.

Even the courts often side with sport when it comes to the acceptance of on-field deviant behavior. They frequently rule that athletes who compete in contact and collision sports are voluntarily and knowingly putting their own health at risk, and even deviant behaviors, such as an illegal hit in football or a fight in hockey, are considered an assumed risk. Only when an act is so criminal that it goes above and beyond the assumed risks of a sport have athletes and coaches been charged by outside law enforcement agencies. Two examples of this in the National Hockey League (NHL) are Marty McSorley's high-sticking slash across the head of Donald Brashear in 2000, and Todd Bertuzzi's blindsided sucker punch to the back of Steve Moore's head in 2004. While Donald

Brashear was fortunate enough to come back and play after his incident, Steve Moore was not as lucky, as his professional hockey career ended that fateful day. However, over the past century of play for both professional football and ice hockey, one will only find a handful of criminal charges for on-field deviant actions. Following these incidents, in 2005, the NHL adopted new rules regarding fair play and fight instigation. More recently, in a response to the number of head injuries and an increase awareness of concussions, the NHL has adopted even stricter rules and harsher penalties for blind-sided hits and intentional hits to the head of opponents.

Professional athletes in contact and collision sports knowingly subject themselves to risks of their sports; however, the consequences for participating in these sports are not limited to the athlete's career. The average length of an NFL career is around 3-4 years; yet, players may face physical and mental problems for the rest of their lives. Former players suffer from a number of issues including being permanently disabled, wheelchair bound, cognitive problems, depression, dementia, and anger (Woods, 2011).

**Use of Performance-Enhancing Substances**

In recent years, one of the most common deviant behaviors discussed in sport has been that of the use of performance-enhancing substances, which are defined as any substance taken to aid and/or help bring about a better performance or outcome, whether the substance is within the rules of play or not. Athletes taking substances to help improve performance is nothing new. As far back as the ancient Olympic Games, athletes have used substances in an attempt to improve their performance (Woods, 2011). What is new is the amount of media attention given to performance-enhancing substances, governing bodies becoming more aware of the use and implementing more aggressive testing procedures, and athletes and scientists developing more sophisticated substances and methods that cannot be detected or that can mask their use (Woods, 2011).

Athletes have taken everything from herbal remedies and vitamins to synthetic drugs. Athletes use and abuse substances for a number of reasons: playing with pain or an injury, a fear of being cut from the team, a need to improve personal performance, and a desire to help the team win, among others. Because of this "do whatever it takes" mindset of many athletes, the temptation to use performance-enhancing substances is even greater, even to the detriment of their own long-term health. Athletes use drugs such as alcohol, marijuana, painkillers and anti-inflammatories to help them mask or overcome injuries, and some use other drugs such as cocaine and amphetamines to give them energy or deal with the anxiety and stress of competition. The culture of performance sports encourages players to "play hurt" or play with injury because it is for the greater good of the team. Coaches and trainers only compound this problem when they allow players to "pop a few pills" in order to minimize pain and get back on the field (Eitzen, 2009).

Another issue related to performance-enhancing drugs is how different teams, leagues, and sports define what is legal and what is not. Many organizations would agree that synthetic steroids and amphetamines should be banned substances, but what about natural supplements and vitamins? What about caffeine and energy drinks? Further, over-the-counter and prescription medications are used on a daily basis by athletes, for reasons ranging from getting over a cold and congestion, to pain relief. Athletes who play with constant pain, and take pain killers to help them function, can be at-risk for becoming addicted to these drugs, as admitted by Pro-Bowl quarterback, Brett Favre in an interview with *Sports Illustrated*'s Peter King (King, 1996). Athletes have taken stimulants for years in an attempt to focus or have more energy. The use of amphetamines, or "greenies," was rampant in Major League Baseball during the 1970's and 1980's. Players played 162 regular season games over the course of six months, meaning players were constantly on the road and, in many cases, playing games six or seven days of the week. They were not getting proper rest and needed help getting ready for games, so they would take greenies to give them the energy and focus needed to play such a demanding schedule. Nowadays, athletes at all levels can buy and use caffeine and energy drinks, although some international governing bodies ban them as well. The use of stimulants is nothing new.

Although the use of steroids is often credited with beginning by being used by former Soviet and Eastern European athletes, North American athletes have been found guilty as well (Woods, 2011). One of the most famous cases was Canadian sprinter, Ben Johnson, who was stripped of his gold medal after testing positive for anabolic steroids at the 1988 Summer Olympics in Seoul. American sprinters Marion Jones and Tim Montgomery were also thrown under a cloud of suspicion and eventually stripped of Olympic medals for their implication in the investigation into BALCO Laboratories in California. BALCO founder, Victor Conte, pleaded guilty to distributing illegal steroids and admitted to supplying performance-enhancing substances to other Olympic and professional athletes, including Barry Bonds (Woods, 2011). Although officially Barry Bonds holds the Major League Baseball single season homerun record (after hitting 73 in 2001), it is marred by controversy because of his relationship with BALCO and alleged use of "clear" and "cream" steroids.

Industry norms help explain why many athletes believe they need to take steroids. As Canadian weightlifter Jacques Demers noted, "To go to international competitions, you have to meet international standards and those based on what the Russians and Bulgarians do. They are the best weightlifters in the world, and they take steroids. So if I go to the Olympics, I must take steroids." (Rozin, 1995). In fact, a 1995 poll of U.S. Olympians and aspiring Olympians (Bamberger & Yaeger, 1997) asked the following questions, and illustrated the extreme overconformity of many elite athletes:

- Scenario One: You are offered a banned performance-enhancing substance, with two guarantees: (1) You will not get caught; (2) You will win. Would you take the substance?
    o  195 said yes, 3 said no
- Scenario Two: You are offered a banned performance-enhancing substance with two guarantees: (1) You will not be caught, (2) You will win every competition you enter for the next five years, and then you will die from the side effects of the substance. Would you take the substance?
    o  Still, more than half the athletes said yes

And the use of performance-enhancing substances is not just restricted to elite athletes. A 2001 survey commissioned by Blue Cross/Blue Shield found that approximately one million adolescent athletes between the ages of 12 and 17 were taking some form of dietary supplement or performance-enhancing drug to make them better athletes (Deam, 2001).

Testing for performance-enhancing substances remains a difficult challenge (Keating, 2005), from both a technological perspective and also a financial perspective. Because different organizations have different lists of banned substances and different policies, it can bring to light many of the issues related to the testing for drug and performance-enhancing substances. For example, MLB and the NFL have instituted strict drug testing policies, and test both during the season and in the off-season; however, the NBA and NHL only test during the season, which leaves the door open for players to use performance-enhancing substances in the off-season when they are training for the upcoming season (Woods, 2011). When it comes to performance-enhancing substances, such as doping, human growth hormone, and steroids, with increasingly better technology comes better performance-enhancing substances (both natural and artificial). This makes it more difficult for drug testing procedures to detect the presence of performance-enhancing substances in an athlete's body, creating what Coakley refers to as "a seemingly endless game of scientific hide and seek" (Coakley, 2007, p. 180).

## Off-Field Violence and Deviant Behavior

In addition to deviance that takes place during athletic competition, there are cases of off-field deviant behavior. This takes several forms, including off-field violence, hazing, and eating disorders.

### Off-Field Violence

Many people believe that it can be difficult for athletes who engage in aggressive and violent behaviors within their sport to just "shut it off" when they leave the field. Former NFL player John Niland once made the comment, "Any athlete who thinks he can be as violent as you can be playing football, and leave it all on the field, is kidding himself" (Falk, 1995, p. 12). Some argue that the use of certain performance-enhancing substances (such as anabolic steroids) can lead to an increase in aggression. In fact, researchers have shown that increased aggression and a heightened sexual drive are side effects of the use of certain performance-enhancing substances, specifically anabolic steroids (Levy, 1993). Others believe that athlete off-field violence is a problem, and suggest that athletes who choose to play contact sports may already be predisposed to violent behavior.

In recent years a number of high-profile athletes and coaches have gained public attention for off-field deviant actions. In 1992, boxing sensation Mike Tyson was found guilty of rape and sentenced to prison time. NFL player, Adam "Pacman" Jones, was implicated in a 2007 shooting in Las Vegas. Former St. Louis Cardinals manager, Tony LaRussa, was arrested for DUI in 2007. Pittsburgh Steelers quarterback, Ben Roethlisberger, was charged in 2010 with sexual assault of woman in a Georgia bar. And former Penn State football defensive coordinator, Jerry Sandusky, was charged for sexual molestation of young boys in 2011.

Eitzen (2009) suggests three reasons why male athletes are more likely than non-athletes to engage in deviant behavior off the field of play: (a) elite male athletes, because of the natural selection process of sports to select those who are more aggressive, dominant, and take risks, are different from their non-athlete peers; (b) athletic teams foster a spirit of exclusivity and solidarity, which encourages exaggerated male bonding and overconformity to fit in with the group; and (c) the celebrity status of athletes results in differential and preferential treatment, resulting in a sense of entitlement. Others, including Woods (2011), also suggest that athletes who go out in public and hang out at bars become the targets for "tough guys," and athletes who must be violent on the field have a difficult time not responding with physical force when they feel their "manhood" is being challenged.

Research examining off-field violence (e.g., violent crimes including assault and rape) involving athletes and coaches compared to the general population is scarce; however, the evidence suggests that although highly publicized, athletes do not commit these crimes as often as the general population (Coakley, 2007). Benedict and Yaeger (1998) found in a sample of NFL players that approximately 21% had been arrested for something more serious than just a minor crime (e.g., traffic violation) at least once since beginning college. In a related study, Blumstein and Benedict (1999) found that about 23% of males living in cities of 250,000 or more people are arrested for a serious crime during their lifetime, suggesting to the authors that the rates of athlete off-field violence are comparable to the general male population. The study also found evidence that the annual arrest rate of NFL players was less than half that of males in the general population. In a *Sports Illustrated*/CBS special investigation of college football programs, Benedict and Keteyian (2011) found that, of the 2,837 student-athletes on NCAA Division-I (FBS) top 25 teams, 7% of players had a criminal record, and nearly 40% of the 277 criminal incidents uncovered involved serious offenses (e.g., assault, battery, domestic violence, sexual offenses). Although the number of off-field criminal incidents involving college and professional athletes may be alarming, the research does show that the majority of athletes who compete in contact and collision sports are good citizens and do not continue their aggressive behavior off the field (Woods, 2011).

Though athletes and non-athletes appear to engage in similar levels of off-field violence, media attention related to the behaviors varies. The celebrity status of many athletes means that the media is more likely to report on their criminal activity. As illustrative examples, sexual assault charges against Kobe Bryant in 2004, and the Thanksgiving 2009 outing of Tiger Woods' infidelity garnered a great deal of national media attention; however, these same issues occur on a daily basis in our society, they just are not made public or played out in the media.

Off-field violence is not just an athlete problem. Spectators and fans can become violent as well. Many times students will "rush the field" at the conclusion of their team winning a big game. This creates a very dangerous environment, in which people may be injured, or even killed, during these mob stampedes. This was the case recently, at the end of the 2011 "Bedlam" football game between the University of Oklahoma and Oklahoma State University. At the conclusion of the game, OSU fans rushed the field after their team beat OU for the first time since 2002, and during the chaos and attempt to tear down the goalposts, over a dozen people were injured, some critically. Also in 2011, fans of the Vancouver Canucks rioted in the streets of Vancouver after their hometown hockey team lost game 7 of the Stanley Cup Finals. Philadelphia Eagle fans are notoriously known for throwing objects at opposing players, including beer and a battery hidden in a snowball.

*Hazing*

The National Federation of State High School Associations (NFHS), which publishes rules for 17 different sports and oversees numerous scholastic extra-curricular activities, defines hazing as, "any action or activity which inflicts physical or mental harm or anxiety, or which demeans, degrades or disgraces a person, regardless of location, intent or consent of participants" (NFHS, 2006). Hazing is often a ritual, or rite of passage, for new members of a group in order to be accepted by the rest of the group. Activities can be dangerous, and even deadly.

Athletes, like many other tight-knit social groups (e.g., fraternities, work groups), form strong bonds because they know exactly what each other go through on a daily basis and what it takes to perform at a high level. Due to a want and need for acceptance, new members to sports teams will often overconform and do whatever it takes to be accepted by teammates. Many teams will have some type of initiation, which often involves hazing, in which rookies will overconform and obey the veterans, even to demeaning and painful levels (Alfred University, 1999b; Woods, 2011). As defined by the NFHS and NCAA, hazing activities can include, but are not limited to, excessive consumption of alcohol, excessive physical punishment, food and sleep deprivation, engaging in sexual acts, vandalism, and other violent behaviors (Woods, 2011). Even after performing embarrassing and demeaning acts, many rookies will not report being hazed because of the need for acceptance and approval from veterans.

After a hazing incident involving the Alfred University football team, the university conducted studies of both high school student-athletes and college student-athletes regarding hazing. The studies (Alfred 1999a, 1999b) found:

- Both male and female student-athletes (at both levels) are at risk for hazing, but male student-athletes are at the highest risk
- For high school student-athletes:
  o Approximately 48% said they had been subjected to hazing activities, as defined by the survey; however, only 14% considered it hazing
  o 30% said they were required to perform an illegal act as part of initiation
  o 71% reported negative consequences as a result of the hazing
- For college student-athletes:
  o Approximately 80% said they had been subjected to hazing activities
  o Overall, 49% reported alcohol being involved in initiation activities
  o The three sports most likely to be involved in hazing activities are lacrosse, soccer, and swimming/diving teams
  o Although men, in general, were subjected to more dangerous, unacceptable initiation activities, women, more often, reported the use of alcohol

A few university athletic programs have made national news, including the cancellation of the 2000 Vermont men's hockey season and the suspension of the 2006 Northwestern women's soccer season, after hazing scandals were brought to the attention of the universities' athletic administrations. Consequences of hazing can be embarrassment, physical injury, and even death. The death of Alfred University student Chuck Stenzel in 1978, was part of the catalyst for the university's 1999 hazing study, and has stimulated national attention and research into hazing. As of 2011, 45 states have some form of ban on hazing, according to the website stophazing.com.

Elite athletes are highly competitive and often put their bodies through extreme measures to maximize their chances of success. Coaches and parents can often encourage this. If losing weight or maintaining a more culturally accepted body figure will help athletes' performance, they are likely to do whatever it takes to achieve this end (Woods, 2011). Eating disorders developed by many athletes is the result of deviant overconformity. Athletes in sports that focus on weight limits or physical appearance, such as cheerleaders, gymnasts, figure skaters, and wrestlers, are generally at the greatest risk for developing an eating disorder. Three of the most common eating disorders among athletes are *anorexia nervosa*, *bulimia nervosa*, and *compulsive or excessive exercise*. Anorexia occurs when people starve themselves and greatly limit their food intake in an effort to achieve or maintain an ideal body image or weight. Bulimia is exhibited by binge eating followed by purging. Excessive or compulsive exercise is characterized by people exercising to the point of overexercising, all in an effort to lose weight or maintain a certain body image (Woods, 2011).

A 1992 University of Washington study found that approximately one-third of female college athletes practiced some form of deviant weight control, and among female college gymnasts, the rate was almost two-thirds (Ryan, 1995). Although eating disorders are more prevalent among female athletes, male athletes do suffer from eating disorders as well (Sundgot-Borgen & Torstveit, 2004). Male wrestlers trying to make a specific weight class perform some of the most extreme weight control methods. University of Michigan wrestler Jeff Reese died after shedding seventeen pounds in two days, by limiting his fluid and caloric intake and wearing a rubber suit while riding a stationary bike in a "sweat room" which had been heated to ninety-two degrees (Fleming, 1998). Although these extreme measures to lose weight by wrestlers has long been the "norm" within the sport, after the death of multiple college wrestlers, the NCAA quickly implemented rule changes related to weight loss methods and the weight-in process before a meet (Eitzen, 2009).

On the flip side, for some athletes, overeating in an attempt to gain weight can be just as much of an issue. This issue is very common in football, especially with offensive and defensive linemen. As the average weight of an American goes up, so too does the weight of athletes. In fact, there were only three players over 300 pounds playing in the NFL in

1980. Jump forward thirty years, and there were 532 players over 300 pounds at NFL training camps in 2010 (Longman, 2011). Coaches encourage lineman to gain weight because being bigger in the trenches can often give a team a distinct advantage. Though this may be an advantage on the field, if weight is not controlled after retirement, it can pose numerous health threats to these athletes. Although research is equivocal, some studies have found that retired NFL players are at a greater risk for high blood pressure, heart disease, diabetes, and stroke, and have a higher mortality rate than the general population (Longman, 2011). Jerry Kramer, a former All-Pro lineman for the Green Bay Packers, once said, "Fat doesn't make you strong and quick. It makes you heavy. We've gotten enamored with the 300-pounder, but give me an offensive guard who's in great shape at 270 or 275 and understands leverage and positioning, and I'll bet he'll whip the fat guy every time" (Longman, 2011, p. 1D). In fact, the weight issue has even spread to high schools, where some studies suggest that over half of high school linemen are overweight (Longman, 2011). If more coaches had the same mindset as Jerry Kramer, the overeating problem among football players may be curved.

Eating disorders are dangerous, and can even be deadly, especially among athletes, who need fluids and nutrients. Coaches and parents need to understand these dangers, and aid athletes in proper eating and weight control methods, whether an attempt to gain or lose weight.

## CURBING DEVIANT BEHAVIOR

As long as athletes and coaches emphasize performance and winning and accept the use of performance-enhancing substances as a means to an end, these values will promote risk taking and self-sacrifice in the pursuit of individual and team goals (Coakley, 2007). Owners, administrators, coaches, sponsors, and other stakeholders often benefit from athlete overconformity, so why would they want things to change? Even in other societal realms, such as business and medicine, those individuals who put in the time and hard work are often praised and rewarded, so why should sport be any different? Because of this, controlling deviant behavior, especially overconformity, can be very difficult, and although deviant underconformity seems to be much easier to identify and punish, it still poses problems to controlling it.

Although rule breaking continues to persist in sports, many believe that improved officiating, clearer rules, and video replay will help curb cheating as a strategy (Dunning, 1999). Rulebooks for some sport organizations are hundreds, or even thousands, of pages long. Organizations like the International Olympic Committee (IOC), the World Anti-Doping Agency (WADA), and the NCAA continue to add new policies and rules every year to address deviant behavior. As new rules are added each year, the penalties for deviant behavior are becoming more severe. At the high school and college levels, player suspensions are more common (and longer in length); and at the professional level players may face fines of thousands of dollars and possible suspensions. Coaches have been fined, suspended, and even fired for deviant behavior and violating rules. Schools and athletic programs can lose out on huge financial rewards if caught violating the rules (Woods, 2011). Punishment for deviant professional athletes has been the subject of much media attention. Fining a NFL player (who makes millions) $10,000 for an illegal hit will not necessarily discourage the deviant behavior. However, handing down suspensions, and therefore prohibiting their ability to participate in the sport they love, might have a more immediate impact on future behaviors.

The leadership and behavior of the coach is paramount for change to occur when it comes to deviant behavior in sport (Bredemeier & Shields, 2006). Those in authority and leadership positions (e.g., administrators, coaches, parents) need to place limits on athletes, especially children and adolescents. Questions need to be raised about the goals and purpose of sport and its meaning in our society. Coaches should place less emphasis on winning and more emphasis on enjoyment and skill development (especially with younger athletes). Resolving drug issues lies with parents, coaches, managers, and other leaders in sport. A new attitude and creative solutions must emerge for any real changes to occur (Woods, 2011). Administrators and coaches also need to educate athletes and parents about the different forms of deviant behavior, the consequences of such behavior, and develop policies to help control and restrict deviant behavior.

Coakley (2007) suggests a few strategies for controlling deviant behavior in sport:

- Critically examine the deep hypocrisy involved in elite power and performance sport.
- Establish rules indicating clearly that certain risks are undesirable and unnecessary in sports.
- Establish rules stating that injured athletes are not allowed to play until certified as "well" by independent doctors.

- Create clear and harsh punishment for managers, coaches, and athletes who engage in deviant behavior.
- Establish educational programs for athletes, coaches, administrators, and parents on deviant behavior and its consequences.

By adopting these steps, sport managers can help to curb deviance in their sport contexts.

## CHAPTER SUMMARY

The nature of competitive sport requires commitment and dedication in order to be successful. Athletes and coaches throughout history have looked for ways to gain an advantage over an opponent, and sometimes this dedication results in deviant behavior. Deviant behavior is condoned, taught, and even rewarded because of the value placed on winning in competitive sport. The expected norm in sport is to push the rules and officials as far as possible, and live on the edge of risk and reward, in order to win. Although the majority of sport-related actions fall within normal ranges of acceptable behavior, when athletes and coaches do engage in deviant behavior, it can take the form of overconformity, or underconformity, to sport and social norms. Whether it is in-game cheating as a strategy or the taking of performance-enhancing substances during training, deviant behaviors in sport will continue unless those who control sport re-examine their motives and reflect on the purpose and meaning of sport in society.

## DISCUSSION QUESTIONS

1. What would you define as "deviant behavior"? Do you think that the range of acceptable behavior changes over time? Why or why not?
2. Do you believe that certain types of deviant behavior are worse than others? If yes, give some examples and explain why. If no, why not?
3. Coaches are teachers, and are often looked up to as parental figures. What lessons are coaches teaching if they ask their players to cheat?
4. Should intimidation be taught, and used, as a strategy to win? How far is too far?
5. What suggestions do you have for sport organizations and governing bodies when it comes to controlling deviant behavior, such as cheating and rule breaking, using violence as a strategy, taking performance-enhancing substances, or engaging in extreme dietary measures?

# RECOMMENDED READINGS

Margolis, J. A. (1999). *Violence in sports: Victory at what price?* Berkeley Heights, NJ: Enslow Publishers. (This book examines how violence in many of today's sports is seen as just part of the game, even if those actions would get you arrested if performed outside of sport. It discusses the influence that parents, coaches and the media have on athletes, reasons for violence within our sporting culture today, and how we as a society need to re-examine our attitudes and values.

McCloskey, J., & Bailes, J. E. (2005). *When winning costs too much: Steroids, supplements, and scandal in today's sports.* Boulder, CO: Taylor Trade Publishing. (This book examines the issue, and place, of performance-enhancing drugs in today's sports. It takes a look at why many coaches encourage the use of performance-enhancing substances, why many athletes are prone to use them, and how much of this motivation is created by our culture placing such a high value on winning. The authors also present possible solutions to the issue of performance-enhancing drug use in sports.)

# REFERENCES

Alfred University. ( 1999a). *High school hazing: How many students are hazed?* Retrieved from http://www.alfred.edu.

Alfred University. (1999b). *National survey of NCAA sports teams.* Retrieved from http://www.alfred.edu.

Bamberger, M., & Yaeger, D. (1997, April, 14). Over the edge: Aware that drug testing is a sham, athletes seem to rely more than ever on banned performance enhancers. *Sports Illustrated*, pp. 62.

Benedict, J., & Keteyian, A. (2011, March 2). College football and crime. *SI.com*. Retrieved from http://si.com.

Benedict, J., & Yaeger, D. (1998). *Pros and cons: The criminals who play in the NFL.* New York, NY: Warner Books.

Blumstein, A., & Benedict, J. (1999). Criminal violence of NFL players compared to the general population. *Chance, 12*, 12-15.

Bredemeier, B. L., & Shields, D. L. (2006). Sports and character development. President's Council on Physical Fitness and Sports. *Research Digest, 7.*

Coakley, J. (2007). *Sports in society: Issues and controversies* (9th ed.). New York, NY: McGraw-Hill.

Deam, J. (2001, September 9). Sports craze. *Denver Post*, pp. 4K.

Deitsch, R. (2009). Dirtiest NFL player: Steelers' Ward. *SI.com*. Retrieved from www.si.com.

Donnelly, P. (1996). The local and the global: Globalization in the sociology of sport. *Journal of Sport and Social Issues, 20*, 239-257.

Dunning, E. (1999). *Sport matters: Sociological studies of sport, violence, and civilization*. London: Routledge.

Eitzen, D. S. (2009). *Fair and foul: Beyond the myths and paradoxes of sport* (4th ed.). Lanham, MD: Rowman & Littlefield Publishers, Inc.

ESPN. (2011). The steroids era. Retrieved from www.espn.com.

Ewald, K., & Jiobu, R. M. (1985). Explaining positive deviance: Becker's model and the case of runners and bodybuilders. *Sociology of Sport Journal, 2,* 144-156.

Falk, W. B. (1995, January 8). Bringing home the violence. *Newsday*, pp. 12-13.

Fleming, D. (1998, January 5). Wrestling's dirty secret. *Sports Illustrated*, pp. 134.

Freeman, M. (1998, September 6). A cycle of violence, on the field and off. *New York Times*. Retrieved from http://www.nytimes.com.

Howe, P. D. (2004). *Sport, professionalism and pain: Ethnographies of injury and risk.* London: Routledge.

Hughes, R., & Coakley, J. (1991). Positive deviance among athletes: The implications of overconformity to the sport ethics. *Sociology of Sport Journal, 8,* 307-325.

Keating, P. (2005, December 5). Baseball has solved its steroid problem – at least that's what they want you to believe. *ESPN The Magazine.*

King, P. (1996, May 27). Bitter pill. *Sports Illustrated.* Retrieved from www.si.com.

Lapchick, R. (1999). Race, athletes and crime. Special Issue, *Sports Business Journal.*

Levy, D. (1993, June 2). Steroid mood effect "dramatic." *USA Today*, pp. 1A.

Longman, J. (2011, January 29). NFL linemen tip the scales. *New York Times*, pp. 1D.

Lumpkin, A., Stoll, S. K., & Beller, J. M. (2003). *Sport ethics: Applications for fair play* (3rd ed.). New York, NY: McGraw-Hill.

Nack, W. (2001, May 7). The wrecking yard. Retrieved from www.si.com.

National Federation of State High School Associations (NFHS). (2006). Sexual harassment and hazing: Your actions make a difference! Retrieved from www.nfshsa.org.

Nixon, H. L. (1993). Accepting the risks of pain and injury in sport: Mediated cultural influences on playing hurt. *Sociology of Sport Journal, 10,* 183-196.

Pilz, G. A. (1996). Social factors influencing sport and violence: On the "problem" of football and hooliganism in Germany. *International Review for Sociology of Sport, 31,* 49-68.

Rozin, S. (1995, June 19). Steroids: A spreading peril. *Business Week*, pp. 177.

Ryan, J. (1995). *Little girls in pretty boxes: The making and breaking of elite gymnasts and figure skaters.* New York, NY: Warner Books.

Schefter, A. (1997, November 22). Chiefs players confirm what the coach won't. *Denver Post*, pp. 7C.

Shields, D. L., & Bredemeier, B. L. ( 1995). *Character development and physical activity.* Champaign, IL: Human Kinetics.

Shields, D. L., Bredemeier, B. L., Gardner, D. E., & Bostrom, A. (1995). Leadership, cohesion, and team norms regarding cheating and aggression. *Sociology of Sport Journal, 12,* 324-336.

Smith, J. (2010). On cue, New York Yankees' Derek Jeter goes into acting mode. Retrieved from www.tampabay.com.

Sundgot-Borgen, J., & Torstveit, M. K. (2004). Prevalence of eating disorders in elite athletes is higher than in the general population. *Clinical Journal of Sport Medicine, 14*, 25-32.

Verducci, T. (2002, June 3). Totally juiced. *Sports Illustrated*, pp. 34-48.

Waldron, J., & Krane, V. (2005). Whatever it takes: Health compromising behaviors in female athletes. *Quest, 57*, 315-329.

White, P., & Young, K. (1997). Masculinity, sport, and the injury process: A review of Canadian and international evidence. *Avante, 3*, 1-30.

Woods, R. B. (2011). *Social issues in sport* (2nd ed.). Champaign, IL: Human Kinetics.

# CHAPTER 11

## SPORT AND COMMUNITY

Stacy Warner

***

**Learning Objectives**

After reading this chapter, you should be able to:

1. Discuss the role that sport can play in creating community.
2. Define a sense of community and the benefits of individuals experiencing a sense of community.
3. Identify the factors that have been found to foster a sense of community within sport.
4. Demonstrate an understanding of the differences between a psychological and sociological perspective.
5. Define social capital, and demonstrate an understanding of how sport can aid in increasing one's social capital.
6. Identify the three primary sporting schemes that can be used to build community.


## INTRODUCTION

Sport is commonly considered a realm that draws people together, a "social glue," and a key contributor to the creation of community (Schimmel, 2003; Spaaij, 2009; Warner & Dixon, 2011). This "community" that sport can foster and enhance is often defined in two important ways (Gusfield, 1975; Heller, 1989): that based on geographical location and boundaries, and that based on the common source of interest or activity for a collective entity. In geographically bound communities, local recreation departments or even professional teams will use sport in an effort to bring together individuals in a defined city, town, or neighborhood. Sport, in this instance, creates a point of identification or a social anchor for members who reside in a specific area. This is especially the case if sport programming or sporting events include competitions against other nearby towns, cities, or rivals. Typically, through a strong identification *and* active membership within a defined neighborhood or city represented by a sports team, individuals can experience a greater identification with their community and an enhanced sense of community.

In the second way community is typically defined, communities of interest, participants or members all have a common interest in being active participants, athletes, or fans of a sport. A local running group or participants in a church softball league would be examples of communities of interest. Another example of a community of interest would be group of New York Yankees fans that gather at a local sports bar to watch their beloved Yankees play. These communities are often referred to as communities of interest because the groups of individuals that make them up share a common devotion to an activity and feel a strong sense of community. Further, it is important to note that contemporary society typically develops community in this type of manner, where interests and skills are more central to the community as opposed to locality (Durkheim, 1933).

Regardless of the type of community sport fosters, a common thread through both definitions of "community" is that individuals who are members of a healthy community will experience a strong sense of community (Bess et al., 2002). That is, individuals who are a part of a healthy geographically bound neighborhood setting or a community centered on her or his sport interests will both experience a strong sense of community. Sense of community is most simplistically defined as an environmental or community characteristic that leads to members feeling a sense of belonging and attachment (cf. Sarason, 1974). It is important to understand, though, that sense of community goes beyond just identification with a community. In other words, an individual can identify with a place or group and still not experience a sense of community. For instance, an individual can identify her- or himself as a resident of Greenville, NC, but that does not imply that the individual feels a strong sense of community. Or students may identify themselves as student members of their university, but not feel a sense of belonging or attachment; hence, their sense of community with the university is nonexistent. In an effort to better understand the role of sport in fostering community, a deeper understanding of the term sense of community and its evolution is necessary. This section will be then followed by sections addressing the benefits of experiencing community, current trends in US society, and a look at how sport intersects with this information.

# SENSE OF COMMUNITY

Sarason (1974) has been credited with first defining and coining the term "sense of community." In his book, *The Psychological Sense of Community: Prospects for a Community Psychology,* he called for the new discipline of community psychology to develop with this concept at its core. Interestingly, Sarason's early work was primarily within the mental health community. It was within this setting that he became dedicated to dispelling the myth that separate residential communities or special classes for individuals with disabilities were a productive way to provide assistance; rather, Sarason asserted that such environments only led to isolation and feelings of not being accepted by others, and thus denied people of the basic need for belonging and a sense of community.

Although his work was primarily geared at advancing the way individuals thought about addressing mental health issues, Sarason soon realized a broad based study of community psychology and this idea of a "sense of community" were important to all individuals across communities and contexts. In fact, the discipline of community psychology continues to operate with this concept at its core and under the premise that a healthy community is one in which a strong sense of community is present for individuals and the collective community (Bess et al., 2002).

At the most fundamental level, sense of community is grounded in Maslow's Theory of Motivation (1943). According to Maslow, after the primary physiological and safety needs are met, individuals have an innate desire and motivation for interpersonal interaction and to feel a sense of belonging. This center or third level of Maslow's Hierarchy of Needs is referred to as Love/Belonging. From an evolutionary standpoint this makes sense, as individuals who were in both intimate and social relationships were not only more likely to reproduce, but they obviously also had a greater chance of survival (cf. Baumeister & Leary, 1995). Thus at the most basic level, Maslow's Theory of Motivation provides the foundation that supports the importance and vitality of belongingness and a sense of community to all individuals.

Considering this, it is not surprising that Sarason described the concept of sense of community as being analogous to hunger—it is a fundamental need, and individuals know when they experience it and when they do not. Although an exact definition of sense of community is still heavily debated in the literature, Sarason (1974) defined sense of community as an environmental characteristic that leads individuals to perceive that support is available from a larger and more stable structure.

## McMillan and Chavis' Sense of Community Theory

McMillan and Chavis (1986) provided further theorizing on the topic of community. They suggested that sense of community was based on four components: *Membership, Influence, Integration and Fulfillment of Needs,* and *Shared Emotional Connections.* The authors also theorized that these elements worked in concert with one another to create a sense of community among individuals. Their theorizing continues to be widely recognized, acknowledged, and accepted in the community psychology literature (Chipuer & Pretty, 1999).

McMillan and Chavis (1986) defined *membership* as having to do with boundaries (e.g., dress, ritual, language, common symbol systems) that created a distinction between those who belong and those who do not belong. Sense of belonging and emotional safety of individuals were also included as important indicators of *Membership.* Effectively, this component results in the formation of in-groups and out-groups (see Cunningham, 2007; Cunningham & Sagas, 2005). An example of this would be athletes and non-athlete groups. Athletes are more likely to feel a sense of *Membership* with other athletes based on the fact that they typically dress similarly and use language and jargon associated with their sport. McMillan and Chavis acknowledged that this component was the most troublesome to researchers because a majority of the existing literature had focused on the deviant behaviors often resulting from group formation, membership, and boundaries. However, McMillan and Chavis were quick to point out that this literature overlooked and almost dismissed the importance that membership and boundaries have in creating an environment where intimate social bonds and emotional safety can be found and fostered.

*Influence* was comprised of actions that led members to being empowered by the group and also feeling empowered to influence the group and its direction. Thus, *Influence* was bi-directional. This particular component was primarily supported by group cohesion research, which has concluded that a positive and significant relationship exists between cohesiveness and a community's influence over a member to conform (see Lott & Lott, 1965). This body of literature also supports the fact that individuals are drawn to communities where they are most likely to be influential. To use the athlete example again, an athlete who feels that she has the ability to inspire or impact her teammates demonstrates the element of *Influence*.

*Integration and Fulfillment of Needs* was based on the idea that resources and support were available at the group level for individuals. Simply, McMillan and Chavis (1986) summed this up as "reinforcement" and concluded that individuals are drawn to others who can provide them with some benefit. For example, an athlete who feels as though his identity and self-esteem are reinforced through the sporting environment exhibits *Integration and Fulfillment of Needs*. Note the similarity to Rappaport's (1977) person-environment fit research, which demonstrates this gravitation of individuals towards environments that are rewarding to them in some way.

*Shared Emotional Connections* was grounded in the idea that it is important for individuals to share a common history and a common set of experiences. This particular component was supported by the contact hypothesis (see Allan & Allan, 1971; Allport, 1954), which argues that individuals who have more contact with one another are more likely to form social bonds. An example of *Shared Emotional Connections* would be athletes experiencing a history of victories or losses together, overcoming a scandal, or even an emotional loss of a loved one.

In sum, McMillan and Chavis' Sense of Community Theory has provided the foundation work for understanding how and when a sense of community developed.

**Sociological View on Sense of Community**

While the concept of a sense of community has its roots in community psychology, researchers have gradually shifted to also viewing the concept from a sociological perspective, with a focus on social structures, social interaction, and institutional factors. In other words, sociologists are concerned with matters of society not matters of individual members. For example, Emile Durkheim, one of the most respected and prolific researchers in sociology, put forth the idea of anomie in two of his classic books, *Suicide* (1951) and *The Division of Labor in Society* (1933), using the term to describe the environmental state in which a breakdown of societal structures and regulations for individuals resulted in feelings of alienation and isolation. Durkheim concluded that anomie and anomic conditions were major contributors to the increases in longitudinal suicide trends that he observed across different societies. This empirical study of a social phenomenon demonstrated how a purely psychological approach to evaluating suicide, an issue many would consider only as an individual problem, would have missed and diminished the crucial role that social structures played in explaining the trends.

Anomie and this sociological perspective are also important to consider because, by definition, anomie is posited as being the direct opposite or antithesis of a sense of community. That is, if a person is experiencing anomie, she or he is not experiencing a sense of community and vice versa. While anomie has sociological roots and has focused on social structures and institutions, sense of community research has typically focused more on just the individual and only the individual's outcomes. This difference is most likely due to sense of community being a derivative of the psychological discipline. Viewing sense of community through a sociological lens (similar to the sociological treatment of anomie) is essential though, as it helps place the focus on the social structures and institutional factors; furthermore, this perspective highlights the important part that sport can play in fostering it. When considering the benefits of experiencing a sense of community and the role sport can play in fostering it for the community as a whole, the value of sport in society becomes more evident.

**Benefits of Experiencing a Sense of Community**

Sense of community and the social structures that foster it are important to understand because of their potential impact on groups of individuals and communities. Research on sense of community has demonstrated it to be a vital factor in enhancing numerous quality of life factors for individuals and communities. For example, greater levels of sense of community are associated with improved well-being (Davidson & Cotter, 1991). Among adolescents, individuals with higher levels of sense of community have significantly less drug use and delinquency behaviors (Battistich & Hom, 1997); this obviously has ramifications for individuals but also benefits the community as a whole. On the other hand, a lack of community (i.e., high anomie) is associated with a host of negative outcomes, including deviant behavior (Agnew, 1997; Carter & Carter, 2007; Hagan & McCarthy, 1997; Hirschi, 1969) and physical and mental health decrements (Berkman et al., 2000; Deflem, 1989). Thus, the importance and ability of fostering community to address a variety of life quality concerns and issues has been well established in literature.

Within the sport literature, numerous scholars have placed significant attention on issues related to better understanding how to retain athletes (e.g., Green, 2005; Lim et al., 2011), understanding how sport employees and participants are impacted by work-family issues (e.g., Dixon & Bruening, 2007; Dixon et al., 2006), and how to reduce athlete burnout (e.g., Smith et al., 2007). Consequently, it is important to note that research has also shown that sense of community has been tied to improved retention (McCarthy et al., 1990; McCole, 2006; Kellett & Warner, 2011), reduced work-family conflict (Royal & Rossi, 1996; Voydanoff, 2004), and reduced burnout (McCarthy et al., 1990). Thus, this provides evidence that increasing sense of community could aid in addressing important issues that have been specifically highlighted in the management of sport as well. Furthermore, considering the current negative trends in relation to individuals and the lack of community in American society, sport may be able to play an important role in reversing trends.

## CURRENT US TRENDS: INDIVIDUALS AND COMMUNITY

As noted by Durkheim (1933) and previously mentioned, contemporary society tends to develop and form communities based on interests and skills rather than around a geographical location or neighborhood setting. Subsequently, the literature has recently noted this type of community (i.e., community of interest) is rapidly declining in American society. Putnam (2000) explicitly highlighted this fact in the popular book, *Bowling Alone: The Collapse and Revival of American Community*. The use of "bowling" in the title helps further capture the role that many believe sports *should* play in the creation of community. Putnam's main thesis of the book, and the title specifically, was that despite the fact that more individuals are bowling than ever before, fewer individuals are participating in bowling leagues and reaping the social benefits of being in community. He went on to further highlight how this decline in community and consequently, declining social connections and social capital, negatively impacted civic participation and social trust.

Social capital refers to the economic benefits that result from the interpersonal relationships with others in and between social networks (Mitchell, 1974). In other words, the more individuals are connected to others, the greater the chances are for them to gain access to important advice, jobs, resources, and even political clout (Kilduff & Tsai, 2007). All of these resources, or social capital attributable to one's social and professional relationships, can have economic and financial benefits. Through these cooperative personal relationships, an individual who possesses social capital will have a dense social network (cf. Warner et al., 2012). A dense social network is one that consists of a variety of diverse social ties and connections. That is, individuals with social capital will have many non-redundant social ties (Kilduff, & Tsai, 2007) and are connected to individuals in many different social circles.

Along with this general decline of social capital and community it is not surprising that research has also demonstrated that social isolation is increasing. McPherson and colleagues' (2006) research further supports the declining trend in individuals experiencing a sense of community. This research explored and compared data from 1985 to 2004, and verified a few noteworthy and alarming trends. McPherson and colleagues' findings indicated that the number of individuals who reported that they do not have anyone to discuss important matters with had tripled over that 20-year span. Overall, the results also signified that individuals were making fewer social contacts through volunteer associations and neighborhoods; consequently, this helped explain why they also found that individuals had few discussion partners and confidants.

These trends are indicative of the fact that individuals are likely not experiencing a healthy community, or in other words, a community in which they feel a strong sense of community towards both the individual and collective levels (Bess et al., 2002). These trends are troubling because they reveal that important socio-emotional needs of individuals are not being met for many individuals in the US, this despite the technological advances seemingly allowing for such connections. Thus, people are more likely to feel isolated. Recent work, nonetheless, has pointed towards sport becoming part of the solution to reversing these alarming trends.

## RECENT WORK IN UNDERSTANDING SENSE OF COMMUNITY

Early research on sense of community was primarily focused on neighborhood settings and continued to utilize and support McMillan and Chavis' Sense of Community Theory (1986). More recently, though, sense of community research has slowly evolved to where researchers have progressively geared their focus away from geographical neighborhood settings. These scholars are now more focused on communities of interest—the more prominent way in which community develops in contemporary society. While previous research within neighborhood contexts clearly supported McMillan and Chavis' (1986) theory, the more current research within communities of interests and other settings has challenged and expanded the boundary conditions of their theory.

As a illustrative example of these dynamics, and perhaps of particular interest to sport, a study on sense of community within the workplace suggested that competition has an impact on a sense of community (Pretty & McCarthy, 1991). More specifically, gender differences may exist among how women and men perceive competition in influencing sense of community in workplace. Pretty and McCarthy (1991) suggested that competition might promote a sense of community for males while it detracts from a sense of community for females in workplace. Consequently, such research outside of neighborhood settings could have many practical applications in various contexts including but not limited to sport contexts.

Despite the fact that numerous sport organizations explicitly state that fostering a sense of community is one of their main goals, a paucity of research exists on how and when this is accomplished through sport. Clopton's (2007, 2008, 2009) along with Warner and Dixon's (2011, in press) research all have recently attempted to fill this noted gap in the literature. While their research has been solely focused on the university sport experience, their findings further point to the academic and quality of life benefits of experiencing a sense of community via sport. For example, improved student retention, overall improved well-being (including evaluated mood), greater attachment to the university, increased social networking opportunities, and increased involvement with other on-campus activities were just a few of the benefits of a sense of community that were identified (Warner, 2010).

## BUILDING COMMUNITY VIA SPORT

In the following section, I outline the ways in which sport can be used as a tool to build community, with a particular focus on participatory sport, community-based sporting events, and fanship and spectatorship. I emphasize that sport needs to be designed and managed so the community experienced for individuals is maximized. In other words, the mere presence of sport does not instantaneously create a community.

### Participatory Sport

Warner and Dixon's (2011, in press) qualitative studies identified seven important factors that were fundamental to fostering a sense of community among athletes: *Administrative Consideration, Common Interest, Competition, Equity in Administrative Decisions, Leadership, Social Spaces,* and *Voluntary Action.* These factors work in concert with one another to facilitate the development of community with a sport setting.

Administrative Consideration involves sport personnel and staff demonstrating they care about the athletes as people, as opposed to just recognizing them as athletes. When sport personnel and staff are intentional and sincere in offering this type of care and concern for athletes, a stronger sense of community is built. Along with this, it is necessary to have a Common Interest. Warner and Dixon identified this as "The group dynamics, social networking, and friendships that resulted from individuals being brought together by the common interest of the sport (and combined with a common goal, shared values, or other unifying factors)."

Warner and Dixon also found Competition to be an important factor in sport settings. This factor entails the challenge to excel against internal (e.g., competing against teammates) and external rivalries (e.g., competing against other teams). It should be noted that Warner and Dixon determined that this particular component was moderated by gender, such that men generally found internal and external competition to foster community; however, only external competition fostered community for women. Furthermore, women in their studies indicated that internal competition (i.e., competing against teammates) was harmful to the community.

It is also important community members perceive Equity in Administrative Decisions. This is vital because it demonstrates to all individuals and community members that everyone will be treated fairly. Intuitively this makes sense because individuals are more likely to thrive in an environment where they perceive fairness.

Leadership Opportunities empower community members to guide and direct activities and others. When Leadership Opportunities are available individuals are more likely to buy into the community. If community members do not feel like they have a voice or leadership opportunities, they are more likely to leave the community (cf. Hirschman, 1970).

When trying to build community through sport, it is also important to consider the role of Social Spaces, or a common physical space where individuals can interact. Swyers' (2005, 2010) ethnographic research on

Chicago Cubs fans captured the essence and importance of having a physical space that allows community to develop. Swyers immersed herself in the culture of being a fan at Wrigley Field and utilized participant observation and informal interviews to guide her work. Her ethnographic research in particular demonstrated that having a certain assigned section of bleachers at Wrigley Field was imperative to the fostering of community. For athletes, this often means a Social Space away from the playing field such as locker rooms or even a designated pub is essential to building community (Kellett & Warner, 2011; Warner & Dixon, 2011).

Voluntary Action involves the participation in a community when little external pressure existed. That is, when members join a community on their own free will and without tangible external incentive or peer pressure, a greater sense of community is fostered. For example, if peers or parents pressure athletes to participate in a sport, it is likely that the athletes will not experience a strong sense of community because Voluntary Action is absent.

This emerging line of research suggests that all the noted factors should be carefully evaluated and considered when considering the role of sport in building community. This work also reiterates the fact that community does not always occur when sport in present. Rather the noted factors must work in concert with one another to build community within sport.

## Community-Based Sporting Events

Another way that sport and community are often intertwined is through community-based sporting events. Communities will host different participatory sporting events, such as bike races, triathlons, 5K runs, and marathons, or even more spectator-based hallmark and mega-events, such as the Tour de France or the Super Bowl. Community members will often serve as volunteers that assist in administering the event or as active sport participants. Again, the events are typically positioned as a means of fostering a sense of community or community development. As a case in point, Chalip (2006a) identified "community development" as one of the five major legitimations or justifications of sport. (Health, salubrious socialization, economic development, and national pride were the other major legitimations Chalip identified.) Numerous other scholars have claimed sporting events are a means of creating social capital, civic pride, and social cohesion (e.g., Chalip, 2006b; Misener & Mason, 2006; Wood, 2006; Ziakas & Costa, 2010). Event planners and organizers will often use this point in their discourse to gain community and leader support of these events. Oftentimes the economic value and impact of a sporting event on a community is overstated (e.g., Jones, 2001; Porter & Fletcher, 2008); consequently, those promoting events are beginning to focus more on the typically immeasurable or difficult to measure and assess social benefits, such as community building.

The celebratory and festival-like atmosphere surrounding community-based sporting events often create an energy and pride that are nearly impossible to measure, but is nonetheless important to note. This energy and pride community members develop as a result of a sporting event is often referred to as *psychic income*. For example, after hosting a marathon in their city, community members may feel a strong sense of pride that their city was showcased to runners who travel to the event. This psychic income is not tangible, but many have argued an important benefit and outcome of a community-based sporting event (see Crompton, 2004). Thus, community-based sporting events are another way sport can be utilized to foster community.

## Fanship and Spectatorship

Professional and college sports team can also play an integral role in nurturing community through fanship and spectatorship. Community can be fostered through watching, cheering on, and attending events related to that sport team. This occurs simply through the fact that a specific city or region is being represented or a passionate community of interest based around supporting that team has developed. Through affiliating with a specific team, individuals begin to identity with others who share that common interest. The team becomes a central point of identification and gives community members a common cause. For example, colleges and universities have been utilizing football and Fall Saturdays in this manner. As Chu (1989) notes, "By affiliating with that [university] team, by caring for its scores, we declare allegiance to an interest greater than oneself – the community" (p. 160). Numerous university leaders believe that football creates a point of attachment for not only students, but also for other stakeholders such as alumni and local community members.

Clopton (2008) found a relationship did exist between college football fan identification and sense of community. However, the direction of this relationship has yet to be determined (see Warner et al., 2011). That is, does a strong sense of community lead to greater fan identification or does greater fan identification lead to a stronger strong sense of community? It is clear though that football games provide an opportunity for individuals to feel membership, a celebratory ritual, and undoubtedly, social spaces are formed through tailgating and even designated sections of seating in the stadium (Clopton, 2007, 2009; Toma, 2003; Warner et al., 2011). Furthermore, Kelly and Dixon (2011) recently observed that creating a sense of community was overwhelmingly the primary strategic reasoning for the university's decision to financially invest and sponsor football.

While Swyers' (2005, 2010) work highlighted the role a professional baseball team played in fostering community among fans, Smith and Ingham (2003) found that a professional sport team divided a community. In this case, the use of public subsides for a professional sports team served as a divisive issue and the professional sports team was not advantageous for fostering community. Taxpayers clearly felt that a professional sports team and facility would not be beneficial to their community. Clearly, professional sport *can* play an important positive role in a community, but this does not occur serendipitously or by happenstance (cf. Warner & Dixon, 2011, in press; Warner et al., 2011). How sport is managed and leveraged is fundamental in determining the outcomes of sport for a community (Chalip, 2006; Sparvero & Chalip, 2007). Both professional teams and sporting events can be leveraged to ensure the maximum value to the community is achieved. Again though, it is important to emphasize this is not occurring with all professional sport teams. Along with realizing greater economic benefit to a community, Sparvero and Chalip (2007) contend that an appropriately leveraged team or sporting event would foster a welcoming social space and gathering place for community members while addressing social welfare issues (see Bradish & Cronin, 2009 and Misener & Mason, 2009). Hence, the ability to build community through way of fanship and spectatorship, along with participatory sport and community-based sporting events, are all an important consideration when assessing the role of sport and community.

## CHAPTER SUMMARY

Sport can play an important function in the community; however, as highlighted in this chapter, this does not automatically occur just because sport is present. Through viewing sport and community from a sociological perspective, it becomes more obvious that the social structures, social interaction, and institutional factors within various sport settings have a significant impact on the benefit sport can provide to a community and its members. Considering current trends suggest fewer individuals are reaping the social and life quality benefits of experiencing a healthy community, the onus for sport to help address this issue is becoming more evident. Through participatory sport, community-based sporting events, and spectatorship, sport provides an important avenue and opportunity for community building.

## DISCUSSION QUESTIONS

1. Should cities and local communities use tax dollars to support or subsidize local sport programs or events? Why or why not? What about for professional sports teams?
2. Recent trends indicate that individuals are not experiencing community and its benefits as much as in the past. What are some practical ways in which a sport in your community could be improved or managed in an effort to foster a greater sense of community?
3. Football is frequently cited as a means of fostering a sense of community on college campuses. In your opinion, does football enhance the sense of community on your campus? Why or why not? What are some factors that are either missing or particularly strong on your campus?
4. Warner and Dixon's Sport and Sense of Community Theory posited that women and men perceive competition and the competitive environment differently. Based on your experiences in sport, do you agree or disagree with this assessment. Why or why not?

## RECOMMENDED READINGS

Kellett, P., & Warner, S. (2011). Creating communities that lead to retention: The social worlds and communities of umpires. *European Sport Management Quarterly, 11*, 475-498. (This article focuses on the importance of community for sport officials and highlights how community for these individuals, who are both important employees in our sport systems yet also tend to be avid consumers of the sport experience, is essential to their retention.)

Swyers, H. (2005). Community America: Who Owns Wrigley Field? *The International Journal of the History of Sport, 22*, 1086-1105. (Swyers' work demonstrates the role a professional sports team can play in a community. Through specifically focusing on the Chicago Cubs and Wrigley Field, Swyers emphasizes the importance of social spaces and a sense of ownership in fostering community via sport.)

Warner, S., Shapiro, S., Dixon, M. A., Ridinger, L. L., & Harrison, S. (2011). The football factor: Shaping community on campus. *Journal of Issues in Intercollegiate Athletics, 4*, 236-256. (This work assesses the community impact of adding college football at Old Dominion University in 2009, challenging the popular notion that football fosters a greater sense of community on campuses. The study also suggests that sense of community influences outcomes related to Satisfaction, Retention, Current Support of Athletics, and Future Support for Athletics.)

## REFERENCES

Agnew, R. (1997). The nature and determinants of strain: Another look at Durkheim and Merton. In N. Passas & R. Agnew (Eds.), *The future of Anomie Theory* (pp. 27-51). Boston: Northeastern University Press.

Allan, T. H., & Allan, K. H. (1971). Sensitivity for community leaders. *Proceedings of the 79th Annual Convention of the American Psychological Association, 6*, 577-578.

Allport, G. W. (1954). *The nature of prejudice*. Cambridge, MA: Perseus Books.

Battistich, V., & Hom, A. (1997). The relationship between students' sense of their school as a community and their involvement in problem behaviors. *American Journal of Public Health, 87*, 1997-2001.

Baumeister, R. F., & Leary, M. R. (1995). The need to belong: Desire for interpersonal attachments as a fundamental human motivation. *Psychological Bulletin, 117*, 497-529.

Berkman, L. F., Glass, T., Brissette, I., & Seeman, T. E. (2000). From social integration to health: Durkheim in the new millennium. *Social Science & Medicine, 51*, 843-857.

Bess, K. D., Fisher, A. T., Sonn, C. C., & Bishop, B. J. (2002). Psychological sense of community: Theory, research and application. In A. T. Fisher, C. C. Sonn & B.J. Bishop (Eds.), *Psychological sense of community: Research, applications, and Implications* (pp. 3-22). New York, NY: Kluwer Academic/Plenum Publishers.

Bradish, C., & Cronin, J. J. (2009). Corporate social responsibility. *Journal of Sport Management, 23*, 691-697.

Carter, E. M., & Carter, M. V. (2007). Social psychological analysis of anomie among National Football League players. *International Review for the Sociology of Sport, 42*, 243-270.

Chalip, L. (2006a). Toward a distinctive sport management discipline. *Journal of Sport Management, 20*, 1-21.

Chalip, L. (2006b). Towards social leverage of sport events. *Journal of Sport Tourism, 11*, 109-127.

Chipuer, H., & Pretty, G. (1999). A review of the Sense of Community Index: Current uses, factor structures, reliability, and further development. *Journal of Community Psychology, 27*, 643-658.

Chu, D. (1989). *The character of American higher education and intercollegiate sport.* Albany: State University of New York Press.

Clopton, A. W. (2007). Predicting a sense of community amongst students from the presence of intercollegiate athletics: What roles do gender and BCS-affiliation play in the relationship? *The SMART Journal, 4*(1), 95-110.

Clopton, A. W. (2008). College sports on campus: Uncovering the link between fan identification and sense of community. *International Journal of Sport Management, 9,* 343-362.

Clopton, A. (2009). Students as spectators: Their academic and social integration. *New Directions for Higher Education, 148,* 83-89.

Crompton, J. L. (2004). Beyond economic impact: An alternative rationale for the public subsidy of major league sports facilities. *Journal of Sport Management, 18,* 40-58.

Cunningham, G. B. (2007). *Diversity in sport organizations.* Scottsdale, AZ: Holcomb Hathaway.

Cunningham, G. B., & Sagas, M. (2005). Access discrimination in intercollegiate athletics. *Journal of Sport and Social Issues, 29,* 148-163.

Davidson, W., & Cotter, P. R. (1991). The relationship between sense of community and subjective well-being: A first look. *Journal of Community Psychology, 19*(3), 246-253.

Deflem, M. (1989). From anomie to anomia and anomic depression: A sociological critique on the use of anomie in psychiatric research. *Social Science & Medicine, 29,* 627-634.

Dixon, M. A., & Bruening, J. (2007). Work-family conflict in coaching I: A top-down perspective. *Journal of Sport Management, 21,* 377-406.

Dixon, M. A., Bruening, J. E., Mazerolle, S. M., Davis, A., Crowder, J., & Lorsbach, M. (2006). Career, family, or both? A case study of young professional baseball players. *Nine: A Journal of Baseball History and Culture, 14*(2), 80-101.

Durkheim, E. (1933). *The division of labor in society translated by George Simpson.* New York: The Free Press.

Durkheim, E. (1951). *Suicide: A study in sociology translated by George Simpson and John A. Spaulding.* New York: The Free Press.

Green, B. C. (2005). Building sport programs to optimize athlete recruitment, retention, and transition: Toward a normative theory of sport development. *Journal of Sport Management, 19,* 233-253.

Gusfield, J. R. (1975). *The community: A critical response.* New York: Harper Colophon.

Hagan, J., & McCarthy, B. (1997). Anomie, social capital, and street criminology. In N. Passas & R. Agnew (Eds.), *The future of Anomie Theory* (pp.124-141). Boston: Northeastern University Press.

Heller, K. (1989). The return to community. *American Journal of Community Psychology, 17,* 1-15.

Hirschi, T. (1969). *Causes of delinquency.* Berkeley: University of California Press.

Hirschman, A.O. (1970). *Exit, voice, and loyalty: Responses to decline in firms, organizations, and states.* Cambridge, MA: Harvard University Press.

Jones, C. (2001). Mega-events and host-region impacts: determining the true worth of the 1999 Rugby World Cup. *The International Journal of Tourism Research, 3,* 241-251.

Kellett, P., & Warner, S. (2011). Creating communities that lead to retention: The social worlds and communities of umpires. *European Sport Management Quarterly, 11,* 475-498.

Kelly, D. D., & Dixon, M. A. (2011). Becoming a "real university": The strategic benefits of adding football for NCAA Division I institutions. *Journal of Intercollegiate Sport, 2,* 283-303.

Kilduff, M., & Tsai, W. (2007). *Social networks and organizations.* London: Sage.

Lim, S. Y., Warner, S., Dixon, M. A., Berg, B., Kim, C., & Newhouse-Bailey, M. (2011). Sport participation across national contexts: A multilevel investigation of individual and systemic influences on adult sport participation. *European Sport Management Quarterly, 11,* 197-224.

Lott, A. J. & Lott, B. E. (1965). Group cohesiveness as interpersonal attraction: A review of relationships with antecedent and variables. *Psychological Bulletin, 64,* 259-309.

Maslow, A. (1943). A theory of human motivation. *Psychological Review, 50,* 370-396.

McCarthy, M., Pretty, G., & Catano, V. (1990). Psychological sense of community: An issue in student burnout. *Journal of College Student Personnel, 31,* 211-216.

McCole, D. (2006). *Sense of community among summer camp staff members.* Paper presented at the 8th Biennial Research Symposium for Coalition for Education in the Outdoors Conference, Bradford Woods, IN.

McMillan, D., & Chavis, D. (1986). Sense of community: A definition and theory. *Journal of Community Psychology, 14,* 6–23.

McPherson, M., Smith-Lovin, L., & Brashears, M. E. (2006). Social isolation in America: Changes in core discussion networks over two decades. *American Sociological Review, 71,* 353-375.

Misener, L., & Mason, D. S. (2006). Creating community networks: Can sporting events offer meaningful sources of social capital? *Managing Leisure, 11,* 39–56.

Misener, L., & Mason, D. S. (2009). Fostering community development through sporting events strategies: An examination of urban regime perception, *Journal of Sport Management, 23,* 770-794.

Mitchell, J. C. (1974). Social networks. *Annual Review of Anthropology, 3,* 279-299.

Porter, P. K., & Fletcher, D. (2008). The economic impact of the Olympic Games: Ex ante predictions and ex post reality. *Journal of Sports Management, 22,* 470-486.

Pretty, G., & McCarthy, M. (1991). Exploring psychological sense of community among men and women of the corporation. *Journal of Community Psychology, 19,* 351-361.

Putnam, R. D. (2000). *Bowling alone: The collapse and revival of American community.* New York: Simon and Schuster.

Rappaport, J. (1977). *Community Psychology: Values, research, and action.* New York: Rhinehart and Winston.

Royal, M., & Rossi, R. (1996). Individual-level correlates of sense of community: Findings from workplace and school. *Journal of Community Psychology, 24,* 395-416.

Sarason, S. B. (1974). *The psychological sense of community: Prospects for a community psychology.* San Francisco, CA: Jossey-Bass.

Schimmel, K. S. (2003). Sport. In Karen Christensen & David Levinson (Eds.), *Encyclopedia of community: From village to virtual world* (pp. 1334-1336*).* Thousand Oaks: Sage Publications.

Smith, A. L., Lemyre, N., & Raedeke, T. D. (2007). Advances in athlete burnout research. *International Journal of Sport Psychology, 38,* 337-342.

Smith, J. M., & Ingham, A. G. (2003). On the waterfront: Retrospectives on the relationship between sport and communities. *Sociology of Sport Journal, 20,* 252-274.

Spaaij, R. (2009). The glue that holds the community together? Sport and sustainability in rural Australia. *Sport in Society, 9,* 1132-1146.

Sparvero, E. S., & Chalip, L. (2007). Professional teams as leverageable assets: Strategic creation of community value. *Sport Management Review, 10,* 1-30.

Swyers, H. (2005). Community America: Who owns Wrigley Field? *International Journal of the History of Sport, 22*(6), 1086-1105.

Swyers, H. (2010). *Wrigley Regulars: Finding community in the bleachers?* Champaign, IL: University of Illinois Press.

Toma, D. (2003). Football U: Spectator sports in the life of the American university. Ann Arbor, MI: University of Michigan Press.

Voydanoff, P. (2004). Implications of work and community demands and resources for work-to-family conflict and facilitation. *Journal of Occupational Health Psychology, 9,* 275-285.

Warner, S. (2010). *Sport and social structures: Building community on campuses.* Unpublished doctoral dissertation. The University of Texas at Austin.

Warner, S., Bowers, M., & Dixon, M. A. (2012). Teambuilding and cohesion: A social networking perspective. *Journal of Sport Management, 1,* 53-66.

Warner, S., & Dixon, M. A. (2011). Understanding sense of community from an athlete's perspective. *Journal of Sport Management, 25,* 258-272.

Warner, S., & Dixon, M. A. (in press). Sport and community on campus: Constructing a sport experience that matters. *Journal of College Student Development.*

Warner, S., Shapiro, S., Dixon, M. A., Ridinger, L. L., & Harrison, S. (2011). The football factor: Shaping community on campus. *Journal of Issues in Intercollegiate Athletics, 4,* 236-256.

Wood, E. H. (2006). Measuring the social impact of local authority events: a pilot study for a civic pride scale. *International Journal Nonprofit Voluntary Sector Marketing, 11,* 165-179.

Ziakas, V., & Costa, C. A. (2010). Between theatre and sport' in a rural event: Evolving unity and community development from the inside-out, *Journal of Sport and Tourism, 15,* pp. 7-26.

# CHAPTER 12

# YOUTH SPORT

## Marlene A. Dixon, Ted Burden, and Mike Newhouse-Bailey

***

**Learning Objectives**

After reading this chapter, you should be able to:

1. Characterize the size and breadth of the youth sport industry in the United States.
2. Discuss socialization and the role of socialization agents in youth sport.
3. Outline the positive and negative effects of sport on youth.
4. Distinguish between instrumental and emotional support.
5. Identify both individual and family outcomes related to participation in youth sport.


## INTRODUCTION

In this chapter, we examine the issue of youth sport in the United States. We begin by placing youth sport within its social and historical context, demonstrating that youth sport is important not only in itself but as part of the sport and social systems in the United States. The chapter then moves into an examination of the process of sport entry, which is largely focused on socialization, or how children learn the values and behaviors of sport. Next, we outline the benefits of sport, exploring the supposed benefits alongside the negative outcomes associated with participation. Finally, we explore the distinct relationship of sport and the family and how each sphere influences the other.

## THE SIZE AND SCOPE OF YOUTH SPORT

In this section we outline a brief history of youth sport in the United States to help establish the context in which today's youth sport system operates.

## Early North American Sport

While it may be difficult to imagine, sport was not always as popular in the United States as it is today. Early European-Americans discarded most leisurely activities for "carving out a living" in this newfound territory. The Native Americans, however, had already established a sense of survival, and therefore dedicated part of their time for play, competition, and rituals for "rites of passage" (Dixon, & Bruening, 2011). In Canada and the United States one such early sport was "lacrosse," which was played as early as 1683 (Robidoux, 2002). And to the south in Mexico, the Mayans celebrated their own version of basketball known as "pok ta pok" (Miller & Houston, 1987). While the rules were basically a combination of basketball and soccer, the losing team not only had to "experience the agony of defeat" but often lost their lives as well.

## The US University and Intercollegiate Sport

Even before America became a nation, it was important that the future statespersons were educated and molded to become the leaders of the new colonies. In 1636, Harvard was given its charter, and became the first of many new colleges and universities that would educate and shape this nation into what it is today. The early universities were designed to teach the liberal arts curriculum of early European institutions; oratory, philosophy, Greek, and Latin, as well as build character through what would become known as "the collegiate way" (Rudolph, 1990). The collegiate way was an environment where the students worshiped together, dined together, shared dormitories, and attended classes together. This campus lifestyle was essential in developing an atmosphere of family, unity, and camaraderie. Eventually the collegiate way would come to include extracurricular activities as well (e.g., rowing, football, baseball, etc.) (Rudolph, 1990).

By the early 19th century, students were competing on campus similar to fraternal and club teams. In 1852, the first intercollegiate competition was held in the form of a boat race, between Harvard and Yale on Lake Winnepesaukee, New Hampshire (Rudolph, 1990). Many other intercollegiate competitions would soon follow:

- 1859: 1st baseball game was held between Amhurst and Williams colleges in Pittsfield, Massachusetts.
- 1869: 1st football game was held between Rutgers and Princeton in New Brunswick, New Jersey.

- 1896: 1st basketball game was held between Wesleyan University and Yale in New Haven, Connecticut.

These early competitions led to increased interest in sport throughout the country, both in the educational setting, and the general community as well. It was not long before strides were made to implement organizations and clubs designed to address this new interest held by America's youth.

## US Interscholastic and Community Sport

In the late 1800's and early 1900's, there was much economic difficulty, and paying jobs were difficult to find. Many city-dwelling young men were engaging in criminal activity with the large amount of free time they had on their hands. It would be 1918 before all states had compulsory school attendance laws, so up to that time many young men did not attend school. Thus, community programs were developed to give these "boys" someplace to expend their energy that was currently being utilized to cause harm. Between 1844 and 1939, no fewer than six major programs would be developed in American communities to involve young men in constructive play and competition: the Young Men's Christian Association (YMCA) in 1844; the Amateur Athletic Union (AAU) in 1888; Federated Boys Club, later named Boys and Girls Club of America in 1906; Police Athletic League (PAL) in 1914; Pop Warner Football in 1929; and Little League Baseball in 1939.

For those attending public education, sport was made available through the National Federation of High Schools (NFHS) in 1920. Today the NFHS represents over 18,500 schools and 11 million students involved in sport and activities (Fellmeth, 2010). The strength of these programs, both community and interscholastic, can be seen in their longevity and track record, as most of them survive and thrive over 100 years in existence.

## Youth Sport Today

In 2008, according to the National Council of Youth Sports (NCYS), approximately 44,000,000 children aged 5-18 participated in organized sports. Based on the 2010 US Census, that means 2 out of every 3 children living in the US participated in youth sports. Of that population, 7.6 million students play sports in US high schools (Fellmeth, 2010).

State and district funding can limit interscholastic sports. Depending on the location and/or wealth of the district, many programs offered to the general public (e.g., swimming, tennis, water polo, etc.), may not be offered in the local schools. These types of sports may be offered, instead, through private organizations or clubs. Such "club" sport offerings and academies are a growing trend in the US as supplemental to or in replacement of interscholastic sport, reflecting a growing trend of privatization of sport in the US (Coakley, 2008).

The trend toward privatization mirrors the increasing trend toward early specialization in sport. Sport specialization advocates believe the sooner one starts specializing in a particular sport, the better the chances are for future success. According to Ericsson, it takes 10,000 hours of specialized training to become an elite athlete (Ericsson et al., 1993). This amount of training for young children can only be accomplished through private organizations where there is less regulation on allowed training and competition hours. This trend toward specialization, though, has become troubling to many child development experts, who contend that early specialization is detrimental to physical, emotional, and psychological development (e.g., Côté, 1999). Such tensions are important from a sociological perspective because they highlight the underlying values of society and a general shift in sport's place as leisure vs. labor.

**US Sport beyond Community and Interscholastic Programs**

In the United States, there is no national sport policy *per se*, as there are in other countries throughout the world. With the exception of the Unites States Olympic Committee (USOC), federal government funding is almost non-existent when it comes to amateur sport (Chalip et al., 1996). Private national governing bodies (NGBs) oversee the elite programs of amateur sport, and if requiring any funding from the USOC must submit participation numbers and program initiatives.

Though other opportunities exist (e.g., private clubs, AAU, professional developmental leagues), primarily for the major sports in the US, most paths beyond community and interscholastic team sports run through the US intercollegiate programs and their scholarships. The probability that young male athletes participating in interscholastic sports will get a scholarship to a participating National Collegiate Athletic Association (NCAA) institution is less than 5%. Less than 0.5% of male athletes competing in interscholastic sport will be drafted by a professional team (National Collegiate Athletic Association, 2011). With the enactment of

1972's Title IX, female athlete scholarship probabilities are higher, but only slightly. Thus, for most athletes in the United States, the end of community and interscholastic sports is also the end of their participation in organized sport programs.

This structure is different than that of other countries, particularly in Europe and Canada, where youth are more likely to continue participation well into adulthood through community-based sport clubs (Lim et al., 2011). Thus, the structure of youth sport impacts who plays, what they play, how long they play, and the values they learn in sport.

The structure of youth sport in the US has several implications for sociologists. First, researchers must continue to explore the social values associated with sport and how sport has changed over time with societal values. Is sport a reflection of social values, and if so, what and whose values does it reflect, particularly in the most prominent sport programs and models? What and whose values does it not seem to reflect? How and why does sport change? How do non-dominant values and voices find a place or expression in and through sport?

In the remainder of this chapter, we explore how children become involved in sport, the benefits they (and their parents) perceive and actually derive from sport, and some of the challenges or problems with youth sport. We conclude with an investigation of the wider issue of sport and the family. Throughout this chapter, consider both how sport shapes society and society shapes sport through the cultural institution and expression of youth sport.

## HOW DO CHILDREN BECOME INVOLVED IN SPORT?

A number of scholars have examined the ways that people enter sport, the people who influence their decisions to participate, and the messages and meanings that sport organizations utilize to help recruit new participants. Green (2005), in her model of sport development, asserts that most new participation is accomplished through "sponsored recruitment," where another person introduces the sport and may even walk through the initial sport experience with the new participant. For children, parents and peers typically serve as "sponsors" in this recruitment process.

Entry into sport is most heavily influenced by parents' decisions (Dixon et al., 2008; Kay, 2000). Parents examine available opportunities and make decisions regarding which sports, which seasons, which leagues, what cost level, and what commitment level is appropriate for their child. In many cases, parents may seek a sport at which they enjoyed or excelled, or they may be influenced by other likeminded parents who are enrolling their children in a sport (Green, 1997). In addition to sport entry, parents are integrally involved in the sport retention process. Parents not only pay for sport, but also provide transportation, equipment, food, laundry, and other daily necessities (Dixon et al., 2008; Fredericks & Eccles, 2002). Thus, children are highly dependent on parental decisions for their sport involvement.

As children grow older, peers also become important in the sport entry and retention process whereby children choose sport based on the opportunity for social interaction with peers (which is particularly important for girls), and sometimes for social status among peer groups (Rees & Miracle, 2000). For example, high school football in Texas carries tremendous social status, and many children and families go to great lengths for the opportunity to play and be part of an elite peer circle (cf., Bissinger, 1990).

## Socialization into Sport

Children are not born knowing what sports to choose and how to behave in sport contexts. Watching young children in sport is often humorous or frustrating because they break the rules that "everyone knows." For example, ask a child to take the ball "to the hole" or "to the rack" or to "post up," and chances are the child will have no idea. Ask an experienced basketball player, and she or he will most likely know exactly what to do. Similarly, the value of sport is not fixed, but malleable and related to other social and cultural norms, patterns, and expectations. Socialization is the process by which people learn the values and norms associated with a particular social sphere and activity. These may include how to act in church, how to behave and respond in school, or how to act in a sport. *Socialization* is defined as an interactive social process whereby individuals are exposed to important forms of information regarding expectations and norms within a particular social setting or role; consequently, they learn to behave in accordance with these expectations and norms (Bandura, 1977; Greendorfer, 1993; Greendorfer & Bruce, 1991; Nixon, 1990; Weiss & Glenn, 1992). Socialization does not just involve exposure to social situations, but it also involves learning and internalization of roles and expectations. It is a two-way interactive process. Children do not just accept all that is taught them; instead they fil-

260

ter experiences and come to form their own identity, values, and behaviors.

Parents, teachers, peers, and coaches all can help in the process of socialization, with parents being the primary influence when children are young, and peers and coaches as children age (e.g., Anderssen et al., 2006; Fredricks & Eccles, 2004; Greendorfer, 1977; Greendorfer & Lewko, 1978; Smith & Smoll, 1990; Weiss & Barber, 1995). In this capacity, they are referred to as agents of socialization. They teach the norms and values associated with a social sphere. The values and expectations learned, especially through parental influence, have both immediate and long-term impact on a child's sport participation (Dixon et al., 2008). Through the socialization process, socializing agents convey both the value of sport to the social circle (e.g., the family), appropriate sports and sport roles based on gender, and the norms of the sport sub-culture.

**The Value of Sport**

By enrolling children in sport, parents communicate that sport is a valued activity in their family and social sphere. As described earlier, this value has changed tremendously over the past 50 years. Early on, sport was viewed as a leisure activity reserved for after work was completed, or for families with means for leisure activities. Prior to World War II, sport was viewed as a valuable way to teach boys their role in society and to train them for toughness and following direction. After World War II, however, as youth were moved out of the labor force, sport was utilized as a place for keeping children (particularly boys) occupied and out of trouble after school and in the summer. Good parents, in this era, enrolled their boys in sport and provided resources for them to participate. During the 1970's and 80's, sport was seen as a valuable leisure activity that filled non-working space, and soon became valuable for both boys and girls, especially after the passage of Title IX in 1972. Interestingly, although sport has become an accepted and even desired activity for girls, much research continues to uncover gender differences in how girls and boys are socialized into sport, the acceptability of different sports for boys and girls, and the impact of sport norms (e.g., competition) on boys' and girls' sport experiences (e.g., Brustad, 1988, 1993, 1996; Coakley & White, 1999; Dixon et al., 2008; Fredricks & Eccles, 2004; Greendorfer, 1977, 1993; Greendorfer & Lewko, 1978; McElroy, 1983; Sage, 1980; Warner & Dixon, 2011; Weiss & Glenn, 1992).

Since the late 1990's participation in sport has become almost an expected part of growing up in most industrialized nations, especially among middle to upper classes. In fact, some would argue that sport has now become children's labor—not a leisure experience that they can choose to do, but something that is expected of them, and as something that is more outcome than process oriented (Brustad, 1993). In some cases, sport is also labor in the sense that it is seen as means to a college scholarship or a form of family income (Ryan, 1995). Parents have poured massive resources into their children's training in sport, and the children are expected to "produce" accordingly. This view of sport has implications not only for its inherent value within society, but also for the social, psychological, and emotional well-being of the children who participate under that premise. There is still much work to be done in this area, where social scientists need to examine the effects of sport as leisure vs. sport as labor on children, families, society, and sport systems.

## Sport Sub-Culture

Socialization into the sport culture is also an important process, especially from a sport development perspective. For children to advance in their sport commitment, both they and their parents/guardians must learn the social roles and expectations associated with their sport (Green, 2005). These are the elements of a sport subculture that "everyone knows" and can be as simple as what clothing to wear or what terms to use, or as complex as where to live and work in order to be successful in a sport. For example, "everyone knows" how a "soccer mom" is supposed to act. "Everyone knows" that Longhorns wear burnt orange while Aggies wear maroon. Terms like "freestyling" or "jibbing" come from the snowboarding subculture, whereas skateboarders utilize terms such as "grinding," "sick," or "carving." People who are immersed in the subculture use these terms, wear the "right clothing," and perform behaviors appropriate to the subculture. The longer they are in the subculture, the more natural they become. Learning these social norms helps immerse and identify a person in a sub-culture and demonstrates commitment to it.

From a sociological perspective, subcultural elements provide powerful cues as to how committed athletes (and their parents) behave in sport. One can understand the power of the social norms by questioning how they came to be or what happens when a person does not follow them. For example, the popular movie *A League of their Own* examined what happens when females enter a male dominated sport (e.g., "There's no crying in baseball!"). These norms are important to understand for a variety of reasons.

Sport managers often take a functionalist perspective on such norms, using them to increase participant buy-in and commitment to sport. For example, sport marketers use sub-cultural norms to convince participants to buy particular brands of clothing or equipment because they are the "right" brands for that sport. Within a sport club, committed parents may socialize new parents into the norms of the sport club, thereby reproducing more committed parents (Green & Chalip, 1997).

From a critical perspective, however, it is important to examine the norms of sport, as they can lead to changes in sport patterns as well as problems and abuses. For example, Ryan's (1995) *Little Girls in Pretty Boxes* examines the social norms of girls' figure skating. It provides a picture of girls who are undernourished and over trained so that they can show commitment to the sport at the highest level. Similarly, a number of scholars have examined the subcultures of girls' finesse sports, such as diving, gymnastics, and distance running. These studies reveal subcultures where eating disorders and unsafe dieting are common practice. Norms in power sports can give rise to such behaviors as performance enhancing drugs, playing injured, and verbal and emotional abuse. Consider the subculture of professional cycling: if doping becomes accepted practice (i.e., a social norm), can athletes who choose not to dope compete at the highest level?

Interestingly, rejection of social norms within a sport or sport community often gives rise to alternative sports. The rise of skateboarding, snowboarding, BMX and other extreme sports can partially be attributed to a rejection of the strict authoritarian subcultures of mainstream sports such as football, basketball, and baseball (Coakley, 2008). Athletes in these sports searched for a means to find more creativity and autonomy in their sport experience. Although some of these sports have now also become more mainstream, one can still find the bulk of athletes at an open park, un-coached, working on their craft in their own time, space, and with their own choice of people. While this is not to suggest that these sports are better than mainstream, they simply reflect how sport norms are not fixed, and how new sports and sport experiences can arise from a critical reflection, and sometimes rejection, of dominant sport values and norms.

# BENEFITS OF SPORT PARTICIPATION

If so many children participate in sport, it must provide some benefits to participants. The benefits attributed to sport are numerous. In fact, reading some youth sport brochures makes one think that sport is the magic wand for all personal and social needs. In this section, we outline some of the benefits associated with youth sport participation and the empirical evidence associated therewith.

As suggested earlier, sport has often been viewed as a place to keep children occupied and safe. In fact, many sport and physical activity programs have been derived with this benefit in mind, and sport programs have generally been effective in achieving this goal, as they provide a supervised, structured activity in which children can participate. It is important to note, however, that while sport programs can provide a "safe" place for children to play, the programs themselves must be delivered in such a way as to prevent such "unsafe" behaviors as bullying, sexual harassment, emotional, physical, and psychological injury. This depends on both the design and delivery of the sport program, including training for the coaches and supervisors (Chalip, 2006; Green et al., 2008).

Sport can also provide social connections and create new social opportunities for children and their parents (Green, 2005; Green & Chalip, 1997). In fact, many parents cite this reason as one of the driving forces in their choice to initially enroll their children in sport (Green, 2005). When designed and managed well, sport can be a source of social opportunity and a significant place for building community both among participants and parents (Dixon et al., 2008; Green & Chalip, 1997; Warner & Dixon, 2011). Some caution must be taken, however, when sport becomes a central community element for parents, as some studies have shown that parental pressure for their children to continue sport when their children want to quit, comes from parents desire to remain a part of the social community (Lally & Kerr, 2008; Dorsch et al., 2009).

Sport participation is also viewed as a means for learning valuable social and "life" skills such as teamwork, cooperation, competitiveness, and perseverance. These skills are seen as valuable for navigating a successful educational and career experience. Again, the experience of these benefits is dependent on the design and delivery of sport programs and the evidence for learning these skills is mixed. For example, there is evidence that high school athletes, as a group, demonstrate more positive attitudes toward school and maintain higher grade point averages than do their non-athlete peers (Rees & Miracle, 2000). However, others have suggested that this relationship likely existed prior to becoming athletes, and that students who are *already* engaged and high performing are more likely to join a high school athletics team (Spreitzer, 1995). Clearly, more longitudinal work is needed in this area before we understand when, where, and what about sport leads to such benefits.

Sport is also viewed as a means toward physical fitness and increased physical activity (Chalip, 2006). Many parents hope their children participate in sport when they are young so they will gain a lifelong love for participation, thereby enabling them to stay active throughout their lives. Based on expectancy-valence theory (Fredericks & Eccles, 2002), numerous studies have demonstrated the importance of parental and coach interpretation of the sport experience for children. Too much parental feedback and pressure causes undue stress in young athletes, and may lead to early burnout. However, appropriate amounts of encouragement and support can increase enjoyment and longevity of the athletes' involvement (Brustad, 1993; Davison et al., 2006; Morgan & Giacobbi, 2006). For example, both Dixon and colleagues (2008) and Morgan and Giacobbi's (2006) studies of American college athletes found that ongoing parental social support was important to helping them overcome obstacles and remain involved in sport.

In summary, sport can indeed provide many benefits for children and their parents; however, these benefits are not automatic nor are they exclusive to sport. It is essential that sociologists continue to explore the ways sport is designed and implemented such that the benefits are maximized and maintained.

## PROBLEMS WITH YOUTH SPORT

In addition to the rewarding benefits one might attain through youth sport participation, there are problems within youth sports as well. The physical and mental demands that youth sport can place on a child can be overwhelming, and those pressures are exacerbated when adolescents enter the sport specialization and "select" or elite realm of youth sport.

According to Smith and Smoll (1990), during the adolescent stage of child development, coaches and peers join parents as the most influential relationships (agents) in a young athlete's life. Therefore, the psychological, psychosocial, behavioral, and moral traits displayed by these "agents" within an athlete's environment can have a dramatic effect on what becomes the "norm" within that child's life. In addition to the psychological and psychosocial aspects of the environment of youth sport participation, there exists a physiological element. What was once play becomes work for many. Children are pushing themselves harder, and more often, than ever before. They are bigger and stronger, play more often, and often pursue the same sport over the course of the entire year. With so much emphasis put on competition and winning, it is not unusual that "reasonable" limits are often exceeded in the quest for socially desirable rewards. This section examines some of the negative aspects of youth sport participation and their effects on children, as well as corrective measures currently in place, and being discussed, to address these issues.

## Physical Injury

Sport participation involves physical exertion. As with any physical activity, the possibility of overuse or injury is not surprising. And while injury is expected, or at least considered, the rate and severity of injury in youth sports is becoming quite alarming.

As previously noted, the NCYS approximates that 44,000,000 children aged 5-18 participate in organized sports. Between 2001 and 2009, it is estimated that 1.8 million emergency visits were made by children 14 years of age and under, specifically related to sport or recreation participation. Of these visits, 6% were for traumatic brain injuries (Safe Kids, 2011). And while one would think the majority of injuries can be attributed to what are considered "contact" sports (e.g., football, hockey, basketball), this is an incorrect assumption. Most childhood injuries come from bicycling, followed by football, baseball/softball, basketball, and skateboarding. Here are some more statistics from the Safe Kids (2011) report:

- Each year, more than 3.5 million children under the age of 14 receive medical treatment for sport injuries.
- Most sport related injuries happen during practice.
- Approximately 715,000 sport and recreation injuries happen each year, in school settings alone.
- Males are six times more likely than females to have a sport injury requiring hospitalization.
- Sport injury hospitalization costs are between $113 - $133 million dollars a year.

While there has been much recent focus on major acute injuries such as concussions or ACL tears, an increasing amount of injuries occur from overuse. Children are often playing sport year round, and particularly specializing in a sport that requires repetitive motion (e.g., pitching in baseball). This repeated patterning, in particular, can lead to inflammation and/or injury. In fact, approximately 50% of injuries in pediatric sport medicine can be attributed to overuse (Brenner, 2007).

## Cheating

In 2001, Danny Almonte pitched a perfect game during the Little League World Series and led his Bronx, New York, team to the semi-finals. Almonte had 46 strike-outs and only allowed 3 hits — feats that are quite remarkable for a 12 year old. The only problem was, Almonte was 14 not 12. His father had given the league officials a false birth certificate so he could dominate in a younger age group. Ten years later, with a 90 mph fastball, his coach felt the incident 10 years earlier is the only thing keeping him out of the professional ranks (King-White, 2010).

Cheating is nothing new, regardless of the level of play. It can be done in many ways: altering scores/results/grades, enhancing one's body or equipment, deceiving regulators and officials. While many advocate that sport is valuable for teaching life lessons, such as teamwork and cooperation, others have suggested that the "performance ethic" in today's youth sport programs just as likely leads to deviance and cheating in an effort to receive social rewards (Coakley, 2008).

In the increasingly competitive atmosphere of youth sports, gaining an advantage on an opponent is critical for winning. Athletes can gain such an advantage through better training, better diet, watching more film, or increased deliberate practice. In many cases, however, these techniques are not as effective or efficient as parents, athletes, or coaches deem them to be. Thus, additional steps are taken which may cross ethical or legal boundaries. For example, middle and high school athletes, particularly boys, may utilize illegal steroids to gain a competitive advantage. Interestingly, after usage rates peaked in the early 2000's, due to educational campaigns and stricter testing policies, steroid use among youth has declined considerably, where 2011 rates among high school boys were only 1.0-1.8% (down from 2.7% in 2006; Johnston et al., 2012).

Within ethical and socially accepted norms, cheating may be blatant and easily recognized. Other times it is not so easy to distinguish, as norms and values change both within and between sport experiences. When does strategy, and technique in coaching, cross the line to become cheating?

From a sociological perspective, one must examine the social norms within society that have led to deviant behavior within sport. What are the contingencies and social rewards within American society that have led to this behavior? One must also examine the sub-cultures within a particular sport to understand the unique reward structures and patterns that shape social values and behaviors within that context. What may be viewed as deviant in mainstream society (e.g., doping) may be accepted practice within a sport culture. Thus, in understanding and controlling cheating, one must first understand the underlying values associated with sport that rewards or condemns such behavior.

## Deviant Behavior

What constitutes bad behavior and abuse? Deviant behavior is difficult to define and govern because it is relative—deviance to one person is acceptable to another. This difficulty in defining deviance is exemplified in the pornography case of *Jacobellis v. Ohio*. In this case, Supreme Court Justice Potter Stewart wrote, "I shall not today attempt further to define [obscenity]; and perhaps I could never succeed in intelligibly doing so. But I know it when I see it..." (NetSafekids, 2003). Such is the case with deviant behaviors experienced within youth sport throughout the world: we know it when we see it. Within sport it is important to understand agreed upon norms that help establish acceptable and unacceptable behavior.

Deviant behavior in sport extends from athletes to parents and coaches who are being fined, arrested, and/or barred from future attendance. In fact, referees and umpires in some states are now required to carry health insurance because of the risk they are exposed to at youth games.

Parents, in particular, have become a major source of problems at youth sport activities. Parents have assaulted opposing players, other players, coaches, officials, and even their own child. One incident ended up with a father of a youth hockey player being arrested, charged, and convicted of murder of another player's father (Rimer, 2002). In another incident, one mother hired an assassin to kill the mother of another cheerleader that had beaten-out her daughter for the opportunity to be on the cheerleading squad (Swartz & Lindem, 1991). Such incidents, and many more minor ones, cause one to question the premier place of youth sport in children's lives and the social status associated with sport, particularly within many American schools.

While deviant behavior is not limited to parents, it is important to recognize the role of parents (and coaches) in the socialization process. Sport may be utilized to teach many "lessons" about values and behavior. Understanding the social rewards and sanctions tied to sport participation, especially from a parent's perspective, can help uncover both problems and solutions for deviance in youth sports.

## Adolescent Dropout and Burnout

Children frequently note they play sports "to have fun." Likewise, when asked why they left sport participation, most respondents will answer "it's not fun anymore." As they age into adolescence, the reasons for remaining in sport become "improve my skills," "competition," "associate with friends," while the reasons for withdrawal are "had other things to do," "didn't like the coach," and "not enough playing time" (Butcher et al., 2002). Depending on the level of sport children soon become aware of the level of expectations and pressures at their particular level. Accepting or rejecting those expectations and pressures can help determine whether an athlete stays in competitive sport or withdraws (Brustad, 1993; Davison et al., 2006; Dixon et al., 2008; Morgan & Giacobbi, 2006).

Researchers have determined and explained that there is a distinct difference between "dropout" and "burnout." First, *dropout* is usually associated with casual team/individual sport participation. *Burnout* on the other hand, is always associated with elite-level athletics and upper level participation. "*Dropout* occurs when fairly high outcomes are exceeded by still higher alternatives" (Schmidt & Stein, 1991), while *burnout* "results from an increase in stress-induced costs" (Smith, 1986, p. 39). Many have suggested that burnout is becoming increasingly common in youth sport, and at younger and younger ages, prompting examination of the policies within sport organization and sport governance.

## SPORT AND THE FAMILY

As outlined in this chapter, youth sport is inexorably tied to children's families. Thus, this chapter concludes with examination of the relationship between sport and the family, with the goal of examining how two important social spheres shape and impact each other within the broader society.

The relationship between youth sport and the family is a reciprocal one. Families and their type and level of support impact the youth sport experience and variables related to the youth sport experience impact the family. Families support youth sport through a variety of resources, and play a vital role in participant commitment to sport. Likewise, the structure and implementation of the youth sport programs are very influential in terms of how the youth sport experience impacts the family.

## Family Support

Families support youth sport participants in a variety of ways. Some examples include providing financial resources or playing an emotionally supportive role. Without proper family support, athletes are less likely to be engaged and more likely to have a negative youth sport experience (Fraser-Thomas et al., 2008).

*Instrumental Support*

One way that families support youth sport is to provide the time and money to play—this is called instrumental support (Dixon et al., 2008; Kay, 2000; Wiersma & Fifer, 2008). The financial requirements vary depending on what type of youth sport league the child is enrolled in, but in a qualitative study with 20 families, Kay (2000) found that the number one cause of ending a sport experience was financial demands. When children begin to specialize in one sport and begin to focus on skill development, the costs of the sport increases dramatically (Côté, 1999). These costs may include league fees, equipment, private lessons, clinics, travel expenses and many others (Côté, 1999).

In addition to the instrumental support of financial means that families provide, they also must make logistical arrangements to accommodate the demands of the league or organization. This includes transportation, scheduling, and arrangements within the family as to who provides transportation, attends practices, attends games, and what role each family member plays in getting the participant ready for his or her activity. The time demand placed on the family has also been referred to as an alteration of family activity patterns (Kay, 2000). Families change work schedules, vacations, and other plans in order to provide enough time to allow the child to participate (Kay, 2000). One of the biggest demands for time that youth sport places on the family is that of deliberate practice. In order for children to reach an elite level for the sport in which she or he is enrolled, families must provide transportation to and from practice, which is often held three or four nights a week (Thompson, 1999; Ericcson et al., 1993).

*Emotional Support*

In addition to providing instrumental support in the form of time and money, families also provide emotional support to participants (Wiersma & Fifer, 2008). These resources contribute to the athlete's well-being and affect her or his level of engagement with the team (Fraser-Thomas et al., 2008). Emotional support can appear in many forms, from post or pre game talks, cheering from the sideline or simply allowing an athlete to have time alone following a loss. Research has shown that, in order for the athlete to have a positive experience, perceived emotional support by the athlete is critical  (Wiersma & Fifer, 2008). Kay (2000) also linked emotional support with talent development, as elite athletes cited emotional support from the family as a key factor helping them stay motivated to attend practices and maintain a positive outlook toward sport.

## Individual and Family Outcomes

As the sport experience will differ for each participant and families vary in how they are structured and the resources available, it is important to understand the impact of youth sport on individual members of the family and the family unit as a whole.

*Individual*

Individual sport-related outcomes for family members may be positive or negative depending on the family and sport variables present. Participants may see an increase in self-esteem, the development of persistence, and gain social skills (Fraser-Thomas et al., 2005). On the other side, participants who have a negative youth sport experience may see increased levels of stress and may see a decrease in self-esteem (Fraser-Thomas et al., 2008; Kay, 2000). In one study, the authors found a direct link between athletic performance and emotions of the participants (Kay, 2000). Those who experienced high levels of athletic performance reached levels of emotional highs, and those who had low levels of athletic performance experienced emotional lows. Beyond sport variables that impact individual outcomes, some athletes are subject to high levels of stress in the form of parental and coach pressure (Fraser-Thomas et al., 2008). Oftentimes when athletes perceive high levels of pressure, they suffer from burnout and are more likely to cease participation. Some athletes participate at levels that are not safe for their age, and as many as 21.5 % of athletes have been asked to participate while injured (Engh, 1999).

Given the large amount of family resources that are needed to facilitate participation, family members who do not participate are also impacted by sport. Some positive benefits include an increased sense of pride for the participant's experience or the addition of more instances of socialization with other individuals (Kay, 2000). Some potential negative impacts include resentment or jealousy on behalf of a sibling (Côté, 1999). In addition, due to lack of time and financial means, some families are not able to partake in additional extracurricular activities (Côté, 1999).

*Family*

While little research has examined the family outcomes from participation in youth sport, it is fair to assume that families may also experience positive or negative outcomes. Potential positive outcomes may include increased closeness or improved family communication (Zabriskie & McCormick, 2001).

Potential negative family impacts include depletion of resources and a conflict of family values with the values of the sport league (Côté, 1999). A study that examined the impact on mothers of elite tennis players found that they felt the entire family suffered burnout like symptoms from the time demands placed on the family (Kay, 1999). Parents have also been shown to have lower levels of physical activity as a result of their children's participation (Dixon, 2009; Thompson, 1999).

In sum, while having a child participate in youth sport may have many positive benefits on the family and the participant, there are also opportunities in which negative outcomes may occur. It is important that families seek out youth sport opportunities that are within their financial means and that are a good fit with family values.

## CHAPTER SUMMARY

In this chapter, we examined youth sport issues in the US. We began by placing youth sport within its social and historical context, illustrating its status in broader society. We also examined socialization, or how children learn the values and behaviors of sport, followed by a discussion of sport outcomes, including the benefits and shortcomings associated with participation. Finally, we examined the distinct relationship of sport and the family and how each sphere influences the other.

## DISCUSSION QUESTIONS

1. What can be done to create, and maintain, a friendly and inviting atmosphere for youth sports?
2. Take into consideration the behaviors of coaches, spectators, parents, and participants. What can be done to prevent negative behaviors and encourage positive ones?
3. Previous researchers have stated that, up to 70% of youth sport participants drop out of participation before their thirteenth birthday. What changes, or accommodations, would you make to help retain these children in sports?
4. How do you feel about the suggestion that score should not be kept in youth sports?
5. Is sponsorship of youth (specifically interscholastic) sport a good thing, especially in light of the economic woes being faced by many public school systems?

## RECOMMENDED READINGS

Ryan, J. (1995). *Little girls in pretty boxes: The Making and breaking of elite gymnasts and figure skaters.* New York: Doubleday. (An excellent sociological examination of the lives and social worlds of figure skaters and gymnasts. In particular, Ryan examines the parental, coach, and social pressures placed on girls at such a young age and the choices the girls make in the quest for Olympic and World status.)

Côté, J. (1999). The influence of the family on the development of sport. *The Sport Psychologist,13,* 395-417. (Cote focuses on the influence that the family has on the development of sport and the different roles the family plays in the different stages of the youth sport continuum, from the early or sampling years, all the way to the high school athlete in the specialization years.)

## REFERENCES

Anderseen, N., Wold, B., & Torsheim, T. (2006). Are parental health habits transmitted to their children? An eight year longitudinal study of physical activity in adolescents and their parents. *Journal of Adolescence, 29,* 513-524.

Bandura, A. (1977). *Social learning theory*. Englewood Cliffs, NJ: Prentice Hall.

Bissinger, H.G. (1990). *Friday night lights: A town, a team, a dream*. Reading, MA: Addison-Wesley.

Brenner, J. S. (2007). Overuse injuries, overtraining, and burnout in child and adolescent athletes. *Pediatrics: Official Journal of the American Academy of Pediatrics, 119,* 1242-1245.

Brustad, R.J. (1988). Affective outcomes in competitive youth sport: The influence of intrapersonal and socialization factors. *Journal of Sport and Exercise Psychology, 10,* 307-321.

Brustad, R.J. (1993). Who will go out and play? Parental and psychological influences on children's attraction to physical activity. *Pediatric Exercise Science, 5,* 210-223.

Brustad, R.J. (1996). Attraction to physical activity in urban schoolchildren: Parental socialization and gender influences. *Research Quarterly for Exercise and Sport, 67,* 316-323.

Butcher, J., Lindner, K., & Johns, D. (2002). Withdrawal from competitive youth sport: A Retrospective ten-year study. *Journal of Sport Behavior, 25,* 145-163.

Chalip, L. (2006). Toward a distinctive sport management discipline. *Journal of Sport Management, 20,* 1-21.

Chalip, L., Stachura, L., & Johnson, A. (Eds.). (1996). *National sports policies: An international handbook* (pp. 404-429). Cheektowaga, NY: Greenwood.

Coakley, J. (2008). *Sports in society: Issues and controversies* (10th ed.). Boston, MA: McGraw-Hill.

Coakley, J., & White, A. (1999). Making decisions: How young people become involved and stay in sports. In J. Coakley and P. Donnelly (Eds.), *Inside Sports* (pp. 77-85). London: Routledge.

Côté, J. (1999). The influence of the family on the development of sport. *The Sport Psychologist, 13,* 395-417.

Davison, K., Downs, D., & Birch, L. (2006). Pathways linking perceived athletic competence and parental support at age 9 years to girls' physical activity at age 11 years. *Research Quarterly for Exercise and Sport, 77,* 23-31.

Dixon, M. A., & Bruening, J. (2011). Youth and community sport. In P. Pederson, J.Parks, J. Quarterman, & L. Thibault (Eds.). *Contemporary Sport Management* (4th ed.). Champaign, IL: Human Kinetics.

Dixon, M.A. (2009). From their perspective: A qualitative examination of physical activity and sport for working mothers. *Sport Management Review, 12,* 34-48.

Dixon, M.A., Warner, S., & Bruening, J. (2008). More than just letting them play: The enduring impact of parental socialization in sport for females. *Sociology of Sport Journal, 25,* 538-559.

Dorsch, T.E., Smith, A.L., & McDonough, M.H. (2009). Parents' perceptions of child-to-parent socialization in organized youth sport. *Journal of Sport and Exercise Psychology, 31,* 44-468.

Engh, F. (1999). *Why Johnny hates sports: Youth sports are failing our children and what we can do about it*. Garden City Park, NY: Avery Publishing Group.

Ericsson, K. A., Krampe, R. T., & Tesch-Romer, C. (1993). The role of deliberate practice in the acquisition of expert performance. *Psychological Review, 100,* 363-406.

Fellmeth, L. (2010). Participation in high school sports tops 7.6 million. *High School Today, October 2010*, pp. 10-11. Retrieved on 20 November, 2011, from www.nfhs.org.

Fraser-Thomas, J.L., Côté, J., & Deakin, J. (2008). Examining adolescent sport dropout and prolonged engagement from a developmental perspective. *Journal of Applied Sport Psychology, 20,* 318-333.

Fraser-Thomas, J.L., Côté, J., & Deakin, J. (2005) Youth sport programs: An avenue to foster positive youth development. *Physical Education and Sport Pedagogy 10*(1), 19-40.

Fredricks, J., & Eccles, J. (2002). Children's competence and value beliefs from childhood through adolescence: Growth trajectories in two male-sex-typed domains. *Developmental Psychology, 38*, 519-533.

Fredricks, J., & Eccles, J. (2004). Parental influences on youth involvement in sports. In M.R. Weiss (Ed.), *Developmental sport and exercise psychology: A Lifespan perspective* (pp. 145-164). Morgantown, WV: Fitness Information Technology.

Green, B. C. (1997). Action research in youth soccer: Assessing the acceptability of an alternative program. *Journal of Sport Management, 11*, 29-44.

Green, B.C. (2005). Building sport programs to optimize athlete recruitment, retention, and transition: Toward a normative theory of sport development. *Journal of Sport Management, 19*, 233-253.

Green, B.C., & Chalip, L. (1997). Enduring involvement in youth soccer: The socialization of parent and child. *Journal of Leisure Research, 29*, 61-77.

Green, B.C., Dixon, M.A., & Smith, B. (2008). *Strategy and Implementation of After-School Sport Program.* Austin, TX. Youth Interactive.

Greendorfer, S. (1993). Gender role stereotypes and early childhood socialization. In G.L. Cohen (Ed.), *Women in Sport: Issues and controversies* (pp. 3-14). Newbury Park, CA: Sage.

Greendorfer, S. (1977). Role of socializing agents in female sport involvement. *Research Quarterly, 48*, 304-310.

Greendorfer, S., & Bruce, T. (1991). Rejuvenating sport socialization research. *Journal of Sport and Social Issues, 15,* 129-144.

Greendorfer, S., & Lewko, J.H. (1978). The role of family members in sport socialization of children. *Research Quarterly, 49*, 146-152.

Johnston, L., O'Malley, P., Bachman, J., & Schulenberg, J. (2012). Monitoring the future national results on adolescent drug use: Overview of key findings, 2011. Ann Arbor, MI: Institute for Social Research, University of Michigan.

Kay, T. (2000). Sporting excellence: A family affair? *European Physical Education Review, 6*(2), 151-169.

King-White, R. (2010). Danny Almonte: Discursive construction(s) of (Im)migrant citizenship in neoliberal America. *Sociology of Sport Journal, 27*, 178-199.

Lally, P., & Kerr, G. (2008). The effects of athlete retirement on parents. *Journal of Applied Sport Psychology, 20,* 42-56.

Lim, S., Warner, S., Dixon, M., Berg, B., Kim, C., & Newhouse-Bailey, M. (2011). Sport participation across national contexts: A Multilevel investigation of individual and systemic factors that impact adult sport participation. *European Sport Management Quarterly, 11*, 197-224.

McElroy, M. (1983). Parent-child relations and orientations toward sport. *Sex Roles, 9*, 997-1004.

Miller, M. E., & Houston, S. D. (1987). The classic Maya ballgame and its architectural setting: A study of relations between text and image. *RES: Anthropology and Aesthetics, 14*, 46-65.

Morgan,T.K., & Giacobbi, P.R. (2006). Toward two grounded theories of the talent development and social support process of highly successful collegiate athletes. *The Sport Psychologist, 20*, 295-313.

National Collegiate Athletic Association (2011). Estimated probability of competing in athletics beyond the high school interscholastic level. Retrieved 10 October, 2011, from www.ncaa.org.

National Council of Youth Sports (NCYS) (2008). Report on trends and participation in organized youth sports: Market research report – NCYS membership survey – 2008 edition. Retrieved November 28, 2011, from www.ncys.org.

NetSafekids, (2003). What is pornography? The National Academy of Science. Retrieved on December 2, 2011 from www.nap.edu.

Nixon II., H. (1990). Rethinking socialization and sport. *Journal of Sport and Social Issues, 14*, 33-47.

Rees, C., & Miracle, A. (2000). Sport and education. In J. Coakley and E. Dunning (Eds.), Handbook of sports studies (pp. 277-290). London: Sage.

Rimer, S. (2002, January 08). Rink manager says hockey father overpowered his victim. *New York Times*, p. 14.

Robidoux, M. A. (2002). Imagining a Canadian identity through sport: A historical interpretation of lacrosse and hockey. *The Journal of American Folklore, (115) 465, Folklore in Canada (Spring, 2002)*, pp. 209-225.

Rudolph, F. (1990). *The American college & university: A history/ by Frederick Rudolph; introductory essay and supplemental bibliography by John R. Thelin* (Rev. ed.). Athens, GA: University of Georgia.

Ryan, J. (1995). *Little girls in pretty boxes: The Making and breaking of elite gymnasts and figure skaters*. New York: Doubleday.

Safe Kids (2011). Sport and Recreation Safety Fact Sheet. Retrieved 11 November, 2011, from www.safekids.org.

Sage, G. (1980). Parental influence and socialization into sport for male and female intercollegiate athletes. *Journal of Sport and Social Issues, 4*, 1-13.

Schmidt, G. W., & Stein, G. L. (1991). Sport commitment: A model integrating enjoyment, dropout, and burnout. *Journal of Sport & Exercise Psychology, 8*, 254-265.

Smith, R. E. (1986). Toward a cognitive-affective model of athletic burnout. *Journal of Sport Psychology, 8*, 36-50.

Smith, R. E., & Smoll, F. L. (1990). Self-esteem and children's reactions to youth sport coaching behaviors: A field study of self-enrichment processes. *Developmental Psychology, 26*, 987-993.

Spreitzer, E. (1995). Does participation in interscholastic athletics affect adult development: A longitudinal analysis of an 18-24 age cohort. *Youth and Society, 25,* 368-87.

Swartz, M., & Lindem, H. (1991, May). The cheerleader murder plot. *Texas Monthly, 19(5),* 106.

Thompson, S.M. (1999). *Mother's Taxi.* Albany, NY: State University of New York Press.

Warner, S., & Dixon, M.A. (2011). Enhancing the sport experience: Understanding sense of community from an athlete's perspective. *Journal of Sport Management, 25,* 257-271.

Weiss, M., & Barber, H. (1995). Socialization influences of collegiate female athletes: A tale of two decades. *Sex Roles, 33,* 129-140.

Weiss, M., & Glenn, S. (1992). Psychological development and females' sport participation: An interactional perspective. *Quest, 44,* 138-157.

Wiersma, L., & Fifer, A.M. (2008). It's our turn to speak: The joys, challenges, and recommendations of youth sport parents. *Journal of Leisure Research, 40(4),* 505-530.

Zabriskie, R. B., & McCormick, B. P. (2001). The influences of family leisure patterns on perceptions of family functioning. *Family Relations, 50,* 281-289.

# CHAPTER 13

# INTERCOLLEGIATE SPORT

## Calvin Nite

***

## Learning Objectives

After reading this chapter, you should be able to:

1. Understand the history of intercollegiate athletics.
2. Identify the two primary lines of thought that guide practices in athletic departments.
3. Recognize the role athletics play on college campuses.
4. Explain how student-athletes are affected by participating in college athletics.


## INTRODUCTION

Within the United States, few phenomena inspire as much passion and enthusiasm as intercollegiate athletics. Every year, millions of students, alumni, and fans spend millions of dollars and countless hours attending games, purchasing memorabilia, and supporting their favorite universities' athletic programs. Countless hours of radio airtime and television broadcasting are devoted every year to following high profile sports. Universities have even created their own, institution-specific television networks devoted solely to providing coverage of their own athletics teams. Interesting enough, the US is one of the few countries in the world that houses and regulates sports within the higher education system (Beyer & Hannah, 2000). Proponents of college athletics contend that athletics are essential to the education process for both the athletes and the student body in general (Bailey et al., 2009; Hyland, 2008). Furthermore, supporters of intercollegiate athletics have asserted that athletic programs are important to the economic viability of universities because they help market and brand the university to the general public through media exposure (Bouchet & Hutchinson, 2010; Putler & Wolfe, 1999). Thus, the inclusion of athletic programs on college campuses presents a myriad of different issues warranting examination.

Per the 2010 NCAA membership report, there are over 1300 NCAA member institutions with more than 400,000 student-athletes competing in a variety of sports (NCAA, 2010). The NCAA is comprised of three divisions, each having different rules governing the affiliated athletic departments. The NCAA sponsors championships for sports in each of these divisions except for football programs competing in the Football Bowl Subdivision (FBS). Even though it uses NCAA rules regarding eligibility, the Bowl Championship Series (BCS) provides the system for determining champions in the FBS. Divisions I and II both offer athletic scholarships to their student-athletes, while Division III universities are not permitted to offer athletic scholarships to their student-athletes. The NCAA is not the sole governing body for college athletics. The National Association of Intercollegiate Athletics (NAIA) has approximately 300 member institutions (NAIA, n.d.). The National Junior College Athletic Association (NJCAA), which is comprised of two-year junior and community colleges, has more than 500 members. Both the NAIA and NJCAA provide scholarship money to student-athletes. Finally, the National Christian College Athletic Association (NCCAA) is comprised of almost 100 Christian/Bible colleges with many of these institutions having dual membership with the NCAA (NCCAA, n.d.).

It should also be noted that most universities competing in intercollegiate athletics are grouped into conferences. Each of these conferences has rules and policies for their member institutions in addition to the rules and regulations of the broad governing bodies. Conferences have rules regarding media revenue distribution to its member institutions along with other bylaws concerning other revenue distributions. Some examples of athletic conferences include the Southeastern Conference, the Big XII, the Big Ten, The Lone Star Conference, and the American Southwest Conference.

There is little denying that intercollegiate athletics and athletic departments have had economic impacts on universities across the nation. Operating an athletic department is a costly endeavor for universities and has both financial and social ramifications. Recent estimates suggest the annual budget for all NCAA affiliated athletic departments totals approximately $10.5 billion (NCAA, n.d.). Yet only 22 athletic departments at the Football Bowl Subdivision (FBS) level were self-sustaining (Fulks, 2011). The fact that most athletic departments often operate with a deficit has resulted in increased efforts to obtain funding from sources outside of universities. This funding is either received through donations to the department or, increasingly, through corporate partnerships (NCAA, n.d.). Without outside sources of funding, universities are left to bear the burden of the financial losses accumulated by the athletic department, which in turn, detracts from other departments and activities of universities. However, campus leaders, state legislators, and the general public willingly bear these financial losses because of the inherent value that has been assigned to athletics (NCAA, n.d.).

In this chapter, I will examine the underlying principles within the broad spectrum on intercollegiate athletics. I begin with an examination of the history of intercollegiate athletics and how commercialism began to shape the actions of athletic departments. This is followed by examination of how both commercial and educational ideologies have shaped intercollegiate athletics and how these ideals currently affect operations, and conclude with a look into how participation in intercollegiate athletics affects student-athletes.

## HISTORY OF INTERCOLLEGIATE ATHLETICS

Athletics have been a part of university life for the better part of the last 200 years. The first athletic competition between universities was a crew race that was held between students at Harvard and Yale universities in 1852 (Barr, 2009). The first intercollegiate baseball game was held in 1859, followed by the first football game between Princeton and Rutgers in 1869 (Barr, 2009). During these first few years, competitions were organized and operated by students from participating colleges. Through the late 1800s, competitions between universities became increasingly more popular among students and the general public, resulting in fierce rivalries between fan and alumni bases with more of an emphasis placed on winning (Barr, 2009; Beyer & Hannah, 2000). As a result, Yale was the first university to hire a coach, William Wood, for their crew team in efforts to realize better performance (Barr, 2009).

As intercollegiate athletic competitions increased in popularity and competitiveness, universities recognized the need to regulate intercollegiate athletics for safety and fairness reasons. The first regulatory body set up to govern intercollegiate athletics was the Big Ten Conference in 1895 (Beyer & Hannah, 2000). Participation in athletics was limited to full-time students who were in good academic standing with their universities. Further regulations resulted from the events of the 1905 football season, which saw the death of 18 football players and at least 150 serious injuries (Beyer & Hannah, 2000). President Theodore Roosevelt pressured university presidents to get control of these athletic competitions. Thus, representatives from 62 colleges and universities formed the Intercollegiate Athletic Association of the United States (IAAUS), which eventually was renamed the National Collegiate Athletic Association (NCAA) (Barr, 2009). Despite the presence of these regulatory bodies, universities did not officially support athletics until the 1920s, at which point they integrated athletics into their physical education departments by appointing coaches to academic positions and providing university funds to support athletic teams (Barr, 2009).

In 1929, the Carnegie Foundation commissioned the first study of inter-collegiate athletics. After visiting 112 colleges and universities, the foun-dation discovered the prevalence of recruiting and academic abuses along with the realization that intercollegiate athletics was highly com-mercialized (Barr, 2009; Thelin, 1994). Ultimately this report led to the evolution of the NCAA regulating more than just the rules used in com-petitions. The NCAA began regulating student-athlete academic eligibil-ity, monitoring recruiting practices, and ultimately establishing rules for amateurism (Barr, 2009). Even though these steps were taken to slow the growth of commercialism, the increasing popularity of intercollegiate athletics lent itself to heightened commercial appeal. The evolution of the game of football in the 1950s and 1960s from a one-platoon system to a two-platoon system further increased the need for more funding in in-tercollegiate athletics (Byers, 1995). Prior to the 1950s and 1960s, football players played both offense and defense during games (one-platoon). Starting in the 1960s, football teams began using separate players for of-fense and defense (two-platoon), with players specializing their skills for certain positions on the football field. Football was already an expensive sport, but the implementation of the two-platoon system essentially doubled the cost of fielding football teams. With the rising costs of inter-collegiate athletics, university leaders needed to find new ways to fund athletics on their campuses.

A new source of funding for intercollegiate athletics came through the selling of television broadcast rights for athletic competitions (Byers, 1995). Prior to the early 1980s, the NCAA regulated and negotiated the television deals for all of college football and limited the number of games that each university could have on television. This practice was eventually deemed illegal because it violated the Sherman Antitrust Act (*NCAA v. Board of Regents*, 1984). This opened the door for individual universities and conferences to negotiate their own television contracts. Thus, it is important to understand that one of the key factors in deci-sion-making for athletic directors and universities became the pursuit of television money. Since about the beginning of the 2000s, the revenue splits that universities have received from television deals were key factors in the last rounds of conference realignments. Perhaps there is no greater example of commercialism in intercollegiate athletics than the presence of multimillion (and even multibillion) dollar television deals.

The commercialism of the intercollegiate athletics culminated in the formation of the Bowl Championship Series (BCS) for college football in 1992 (Byers, 1995). Originally, the BCS was a partnership between the top six intercollegiate athletic conferences, three bowls (Orange, Rose, and Fiesta), and network television. Initially the winners of each conference competed against the winner of another conference. This system has evolved and expanded where now there are five BCS bowls (Orange, Rose, Fiesta, Sugar, and National Championship), with the top six conference winners receiving automatic bowl bids and four other teams receiving "at-large" bids. Playing in these bowl games results in millions of dollars being distributed to universities and their conference affiliates.

The push for competing in BCS bowls and being affiliated with a BCS automatic qualifying conference has led to universities spending millions of dollars on high-profile coaches and state of the art facilities. Though football is the primary revenue generator for athletic departments, universities have begun to invest millions of dollars into upgrading facilities for other sports as well in order to attract top-level coaches and athletes. This trend has shown no signs of slowing and is, in fact, probably gaining momentum.

In response to the increased commercialism of intercollegiate athletics, the Knight Foundation created the Knight Commission with the purpose of reforming intercollegiate athletics. The Knight Commission consisted of university presidents, corporate presidents and CEOs, and members of Congress (Barr, 2009). Initial studies conducted by the Knight Commission found that many of the problems first reported by the Carnegie foundation still existed in intercollegiate athletics (Barr, 2009; Byers, 1995). Further, the Knight Commission offered suggestions for regulating college athletics, which have led to many of the current NCAA regulations (Barr, 2009; Knight Commission, 1999). The Knight Commission is still active today. In its 2010 report, the Commission highlighted the need to limit and reduce commercialism in intercollegiate athletics. Many are skeptical of the impact that the Knight Commission has had on reforming intercollegiate athletics. As it stands today, commercial involvement with intercollegiate athletics is at an all-time high and numerous scandals and recruiting violations still occur.

## COMMERCIAL AGENDA *vs* EDUCATIONAL VALUES

The world of intercollegiate athletics seems to be paradoxical in nature with divergent ideas factoring into the decision-making of university and athletic department administrators. This makes for an interesting dynamic because it often leaves decision-makers in a position where values, whether they be commercial or educational in nature, may be compromised depending on which line of thought is most prevalent. The two primary lines of thinking can be characterized as "commercial" and "educational" (Shulman & Bowen, 2001; Southall et al., 2008). Both of these ideas have become so engrained within intercollegiate athletics that they are dependent on each other for the survival of the institution that is intercollegiate athletics. Simply, athletic departments would not be able to remain competitive or viable in the current climate without operating in a commercialized manner. However, completely ignoring or abandoning educational values would result in the demise of intercollegiate athletics because they are housed within the higher education system, which still requires at least a minimal commitment to educational values. Let us examine these two lines of thought in depth.

### Commercial Agenda

As previously discussed, the history of college athletics suggests commercialism has been an issue within intercollegiate athletics since the inception of athletic competitions. In the current climate of intercollegiate athletics, commercialism can be seen in numerous aspects, including: conference realignments, television deals, athletic facilities expansions, and coaches' salaries.

*Conference Realignments*

In recent years, few events in intercollegiate athletics have garnered as much attention as conference realignments. Conference realignment is the process in which universities disassociate with their current conferences in order to join other conferences. This process has been driven by commercial concerns, notably television (discussed in detail below). Notable universities that have switched conferences from 2009-2011 include: Nebraska, Utah, Boise State, Colorado, Missouri, Texas A&M, Syracuse, Texas Christian University, West Virginia, and Pittsburgh. Many of these universities abandoned traditional rivalries for what they perceived to be a better financial situation for their athletic departments and universities. However, most of the decisions surrounding conference realignments focused primarily on the benefits that would be incurred by football with little attention being paid to other sports. It would appear that universities have demonstrated little concern for the geographical fit and subsequent travel issues for other sports that were created by these realignments. Increased frequency of missed classes for student-athletes also seemed to matter little in conference realignments. This is an example of commercial agendas trumping educational values in intercollegiate athletics.

*Television Deals*

From the time that conferences and universities were allowed to negotiate their own television deals, the pursuit of television money has influenced numerous decisions for university and athletic department administrators. This quest has been a primary motivation behind recent conference realignments and expansions. As of 2011, the Southeastern Conference (SEC) has television deals with CBS (15 years/$825 million) and ESPN (15 years/$2.25 billion) (Mandell, 2009). The Big Ten Network's deal with FOX is worth $2.8 billion over the next 25 years (Kuriloff & Mildingburg, 2011). The Pac 12 has secured a multi-network deal that is worth approximately $3 billion over the next 12 years (Pucin, 2011). The Big XII has deals with ABC/ESPN and FOX that are worth approximately $150 million a year (Associated Press, 2011). Television contracts are important because conference television money is distributed to the universities that comprise each conference. Individual universities have also struck their own television deals. Notre Dame has a long standing television contract with NBC, and the University of Texas partnered with ESPN to launch the Longhorn Network, worth $800 million over the next 20 years (Kuriloff & Mildenburg, 2011). Brigham Young University also has a television contract with ESPN (Davis, 2010). Television money increases athletic budgets, which allows athletic departments to increase coaches' salaries and improve facilities.

The governing bodies of intercollegiate athletics also benefit from lucrative television contracts. The NCAA has secured a 14-year, $10.8 billion television deal with CBS and Turner Sports to broadcast the NCAA Men's Basketball tournament. Annually, $740 million of this will be distributed to its member institutions (Wolverton, 2010). ESPN currently holds the broadcasting rights to all BCS bowl games. This deal totals about $125 million dollars per year (Tillman, 2008). Similar to the NCAA, the money from BCS bowls is distributed to the conferences, which then distribute those funds to their member institutions. Each of the "automatic qualifying" conferences (SEC, Big XII, Big Ten, Big East, ACC, Pac 12) receive the largest portion of the money. Consequently, many universities have tried to position themselves to receive invites to join these conferences.

*Athletics Facilities Expansions*

Athletic departments and universities spend millions of dollars every year on facilities. In recent years, numerous universities have either built new athletic facilities or have renovated existing facilities in order to lure highly rated recruits and to increase the ticket sales to their events. Some have estimated that throughout the mid 2000s, athletic departments raised close to $4 billion from private donors to fund athletic facilities (Sander & Wolverton, 2009). The University of Minnesota, Oklahoma State, and the University of Michigan have all spent over $250 million on upgrades and remodels to their football stadiums (Sander & Wolverton, 2009). The money that was not raised through private donations was secured using debt financing (Sander & Wolverton, 2009). This is significant because it is another example of universities and athletic departments yielding to the commercial aspects of intercollegiate athletics. The financial burdens of athletic departments are typically absorbed by their universities, thereby diminishing the funds that can be used for other projects that would likely enhance the academic missions of universities.

It should also be noted that many athletic departments have been (or are in the process of) constructing multi-million dollar academic facilities to support the academic growth of their student-athletes. These centers have been used to house study halls, computer labs, academic advisors, and academic tutors. Some have questioned the fairness of providing student-athletes with this level of support suggesting that these facilities give student-athletes an unfair advantage over other students in the classroom (Wolverton, 2008). Despite this debate, it appears that athletic departments and universities are demonstrating academics are as important as the athletic endeavors of their student-athletes. However, critical examination of this issue suggests that these academic facilities are still meant to serve the commercial side of intercollegiate athletics. That is, these facilities and their personnel are meant to keep underachieving student-athletes eligible so that their teams can remain successful in their athletic competitions. These facilities may also aid in recruiting highly talented athletes who may be ill prepared for college academic life. Therefore, even the academic facilities in athletic departments may in fact serve commercial purposes.

*Coaches Salaries*

The final commercial issue that I highlight is the exorbitant coaches' salaries of intercollegiate athletics. Coaches' salaries have steadily risen over the past few decades to the point where many college coaches are compensated as well as professional coaches. In many cases (especially at the FBS and Division I level), coaches have salaries exceeding their university presidents' and athletic directors'. What is more, in some states, the highest paid government employees are coaches. Consider the state of Texas. The *Texas Tribune* reported in 2011 that the two highest paid state employees of Texas were Mack Brown (Head Football Coach at the University of Texas, $5.1 million/year) and Rick Barnes (Head Men's Basketball Coach at the University of Texas, $2.2 million/year). In comparison, the salary of the president of the University of Texas that year was $613,612, while the Athletic Director made approximately $700,000.

The justifications for the excessive coaches' salaries are typically commercial in nature. Coaches are paid so well because their teams generate substantial revenues for their universities; therefore, just as any CEO at a successful firm, coaches should be compensated in relation to the amounts of money that they bring into the athletic department and university. Whether or not college coaches deserve these salaries could be an endless conversation. The point is that these salaries are supposedly driven by commercial principles with little regard given to the educative side of the coaching profession. In fact, one could argue that many coaches who have emphasized the educational aspects of participation in intercollegiate athletics have been fired from their jobs because they did not win enough games to satisfy the commercial aspects of coaching.

**Educational Values**

For most sports and athletes in the United States, the highest level of amateur athletics is housed within the higher education system. Therefore, athletes, coaches, and other athletic administrators cannot focus solely on the athletic side of sports and must be attentive to educational values. Historically (and many argue presently), stakeholders in intercollegiate athletics had ignored or minimized the academic aspect of intercollegiate athletics. Therefore, the NCAA and other governing bodies have tried to set baseline standards of academic requirements that all student-athletes must meet in order to participate in intercollegiate athletics. These measures were meant to ensure the educational values of the higher education system were not neglected. Further, in order to root out professional influence and preserve amateurism, the NCAA has also set forth regulations governing the amateur status of student-athletes. These steps were taken to combat the commercial aspects of intercollegiate athletics and maintain, at the very least, a minimal adherence to educational values.

*Amateurism*

One of the principle purposes of the NCAA is to regulate and maintain the amateur status of student-athletes and intercollegiate athletics in general. This idea is the foundation for many of their rules and regulations. Amateurism is used to explain the NCAA's reluctance to compensate student-athletes beyond scholarships or financial aid agreements. Because of the adherence to amateur values, the NCAA also regulates the contact that student-athletes can have with agents. Critics of this routinely point to the amount of money that is generated by football and men's basketball and have suggested that student-athletes are exploited (Donnor, 2005). Some would argue that the NCAA operates to protect the myth of amateurism in an effort to maintain their status as a not-for-profit organization (Sack & Staurowsky, 1998). However, the NCAA has argued that most athletic departments, sports, and championship events typically operate at a deficit (NCAAc, n.d.). Regardless, the NCAA has attempted to preserve some semblance of amateurism in intercollegiate athletics. A key aspect of amateurism for the NCAA is upholding the educational values of participation in sport at the college level. The NCAA has routinely suggested that deviating from its amateur status would jeopardize the role of education in intercollegiate athletics (NCAAc, n.d.). To this point, they have remained steadfast that "Student-athletes are students first and athletes second. They are not university employees who are paid for their labor" (NCAAc, n.d.). Using this mindset, the NCAA has adopted extensive rules and requirements concerning academic eligibility, rules for participation, and institutional regulations in order to remain aligned with the educational values of higher education.

*Eligibility Requirements*

Historically, the NCAA has maintained the position that participation in intercollegiate athletics is an important part of higher education. The NCAA regards "that participation in intercollegiate athletics is part of the higher education experience and teaches values that are difficult to learn in a classroom" (NCAA, 2010b). In order to propagate this idea and counter the negative publicity, the NCAA began using the term "student-athletes" in the 1950s to describe athletes who participate in intercollegiate athletics (Staurowsky & Sack, 2005). Some have become critical of the term "student-athlete" because it "reflects the intention of the NCAA and college administrators to obscure exploitative practices that profited the institutions involved while violating the fundamental tenets of higher education and human rights" (Staurowsky & Sack, 2005, p. 107). Regardless of the original intent for its usage, the term "student-athlete" suggests that participants in athletics must at least feign some level of academic concern.

In this regard, the NCAA has taken steps to address certain academic concerns. One notable step occurred in 1983 with the adoption of Proposition 48 (NCAA, 2010b). Proposition 48 established that student-athletes must maintain a minimum grade point average of 2.0. Included in this, first-year athletes must also have scored a minimum of a 700 on the SAT or a 15 on the ACT. Further, entering first-year student-athletes must have also passed 11 core classes prior to enrollment. Eventually in 1992, Proposition 16 was adopted to heighten the academic eligibility requirements. Proposition 16 introduced a "sliding scale" that took into account an entering individual's high school grade-point average along with the student's SAT or ACT scores (NCAA, 2010b). In recent years, the NCAA has instituted further reforms to their eligibility requirements. The NCAA implemented the Graduation Success Rate (GSR) and Academic Success Rate (ASR) in order to instill accountability within athletic departments and universities in regards to the academic achievement of their student-athletes. The NCAA continues to update and reform its eligibility requirements for student-athletes and has also begun to penalize universities that frequently do not meet minimal GSR and ASR standards.

Other governing bodies of intercollegiate athletics also have admission requirements. The NAIA is generally less restrictive than the NCAA, yet they still require that universities only admit athletes "under admission standards that are equal to or higher than those applied to the general student body of that institution" (NAIA, 2011, p. 33). Entering first-year students within the NAIA must score at least an 860 on the SAT or an 18 on the ACT. Even though rules for eligibility are often stretched or violated, most intercollegiate athletic governing bodies maintain academic eligibility requirements for student-athletes in order to comply with the educational values of the system of higher education.

Having examined the two primary lines of thought influencing operations within intercollegiate athletics, in the next section, I focus on how intercollegiate athletics influence and shape student-athlete development. When examining student-athletes, one should be able to recognize the influences of both commercial and educational aspects in regards to student-athlete development. This shall be the focus of the remainder of this chapter.

## STUDENT-ATHLETE DEVELOPMENT ISSUES

As previously discussed, the world of intercollegiate athletics operates within both commercial and educational lines of thought. Both of these impact the student-athletes and their overall development as people. Many of the challenges that student-athletes face while in college are not necessarily unique to their situations. That is, student-athletes encounter obstacles to their growth and development that are similar to other students. However, participation in intercollegiate athletics presents some unique challenges for student-athletes as they progress through college. Most notably, student-athletes must manage the pressure and fame that is inherent with intercollegiate athletics (Adler & Adler, 1991; Parham, 1993). Let us further examine some of these issues.

Student-athletes wear many hats while they are in college. In particular, scholars have suggested that student-athletes occupy the roles of "student," "athlete," and "socialite" (Adler & Adler, 1991). However, student-athletes tend to identify more with the athlete role than any of the other roles (Adler & Adler, 1991; Miller & Kerr, 2003; Valentine & Taub, 1999). This can be attributed to many factors. First, student-athletes spend most of their time and energy attending to athletic concerns rather than to the athletic or social aspects of their lives (Adler & Adler, 1991; Valentine & Taub, 1999). Specifically, they spend countless hours in practice, traveling to games, in team meetings, and watching film. To limit athletics consuming the lives of student-athletes, the NCAA has tried to regulate the amount of time coaches can spend with student-athletes. Despite this, coaches can find ways to bend these NCAA rules (and some break them altogether, such as basketball coach John Calipari during his time at the University of Massachusetts and the University of Memphis) (King, 2009). Also, it is difficult to keep student-athletes from spending their own time practicing or thinking about their respective sports; therefore, the majority of student-athletes' time and energy is spent attending to athletic endeavors.

The glorification and positive affirmation that accompany participation in intercollegiate athletics also attribute to student-athletes focusing more to athletics than academics (Adler & Adler, 1991; Yopyk & Prentice, 2005). Once student-athletes step onto their respective campuses, they become somewhat public figures who are lauded for their athletic prowess. This fame and celebrity status leads many student-athletes to neglect their academic endeavors because it is their athleticism for which they are glorified. Further, student-athletes tend to receive more positive feedback concerning their athletic performances than they do for their academic achievements. The media, coaches, family members, and even members of the academic community often focus on the student-athletes' athletic achievements, sending the message that athletics are most important. Research has suggested that student-athletes often deemphasize the importance of academics and other non-athletic aspects of their lives because they receive limited reinforcement of these roles by important people in their lives (i.e. coaches and family members; Adler & Adler, 1991; Singer & Armstrong, 2001). Further, student-athletes (especially male student-athletes) often hold onto the dream that they are going to play their sport professionally. Despite indicators otherwise, they hold onto these dreams because of the fame, glory, and large salaries of professional athletes. This leads many student-athletes to neglect developing in areas that do not directly contribute to their growth as athletes. Finally, student-athletes are often subjected to negative stereotypes concerning their academic abilities (Engstrom & Sedlacek, 1991; Sharp & Sheilley, 2008). Many professors also hold negative feelings toward student-athletes because they perceive that student-athletes receive special treatment (Baucom & Lantz, 2001; Valentine & Taub, 1999). Thus, the negative reinforcement from academic stakeholders further results in student-athletes identifying more as athletes rather than students.

Student-athletes often face developmental challenges, which can be directly attributed to them focusing so much of their time and energy on athletics (Valentine & Taub, 1999). Of primary concern, student-athletes often neglect their academic development because they focus their attention on athletics (Astin, 1993; Pascarella & Truckenmiller, 1999). Research has indicated that student-athletes often enter college with lower SAT scores than the general student body (Aries et al., 2004) and frequently maintain lower grade-point averages (GPAs) than their non-athlete peers (Robst & Keil, 2000; Simons et al., 1999). This is particularly problematic because student-athletes have also been found to experience delayed career development (Murphy et al., 1996). Simply put, student-athletes often neglect thinking beyond their athletic careers and fail to think about their future employment. Perhaps this can be attributed to the belief that they will somehow be able to play their chosen sport professionally. This is troubling because statistics have indicated that generally, less than 2% of student-athletes will become professional athletes (NCAAb, n.d.).

Despite these developmental concerns, student-athletes also realize notable advantages from competing in intercollegiate athletics. Relative to their counterparts, they score higher on measures of well-being (Snyder & Spreitzer, 1992), tend to experience fewer instances of depression and suicidal tendencies (Miller & Hoffman, 2009) and are more apt to remain physically active throughout their lives (Bailey et al., 2009). Further, many student-athletes receive some level of financial aid associated with their participation in athletics. This often means that student-athletes tend to have less debt when they graduate because they have not been forced to finance their educations with student loans. Thus, even though student-athletes may experience certain setbacks from competing in intercollegiate athletics, they still garner some benefits from their participation.

## SUMMARY

In this chapter, I discussed the two prevalent lines of thought that guide decision-making in intercollegiate athletics. Specifically, intercollegiate athletics operate with commercial and educational intents. Stakeholders within intercollegiate athletics must satiate both commercial and educational ideals in order to remain viable. Commercialism has permeated intercollegiate athletics to the point that athletic departments and universities have been forced to pursue commercial endeavors in order to remain competitive in athletics. However, stakeholders in intercollegiate athletics must also adhere to the educational values of the higher education system, or they risk sanctions from governing bodies that will limit their ability to compete in athletics. The NCAA has used the concept of amateurism as the foundation for committing to education in athletics. Finally, competing in intercollegiate athletics presents numerous developmental issues for student-athletes. Student-athletes often neglect academics and their future non-athletic careers while competing in intercollegiate athletics. Even though student-athletes do realize certain benefits from competing in intercollegiate athletics, some have questioned whether these benefits outweigh the setbacks.

## DISCUSSION QUESTIONS

1. How does the presence of two divergent lines of thought affect administration and management decisions within athletic departments?
2. How could these commercial agendas and educational agendas impact student-athletes from a developmental standpoint?
3. Should intercollegiate athletics still operate under the guise of amateurism?
4. What would be some of the drawbacks and benefits to compensating student-athletes?
5. How can stakeholders slow down commercialism within intercollegiate athletics and reemphasize the educational values of higher education? Is this even possible?

## RECOMMENDED READINGS

Adler, P. A. & Adler, P. (1991). *Backboards and Blackboards: College Athletes and Role Engulfment.* New York: Columbia University Press. (This seminal work conducted by two sociologists examined the impact of intercollegiate athletics on the development of student-athletes.)

Bowen, W. G. & Shulman, J. L. (2001). *The game of life: College sports and educational values.* Princeton, NJ: Princeton University Press. (This book examines the interplay between college sport and education.)

Gerdy, J. R. (2006). *Air ball: American education's failed experiment with elite athletics.* Jackson, MS: University of Mississippi Press. (This book examines the place of intercollegiate sport in higher education.)

Sperber, M. (2000). *Beer and circus: How big-time college sports is crippling undergraduate education.* New York: Henry Holt and Company. (This book is a critical examination of intercollegiate athletics and how commercialism within sport undermines higher education.)

# REFERENCES

Adler, P. A. & Adler, P. (1991). *Backboards and blackboards: College athletes and role engulfment*. New York: Columbia University Press.

Aries, E., McCarthy, D., Salovey, P., & Banaji, M. R. (2004). A comparison of athletes and non-athletes at highly selective colleges: Academic performance and personal development. *Research in Higher Education, 45*, 577-602.

Associated Press (2011). *Big 12, Fox Sports agree to TV deal*. Retrieved from http://sports.espn.go.com.

Astin, A. W. (1993). *What matters in college? Four critical years revisited*. San Francisco: Jossey-Bass.

Bailey, R., Armour, K., Kirk, D., Jess, M., Pickup, I., & Sandford, R. (2009). The educational benefits claimed for physical education and school sport: An academic review. *Research Papers in Education, 24*(1), 1-27.

Barr, C. (2009). College Sport. In L. Masteralexis (Ed.), *Principles and practice of sport management* (3rd ed., pp.145-166). Boston, MA: Jones and Bartlett Publishers

Baucom C. & Lantz, C. D. (2001). Faculty attitudes toward male division II student-athletes. *Journal of Sport Behavior, 24*, 265-276.

Beyer, J. M. & Hannah, D. R. (2000). The cultural significance of athletics in U.S. higher education. *Journal of Sport Management, 14*, 105-132.

Bouchet, A. & Hutchinson, M. (2010). Organizational escalation to an uncertain course of action: A case study of institutional branding at Southern Methodist University. *Journal of Issues in Intercollegiate Athletics, 3*, 272-295.

Byers, W. (1995). *Unsportsmanlike conduct: Exploiting college athletics*. Ann Arbor, MI: University of Michigan Press.

Davis, N. (2010). *ESPN, BYU Sign Television Contract*. Retrieved from http://www.mediabistro.com.

Donnor, J. K. (2005). Toward an interest-convergence in the education of African American football student-athletes in major college sports. *Race, Ethnicity, and Education, 8*(1), 45-67.

Engstrom, C. M. & Sedlacek, W. E. (1991). A study of prejudice toward university student-athletes. *Journal of Counseling and Development, 70*, 189-193.

Fulks, D. (2011). *Revenues and Expenses Division I Report: 2004-2010*. Retrieved from http://www.ncaapublications.com.

Hyland, D. A. (2008). Paidia and paideia: The educational power of athletics. *Journal of Intercollegiate Sport, 1*(1), 66-71.

King, J. (2009). *John Calipari's Final Four Erased...Again*. Retrieved from http://bleacherreport.com.

Knight Commission (1999). *Reports of the Knight Foundation Commission on Intercollegiate Athletics (1991-1993)*. Retrieved from http://www.knightcommission.org.

Knight Commission (2010). *Restoring the Balance: Dollars, Values, and the Future of College Sports*. Retrieved from http://www.knightcommission.org.

Kuriloff, A & Mildenburg, D. (2011). *ESPN Longhorn Network Cash Tips College Sports into Disarray*. Retrieved from http://www.businessweek.com.

Mandell, S. (2009). *De facto TV network will push SEC even further ahead of competitors.* Retrieved from http://sportsillustrated.cnn.com.

Miller, K. E. & Hoffman, J. H. (2009). Mental well-being and sport-related identities in college students. *Sociology of Sport Journal, 26,* 335-356.

Miller, P. S. & Kerr, G. A. (2003). The role experimentation of intercollegiate student athletes. *The Sport Psychologist, 17,* 196-219.

Murphy, G. M., Petitpas, A. J., & Brewer, B. W. (1996). Identity foreclosure, athletic identity, and career maturity in intercollegiate athletes. *The Sport Psychologist, 10,* 239-246.

NAIA (2011). *2011 Official & Policy Handbook.* Retrieved from http://naia.cstv.com.

NAIA (n.d.). *Member Institutions.* Retrieved from http://naia.cstv.com.

NCAA (2010a). *2009-1010 NCAA Membership Report.* Retrieved from http://catalog.proemags.com.

NCAA (2010b). *History of Academic Reform.* Retrieved from http://www.ncaa.org.

*NCAA v. Board of Regents,* 468 U.S. 85 (1984).

NCAAa (n.d.). *Commercialism.* Retrieved from http://www.ncaa.org.

NCAAb (n.d.). *Estimated Probability of Competing in Athletics Beyond the High School Interscholastic Level.* Retrieved from http://www.ncaa.org.

NCAAc (n.d.). *Why Student-Athletes are not Paid to Play.* Retrieved from http://www.ncaa.org.

NCCAA (n.d.). *About the NCCAA.* Retrieved from http://www.thenccaa.org.

NJCAA (n.d.). *Opportunities.* Retrieved from http://www.njcaa.org.

Parham, W. D. (1993). The intercollegiate athlete: A 1990s profile. *The Counseling Psychologist, 21,* 411-429.

Pascarella, E. T. & Truckenmiller, R. (1999). Cognitive impacts of intercollegiate athletic participation. *Journal of Higher Education, 70*(1), 1-26.

Pucin, D. (2011). *Pac-12 to feast on new TV deal.* Retrieved from http://articles.latimes.com.

Putler, D. S., & Wolfe, R. A. (1999). Perceptions of intercollegiate athletics programs: Priorities and tradeoffs. *Sociology of Sport Journal, 16,* 301-325.

Robst, J. & Keil, J. (2000). The relationship between athletic participation and academic performance: Evidence from NCAA division III. *Applied Economics, 32,* 547-558.

Sack, A. L. & Staurowsky, E. J. (1998). *College Athletes for Hire.* Westport, CT: Praeger Publishers.

Sander, L. & Wolverton, B. (2009). *Debt Loads Weigh Heavily on Athletics Programs.* Retrieved from http://chronicle.com.

Sharp, L. A. & Sheilley, H. K. (2008). The institution's obligations to athletes. *New Directions for Higher Education, 142,* 103-113.

Shulman, J. L. & Bowen, W. G. (2001). *The game of life: College sports and educational values.* Princeton, NJ: Princeton University Press.

Simons, H. D., Van Rheenan, D., & Covington, M. V. (1999). Academic motivation and the student athlete. *Journal of College Student Development, 40,* 151-162.

Singer, J. N. & Armstrong, K. L. (2001). Black coaches' roles in the holistic development of student-athletes. *Academic Athletic Journal, 15*(2), 114-131.

Snyder, E. E. & Spreitzer, E. (1992). Social psychological concomitants of adolescents' role identities as scholars and athletes: A longitudinal analysis. *Youth & Society, 23*, 507-522.

Southall, R. M., Nagel, M. S., Amis, J. M., & Southall, C. (2008). A method to march madness? Institutional logics and the 2006 national collegiate athletic association division I men's basketball tournament. *Journal of Sport Management, 22*, 677-700.

Staurowsky, E. J. & Sack, A. L. (2005). Reconsidering the use of the term student-athlete in academic research. *Journal of Sport Management, 19*, 103-116.

The Texas Tribune. (n.d.). *Government Employee Salaries.* Retrieved from http://www.texastribune.org.

Thelin, J. (1994). *Games Colleges Play: Scandal and reform in Intercollegiate Athletics.* Ann Arbor, MI: The University of Michigan Press.

Tillman, S. (2008). *Latest BCS-TV Deal Likely to Pilfer Fans' Pockets in Future.* Retrieved from http://www.cbssports.com.

Valentine, J. J. & Taub, D. J. (1999). Responding to the developmental needs of student athletes. *Journal of College Counseling, 2*, 164-179.

Wolverton, B. (2008). *Rise in Fancy Academic Centers for Athletes Raises Questions of Fairness.* Retrieved from http://chronicle.com.

Wolverton, B. (2010). *NCAA Agrees to $10.8 Billion Deal to Broadcast Its Men's Basketball Tournament.* Retrieved from http://chronicle.com.

Yopyk, D. J. A. & Prentice, D. A. (2005). Am I an athlete or a student? Identity salience and stereotype threat in student-athletes. *Basic and Applied Social Psychology, 27*, 329-336.

# CHAPTER 14

# RACE MATTERS IN SPORT AND PHYSICAL ACTIVITY

## John N. Singer

***

## Learning Objectives

After reading this chapter, you should be able to:

1. Discuss why race is significant in sport and society.
2. Discuss the major tenets of critical race theory and how each applies to sport.
3. Discuss the Black-White binary and why it is important to understanding the social construction of race and ethnicity in sport and society.
4. Identify and discuss some race matters that are salient to the different racial and ethnic minority groups in the American sport industry.

## INTRODUCTION

"We talked about what *race matters* have meant to the American past and how much *race matters* in the American present."
    Cornell West, *Race Matters* (1993, p. xvi)

Dr. West's quote, which is in reference to a conversation that he and his wife had one day as they rode in a cab from New York City back to Princeton University where he was a professor, is indicative of two different, yet interrelated meanings that he attached to the title of his best-selling book, *Race Matters*. On the one hand, *race matters* refers to the many problems and issues that emerged when racial categories were created or socially constructed and embedded in the American legal system to empower and privilege the majority racial group (i.e., Whites) and to oppress and marginalize racialized others (i.e., people of color) (see Coates, 2003; Haney Lopez, 1996; see also Omni & Winant, 1994 for a discussion of *racial formation theory*). As a result, *Whiteness* (i.e., being considered a part of the White "race") has historically been, and continues to be positioned at the top of the American racial order with other non-White racial groups (e.g., Blacks/African Americans, Native Americans/American Indians, Latinos/Hispanics, Asians/Pacific Islanders) falling somewhere below this group. As Chideya (1999) cleverly put it, "in the basest and most stereotypic terms, white Americans are considered 'true' Americans: black Americans are considered inferior Americans; Asian and Latinos are too often considered foreigners; and Native Americans are rarely thought of at all" (p. 7). Indeed, many of the historical and contemporary issues and problems pertaining to race (and ethnicity) in American society can be traced and attributed to this positioning of Whiteness as the optimal status criterion, and to the predominant emphasis and preference that has been placed on the social histories, perspectives, and interests of White people.

On the other hand, *race matters* is also a declaration that speaks to the significance of and need for engaging with race and understanding the impact it has on various racial and ethnic groups within American society. *Racism,* which stems from the social construction of race and the racial categories and hierarchies that have emerged, has been described as "an individual's negative prejudicial attitude or discriminatory behavior toward people of a given race, as well as institutional personnel, policies, practices, and structures (even if not motivated by prejudice) that subordinate people of a given race" (Waller, 1998, p. 47). What this description might suggest to some is that individuals and groups from all racial backgrounds (not just Whites) could hold racist attitudes or even engage in different kinds of blatant, overt acts of racism against racial others (e.g., racial hate crimes, racially insensitive comments; see Blum, 2002 for an interesting discussion on power and the extent to which historically marginalized racial groups or non-Whites could practice racism). However, the primary focus of this chapter will be on the systemic, institutionalized, covert forms of White racism (see Feagin, 2006) and White supremacy, which is "a political, economic and cultural system in which Whites overwhelmingly control power and material resources, conscious and unconscious ideas of white superiority and entitlement are widespread, and relations of white dominance and non-white subordination are daily re-enacted across a broad array of institutions and social settings" (cited in Stoval, 2006, p. 245).

The sport industry is one social institution in American society where race is indeed an important consideration, and matters pertaining to it are real and have consequences for different racial and ethnic groups. Sport is often heralded as a race-neutral, colorblind space and a place where the notion of a meritocracy and a level playing field operates (see

Brown et al., 2003 for empirical support for this notion). The increased number and visibility of people of color (particularly Blacks/African Americans) who have become well-known millionaire sporting celebrities (e.g., athletes, media personalities, coaches) further perpetuates this belief (see King et al., 2007). Moreover, in a broader sense, the work of scholars such as prominent sociologist, William Julius Wilson (1978), and others (e.g., D'Souza, 1995; Robinson, 1998) who have suggested the impact of race (and racism) is declining, and becoming less significant, particularly in American society, has contributed greatly to this discourse. Therefore, in light of the many conservative voices that "have sought to reformulate the debate over the causes of persisting racial inequality with arguments about the 'declining significance of race' and 'the end of racism'" (Sage, 1998, p. 82) in favor of class-based arguments, I attempt, in this chapter, to offer a counter-narrative to those conservative voices spoken of above.

The purpose of this chapter is to argue against the notion of a post-racial society (see Wise 2010) while discussing the increasing significance of race in society and sport, and some of the salient race-related issues specific to racial and ethnic minority groups in various sport industry segments, particularly within the USA. I argue race is actually increasing in significance, not declining, for two primary reasons. First, despite the racial progress that has been made since chattel slavery, the Jim Crow segregation era, and the Civil Rights Movement, Whites continue to hold onto and maintain inordinate amounts of power, privilege, resources, and influence in American society, and racial minority groups continue to struggle for equal opportunities, equitable treatment, and the achievement of the "American Dream." For example, although the historic 2008 election of Barack Obama as USA President certainly signals racial progress, the widespread racial disparities that have existed (and continue to exist) between Blacks and Whites in poverty, educational attainment, school funding, unemployment rates, median income, male prison inmates, and infant mortality rates, among other social indicators, (see Anonymous, 2009; Bowser, 2007; Kozol, 1991, 2005; Milner, 2010; Oliver & Shapiro, 1995; Shapiro, 2004) point to the tangibly manifested effects of systemic racism or the race-based injury, inherited disadvantage, and ongoing discrimination Black people in American society have endured (Wise, 2010).

The second major reason I argue race is increasing in significance and worthy of our attention has to do with the changing racial demographic landscape in the USA. The White race has historically been the dominant group and majority in terms of power and privilege as well as actual numbers in the population; however, Whites are not reproducing at an equal pace or frequency compared to members of the Black, Latino, and Asian communities, in particular (Chideya, 1999; Pulera, 2002). According to demographers, it is expected that by approximately 2040 racial and ethnic minorities will overtake Whites as the numerical majority in the USA (see Roberts, 2008). This is already the case in states such as Texas, New Mexico, California, and Hawaii. This reality has not been lost on some groups and individuals, particularly those who desire to see the current racial status quo remain intact. For example, in his book, *The Death of the West*, White political conservative, Pat Buchanan (2002) complained that the declining birth rates of Whites in Europe and the USA and the increasing birth rates of racial and ethnic minority populations — many of whom are immigrating from Africa, Asia, and Latin America into the USA and other countries in the Western hemisphere — is leading to a society that is far different from the one he grew up in and desires to maintain. Buchanan's use of the subtitle, *"how dying populations and immigrant invasions imperil our country and civilization"*, reveals a deep-seated fear and resentment about the possibility that this increasing racial diversity might alter the power dynamics between racial and ethnic groups, and create a new social order and way of life in the USA and throughout the world.

Because sport is a pervasive social institution across many societies, several sociologists, scholars, and journalists interested in sport have written on the topic of race (racial diversity) and sport from a critical perspective. For example, the work of Harry Edwards (1969, 1973), arguably the leading pioneer of the sociology of sport as a subdiscipline, helped lay the foundation and set the tone for the systematic study of sport as a social institution and cultural practice in American society in particular. In addition, several scholars and writers from within the American context (e.g., Andrews, 1996; Hartmann, 2000; Hawkins, 2001; Lapchick, 1991; McDonald, 2005; Shropshire, 1996; Smith, 2007) as well as from outside the American context (e.g., Adair & Rowe, 2010; Carrington & McDonald, 2001; Hylton, 2009; Long, Robinson, & Spracklen, 2005; Massao & Fasting, 2010; Tatz, 2011) have continued to build the literature by embracing a critical approach to the study of race and ethnicity in the domain of sport and sporting institutions across the globe.

My goal in this chapter is to add to this dialogue by specifically embracing critical race theory (CRT), which calls for the centralizing of race in the study and analysis of the legal system and the various social institutions in American society (see Crenshaw et al., 1995; Taylor, 1998), to challenge readers to better understand, confront, and ultimately, think about how to transform aspects of social life—particularly in the domain of sport and physical activity contexts—that involve exploitation and oppression based on race. In the sections to follow, I situate the discussion of race matters within the context of the CRT framework. More specifically, I begin with a general introduction to CRT and some of its major tenets; and discuss a) the historical significance of Black-White race relations, and b) the social construction of race and how it relates to ethnicity. This approach allows me to demonstrate CRT's explanatory power and utility as an analytic tool for understanding historical and contemporary issues related to race and ethnicity in American society and sport. This chapter concludes with some examples of how race and racism have been relevant to and impacted racial and ethnic minority groups across a few of the major sport industry segments.

## FOUNDATIONS OF CRITICAL RACE THEORY

As a conceptual framework that has its intellectual genealogy in ethnic studies and several epistemological traditions such as cultural nationalism, internal colonialism, feminisms, Marxism, and Neo-Marxism (see Yosso, 2005), CRT is a form of oppositional (to the White racial status quo) scholarship that is rooted in the mission and struggles of the Civil Rights Movement. CRT is an academic and activist movement that emerged from the disenchantment that a group of racial minority legal scholars had with the limitations of the critical legal studies approach and the stalled progress of traditional civil rights litigation to produce meaningful racial reform (Taylor, 1998). These scholars emphasized "the many ways that race and racism were fundamentally ingrained in American social structures and historical consciousness and hence shaped U.S. ideology, legal systems, and fundamental conceptions of law, property, and privilege" (Lynn & Adams, 2002, p.88). Derrick Bell (1980, 1987, 1992), Kimberle Crenshaw (1988), Mari Matsuda (1991), and Richard Delgado (1995) are considered to be some of the major pioneers of the CRT movement.

There are several core principles or major tenets that developed from the work of these and other scholars in the movement. First, racism is viewed as being a normal fixture and occurrence in American society, and reproduced through routine and extraordinary customs, traditions, and experiences which critically affect the quality of life and opportunities of racial groups (Brown, 2003). This embedded nature and permanence of racism is reflected in America's many social systems and institutions, including sport. Second, "Whiteness" has been deemed a property interest (Harris, 1993) or valuable commodity resulting from the historical social construction of race and the role the legal system played in reifying conceptions of race (see Haney-Lopez, 1996). According to Frankenberg (1993), Whiteness has the following linked dimensions: (a) it is a location of structural advantage, of race privilege, (b) it is a standpoint or place from which White people look at themselves, at others, and at society, and (c) it refers to a set of cultural practices that are usually unmarked and unnamed. Whiteness in American society has been positioned as the gold standard upon which all other racial groups are judged and evaluated. Third, CRT offers a critique of liberalism by exposing the limitations of civil rights law. Scholars have suggested that legislation designed to address racial inequality (e.g., Title VII of the Civil Rights Act of 1964) are often undermined before they can be fully implemented (Crenshaw, 1988). For example, as it relates to African Americans and sport, Davis (1999, p. 2) asserted, "Because of the subtle nature of aversive racism, traditional anti-discrimination laws are of dubious value in ameliorating its adverse impact on African Americans in sports."

Fourth, CRT rejects the notion that racism is outdated or a thing of the past, and argues against ideas such as objectivity, color blindness, and meritocracy which have been advanced by many people from various racial and ethnic groups in society. Instead, scholars argue this is a camouflage for the power, privileges, and advantages Whites have gained and maintained throughout American history (Tate, 1997). Fifth, (counter)-storytelling is an important tenet of CRT because it can be used (particularly by subordinated groups) to combat the pervasiveness of the privileged discourses of the majority (DeCuir & Dixson, 2004). The narratives and stories of subordinated groups, and those who work on their behalf (including Whites), have potential to counter the "taken-for-granted" assumptions of the status quo and cast doubt upon the master narratives widely espoused in society and sport. Finally, the interest convergence principle — which posits that Whites will tolerate or support the advancement of racially under-represented groups, particularly when it promotes their own self-interest — is an integral part of CRT and the aforementioned arguments. This tenet of CRT focuses on how racial equality and equity will be promoted and pursued when they converge with the interests, needs, expectations, and ideologies of Whites (Milner, 2008). In the sport context, scholars have asserted the integration of Jackie Robinson as the first Black/African American ball player into America's pastime (Major League Baseball, MLB) is a great example of the interest-convergence principle (see DeLorme & Singer, 2010).

## The Black-White Binary

As one might surmise from reflecting on the tenets above, CRT provides a framework for exploring race and racism in society, taking into account the role of institutions (such as sport) and drawing on the experiences of those most affected by systemic racism (typically, racial minorities). In this chapter, I primarily draw from CRT to challenge the experiences and perspectives of Whites as the normative standard, and instead, ground the work in the distinctive experiences and perspectives of people of color, particularly Blacks/African Americans. Beginning with the influential work of Black legal scholar, Derrick Bell—widely considered the founder of critical race theory—CRT's initial aim and focus centered on Black-White race relations. In discussing the permanence of racism in American society, Bell (1992) described Blacks/African Americans as those "faces at the bottom of the well" and stressed the need to focus first and foremost on the unparalleled struggles of Black people in society. Sage (2000) provided credence for this perspective when he acknowledged that Blacks are the only racial group in America that a) has been subjected to an extended period of slavery, and b) had segregation laws passed against them that were fully sanctioned and supported by the Supreme Court. Martin's (2010) discussion of the racial policies and practices that initially excluded *only* Blacks from historically White southern universities (even Native Americans, who experienced horrific treatment at the hands of Whites, were legally permitted to enroll in these colleges and normally allowed to participate in athletics) reveals how Black peoples' sojourn in American society and sport "has been a unique and insidious heritage of injustice" (Sage, 2000, p. 2) in comparison to other racial and ethnic groups.

It is my contention that one cannot begin to fully understand any current race-related issues in American society and sport, regardless of what race(s) or ethnic groups are involved, until at least a rudimentary knowledge of and appreciation for the history of Black-White race relations has been achieved. Moreover, since the construction of White identity and the ideology of racial hierarchy were intimately tied specifically to the evolution and expansion of the system of chattel slavery (Harris, 1993), which led to the creation and positioning of Whiteness as being superior and Blackness as inferior, it is appropriate to use the Black-

White binary as a starting point for the analysis and discussion of race and ethnicity in American sport. In following the example of Sammons (1994) in his critical, historical examination of race and sport, this chapter places Black people at the center of their history and utilizes Black history as an important and primary context through which to analyze past, present, and future race relations in American society and sport. This, I believe, will allow me to better speak to the effects that race and racism have had on all racial and ethnic groups in American society and sport.

This emphasis on the Black-White binary is certainly not to minimize or trivialize the plight of other racial and ethnic groups or the struggle for basic human and civil rights they have had to endure throughout American history. It is also not to imply that we should only focus on the Black experience as a way to understand and appreciate race matters in society and sport. Most certainly, an examination and understanding of the myriad of issues that other marginalized, historically underrepresented racial and ethnic groups have faced and continue to face in American society is very important for students, scholars, and educators to consider. Several critical race scholars would agree with this as evidenced by the emergence of literature that suggests the Black-White binary limits our understanding of the multiple ways that African Americans, Asians/Pacific Islanders, Native Americans, Latinos, and Chicanos continue to experience, respond to, and resist racism and other forms of oppression. For example, Latino critical race (LatCrit) theory (e.g., Delgado Bernal, 2002), Asian critical race (AsianCrit) theory (e.g., Chang, 1993), and Tribal critical race (TribCrit) theory (e.g., Brayboy, 2005) emerged as branches of CRT to move beyond the Black-White binary and specifically address the racialized experiences of these particular communities of people. The final section of this chapter will not only highlight some of the race matters pertaining to Blacks/African Americans, but also those specific to these other racial and ethnic minority groups in various sport industry segments in the USA context.

## The Social Construction of Race

In utilizing CRT to make sense of the racialized experiences of Blacks and other marginalized racial and ethnic minority groups in American society it is important to understand "race" as a social construct. According to Coakley (2009), race "refers to a population of people who are believed to be naturally or biologically distinct from other populations" (p. 276). Coakley discussed how race involves a reference to genetically-based physical traits, but it is ultimately based on a socially constructed classification system developed around the meanings that people (usually those with power and privilege) have given to the particular physical traits (e.g., skin color, eye shape, hair texture) associated with different populations of people. More specifically, in North American society, "European attempts to legitimate settlement, conquest, colonization, and slavery made skin color and phenotype meaningful while simultaneously imagining white subjectivities as superior to (especially) indigenous and African bodies" (McDonald, 2005, p. 248). This exploitation and denigration of Native Americans (i.e., the seizure and appropriation of land) and Black Africans (i.e., via the seizure and appropriation of labor) set the tone for the social construction of race in the USA (Harris, 1993).

According to Coakley (2009), the idea of race has had a powerful impact on history and society but it has little to do with the biological diversity among different populations of people. Coakley discussed how many social scientists view race as a myth based on socially created ideas about variations in human potential and abilities that are assumed to be biological. Sociologists have argued instead that race is really based on categories and classifications that people have developed for social, political, and economic reasons at different points in American history (Omni & Winant, 1994). This argument runs counter to those made by Hernstein and Murray (1994), who argued in their book, *The Bell Curve*, that there are fixed and enduring racial differences in intelligence between the races (i.e., Whites are superior to Blacks). In addition, the notion of race as a social construct also challenges the major thesis of Jon Entine's (2000) controversial book, *Taboo: Why Black Athletes Dominate Sports and Why We Are Afraid to Talk About It*, which argues that genetics, and to a lesser degree, cultural factors help to explain Black athletic superiority in certain sports (i.e., football, basketball, and running). While biological arguments such as those mentioned above remain a part of the discourse on race matters, they are routinely challenged and refuted by sociologists and other social scientists.

In arguing for the notion of race as a social construct, it is important to also understand the complex relationship between race and ethnicity. Adair and Rowe (2010) discussed how an engagement with both race and ethnicity is integral to our understandings of identity, commonality, difference, diversity, and discrimination in sport and society. According to (Coakely, 2009), ethnicity is different than race in that it refers to "a particular cultural heritage that is used to identify a particular population" (p. 276). It is not based on biology or genetically transmitted traits; rather, it is based on cultural traditions and history. In this regard, an ethnic population is "a category of people regarded as socially distinct because they share a way of life, a collective history, and a sense of themselves as a people" (p. 276). Coakley also discussed how some people become confused when they use the term minority to talk about racial or ethnic populations. From a sociological perspective, a minority is "a socially identified population that suffers disadvantages due to systemic discrimination and has a strong sense of social togetherness based on shared experiences of past and current discrimination" (p. 276).

Based on the definitions above, there are several racial and ethnic groups that at different points throughout American history would be considered racial minorities. For example, at one point in American history the Italians as an immigrant ethnic group from Europe were initially categorized as racially "other" in relation to White, Anglo-Saxons; and they faced discrimination because of their racial status. It was not until well into the twentieth century that this ethnic group was legally accepted into the White racial category (Omni & Winant, 1994). However, it is important to note that the "immigration experience" has been quite different for White ethnic groups (e.g., Italians, Irish, Germans) than it has been for non-White ethnic groups, such as African-Americans, who were brought in chains and enslaved for hundreds of years. Likewise, Japanese-Americans, unlike their German-American and Italian-American counterparts, were put in internment camps during World War II (Chong-Soon Lee, 1995). Even when different populations of people are referred to in terms of their ethnicity or ethnic background, it is important to understand and acknowledge how "race," and, more specifically, issues of Whiteness are linked to ethnic identity.

This discussion thus far is demonstrative of the conceptual entanglements of the social construction of race and ethnicity, and how, based on the racial classification system that developed in American society, ethnic groups become racialized or "raced" (see Armstrong, 2011; Higginbotham & Anderson, 2009). Therefore, while race and ethnicity have been defined as distinct concepts—where the former emphasizes skin color and biology, and the latter emphasizes culture—the differences between these concepts are not always clear and obvious. As Card (1999) exclaimed, "Both suggest birthplaces and birthrights. Both races and ethnicities may become dispersed through the homelands of others. Like 'national', 'ethnic' may suggest geographic origins. Like 'race', it suggests heritage" (p. 259).

The discourse surrounding professional golfer, Tiger Wood's racial identity provides a good example of this conceptual entanglement between race and ethnicity. His father identified as Black or African American with American Indian ancestry, and mother as being of Thai, Chinese and Dutch ancestry; as such, Woods has self-identified racially as "Cablinasian," creating his own racial category to honor and pay homage to his Caucasian, Black, American Indian, and Asian heritages. Nevertheless, people in the (sport) media and other observers have widely viewed him as being the first "Black" or "African American" to the win the prestigious Masters Golf tournament in 1997, fifty years after Jackie Robinson broke the color barrier in MLB. He continues to be identified as such by many people, despite the fact he has constantly embraced his mixed-race ancestry and heritage.

This example underscores the complexities associated with the social construction of race and ethnicity in American society. In the book entitled, *Who is Black?*, Davis (2001) discussed how the answer to that question is any person with any known Black African ancestry has been considered "Black" or "African American" or some other identity moniker related to African ancestry (see Smith, 1992 for a discussion on the changing racial labels for people of African descent throughout American history). This definition, according to Davis, reflects the long experience in the USA with chattel slavery and later with Jim Crow segregation. In the American South, this idea became known as the "one-drop rule", meaning that a single drop of "Black blood" makes a person Black. This phenomenon is unique to the USA. Perhaps this explains why mixed-raced people in American society (e.g., Barack Obama, Halle Berry) and sport (e.g., Tiger Woods, Derek Jeter) have been described or classified as Black, even though a parent or multiple grandparents might be White, Latino, Asian, or a combination of these or some other racial and ethnic classifications.

This convoluted relationship between race and ethnicity has led many people in American society to use the terms interchangeably without taking into consideration "that one is based on a classification of physical traits and the other on the existence of a shared culture" (Coakley, 2009, p. 277). Coakley further stated:

> Sociologists attempt to avoid this conceptual confusion
> by using the term "race" only to refer to the social mean
> ings that people have given to these physical traits.
> These meanings, they say, have been so influential in so-

ciety that shared ways of life have developed around them. Therefore, many sociologists today focus on ethnicity rather than race, except when they study the social consequences of widespread ideas and beliefs about skin color (p. 277).

In this chapter, I acknowledge the relationship and distinction between race and ethnicity, but chose to focus primarily on the concept of "race" because I am interested in discussing how the widespread ideas and beliefs about one's skin color and other physical traits has led to stereotypes and discrimination against racial and ethnic minority groups in American society and sport.

## CRITICAL RACE THEORY AND SPORT

Thus far, this chapter has employed a CRT approach to the discussion of some reasons why race matters and still is a significant sociological concern in American society and sport. The remainder of this chapter will focus on some race matters in the sport industry by analyzing the experiences of different racial and ethnic minority groups, and discussing some examples of key issues each of these groups have faced. In efforts to focus and simplify the discussion in each section, I will concentrate on only one or two race matters relevant to the particular group being discussed. While I acknowledge there are several issues pertaining to race that could be discussed and applied to various sport industry segments, I focus primarily on a few areas where the research and literature is more abundant. It is important to note that this discussion is in no way meant to be an exhaustive one; rather, the point here is to expose readers to some of the race matters that have impacted (or will impact) different racial and ethnic minority populations in American sport. Readers are encouraged to reflect upon other race matters in sport (within the American context as well as throughout the world) that might not be mentioned here.

### Integration of Blacks/African Americans

In 1996, HBO aired a two-part documentary, *The Journey of the African American Athlete*, which chronicled the trials, tribulations, and triumphs of Blacks in American sport and society from the latter part of the 19th Century (i.e., 1875) to the end of the 20th century (i.e., 1990s). More specifically, it provides insight into and demonstrates how some of the same ideological assumptions and limitations placed on Black people in the broader American society were also prevalent in the sport industry, particularly within the professional and major college sport segments. It also highlights the various forms of overt and covert racism that Black athletes—in sports such as horse racing, cycling, boxing, football, baseball, track and field, tennis, golf, and basketball—faced and endured. The documentary also discusses some of the policies and practices that were put into place in sport organizations to deny Blacks access to participation in sports with Whites, such as the Jockey Club in horse racing.

*The Journey of the African American Athlete* tells the stories and documents the experiences of several Black athletes, and how many of them rebelled and engaged in social and political activism against the White establishment in response to the racism in American society and sport (e.g., 1968 Olympic protests at the Mexico City Games). These Black women and men helped pave the way for future generations of Black athletes in terms of access and participation opportunities in various sports, endorsement deals with corporate America, and coaching and administration opportunities in sport organizations. In many respects, this documentary reveals how the integration of the Black athlete into the White sports establishment played arguably the most significant role in the tremendous commercial growth and development of American sport (particularly in major college and professional sport).

Although it should be acknowledged Blacks/African Americans have made great strides in American sport from slavery on up to today, there are still some important race matters that warrant our attention. This is the case across the various sport industry segments in American society. For example, in the youth sport context Glover (2007) adopted a CRT framework to expose the elements of racism embedded within the seemingly "color-blind" policies in America's most popular children's sport, Little League Baseball. Within college sport, the issue of race and racism at predominantly White institutions of higher education (PWIHE) has received considerable attention from sport sociologists and other scholars since the gradual and steady integration of Black/African American athletes into these educational contexts in the years following the historic 1954 *Brown v. Board of Education* decision (see Adler & Adler, 1991; Brooks & Althouse, 1993; Davis, 1995; Edwards, 1984, 1985; Purdy et al., 1982; Sage, 1998; Spivey & Jones, 1975). More recently, scholars have embraced CRT and other critical approaches in analyzing the economic and academic exploitation of Black male athletes in the revenue-producing sports of football and basketball (see Benson, 2000; Donnor, 2005; Eitzen, 2003; Grant, 2003; Hawkins, 2001; Harrison et al., 2011; Hodge et al.,

2008; Singer, 2005, 2008, 2009, in press; Smith, 2007). Essentially, this research has illuminated and interrogated some of the historical, legal, social, cultural, organizational, and individual level factors that have contributed to the negative exploitation of this group.

Although research pertaining specifically to Black female college athletes is limited, scholars have begun examining the role race and gender has played in the experiences of Black female athletes. For example, in posing the question, "Are all the women White, and all the Blacks men," Bruening (2005) highlighted the double jeopardy (i.e., sexism and racism) Black female athletes face and discussed the need for research that empowers and gives voice to this historically marginalized group. She and her colleagues embraced a race-based framework (i.e., Black Feminist Thought) in their research with Black female athletes that examined the sport participation patterns of this population and how they are silenced by the media, athletics administrators, coaches, and other athletes (Bruening et al., 2005). Carter and colleagues also adopted a critical race feminist approach in calling for the need to empower and give voice to Black female athletes. These scholars discussed issues related to academic advising (Carter, 2008), mentorship (Carter & Hart, 2010), and coping mechanisms (Carter & Hawkins, 2011), and how these areas are crucial to addressing the culturally relevant needs and unique challenges of Black female athletes at PWIHE. Finally, scholars have also employed critical approaches to examine (a) how the media silences, trivializes, and sexualizes women's sports, (b) media representations of African American women in the USA have historically reproduced racism and sexism, and (c) how issues of race and class relations differentially shape dominant understandings of Black women's participation in sport (Cooky et al., 2010; Gill, 2011).

Other researchers have focused on the dearth of African Americans in leadership positions (i.e., head coaches, athletic administrators) and the hiring practices of PWIHE athletic departments. Some scholars have suggested it is problematic that Blacks/African Americans are granted access to the entry level positions within these athletic departments as athletes but have a far more difficult time breaking through the barriers to those positions where the power lies and major decision-making takes place (Sage, 2000; Singer et al., 2010). Since the early 1990s, Richard Lapchick has published the *Racial and Gender Report Cards* (RGRC), which provides a definitive assessment of how the hiring practices in major college and professional sport in the USA impact women and racial minorities. It considers the composition—assessed by racial and gender makeup—of players, coaches, and administrators in various sport organizations. Since the publication of the first RGRC, some progress has been made in the areas of coaching and administration opportunities for racial minorities, particularly African Americans. For example, the 2010 report card for college sports (see Lapchick et al., 2011) reveals that NCAA member institutions have improved in the area of hiring head football coaches for Football Bowl Subdivision (FBS) schools.

Perhaps a major reason there have been improvements in the hiring of Blacks/African Americans into some of these positions, particularly the head football coach position, is because since 2004 the Black Coaches & Administrators (BCA) has published the BCA Hiring Report Card (HRC) on an annual basis. The goal of the BCA HRC has been to place the hiring process of NCAA college football programs at PWIHE under public scrutiny, with the ultimate goal of changing the way these programs hire head football coaches. In this regard, despite the optimism that might arise as a result of these improvements reported by Lapchick and colleagues, there is still a need to continue scrutinizing the hiring process in efforts to illuminate some of the major forces that have contributed to the slow progress in schools seeking out and hiring Blacks/African Americans and other racial minorities into various leadership positions. This is particularly the case, for example, if you take into account that not a single Black female holds the athletic director position at an FBS school (Lapchick et al., 2011).

Shifting the attention now to the professional sport context, the negative backlash that NBA all-star, LeBron James, received for "The Decision" in 2010 (see Bunton, 2010) is an example of a race matter that could be explored from a CRT perspective; a closer look at this issue could help illuminate broader issues pertaining to race in North American professional sport leagues more generally. According to sportswriter, J.A. Adande (2010), "As long as the NBA features predominantly black athletes playing for predominantly white owners who are selling their sport to predominantly white ticket buyers, there will be a race factor". In this regard, while several critics have questioned LeBron's decision and the manner in which he went about making it (i.e., announcing live to a national television audience on ESPN that he was leaving Cleveland and taking his "talents to South Beach") and claimed that race had nothing to do with the negative backlash he received, I contend that some of the vitriol with which the critics of his decision spoke should encourage people to engage in a deeper, critical race analysis of the issue.

Agyemang and I (Agyemang & Singer, 2012) conducted a case study with Black male players, scouts, coaches, and media personnel from an NBA team, and the research sheds light on this issue. These participants believed the negative backlash against James was racially motivated. They made particular reference to White team owner Dan Gilbert referring to James's actions as a "cowardly betrayal" and as a "heartless and callous action" (see Plain Dealer Staff and wire reports, 2010). These comments were viewed by some of these participants as an example of a person who exhibited a slave master's mentality. From a CRT perspective, the LeBron James situation brings to the fore issues of power, privilege, and property rights. A central tenet of CRT is the notion of race as property (Harris, 1993), and some scholars have discussed how historically Blacks/African Americans, in particular, were constructed as property in the sense that they could be owned by others (i.e., White males). This, of course, was the whole idea behind chattel slavery in the USA. And although chattel slavery was abolished in the 1800s, Rhoden argued that Black athletes' "evolution" has merely been a journey from literal plantations — where sports were introduced as diversions to quell revolutionary strivings — to today's figurative ones, in the form of collegiate and professional sport organizations (Rhoden, 2006).

Many people might disagree with or even be offended by Rhoden's argument, especially when considering that many of these Black athletes are indeed millionaire celebrities. However, in judging the merits of this argument and how Gilbert's comments and his reactions to James's decision to leave Cleveland might actually corroborate or provide support for Rhoden's argument, it is important to consider the concept of free agency and the nature of player movement in the NBA. In simple terms, a free agent is a player who has fulfilled his contractual agreement with a particular franchise, and thus, reached the point where he has the right to negotiate with other franchises that might be interested in his services. However, when one considers that team owners and executives reserve the right to waive or trade a player at anytime, even against that player's will, it should become clear that the power dynamics between the owner and player are skewed in favor of the owner. In fact, it is commonplace for team executives to make these types of personnel decisions, and many players have come to accept this as the "nature of the business" or how things are done in professional sport.

LeBron James's free agency, from his collaboration with fellow free agents Dwayne Wade and Chris Bosh to the unique approach he took to announce his decision, certainly went against how things had typically been done in the business of professional basketball. It was Gilbert's contention that is was not necessarily James's decision to leave for another team that angered and offended him; rather, it was the manner in which he did so. Although some people (including James himself) have suggested he could have done things differently, the bigger issue, from a CRT perspective, centers on the issue of labor rights and these players' desire to dictate what is in their best interests.

In thinking about the notion of White power and privilege in sport, Gilbert's (and other owners who might have echoed his sentiments) reaction to James's decision conveys an attitude—be it conscious or subconscious—that he was not only the owner of the Cleveland Cavaliers, but also, the owner of LeBron James the individual. As civil rights leader, Jesse Jackson exclaimed, Gilbert's "feelings of betrayal personify a slave master mentality...he sees LeBron as a runaway slave. This is an owner-employee relationship—between business partners—and LeBron honored his contract" (Cherner, 2010). Dan Gilbert's (and other critics of Jesse Jackson) predictable denial of and disagreement with Jackson's claims does not mean that they do not carry weight. Although these claims might be controversial and make certain people uncomfortable, they can be viewed as a challenge to White power and privilege in professional sport in American society.

**Native Americans and Sport Team Mascots**

According to Pulera (2002), "Before the first whites came to the New World, Native Americans referred to themselves by their tribal identifiers and often fought acrimonious wars with their enemies" (p. 30). Pulera further discussed how Native Americans only began to develop a panethnic identity in response to the discrimination by White society and Whites' definition of Indians as a singular racial entity. Although the U.S. census has counted Native Americans as a single demographic category, they comprise several diverse cultural populations and the differences between these populations are socially significant (Coakley, 2009). American Indians are Cherokee, Navajo, Sioux, Chippewa, and Choctaw; the Pueblo, Apache, and Lumbee tribes claim several thousand coethnics, and this category includes thousands of Eskimos and Aleutians (Pulera, 2002). Despite this diversity, most people who are not Native American "tend to erase these differences by referring generally to 'Indians' and envisioning stereotypical habits and dress—long hair, feathers, buckskin, moccasins, bows and arrows, horseback riding, war-whooping, tomahawk-chopping, and half-naked, even in cold northern states" (Coakley, 2009, p. 294).

A major issue worthy of discussion and that has received considerable attention in the academic literature is the use of Native American mascots in professional, college, and high school sport organizations. Several commentators have weighed in on this contentious issue. On one side of the debate, several students, fans, casual observers, and others have taken the position that there is nothing inappropriate about sport teams having Native Americans as mascots. They have suggested that critics of the Native American mascot are blowing things out of proportion and offer several rationales for having these mascots. For example, some claim that teams such as the Washington Redskins of the NFL, the Atlanta Braves of MLB, the Chicago Blackhawks of the NHL, the Golden State Warriors of the NBA, the Illinois Fighting Illini of the NCAA, and several college and high school teams are actually honoring and paying homage to the cultural heritage of Native Americans by having these mascots (Eitzen & Sage, 2003). In addition, some of these sport teams might be reluctant to jettison the mascot because they believe it would go against the tradition and history of the team name, and have a potentially negative impact on the identity of the sport organization. Moreover, representatives of these sport organizations might even solicit the support from members of Native American tribes to justify and continue their usage of the team mascots (e.g., Florida State Seminoles claiming they had tribal permission to use the Seminole name and logo image in an honorable way; see Staurowsky, 2007). Finally, students I have had in my classes over the years have also advanced the argument that other racial and ethnic groups have been used as sport team mascots (e.g., Notre Dame Fighting Irish), and these groups accept the use of their names with no problem (see Eitzen & Sage, 2003).

On the other side of the debate, advocates have argued that the mascot is disrespectful, and it denigrates, not celebrates, this historically marginalized racial and ethnic group in American society. As Coakley (2009) notes, the use of Native American stereotypes is so common that people take it for-granted. Nevertheless, their use belittles and misrepresents Native Americans' histories, traditions, and culture. He further contends that by using Native American names and mascots these sport teams enable fans to express their ignorance and/or racist ideas. He further intimated that when fans and team stakeholders engage in their insensitive displays, chants, and actions at games they are misrepresenting the histories, cultural traditions, and religions of many Native American tribes and nations in the USA today. Coakley used the example of a White European American student who paints his face, puts on a head-band and a colorful shirt, carries a feather-covered spear, and rides into the football stadium on a horse named Seminole (as they have done for years at Florida State University) to further convey his point that White privilege and power is real and Native Americans continue to be subject-ed to various forms of "cultural identity derogation and theft" in Ameri-can sport.

This race matter has become so prominent that the *Journal of Sport and Social Issues* (2004, volume 28, number 1) dedicated an entire issue to the topic, and several scholars have adopted a critical approach in analyzing the topic (e.g., Staurowsky, 2007). They suggest that proponents of hav-ing Native American team names and mascots are more concerned with their own self-interests than they are with the interests of the group that is most negatively impacted by it (i.e., Native Americans). One of the major tenets of tribal critical race theory is that USA policies toward In-digenous people are rooted in imperialism, White supremacy, and a de-sire for material gain (Brayboy, 2005). Although some states and school districts have policies banning the use of Native American names, logos, and mascots, and the NCAA has banned the display of them on uni-forms and other clothing and at NCAA playoff games and champion-ships, there are still several sport organizations that remain steadfast in their commitment to the use of Native American names, logos, and mas-cots.

Castagno and Lee (2007) utilized CRT and the interest convergence prin-ciple to demonstrate how PWIHE ultimately act in their own self-interests in how they address the issue. These scholars applied it to a university's policy that discourages, but does not prohibit, opposing teams from bringing their American Indian mascot to the university for competition. Furthermore, the university will not schedule a competition against an opponent with an American Indian mascot unless that team is a "traditional rival or a conference member" (p. 6). Castagno and Lee (2007) believe the interest convergence principle is demonstrated in the "traditional rival/conference member" component of the policy, insofar as:

> The institution clearly recognizes and honors the inter-
> ests of the Native community on campus by refusing to
> schedule games with some teams who have Native mas-
> cots, but the institution is even more protective of its

own interests by still scheduling games with teams with whom they have long standing commitments (p. 7).

This case represents just one of many instances where sport organizations, the majority of which are controlled by White powerbrokers, choose to place the goals and financial interests of the organization over the interests of a racial and ethnic minority group that has suffered a history of oppression at the hands of the White establishment.

### Hispanics and Latinos in America's Pastime

In terms of numbers in the population, Latinos or Hispanics are the largest racial and ethnic minority group in the USA (Coakley, 2009). The racial descriptor Latino or Hispanic refers to persons of Spanish origin who come from Spanish-speaking Latin America, as well as from the Iberian Peninsula (Cashmore, 1996). According to Alcoff (2006), the term "Latino" signifies people from an entire continent, subcontinent, and several large islands, with diverse racial, national, ethnic, religious, and linguistic aspects to their identity. She further discussed how the pan-Latino or Hispanic identities have replaced or overtaken identity monikers such as "Cuban," "Puerto Rican," "Dominican," "Mexican," and so on in national discourses on race across the USA. The Hispanic population in the USA is largely comprised of Mexicans, with this ethnic group accounting for the majority of this population (Pulera, 2002). But it is also important to note that some people of Mexican descent prefer the term Chicano rather than Latino because the former better reflects their political development and interests than the latter (Cashmore, 1996). Therefore, although the terms "Latino" and "Hispanic" are often used interchangeably and are commonly used to describe this particular racial and ethnic population, readers should be mindful of the diverse ways in which members of this population might identify themselves.

When dealing with sport in the USA, Coakley (2009) discussed the need to distinguish between three categories of Latinos or Hispanics: (a) native born and naturalized citizens, (b) Latin Americans working as athletes in the USA, and (c) workers and their family members who are in the USA without legal approval. Although there certainly are some interesting race matters related to each of the groups mentioned above, I will focus briefly here on Latin Americans working as athletes, particularly in professional baseball, in the USA. According to the 2011 RCRC for MLB (see Lapchick et al., 2011), 27% of the players on opening day rosters were Latino. While some of these MLB players were born in the USA, the majority of them are from Latin American countries.

Eitzen and Sage (2003) discussed two primary reasons there are so many MLB players who emigrate from Latin American countries. First, baseball is an extremely popular sport in these countries, and many young boys play year-round developing their skills with the hope that baseball is their meal ticket out of a life of poverty. Furthermore, they are motivated by the success they have seen from other players who left their countries and became stars in MLB. Second, once MLB executives realized there was so much talent in countries such as the Dominican Republic, they began building training academies in the 1970s to gain access to the young players and then assess, develop, and ultimately control them (Coakley, 2009). In many instances, this process has led to the "mining of baseball talent" (Eitzen & Sage, p. 290), where these MLB teams sign these players and pay them much less than they would pay a U.S.-born player. In addition, some of these teams will also sign too many players, which is known as the "boatload mentality." Oftentimes, this leads to a situation where the vast majority of these players who sign contracts never make it to the Major Leagues, and for that matter, never play at any level in the USA. Although some people in Latin American countries have made efforts to regain some control over their own talent so that MLB teams do not just take all the best players and destroy the local leagues and teams, some of the recruitment practices of MLB teams in Latin American countries continues to be a problem.

In analyzing this race matter through a CRT lens, two tenets are particularly useful. The first is the interest-convergence principle. In this vein, while it is true that some Latin American ball players have benefited from the academies that MLB executives have created and their recruitment to the minor and major league teams in the USA have lead to great financial rewards and successful careers for these individuals, this reality is never experienced by most of these athletes. As Eitzen and Sage (2003) put it:

> The ones who make it to the United States but fail to make a team tend to stay in the country as undocumented immigrants, working for low wages rather than returning home as "failures" ... These castoffs represent the underside of the Sammy Sosa story, the rule rather than the exception in the high-stakes recruitment of ball players from Latin America and the Caribbean. (p. 291)

Thus, the second tenet of CRT that is relevant to the discussion here is the (counter)-storytelling component. The experiential knowledge derived from the stories of oppression and exploitation as told by these athletes could expose the unethical practices of MLB and provide a counter-narrative to the belief that MLB is being socially responsible in its recruitment practices. An example is observed in *Stealing Lives: The Globalization of Baseball and the Tragic Story of Alexis Quiroz* (see Marcano Guevara & Fidler, 2003), where the authors tell the story of a Venezuelan teenager as one of many examples to help expose the ways in which MLB teams violate basic human rights in their efforts to secure cheap labor. Issues of MLB scouts stealing money from players, underpaying these players for their services, inhumane living conditions for players playing in MLB summer leagues based in Latin America (i.e., Dominican Republic), lack of medical care, hazardous playing conditions, and many other practices plagued the lives of these racial minorities. Essentially, stories such as this one reveal how MLB and its affiliated teams have condoned blatant and subtle forms of racism against this particular group.

### Asians in American Professional Sport

The "Asian" racial or ethnic identity moniker has long been assigned to people with origins in the Far East, Southeast Asia, or the Pacific Islands. These areas have included China, Japan, Korea, Vietnam, the Philippine Islands, Samoa, and several other countries. The legacy of wars and the global migration of labor brought people from many Asian Pacific cultures to the USA (Coakley, 2009). This diverse group of people has a long history in this country, and has had a profound impact on the economic development and culture of the USA. For example, large-scale Chinese immigration began with the Gold Rush in 1849, and for more than three decades, Chinese labor contributed greatly to the rapid economic development of the new nation (Cashmore, 1996). Cashmore (1996) also discussed how the continuing need for labor led to the recruitment of other people of Asian descent (e.g., Japanese in 1884). However, Chinese and Japanese people—like many other members of this diverse racial and ethnic group—have experienced racial prejudice and discrimination throughout American history. Some Asians have roots in America that go back to the middle of the 1800s, but a large majority of Asians since that time are immigrants to the USA (Cashmore, 1996).

A few people of Asian descent have become stars in professional American sports such as baseball, figure skating, martial arts, gymnastics, diving, basketball, and golf (Coakley, 2009; Eitzen & Sage, 2003). For example, the success of Chinese basketball player Yao Ming in the NBA during the first decade of the 2000s, and the meteoric rise of Asian American NBA basketball player, Jeremy Lin (who was born in the USA to Taiwanese parents), who emerged as the starting point guard for the New York Knicks in 2012, garnered these individuals a great deal of attention from various stakeholders in sport. In fact, Lin's initial success as the Knicks point guard attracted international attention and garnered several headlines—both positive and negative. In response to what many people believed to be racially charged language and insensitive comments made about Lin by fans, people in the sport media, as well as other professional athletes (of diverse racial backgrounds), the Asian American Journalists Association (AAJA) issued a set of guidelines on how and how not to report on this NBA sensation (see Schurmann, 2012).

While the global popularity of Yao Ming and Jeremy Lin has received considerable attention, the success, and in some regards, dominance in the early part of the 21st Century of Asian players (particularly foreign-born women from Korea) on the Ladies Professional Golf Association (LPGA) Tour, is of particular note. More specifically and as it relates to the point of this chapter, the "English only" policy that the LPGA Tour proposed in 2008 is an example of a race matter that could be examined through a CRT lens. Although the LPGA eventually reversed its thinking on this policy (only after being severely criticized for it), the fact that it was ever suggested and attempts were made to implement such a policy warrants further examination.

The initial policy called for LPGA Tour members to undergo "oral evaluations" of their proficiency in speaking English and suspension from the Tour if they failed the exam (Kelly, 2008). An initial justification for such a rule was that it would be beneficial from a business standpoint to have players who were proficient in the English language representing the LPGA (Claussen, 2010). From a CRT perspective, the question becomes, "beneficial for whom"? The LPGA Tour, at the time, included 126 international players from 26 countries, and 45 of those players were from South Korea (Claussen, 2010). Many of these Korean players during this time period were dominating on Tour, winning tournaments on a regular basis.

Given that English is not the native language for most of these Asian players, this proposed policy served as a form of treatment discrimination against this particular racial and ethnic group, especially given that this "unwritten, internal regulation was initially only announced at a mandatory meeting of the Korean players" (Claussen, 2010, p. 137). From a CRT perspective, the Whiteness as property tenet serves as a robust explanatory tool for examining this issue. Briefly, scholars and journalists have documented the negative sentiments that some of the White players on Tour expressed about the influx of Asian players and how it could have a negative effect on the "attractiveness" of the tour to fans and corporate sponsors (Claussen, 2010; Kelly, 2008). This stated concern suggests that Whiteness is and should be the face of this particular sport organization; and that this Asian presence is a challenge to Whiteness, and therefore, detrimental to the future of the LPGA Tour.

## CHAPTER SUMMARY

This chapter utilized the theme of Cornel West's best-selling book, *Race Matters*, to discuss the increasing significance of race and ethnicity, and some of the salient issues and problems that various racial and ethnic minority groups have experienced in American society and sport as a result of the social construction of race and ethnicity in the USA. I utilized critical race theory as a theoretical lens through which to examine some of the historical and contemporary race matters in society and sport. In doing so, I attempted to (a) highlight Black-White race relations and how the early encounters between White European colonists and Black African slaves was the impetus for the racial categorization of various groups of populations in the USA, and (b) clarify the nature of the complex relationship between race and ethnicity in American society. The latter part of the chapter discussed specific race matters related to (a) the integration of Black/African American males and females into the White sport establishment and the myriad of challenges they face in youth, college, and professional sport, (b) the Native American mascot issue in team sports and the denigration of this group's culture, (c) the exploitation of Latin American professional baseball players, and (d) the treatment discrimination faced by female Asian professional golfers.

In conclusion, this chapter has focused specifically on the interrogation of Whiteness and how systemic racism rooted in White supremacy has led to a myriad of issues and problems faced by racial and ethnic minority groups in American society and sport. However, it is important to note that this emphasis on White racism in American society and sport is not meant as an indictment of the White race as a whole, or condemnation of individuals who happen to be members of this population. Whiteness is structural, not personal. It also does not suggest that members of historically marginalized, oppressed racial and ethnic minority groups should be pardoned or excused from racial prejudice or discrimination against any other groups, including Whites. However, what this chapter does argue and maintain is that it is important for readers to understand that there is a certain legacy of power and privilege that continues to be associated with being White in the USA. An acknowledgement of and desire to address this reality will go a long ways in improving race relations between different racial and ethnic groups in American society and sport.

## DISCUSSION QUESTIONS

1. This chapter argued that race matters or is still significant in American society and sport today. Do you agree with this? Why or why not?
2. Several race matters specific to various racial and ethnic minority groups were discussed. What are some additional examples of race matters in sport both domestically and internationally?
3. How do you identify yourself racially? Ethnically? Why? What implications might that have for your experiences in sport and society?

## RECOMMENDED READINGS

Blum, L. (2002). *"I'm not a racist, but…": The moral quandary of race.* Ithaca, NY: Cornell University Press. (The author views "race" as fundamentally a moral problem, and examines contemporary attitudes, behaviors, and beliefs about race in the USA; the author challenges readers to recognize and distinguish the various manifestations of racism.)

Snyder, B. (2006). *A well-paid slave: Curt Flood's fight for free agency in professional sport.* New York: Viking. (Provides an in-depth look into how Black professional baseball player, Curt Flood sacrificed his career to battle MLB's reserve clause [a clause in standard player contracts that bounded them to teams for life]; it chronicles the lawsuit Flood brought against MLB and how his activism was the catalyst for free agency in professional sports.)

## REFERENCES

Adair, D., & Rowe, D. (2010). Beyond boundaries? 'Race', ethnicity and identity in sport. *International Review for the Sociology of Sport*, 45, 251-257.
Adande, J. A. (2010, October 1). LeBron James, race and the NBA. Retrieved on February 29, 2012 from http://espn.go.com.

Adler, P. A., & Adler, P. (1991). *Backboards and blackboards: College athletes and role engulfment.* New York: Columbia University Press.

Agyemang, K. J. A., & Singer, J. N. (2012). Race in the present day: NBA stakeholders sound off on race and racism. *Unpublished Manuscript.*

Alcoff, L. M. (2006). *Visible identities: Race, gender, and the self.* New York: Oxford University Press.

Andrews, D. L. (1996). The fact(s) of Michael Jordan's blackness: Excavating a floating racial signifier. *Sociology of Sport Journal, 13,* 125-158.

Anonymous. (2009). A black man is in the white house: But established racial inequalities remain....*Journal of Blacks in Higher Education, 64,* 6.

Armstrong, K. L. (2011). 'Lifting the veils and illuminating the shadows': Furthering the explorations of race and ethnicity in sport management. *Journal of Sport Management, 25,* 95-106.

Bell, D. (1980). *Brown vs. Board of Education* and the interest-convergence principle. *Harvard Law Review, 93,* 518-533.

Bell, D. (1987). *And we are not saved: The elusive quest for racial justice.* New York: Basic Books.

Bell, D. (1992). *Faces at the bottom of the well: The permanence of racism.* New York: Basic Books.

Benson, K. F. (2000). Constructing academic inadequacy: African American athletes' stories of schooling. *Journal of Higher Education, 71,* 223-246.

Blum, L. (2002). *"I'm not a racist, but...": The moral quandary of race.* Ithaca, NY: Cornell University Press.

Bowser, B. P. (2007). *The black middle class: Social mobility – and vulnerability.* Boulder, CO: Lynne Rienner Publishers.

Brayboy, B. M. J. (2005). Toward a tribal critical race theory in education. *The Urban Review, 37,* 425-446.

Brooks, D. & Althouse, R. (Eds.) (1993). *Racism in college athletics: The African American athlete's experience.* Morgantown, WV: Fitness Information Technology.

Brown, T. N. (2003). Critical Race Theory speaks to the sociology of mental health: Mental health problems produced by racial stratification. *Journal of Health and Social Behavior, 44*(3), 292-301.

Brown, T. N., Jackson, J. S., Brown, K. T., Sellers, R. M., Keiper, S., & Manuel, W. J. (2003). "There's no race on the playing field": Perceptions of racial discrimination among white and black athletes. *Journal of Sport and Social Issues, 27,* 162-183.

Bruening, J. E. (2005). Gender and racial analysis: Are all the women white, and all the blacks men? *Quest, 57,* 330-349.

Bruening, J. E., Armstrong, K. L, & Pastore, D. L. (2005). Listening to the voices: The experiences of African American student-athletes. *Research Quarterly for Exercise and Sport, 76,* 82-100.

Buchanan, P. J. (2002). *The death of the west: How dying populations and immigrant invasions imperil our country and civilization.* New York: St. Martin's Press.

Bunton, K. (2010, October 1). LeBron James: It isn't a race issue we have with you...you are the issue. Retrieved on February 29, 2012 from http://bleacherreport.com.

Card, C. (1999). On race, racism, and ethnicity. In L. Harris (Ed.), *Racism: Key concepts in critical theory* (pp. 257-266). Amherst, NY: Humanity Books.

Carrington, B., & McDonald, I. (Eds.) (2001). *"Race", sport, and British society*. London & New York: Routledge.

Carter, A. R. (2008). Advising champions: Black female student-athletes. In A. Leslie-Toogood & E. Gill (Eds.), *Advising student-athletes: A collaborative approach to success*. (NACADA Monograph No. 18) (pp. 163-66). Manhattan, KS: National Academic Advising Association.

Carter, A. R. & Hart, A. (2010). Perspectives of mentoring: The Black female student-athlete. *Sport Management Review 13*, 382-394.

Carter, A. R. & Hawkins, B. J. (2011). Coping strategies among African American female collegiate athletes' in the predominantly white institution. In K. Hylton, A. Pilkington, P. Warmington, & S. Housee (Eds.), *Atlantic crossings: International dialogues in critical race theory* (pp. 61-92). Birmingham, United Kingdom: Sociology, Anthropology, Politics (C-SAP), The Higher Education Academy Network.

Cashmore, E. (1996). *Dictionary of race and ethnic relations* (4th ed.). London: Routledge.

Castagno, A. E. & Lee, S. J. (2007). Native mascots and ethnic fraud in higher education: Using Tribal Critical Race Theory and the interest convergence principle as an analytic tool. *Equity & Excellence in Education, 40*(1), 3-13.

Chang, R. (1993). Toward an Asian American legal scholarship: Critical race theory, post-structuralism, and narrative space. *California Law Review, 81*, 1243.

Cherner, R. (2010, July 12). Eye opener: Was Jesse Jackson right in his criticism of Dan Gilbert? Retrieved from www.usatoday.com.

Chideya, F. (1999). *The color of our future*. New York: William Morrow and Company, Inc.

Chong-Soon Lee, J. (1995). Navigating the topology of race. In K. Crenshaw, N. Gotanda, G. Peller, & K. Thomas (Eds.), *Critical race theory: Key writings that formed the movement*, (pp.441-449), New York: The New Press.

Claussen, C. L. (2010). The LPGA's English proficiency rule: An-e-yo, kamsa-hamnida. *Journal of Legal Aspects of Sport, 20*(2), 135-150.

Coakley, J. (2009). *Sports in society: Issues and controversies* (10th ed.). Boston: McGraw-Hill.

Coates, R. D. (2003). Law and the cultural production of race and racialized systems of oppression: Early American court cases. *American Behavioral Scientists, 47*(3), 320-351.

Cooky, C., Wachs, F. L., Messner, M., & Dworkin, S. L. (2010). It's not about the game: Don Imus, race, class, gender and sexuality in contemporary media. *Journal of Sport and Social Issues, 27*, 139-159.

Crenshaw, K. (1988). Race, reform, and retrenchment: Transformation and legitimation in antidiscrimination law. *Harvard Law Review, 101*, 1331-1387.

Crenshaw, K., Gotanda, N., Peller, G., & Thomas, K. (Eds.) (1995). *Critical race theory: Key writings that formed the movement.* New York: The New Press.

D'Souza, D. (1995). *The end of racism.* New York: Free Press.

Davis, F. J. (2001). *Who is black? One nation's definition.* University Park, PA: The Pennsylvania State University Press.

Davis, T. (1995). The myth of the superspade: The persistence of racism in college athletics. *Fordham Urban Law Journal, 22,* 615-698.

Davis, T. (1999). Racism in athletics: Subtle yet persistent. *University of Arkansas at Little Rock Law Review, 21,* 881.

DeCuir, J. T., & Dixson, A. D. (2004). "So when it comes out, they aren't that surprised that it is there": Using Critical Race Theory as a tool of analysis of race and racism in education. *Educational Researcher, 33*(5), 26-31.

Delgado, B. D. (2002). Critical race theory, LatCrit theory and critical race-gendered epistemologies: Recognizing students of color as holders and creators of knowledge. *Qualitative Inquiry, 8*(1), 105-126.

Delgado, R. (1995). *Critical race theory: The cutting edge.* Philadelphia: Temple University Press.

DeLorme, J., & Singer, J. N. (2010). The interest convergence principle and the integration of major league baseball. *Journal of Black Studies, 41,* 367-384.

Donnor, J. (2005). Towards an interest-convergence in the education of African-American football student athletes in major college sports. *Race Ethnicity and Education, 8*(1), 45-67.

Edwards, H. (1969). *The revolt of the black athlete.* New York: The Free Press.

Edwards, H. (1973). *Sociology of sport.* Homewood, IL: The Dorsey Press.

Edwards, H. (1984). The collegiate athletic arms race: Origins and implications of the "rule 48" controversy. *Journal of Sport and Social Issues, 8*(4), 4-22.

Edwards, H. (1985). Beyond symptoms: Unethical behavior in American collegiate sport and the problem of the color line. *Journal of Sport and Social Issues, 9*(3), 3-13.

Eitzen, D. S. (2003). *Fair and foul: Beyond the myths and paradoxes of sport* (2nd ed.). Lanham, MD: Rowman & Littlefield Publishers, Inc.

Eitzen, D. S. & Sage, G. H. (2003). *Sociology of North American Sport* (7th ed.). New York: McGraw Hill.

Entine, J. (2000). *Taboo: Why black athletes dominate sport and why we're afraid to talk about it.* New York: PublicAffairs.

Feagin, J. R. (2006). *Systemic Racism: A Theory of Oppression.* New York: Routledge.

Frankenberg, R. (1993). *White women, race matters: The social construction of whiteness.* Minneapolis, MN: University of Minnesota Press.

Gill, E. L. (2011). The Rutgers women's basketball & Don Imus controversy (RUIMUS): White privilege, new racism, and the implications for college sport management. *Journal of Sport Management, 25,* 118-130.

Glover, T. (2007). Ugly on the diamonds: An examination of white privilege in youth baseball. *Leisure Sciences, 29,* 195-208.

Grant, O. B. (2003). African American collegiate football players and the dilemma of exploitation, racism and education: A socio-economic analysis of sports law. *Whittier Law Review, 24,* 645-661.

Haney Lopez, I. F. (1996). *White by law: The legal construction of race*. New York: New York University Press.

Harris, C. (1993). Whiteness as property. *Harvard Law Review, 106*, 1707-1791.

Harrison, L., Sailes, G., Rotich, W. K., & Bimper, A. Y. (2011). Living the dream or awakening from the nightmare: Race and athletic identity. *Race, Ethnicity and Education, 14*(1), 91-103.

Hartmann, D. (2000). Rethinking the relationship between sport and race in American culture: Golden ghettos and contest terrain. *Sociology of Sport Journal, 17*, 229-253.

Hawkins, B. (2001). *The new plantation: The internal colonization of black student athletes*. Winterville, GA: Sadiki Press.

Hernstein, R. J., & Murray, C. (1994). *The bell curve: Intelligence and class structure in American life*. New York: Free Press.

Higginbotham, E., & Anderson, M. L. (2009). *Race and ethnicity in society: The changing landscape* (2nd ed.). Belmong, CA: Wadsworth.

Hodge, S. R., Harrison, L., Burden, J. W., & Dixson, A. D. (2008). Brown in black and white—then and now: A question of educating or sporting African American males in America. *American Behavioral Scientist, 51*, 928-952.

Hylton, K. (2009). *'Race' and sport: Critical race theory*. London & New York: Routledge.

Kelly, B. (2008, August 26). LPGA adopts English-proficiency rules. Retrieved on March 5, 2010 from www.golf.com.

King, C. R., Leonard, D. J., & Kusz, K. W. (2007). White power and sport: An introduction. *Journal of Sport & Social Issues, 31*(1), 3-10.

Kozol, J. (1991). *Savage inequalities: Children in America's schools*. New York: Harper Perennial.

Kozol, J. (2005). *The shame of the nation: The restoration of apartheid schooling in America*. New York: Crown Publishers.

Lapchick, R. (1991). *Five minutes to midnight: Race and sport in the 1990s*. Lanham, MD: Madison Books.

Lapchick, R., Cloud, C., Gearlds, A., Record, T., Schulz, E., Spiak, J., & Vinson, M. (2011, April 21). *The 2011 Racial and gender report card: Major League Baseball*. The Institute for Diversity and Ethics in Sport, University of Central Florida: Orlando, Florida.

Lapchick, R., Hoff, B., & Kaiser, C. (2011, March 3). *The 2010 Racial and gender report card: College Sport*. The Institute for Diversity and Ethics in Sport, University of Central Florida: Orlando, Florida.

Long, J., Robinson, P., & Spracklen, K. (2005). Promoting racial equality within sport organizations. *Journal of Sport & Social Issues, 29*, 41-59.

Lynn, M., & Adams, M. (2002). Introductory overview to the special issue critical race theory and education: Recent developments in the field. *Equity & Excellence in Education, 35*(2), 87-92.

Marcano Guevara, A. J., & Fidler, D. P. (2002). *Stealing lives: The globalization of baseball and the tragic story of Alexis Quiroz*. Bloomington, IN: Indiana University Press.

Martin, C. H. (2010). *Benching Jim Crow: The rise and fall of the color line in southern college sports, 1890-1980.* Urbana, IL: University of Illionois Press.

Massao, P. B., & Fasting, K. (2010). Race and racism: Experiences of black Norwegian athletes. *International Review for the Sociology of Sport*, 45, 147-162.

Matsuda, M. (1991). Voices of America: Accent, antidiscrimination law and jurisprudence for the last reconstruction, *Yale Law Journal*, 100, 1329-1407.

McDonald, M.G. (2005). Mapping whiteness and sport: An introduction. *Sociology of Sport Journal*, 22, 245-255.

Milner, H. R. (2008). Critical race theory and interest convergence as analytical tools in teacher education policies and practices. *Journal of Teacher Education*, 59, 332-346.

Milner, H. R. (2010). *Start where you are, but don't stay there: Understanding diversity, opportunity gaps, and teaching in today's classrooms.* Cambridge, MA: Harvard Education Press.

Oliver, M. L., & Shapiro, T.M. (1995). *Black wealth/white wealth: A new perspective on racial inequality.* New York & London: Routledge.

Omni, M., & Winant, H. (1994). *Racial formation in the United States: From the 1960s to the 1990s* (2nd ed.). New York: Routledge.

Plain Dealer Staff and wire reports (2010, July 8). *Dan Gilbert's open letter to fans: James' decision a 'cowardly betrayal' and owner promises a title before heat.* Retrieved from www.cleveland.com.

Pulera, D. (2002). *Visible differences: Why race will matter to Americans in the twenty-first century.* New York: Continuum.

Purdy, D. A., Eitzen, D. S., & Hufnagel, R. (1982). 'Are athletes also students? The educational attainment of college athletes'. *Social Problems*, 29, 439-448.

Rhoden, W. C. (2006). *Forty million dollar slaves: The rise, fall, and redemption of the black athlete.* New York: Three Rivers Press.

Roberts, S. (2008, August 14). *In a generation, minorities may be the U.S. majority.* Retrieved from www.nytimes.com.

Robinson, J. L. (1998). Blacks exaggerate the problem of racism. In J.A. Hurley (Ed.), *Racism: Current controversies* (pp. 44-51), San Diego, CA: Greenhaven Press, Inc.

Sage, G. H. (1998). *Power and ideology in American sport: A critical perspective* (2nd ed.). Champaign, IL: Human Kinetics.

Sage, G. H. (2000). Introduction. In D. Brooks & R. Althouse (Eds). *Racism in college athletics: The African American Athlete's Experience* (2nd ed.), pp. 1-12, Morgantown, WV: Fitness Information Technology.

Sammons, J.T. (1994). "Race" and sport: A critical, historical examination. *Journal of Sport History*, 21, 203-278.

Schurmann, P. (2012, February 28). AAJA issues guidelines on Lin reporting. Retrieved from www.newamericanacademic.com.

Sharpiro, T. M. (2004). *The hidden cost of being African American: How wealth perpetuates inequality.* New York: Oxford University Press.

Shropshire, K. L. (1996). *In black and white: Race and sports in America.* New York: New York University Press.

Singer, J. N. (2005). Understanding racism through the eyes of African American male student-athletes. *Race, Ethnicity and Education, 8,* 365-386.

Singer, J. N. (2008). Benefits and detriments of African American male athletes' participation in a big-time college football program. *International Review for the Sociology of Sport, 43,* 399-408.

Singer, J. N. (2009). African American football athletes' perspectives on institutional integrity in college sport. *Research Quarterly for Exercise and Sport, 80,* 102-116.

Singer, J. N. (in press). Stakeholder management in big-time college sport: The educational interests of the African American male athlete. In D. Brooks & R. Althouse (Eds.), *Racism in College Athletics* (3rd ed.).

Singer, J. N., Harrison, C. K., & Bukstein, S. J. (2010). A critical race analysis of the hiring process for head coaches in NCAA college football. *Journal of Intercollegiate Sport, 3,* 270-296.

Smith, E. (2007). *Race, sport and the American dream.* Durham, NC: Carolina Academic Press.

Smith, T. W. (1992). Changing racial labels: From "colored" to "Negro" to "black" to "African American". *Public Opinion Quarterly, 56,* 496-514.

Spivey, D., & Jones, T.A. (1975). Intercollegiate athletic servitude: A case study of the black Illini student-athletes, 1931-1967. *Social Science Quarterly, 55,* 939-847.

Staurowsky, E. J. (2007). "You know, we are all Indian": Exploring white power and privilege in reactions to the NCAA Native American mascot policy. *Journal of Sport and Social Issues, 31,* 61-76.

Stovall, D. (2006). Forging community in race and class: Critical race theory and the quest for social justice in education. *Race, Ethnicity, and Education, 9,* 243-259.

Tate, W. F. (1997). Critical race theory and education: History, theory, and implications. In M. Apple (Ed.), *Review of Research in Education* (pp. 191-243). Washington, DC: American Educational Research Association.

Tatz, C. (2011). Race matters in Australian sport. In J. Long & K. Spracklen (Eds.), *Sport and challenges to racism,* (pp. 100-114), England: Palgrave Macmillan.

Taylor, E. (1998). A primer on Critical Race Theory. *The Journal of Blacks in Higher Education, 19,* 122-124.

Waller, J. (1998). *Face to face: The changing state of racism across America.* New York: Plenum Press.

West, C. (1993). *Race matters.* New York: Vintage Books.

Wilson, W. J. (1978). *The declining significance of race.* Chicago: The University of Chicago Press.

Wise, T. (2010). *Color-blind: The rise of post-racial politics and the retreat from racial equity.* San Francisco: City Lights Books.

Yosso, T.J. (2005). Whose culture has capital? A critical race theory discussion of community cultural wealth. *Race, Ethnicity, and Education, 8*(1), 69-91.

# CHAPTER 15

# GENDER ISSUES IN SPORT & PHYSICAL ACTIVITY

## Melanie L. Sartore-Baldwin

***

**Learning Objectives**

After reading this chapter you should be able to:

1. Define the terms "sex" and "gender," and discuss how gender influences participation and discourses in sport, physical activity, and physical education.
2. Discuss the gendered physical body and the concept of hegemonic masculinity within the contexts of sport, physical activity, and physical education.
3. Define 'sport ideology' and 'gender ideology' and discuss how they intertwine.
4. Discuss the significance of Title IX of the 1972 Educational Amendments to the 1964 Civil Rights Act.
5. Discuss the relationship between gender, sexuality, and sexual orientation.

## INTRODUCTION

In 2009, 18-year old South African middle-distance runner, Caster Semenya won the gold medal in the Women's 800 meters at the World Championships in Athletics with a time of 1:55.45. Shortly after her win, questions arose concerning her sex because of her exceptional performance and "masculine" physical features. In response, the International Association of Athletics Federation (IAAF) ordered Semenya to undergo a battery of, what the organization refers to as "gender" verification tests to determine whether or not the medal should be revoked. After making Semenya wait nearly a year for a decision, the IAAF finally ruled that Semenya would be allowed to keep her medal and continue competing as a female. What were not included in this ruling were the results of the "gender" verification tests, as they remained confidential. Regardless of the results, however, the damage had been done. The questioning of Semenya's sex, gender, gender identity, and even her sexual orientation have labeled her as something "other" than female and likely resulted in her experiencing some degree of psychological stress (Wackwitz, 2003). Indeed, one's sex and gender identity is a fundamental component of one's overall self (Wiesemann, 2010).

Questioning the femininity of females who exhibit exceptional athletic and physical prowess is not a new phenomenon, nor is the criticizing of the process by which claims of "gender" falsification are tested (Ljungqvist et al., 2006). In actuality, biological sex differences are questioned on the basis of socially constructed gender characteristics (Wackwitz, 2003). Thus, if one were to investigate the physical differences between women and men, she or he would be accurate in using the term sex (Wiesemann, 2010). This is not to say, however, that all persons can be neatly categorized as being female or male. Likewise, it is presumptuous to believe that all men are masculine and all women are feminine. Such ideological beliefs, however, are so deeply embedded in both mainstream society and the contexts of sport and physical activity that they inform the cognitive, emotional, and behavioral processes of individuals, groups, teams, organizations, and the like.

In this chapter, I detail why and how these processes are influenced by gendered beliefs. In the first section, I define and discuss various terms surrounding the topics of sex and gender. The hegemonic nature of gender is next related to the physical body, followed by a discussion of how the acquisition of gendered meanings influences one's own understanding of gender within physical activity and sport throughout one's lifetime. The chapter next includes a brief section on the gendered discourse within the context of sport organizations and concludes with a discussion of how gender intersects with other social structures.

## CONCEPTUALIZING SEX AND GENDER

What is gender? While the answer to this question is presumably straightforward, discussions of gender are often misinformed, as the terms *sex* and *gender* are oftentimes used synonymously. While the concepts are indeed overlapping (West & Zimmerman, 1987), it is important to individually define the two for the purposes of clarity. Sex and sex differences refer to the biological and anatomical characteristics (e.g., chromosomes, hormones levels, and genitalia) assigned to women and men. Gender and gender differences refer to the societal and contextual implications of sex characteristics (Deaux, 1985; Lorber, 1993; West & Zimmerman, 1987). Specifically, and as discussed by Butler (1990), gender exists in the form of gendered norms and gender practices that have been accorded women and men over time, stereotypes that have emerged as a result of such traditional norms, individual gender identity or the extent to which one feels they belong to a gender category (i.e., masculine or feminine), and the degree to which one is attracted and aroused by the opposite or same sex (i.e., sexual orientation). Lorber (1996) identified gender beliefs and displays, marital and procreation status, and work and family roles as additional components of gender.

The conventional understanding of gender is that following one's assignment to a dichotomous sex category (i.e., female or male), an individual possesses congruent gender roles, beliefs, identity, and displays, and sexual orientation (Lorber, 1996). A man would therefore have congruous masculine roles, beliefs, displays and a congruent masculine identity. Likewise, he would be attracted only to the opposite sex. Correspondingly, women possess femininity and congruent feminine roles, beliefs, and so on. This conceptualization strengthened the polarization of the sexes by conveying that what women are, what men are not, and vice versa. As Lorber noted, however, it is naïve to believe that all of the components of one's gender will "line up neatly on one side of the binary divide" (p. 147). Thus, the assumption that females are feminine, males are masculine, and both are heterosexual, lacks meaning and overlooks individuals who fall beyond these boundaries such as the intersexed, lesbians, gays, bisexuals, and the transgendered. Further, the gender binary ignores the blatant similarities and differences that exist between men and women. For instance, female and male bodies possess the same bones, muscles, and, with the exception of reproductive systems, organs. As Fausto-Sterling (1993) points out, however, despite possessing different sex organs, male and female genitalia are developed from the same fetal tissue. Thus, male and female bodies possess the same tissue, cells, bones, and so on, as well as move in the same manner and perform the same physiological functions. Despite similarities such as these, Western cultures' rigid construction of two and only two sexes has led to the negation of similarities such as these and the reinforcement of dichotomous sex and gender differences (Fausto-Sterling, 1993).

The intertwining of sex and gender has led to the formation of corresponding binaries. Like sex, gender has traditionally been conceptualized as two opposite, yet complementary, one-dimensional constructs. On one end of the binary there are males and masculinity, and on the opposite end are females and femininity (Spence, 1993). Over time, however, researchers have identified masculinity and femininity as multidimensional and unrelated facets. First challenged by Constantinople (1973) and later by Lewin (1984), the assumptions that masculinity and femininity were a-theoretical, simplistic, and fixed began to be abandoned. As such, researchers like Bem (1974, 1981a, 1981b) and Spence (1993; Spence & Helmreich, 1972) began to offer theoretical explanations of gender and measures by which gender could be assessed. While many of these measures continue to be used today, emerging literature has begun to view femininity as both sociological and psychological constructs, thus representing gender as behavioral differences between the sexes and the differences in masculinity and femininity within individuals (Hoffman, 2001; Lippa, 2005). These differences have received considerable theoretical attention.

There are several ways that researchers have tried to shed light onto *why* similarities and differences exist between the sexes and *how* gender differences materialize and endure as a result. Broadly speaking, there are those who study the biological determinants (i.e., nature) of similarities and differences, those who study the social and environmental determinants (i.e., nurture), and those who study both. Lips (2005) identified six general theoretical realms through which sex and gender are studied: psychoanalytic, structural, evolutionary, environmental, developmental, and interactional. While several theories are housed within these realms, the predominance of their underpinnings include things such as personality, identification, genetic adaptation, cognition, and social and cultural influences, as ways to understand sex and gender. Lips also identified several methods, ranging from the use of case histories and narratives to constructing experiments on both humans and animals, by which these theoretical perspectives have been and can be employed. As such, there exists a considerable amount of literature, operating from various theoretical perspectives and paradigms, exploring the topics of sex and gender. Despite the abundance of research attention paid to the topics, there are few, if any, definitive answers with regard to the *why* and *how* of sex and gender. Thus, the nature-versus-nurture debate persists between some researchers, while others explore the roles of both nature and nurture in the complex relationship between the two concepts. Recognizing the profound impact of both nature and nurture on cognition and behavior, I adopt the latter approach so that the term gender can be better contextually understood.

Gender, when understood as both sociological and psychological constructs, does not take the form of truth, but rather takes the form of a social category and an individual identity. As such, gender is constructed, performed, understood, and reproduced through everyday discursive practices (Potter, 1996). Discursive practices are collaborative, regularly occurring interactions whereby uniform talk, thoughts, interactions, and actions are produced and reproduced (Potter, 1996). They are reflective of a discourse, or a societal structuring principle, that accepts certain societal aspects as unquestionable givens (Foucault, 1984). The discursive practices that construct gender have shaped it as an institution whereby women and men are accorded different levels of social status and power and thus differential access to resources and opportunities (e.g., Connell, 1987; Lorber, 1996). Such gendered practices embody traditional gender beliefs and gender stereotypes that, in turn, perpetuate gender as an institution (West & Zimmerman, 1987). Thus within this institution, women are to be compassionate, emotional, gentle, and passive (i.e., feminine), whereas men are to be confident, assertive, strong, and independent (i.e., masculine). As Connell (2005a) contended, it is only within a gendered institution where hegemonic gendered order is pronounced that results in gendered behavior. This latter notion is particularly pertinent to the sport and physical activities domains.

Sport, physical activity, and physical education can be viewed as institutionalized domains where gendered discourses surround the physical body, inform identities and interactions, dictate behaviors, work or otherwise, and influence the structures of organizations (Connell, 1987; Hall, 1988; Hargreaves, 1986; Shaw & Hoeber, 2003). We are inundated with powerful messages of what is gender appropriate within these domains, the likes of which contribute to the perpetuation of gender stereotypes and appropriateness. While women have experienced profound increases in the number of sport and physical activity opportunities afforded to them (e.g., Acosta & Carpenter, 2010), and while there has been some progress in deconstructing the gendered order over the past few decades (e.g., Kane & Buysse, 2005), the assumption remains that "there are two, and only two, mutually exclusive sexes that necessarily correspond to stable gender identity and gendered behavior" (Birrell & Cole, 1990, p. 3). For men this assumption confirms their natural occupancy within the masculine contexts of sport and physical activity. For women, this assumption has long labeled them as outsiders and intruders. As Messner (1990) pointed out, however, gender identity, and to some extent gendered behavior, is a developmental process that is never completed and always influenced by social context. This contradiction is explained below.

# GENDER AND THE BODY

Female and male bodies are not only expected to behave a certain way, but they are also expected to look and be presented in a certain manner. After all, "bodily difference is the arena in which gender relations are defined" (Connell, 2005b, p. 13). Thus, the physical characteristics of men and women should match their socially constructed gender beliefs. The current (Western) cultural body ideals of women and men are such that women are to be demurely slender yet slightly toned, while men are to be athletically muscular. This contrast is indicative of three interrelated effects (Choi, 2003; Krane, 2001). First, it reinforces the placement of women as weaker than and subordinate to men, thus securing a social position that accords them lower societal power and status. Second, it presents a dilemma for women who wish to be recreationally and competitively physically active (Krane et al., 2004a). Third, as both ideals do involve some degree of muscularity, the opportunity is presented for both men and women to challenge the notion of various hegemonic masculinities (Anderson, 2005; Bridges, 2009; Connell, 2005a).

*Hegemony* refers to how the ideas of one social group within a system are used to exert power and dominance over another social group (Bates, 1975). Hegemonic power is thus an institutionalized form of dominance that is accepted by subordinates and dominants as self-explanatory and rational (Connell, 2005a). In his discussion of the gender system, Connell defined *hegemonic masculinity* as, "the configuration of gender practice which embodies the currently accepted answer to the problem of the legitimacy of patriarchy, which guarantees (or is taken to guarantee) the dominant position of men and the subordination of women" (p. 77). Simply put, it is the process by which the most dominant form of masculinity exerts power and control over other masculinities and femininity. In general, hegemonic masculinity takes form in White, middle-class, heterosexual men, thus rendering other masculinities and femininity, or the absence of or a lack of (hegemonic) masculinity, as subordinate (Connell, 1987; Kessler & McKenna, 1978; Paechter, 2006). In contexts where the body is of significance, muscularity is included as a component of hegemonic masculinity, as bodies are vital to the social construction of gender and gendered order through the fostering of gender capital (Connell, 1987; Bourdieu, 1984). As indicated by Bridges (2009), this process has clear implications for, above all else, body image within the contexts of sport and physical activity.

According to Krane et al., (2004b), exercise and competitive sport environments are settings where participants feel an extraordinary amount of pressure to conform to Western society's gendered ideal body shapes. As Thereberge (1993) noted, "the centrality of the body and physical performance to athletic experiences makes sport a particularly powerful site for the construction and confirmation of gender ideologies (p. 312). Indeed, several authors have argued that the contexts of sport and physical activity augment such gendered body standards (e.g., Messner, 1988). For women, the ideal body epitomizes feminine beauty, a concept that has become synonymous with toned thinness (Choi, 2003). Men, on the other hand, have come to learn that muscularity is tantamount to masculinity, and as such, the ideal body is big, strong, and lean (Galli & Reel, 2009; Luciano, 2007). While both ideals suggest that attaining the optimal body is as simple as leading a healthy and active lifestyle, there are several other issues involved when the body is put on display in exercise and sport settings. These issues revolve around the performance of gender.

Today's athlete is more visible than ever before. However, across all sport media outlets male and female athletes are presented differently, both in type and frequency (e.g., Clavio & Eagleman, 2011; Kane & Buysse, 2005). Male athletes are prominently displayed in the media and are almost always depicted as brave, strong, and powerful – the personification of masculinity. Female athletes, on the other hand, are underrepresented in the media and when they do receive attention, are often trivialized or sexualized. These profound messages not only reproduce gender order, but also communicate unrealistic expectations to society (Connell, 2005a; Messner et al., 2003). For instance, Daniels (2009) found that images of female athletes performing their sport had an empowering effect on females, as they were more likely to describe themselves in terms of what their bodies can do versus what their bodies looked like. Conversely, participants who viewed images of female athletes in sexualized poses experienced dissatisfaction with their bodies, as they negatively evaluated both their appearance and physicality. Some men have also been found to exhibit body dissatisfaction related to the media portrayal of the muscular male body ideal (Galli & Reel, 2009; Leit et al., 2002).

Self-objectification theory posits that individuals not occupying the dominant physical ideal within a culture will negatively evaluate themselves, the result of which can be detrimental to one's physical and psychological health (e.g., Daniels, 2009; Martins et al., 2007; Slater & Tiggemann,

2011). As the physical ideal within the contexts of sport and physical activity has been constructed through the gaze of hegemonic masculinity (Azzarito, 2009), the bodies of women and subordinate men are particularly susceptible to objectification and its negative consequences. At one extreme, objectification may lead to avoiding all or specific sport and physical activities (Fredrickson & Roberts, 1997). At another extreme, objectification can lead to a negative body image and subsequent harmful behaviors (Martins et al., 2007). The gendered nature of body image suggests that for men these behaviors often include going to great lengths to achieve muscularity. An example would be the use of steroids. Women, on the other hand, are more inclined to develop dangerous exercise and eating behaviors, such as anorexia nervosa, to attain thinness. Such behaviors have not only been linked to the endorsement of traditional gender norms (Smolak & Murnen, 2008), but Azzarito noted that, as a result of institutional practices determined to establish a hierarchy of normalized bodies, "individuals police and discipline themselves to achieve or maintain a specific shape, size and muscularity to perform ideals of masculinity and/or ideals of femininity" (p. 21). Thus, the social sanctions experienced and the self-regulatory behaviors learned from early exposure to these institutional practices continue to inform one's gender development throughout one's lifetime (Bussey & Bandura, 1999).

## GENDER, YOUTH, AND PHYSICAL ACTIVITY

Children learn to negotiate their bodies and construct their identities in accordance with sex and gender at a very young age. As many researchers have illustrated, gender identities are neither passively constructed, nor are they fixed across contexts (Butler, 1990; Connell, 2005a). Rather, gender identities take the forms of many masculinities and femininities that are numerous, diverse, and contextual. The contexts of sport and physical activity are of particular importance, as within these contexts gender identities are performed, constructed, and reproduced through social practice such that the illusions of proper, natural, and fixed gender identities act to inform how young children construct their gendered selves (Butler, 1990; Messner, 2002; Therberge, 1993).

In a study of nursery school children, Bussey and Bandura (1992) found that children as young as four abided by the gender stereotypes placed upon themselves and others. Specifically, children sanctioned themselves and others to play with toys that were congruent with their perceived genders. Research also suggests similar sanctioning occurs when children engage in physical activities and sport, the likes of which have led to differing perceptions of both appropriateness and competence between young girls and boys (Messner, 2002). This is not to suggest children do not play an active part in gendering activities; however, even at this young age, they are performing gender (Messner, 2002). Drawing from his observations of children playing soccer in the American Youth Soccer Organization, Messner explained how gender performances were evident within and between a young girl's team and a young boy's team. Specifically, the girls performed femininity by first naming their team "The Barbie Girls" and subsequently dancing and singing while the boys performed masculinity by naming their team "The Sea Monsters" and subsequently acting aggressively, particularly toward "The Barbie Girls." These names and actions clearly defined the two oppositional categories of boys vs. girls. They also highlighted the manner in which boys and girls reconstructed sex and gender binaries by "doing gender" in the sport context.

As Messner (2002) points out, the social construction of gender is a multileveled ideological construct that permeates interactions, institutional structures, and cultures. This is perhaps most true within the context of sport and physical activity, where children learn which activities are gender-appropriate from parents, peers, schools, media outlets, the community, and contextual practices and observations (Azzarito, 2009; Messner, 2002). Activities are consequently classified on the basis of gender characteristics and expectations. Based on the original classification by Metheny (1965), several researchers have demonstrated that activities such as football, ice hockey, wrestling, and boxing require a great deal of strength and power and are dangerous, risky, and violent; therefore, they continue to be considered male-appropriate and masculine (Koivula, 2001; Riemer & Visio, 2003). Activities such as gymnastics, aerobics, volleyball, and figure skating involve aesthetics, grace, and beauty and/or are dominated by women and, thus, remain feminine and female-appropriate (Riemer & Visio, 2003; Hardin & Greer, 2009). Other activities and sports, such as tennis and swimming are generally identified as gender neutral and are appropriate for the participation of both girls and boys. While there is increasing acceptance of girls and women in activities deemed masculine, boys and men who cross the gender boundary and partake in feminine activities risk harsh consequences, particularly as they enter adolescence (Alley & Hicks, 2005).

Many researchers have identified adolescence as a time where the social worlds of young boys and girls begin to expand (Bussey & Bandura,

1999; Leszczynski & Strough, 2008). It is during this time that adolescents gravitate toward their peers, form social identities, and begin to make their own choices. It is also during this time that the saliency of gendered understandings becomes highly pronounced and gender boundaries become increasingly enforced (Laberge & Albert, 1999). As such, gender beliefs and stereotypes are factors that influence the decisions that adolescents make, one of which is whether or not they will participate in physical activity and sport. As Elling et al. (2001) illustrated, there are several factors that influence these choices, such as peer acceptance, contextual participation norms, and culturally normative images (Elling et al., 2001). Further, and as noted by Elling and Knoppers (2005), because these factors exist in relation to both cultural gender norms and sport's hegemonic practices they may act to uphold ideologies, further marginalize subordinate groups, and subsequently result in a gendered pattern of attrition.

Despite the lifelong positive health and psychological benefits that can result from physical activity, a vast amount of research has shown that adolescents are highly likely to dropout of sport and physical activities, and the rates are more pronounced for girls than for boys (Azzarito & Solomon, 2005; Kirshnit et al., 1989). In general, the attrition of both girls and boys is a result of a lack of time and enjoyment for specific activities. Higher instances of withdrawal amongst adolescent girls, however, have been attributed to gendered expectations of body performances. In their study of adolescent girls and boys, Butcher et al. (2002) found that young girls were more likely than boys to cite perceived performance and ability deficiencies as primary reasons for withdrawal from sport. Slater and Tiggemann's (2011) findings cited teasing and body image concerns as contributors to sport and physical activity attrition amongst girls. Taken together, and consistent with Lenskyj (1990), these perceptions manifested within the young girls as a result of receiving continuous cues of gender appropriateness. Adolescent boys also suffer as a result of gendered cues, as any indication of a gender transgression (i.e., taking part in a so-called women's sport or physical activity) is indicative of possessing less masculinity and being less than a man (Laberge & Albert, 1999). These cues are found in various contexts throughout one's childhood and adolescence. Within the physical education setting, cues are present in the gendered discourse that surrounds the physical body (Azzarito & Solomon, 2005). Within the competitive sport setting, gendered cues become more and more prevalent and augmented as one moves through early to late adolescence and into adulthood, as they are endorsed by the media, parents, siblings, peers, and coaches (Vilhjalmsson & Kristjansdottir, 2003).

## SPORT IDEOLOGY

It is not uncommon to hear a physical education teacher, coach, parent, and so on use the phrases, "throw like a girl" or "play like a girl." Both phrases have profound meaning, as they exemplify male superiority within the contexts of sport and physical activity. As Azzarito and Solomon (2005) pointed out, young boys and men are often told that they throw like girls as a way to communicate inferior athletic skill and prowess – tantamount to the skills and prowess of girls. Constructing the female body as inferior has been a common occurrence throughout history (Messner, 2011). In fact, during the Victorian age, the female body was viewed as so frail that for fear of incurring irreparable damage to their reproductive systems, doctor's discouraged women from engaging in strenuous activity (Cahn, 1994). Gendered understandings like this have shaped the sport realm as solely masculine, thus paving the way for the exclusion of women. They have also created males as active, females as passive, and perpetuated the tendency for women to underestimate their athletic abilities (Connell, 2005a; Young, 1980). Finally, gendered understandings have created the fear that women who do engage in sport and physical activity and possess skills and abilities equivalent to or better than those of men, will become masculinized (Cahn, 1994).

Over time and despite the oppressive connotation of the aforementioned phrases, women have become empowered by the notion of throwing or playing like a girl. The newfound athleticism and strength of women has fostered action, power, autonomy, and resistance hegemonic masculinity (Dworkin & Messner, 2002; Messner, 2011). Arguably, the source of this empowerment is the passing of Title IX. Title IX of the 1972 Educational Amendments to the 1964 Civil Rights Act (P.L. 92-318, 20 U.S.C.S § 1681) mandated that "No person in the United States shall, on the basis of sex, be excluded from participation in, be denied the benefits of, or be subjected to discrimination under any educational programs or activities receiving federal financial assistance." Despite not possessing the words, "sport," "athlete," or "physical education," Title IX has had a profound impact on the sport experiences of young women at the high school and collegiate levels. According to the Women's Sport Foundation, female participation rates have increased approximately 900% and nearly 500% within interscholastic and intercollegiate athletic programs, respectively. This progress has not come easily, however, as even after 1978, the year in which all federally funded educational institutions were required to comply with Title IX, gender equity remained elusive at best due to the variable interpretations of the law. Subsequent letters of clarification in 1996, 1998, and 2003, a manual, and case law were necessary to further define the true meaning of Title IX (Carpenter & Acosta, 2005).

The passing of Title IX has provided the young women and girls of to-day and tomorrow vast amounts of participation opportunities in sport and physical education. This is not to say, however, that women did not partake in sport or organize sport leagues prior to this time. Several female-driven sport organizations were present from as early as 1899 (Carpenter & Acosta, 2005). The significance of Title IX rests in how its passage reflected social change within American society-at-large. Driven by the civil rights movement of the 1950's and 1960's and the women's movement of the 1970's, Title IX provided women access to a domain where they were once forbidden. As Birrell (1988) noted, "Title IX ushered in an era of participation unequaled in women's sport history" (p. 472). As such, the experiences of sporting and physically active girls and women within the pre-Title IX era would presumably be different than those of the post-Title IX era, particularly amongst those within institutions directly affected by the law. Blinde's (1986) findings support this rationale, as the post-Title IX female intercollegiate athletes and pre-Title IX male intercollegiate athletes in her study exhibited similar orientations and reactions to their sport experiences.

Whereas a clear trend of increased sport participation amongst females has been identified since its passing (Carpenter & Acosta, 2005; Sartore & Sagas, 2007), Title IX has had little, if any, impact on the hegemonic masculinity that remains endemic in sport and physical activity settings. In fact, the inclusion of women and consequently, femininity, into these realms prompted men to assert their superordinate position in two primary ways. The first way is through the physical use of their bodies (Messner, 1990). The second way is through institutionalized organizational practices (Cunningham, 2008; Shaw & Hoeber, 2003; Shaw, 2006). Both ways are discussed in detail below.

**Physicality and Masculinity**

Coupled with the muscular physique of the male body, the violent and aggressive behaviors performed by the male body have become the exemplification of masculinity and 'natural superiority' within American society (Connell, 1987, 2005a). Messner, Dunbar, and Hunt's (2000) study of sport media substantiates this, as the predominant themes within sport commentary, programming, and commercials conform to and perpetuate the ideals of hegemonic masculinity by focusing on White males and aggressive performances. As they point out, these themes present messages that discipline the bodies, minds, and choices of boys and men such that they strive to display exemplary muscularity, aggression and violent behaviors (Connell, 2005a; Galli & Reel, 2009). Women, on the other hand, are expected to display the opposite, an expectation that the media perpetuates through the underrepresentation and persistent portrayal of female athletes in (hetero)sexualized poses (Knight & Giuliano, 2003; Krane, et al., 2004b). These messages can be problematic, as sport and physical activity are contexts where bodies are gazed upon, harshly compared, policed through gendered discourse, and sexually objectified (Butler, 1990; Daniels, 2009; Galli & Reel, 2009).

In their study of intercollegiate female athletes, Krane and colleagues (Krane et al., 2004a) identified physically active women as facing a gendered dilemma whereby they are expected to exude femininity, both in physicality and behavior, within a context that values masculinity and muscularity. The same dilemma was found amongst college-aged female recreational exercisers as well (Krane et al., 2004b). Indeed, female athletes, coaches, fitness instructors, and recreational exercisers, just to name a few, are likely to encounter expectations of stereotypically feminine behaviors and appearance (Krane & Barber, 2005; Sartore & Cunningham, 2007a). Further, and to the extent that women do not represent the feminine ideal, they represent an "image problem" and face negative consequences as a result (Harris, 2005). As such, physically active women and female athletes often "…perform femininity to protect themselves from prejudice and discrimination" (Krane, 2001, p. 120). Specifically, women often do things like wear make-up and ribbons in their hair when competing in sport or being physically active. These outcomes and behaviors are a result of the inextricable link between gender and (hetero)sexuality (Butler, 1990; Connell, 2005a).

As mentioned at the beginning of the chapter, there is a socially constructed dichotomy of two sexes and two corresponding genders, the likes of which are expected to be attracted to one another only. As such, heterosexuality is proclaimed to be natural, normal, and a characteristic of "real men and women" (Elling & Janssens, 2009, p. 72). Thus, heteronormativity has been established and subsequently serves as a fundamental aspect of hegemonic masculinity and used as an organizing principle within sport (Connell, 2005a; Elling & Janssens, 2009). On the basis of heteronormativity, women who exhibit less than the epitome of femininity and (subordinate) forms of masculinity are often perceived to be lesbians, as lesbians are suspected to be more masculine than heterosexual women (Harris, 2005). Likewise, heterosexual men who exhibit femininity or subordinate masculinities are believed to be gay, as gay men stereotypically possess more femininity than heterosexual men. Thus, lesbians, gay men, and heterosexual men who possess subordinate masculinities often experience prejudice and discrimination, are relegated to the out-group, and believed to be incompatible with the sport setting (Anderson, 2002; Krane & Barber, 2005; Plummer, 2006). This is consistent with the social categorization framework, which posits that individuals classify themselves and others into various social categories based on salient differences (Tajfel & Turner, 1979; Turner et al., 1987).

To the extent that identifying with a particular social category within a specific context fosters self-esteem, individuals classify those whom they perceive to be members of the same social category as comprising one's in-group (Tajfel & Turner, 1979; Turner, 1987). In-group members are subsequently evaluated more positively than members outside of this group, or out-group members (Gaertner & Dividio, 2000). As self-esteem comprises feelings of acceptance, respect, and worthiness, the formation of in-groups and out-groups is also influenced by ideological beliefs and the need to both procure and secure societal status and power (Crocker & Major, 1989; Sidanius et al., 1994, 2004). Within the sport and physical activity context then, it is somewhat reasonable that men would not only identify as and with the established in-group (i.e., that of hegemonic masculinity), but also that they would take measures to ensure the in-group remains intact and powerful. This logic has resulted in several modern developments. First, it has led to the continued marginalization of women, particularly those who are not overtly feminine (Messner, 1988; Knight & Giuliano, 2003; Krane, 2001). Second, it has led to the silence amongst non-heterosexuals, most markedly amongst gay males (Anderson, 2002; Elling & Janssens, 2009; Plummer, 2006). Finally, it has led to the gendering of sport organizations (Cunningham, 2008; Shaw & Hoeber, 2003; Shaw, 2006).

**Sport Organizations**

Whereas the passage of Title IX has provided exponential gains in participation opportunities to girls and women, the exact opposite has occurred for leadership opportunities (Acosta & Carpenter, 2010; Sartore & Sagas, 2007). Women at all levels of sport are underrepresented as administrators, head coaches, assistant coaches, and managers. Further, women in these leadership positions often receive lower pay than their male counterparts and are ascribed traditional gender stereotypes (Sartore & Cunningham, 2007b). Indeed, several types of inequities between the sexes still exist at various levels within sport organizations that can be attributed to hegemonic masculinity's gendered discourse (Claringbould & Knoppers, 2008; Cunningham & Sagas, 2008; Shaw & Hoeber, 2003). As Cunningham (2008) suggested, the norm of masculinity and the corresponding negative effects experienced by women within sport organizations are institutionalized practices, such that they represent "the way things are done" within that context (see also Scott, 1987). Cunningham further identified that various pressures and tools are necessary to deconstruct the gender inequities that are endemic in sport organization practices. In other words, these pressures and tools are of use to managers and researchers as means to undo gendered processes, challenge existing ideologies, regain gender-neutral organizational logic, and provide women more power in sport organizations (Acker, 1992; Claringbould & Knoppers, 2008). As Connell (2005a) notes, however, hegemony is established when cultural ideals and institutional power correspond. As such, de-gendering the sport and sport organization practices that embody the ideals of hegemonic masculinity can be difficult in a patriarchal society. The de-gendering process is even more difficult when placed in the context of a racialized and patriarchal society.

## GENDER AND OTHER SOCIAL STRUCTURES

The discussion of gender thus far has revolved around the topic of hegemonic masculinity. What has not been discussed, however, is the assumption that the epitome of hegemonic power is a White, able-bodied, young, middle-class, heterosexual male (Connell, 2005a). This is consistent with what Messner et al. (2000) found to dominate the sport media, as well as what Fink et al. (2001) identified as the prototypical employee in intercollegiate athletic departments. Thus, when discussing gender in sport, one must also examine the other characteristics of hegemonic masculinity. Despite the fact that sport has not been as formally arranged by race, ethnicity, and social class as it has with gender, the gendered discourse surrounding members of these social groups is unique, particularly within the sport media where racializing bodies has been used to naturalize differences between groups (Butler, 1990).

The most prevalent racialized beliefs in sport and physical activity revolve around Black participants and athletes. For instance, the belief that

Black male athletes are naturally physically superior, yet intellectually inferior, to their White male counterparts is repeatedly communicated through sport media outlets (Hardin et al., 2004; Harrison et al., 2004). Black female athletes, relative to their White female athlete counterparts, suffer harsh scrutiny within the media, as they are both racially and sexually different from the feminine ideal imposed upon sport bodies by hegemonic masculinity (Cooky et al., 2010; Cahn, 1994). Further, they are often affected by the implications of occupying lower levels of social class. Thus, the experiences of Black female athletes are influenced by race, gender, and social class (Bruening et al., 2005). Indeed, Black women of all ages, as well as women occupying other racial and ethnic minority groups, are influenced by these social structures in nearly every physical activity and sport context (e.g., Boyle, 2005; Gordon-Larsen et al., 2000; Hunter et al., 2004).

It is important to note, though, that the social construction of gender and constraints of patriarchy can vary from culture to culture (Pyke & Johnson, 2003). That is, cultural understandings of gender can be imposed upon and carried out by women (e.g., With-Nielsen & Pfister, 2011). Simply put, beyond the strict definitions of femininity imposed upon all women, racialized femininities may be imposed upon women of color and varied ethnic backgrounds. Women within the sport and physical activity context seemingly must "do" their respective gender performances in order to participate, just as boys and men seemingly must also adhere to their assigned masculinities. Such is not the case; however, gender transgressions have been occurring more frequently, and as a result, they subsequently inform the process of deconstructing discourse of hegemonic masculinity (Anderson, 2005; Boyle, 2005; McGrath & Chananie-Hill, 2009).

## CHAPTER SUMMARY

The purpose of this chapter was to provide an overview of how sex and gender affect sport and physical activity. As one can see from the case of Caster Semenya, sex and gender binaries are still enforced and gender transgressors often punished in some fashion. In this chapter, I discussed how the gendered practices responsible for gender binaries have materialized and why they persist. Likewise, I outlined how gendered meanings inform our understanding of the body and how the body performs gender within the sport and physical activity contexts. Special attention was paid to the manifestation of hegemonic masculinity and its effects on participants, athletes, sport organizations, and racial and ethnic minorities.

## DISUCSSION QUESTIONS

1. The terms sex and gender are often used interchangeably. What are the definitions of these terms and how are they intertwined?
2. What are some stereotypical feminine characteristics? What are some stereotypical masculine characteristics? How do these relate to sport and physical activity?
3. What is meant by the terms hegemony and hegemonic masculinity?
4. How do girls, boys, men, and women "do" or "perform" gender in the contexts of sport and physical activity?
5. What impact did Title IX have in the context of sport and physical activity?

## RECOMMENDED READINGS

Anderson, E. (2005). In the game: *Gay athletes and the cult of masculinity.* Albany, NY: State University Press of New York. (The author discusses his own experiences and the experiences of other gay men within the sport context; presents an illuminating picture of how masculinity is strictly constructed, defined, and enforced.)

Cunningham, G. B. (2011). *Diversity in sport organizations* (2nd ed.). Scottsdale, AZ: Halcomb Hathaway. (Provides a thorough theoretical discussion of gender issues within sport organizations, particularly within the chapter "Sex and Gender in Sport Organizations.")

Hargreaves, J. A. (1994). *Sporting females: Critical issues in the history and sociology of women's sport.* New York, NY: Routledge. (Offers a critical discussion of women in sport).

## REFERENCES

Acker, J. (1990). Jobs, bodies: A theory of gendered organizations. *Gender and Society, 4*, 139-158.

Acosta, R. V., & Carpenter, L. J. (2010). Women *in intercollegiate sport: A longitudinal study-thirty-three year update-1997-2010.* Unpublished manuscript, Brooklyn College, Brooklyn, NY.

Alley, T. R., & Hicks, C. M. (2005). Peer attitudes toward adolescent participants in male- and female-oriented sports. *Adolescence, 40*, 273-280.

Anderson, E. (2002). Openly gay athletes: Contesting hegemonic masculinity in a homophobic environment. *Gender & Society, 16*, 860-877.

Anderson, E. (2005). Orthodox and inclusive masculinity: Competing masculinities among heterosexual men in a feminized terrain. *Sociological Perspectives, 48*, 337-355.

Azzarito, L. (2009). The Panopticon of physical education: Pretty, active and ideally white. *Physical Education and Sport Pedagogy, 14*, 19-39.

Azzarito, L., & Solomon, M. A. (2005). A reconceptualization of physical education: The intersection of gender/race/social class. *Sport, Education, and Society, 10*, 25-47.

Bates, T. R. (1975). Gramsci and the theory of hegemony. *Journal of the History of Ideas, 36*, 351-366.

Bem, S. L. (1974). The measurement of psychological androgyny. *Journal of Clinical and Consulting Psychology, 42*, 155-162.

Bem, S. L. (1981a). Gender schema theory: A cognitive account of sex typing. *Psychological Review, 88*, 354-364.

Bem, S. L. (1981b). The BSRI and gender schema theory: A reply to Spence and Helmreich. *Psychological Review, 88*, 369-371.

Birrell, S. (1988). Discourses on the gender/sport relationship: From women in sport to gender relations. *Exercise and Sport Science Reviews, 16*, 459-502.

Birrell, S., & Cole, C. L. (1990). Double fault: Renee Richards and the construction and naturalization of difference. *Sociology of Sport Journal, 7*, 1-21.

Blinde, E. M. (1986). Contrasting orientation toward sport: Pre- and post- Title IX athletes. *Journal of Sport and Social Issues, 10*, 6-14.

Bourdieu, P. (1984). *Distinction*. Cambridge, MA: Harvard University Press.

Boyle, L. (2005). Flexing the tensions of female muscularity: How female body builders negotiate normative femininity in competitive bodybuilding. *Women's Studies Quarterly, 33*, 134-149.

Bridges, T. S. (2009). Gender capital and male bodybuilders. *Body & Society, 15*, 83-108.

Bruening, J. E., Armstrong, K. L., & Pastore, D. L. (2005). Listening to the voices: The experiences of African American female student athletes. *Research Quarterly for Exercise and Sport, 76*, 82-100.

Bussey, K. & Bandura, A. (1992). Self-regulatory mechanisms governing gender development. *Child Development, 63*, 1236-1250.

Bussey, K., & Bandura, A. (1999). Social cognitive theory of gender development and differentiation. *Psychological Review, 106*, 676-713.

Butcher, J., Lindner, K.J., & Johns, D.P. (2002). Withdrawal from competitive youth sports: A retrospective ten-year study. *Journal of Sport Behavior, 25*, 145-163.

Butler, J. (1990). *Gender trouble: Feminism and the subversion of identity*. New York: Routledge.

Cahn, S. K. (1994). *Coming on strong: Gender and sexuality in twentieth-century women's sport*. Cambridge, MA: Harvard University Press.

Carpenter, L. J., & Acosta, R. V. (2005). *Title IX*. Champaign, IL: Human Kinetics.

Choi, P. Y. L. (2003). Muscle matters: Maintaining visible differences between women and men. *Sexualities, Evolution, and Gender, 5*, 71-81.

Claringbould, I., & Knoppers, A. (2008). Doing and undoing gender in sport governance. *Sex Roles, 58*, 81-92.

Clavio, G., & Eagleman, A. N. (2011). Gender and sexually suggestive images in sports blogs. *Journal of Sport Management, 7*, 295-304.

Connell, R. W. (1987). *Gender and power: Society, the person and sexual politics.* Stanford, CA: Stanford University Press.

Connell, R. W. (2005a). *Masculinities* (2nd ed.). Berkeley, CA: University of California Press.

Connell, R. W. (2005b). Growing up masculine: Rethinking the significance of adolescence in the making of masculinities. *Irish Journal of Sociology, 14*, 11-28.

Constantinople, A. (1973). Masculinity – Femininity: An exception to a famous dictum? *Psychological Bulletin, 80*, 389-407.

Cooky, C., Wachs, F. L., Messner, M., & Dworkin, S. L. (2010). It's not about the game: Don Imus, race, class, gender and sexuality in contemporary media. *Sociology of Sport Journal, 27*, 139-159.

Crocker, J., & Major, B. (1989). Social stigma and self-esteem: The self-protective properties of stigma. *Psychological Review, 96*, 608-630.

Cunningham, G. B. (2008). Creating and sustaining gender diversity in sport organizations. *Sex Roles, 58*, 136-145.

Cunningham, G. B., & Sagas, M. (2008). Gender and sex diversity in sport organizations: Introduction to a special issue. *Sex Roles, 58*, 3-9.

Daniels, E. A. (2009). Sex objects, athletes, and sexy athletes: How media representations of women athletes can impact adolescent girls and college women. *Journal of Adolescent Research, 24*, 399-422.

Deaux, K. (1985). Sex and gender. *Annual Review of Psychology, 36*, 49-81.

Dworkin, S. L., & Messner, M. A. (2002). Just do…what? Sport, bodies, gender. In S. Scranton, & A. Flintoff (Eds.). *Gender and Sport: A reader* (pp. 17-29). New York, NY: Routledge.

Elling, A., De Knop, P., & Knoppers, A. (2001). The social integrative meaning of sport: A critical and comparative analysis of policy and practice in the Netherlands. *Sociology of Sport Journal, 18*, 414-434.

Elling, A., & Janssens, J. (2009). Sexuality as a structural principle in sport participation: Negotiating sport spaces. *International Review for the Sociology of Sport, 44*, 71-86.

Elling A., & Knoppers, A. (2005). Sport, gender, and ethnicity: Practices of symbolic inclusion/exclusion. *Journal of Youth and Adolescence, 34*, 257-268.

Fausto-Sterling, A. (1993). The five sexes: Why male and female are not enough. *The Sciences, April/March*, 20-25.

Fink, J. S., Pastore, D. L., & Riemer, H. A. (2001). Do differences make a difference? Managing diversity in Division IA intercollegiate athletics. *Journal of Sport Management, 15*, 10-50.

Foucault, M. (1984). Truth and power. In P. Rabinow (Ed.), *The Foucault reader: An introduction to Foucault's thought* (pp. 51-76). London: Penguin.

Fredrickson, B. L., & Roberts, T. (1997). Objectification theory: Toward understanding women's experiences and mental health risks. *Psychology of Women Quarterly, 21*, 173-206.

Gaertner, S. L., & Dovidio, J. F. (2000). *Reducing intergroup bias: The Common Ingroup Identity Model*. Philadelphia, PA: Psychology Press.

Galli, N., & Reel, J.J. (2009). Adonis or Hephaestus? Exploring body image in male athletes. *Psychology of Men and Masculinity, 10*, 95-108.

Gordon-Larsen, P., McMurray, R. G., & Popkin, B. M. (2000). Determinants of adolescent physical activity and inactivity patterns. *Pediatrics, 105*, 1-9.

Hall, M. A. (1988). The discourse of gender and sport: From femininity to feminism. *Sociology of Sport Journal, 5*, 330-340.

Hardin, M., Dodd, J. E., Chance, J., & Walsdorf, K. (2004). Sporting images in Black and White: Race in newspaper coverage of the 2000 Olympic Games. *The Howard Journal of Communications, 15*, 211-227.

Hardin, M., & Greer, J. D. (2009). The influence of gender-role socialization, media use and sports participation on perceptions of gender-appropriate sports. *Journal of Sport Behavior, 32*, 207-226.

Hargreaves, J. A. (1986). Where is the virtue? Where is the grace? A discussion of the social production of gender relations in and through sport. *Theory, Culture, & Society, 3*, 109-121.

Harris, J. (2005). The image problem in women's football. *Journal of Sport and Social Issues, 29*, 184-197.

Harrison, Jr., L., Azzarito, L., & Burden Jr., J. (2004). Perceptions of athletic superiority: A view from the other side. *Race, Ethnicity and Education, 7*, 149-166.

Hoffman, R. M. (2001). The measurement of masculinity and femininity: Historical perspective and implications for counseling. *Journal of Counseling and Development, 79*, 472-485.

Hunter, G. R., Weinsier, R. L., Zuckerman, P. A., & Darnell, B. E. (2004). Aerobic fitness, physiologic difficulty and physical activity in Black and White women. *International Journal of Obesity, 28*, 1111-1117.

Kane, M. J. & Buysse, J. M. (2005). Intercollegiate media guides as contested terrain: A longitudinal analysis. *Sociology of Sport Journal, 22*, 214-238.

Kessler, S., & McKenna, W. (1978). *Gender: An ethnomethodological approach*. New York, NY: Wiley & Sons.

Kirshnit, C. E., Ham, M, & Richards, M. H. (1989). The sporting life: Athletic activities during early adolescence. *Journal of Youth and Adolescence, 18*, 6001-615.

Knight, J. L., & Giuliano, T. A. (2003). Blood, sweat, and jeers: The impact of the media's heterosexist portrayals on perceptions of male and female athletes. *Journal of Sport Behavior, 26*, 272-284.

Koivula, N. (2001). Perceived characteristics of sports categorized as gender-neutral, feminine, and masculine. *Journal of Sport Behavior, 24*, 377-393.

Krane, V. (2001). We can be athletic and feminine, but do we want to? Challenging hegemonic femininity in women's sport. *Quest, 53*, 115-133.

Krane, V., Choi, P. Y. L., Baird, S. M., Aimar, C. M., & Kauer, K. J. (2004a). Living the paradox: Female athletes negotiate femininity and muscularity. *Sex Roles, 50*, 315-329.

Krane, V., Waldron, J., Stiles-Shipley, J. A., & Michalenok, J. (2004b). Relationships among body satisfaction, social physique anxiety, and eating behaviors in female athletes and exercisers. *Journal of Sport Behavior, 24*, 247-264.

Krane, V., & Barber, H. (2005). Identity tensions in lesbian intercollegiate coaches. *Research Quarterly for Exercise and Sport, 76*, 67-81.

Laberge, S., & Albert, M. (1999). Conceptions of masculinity and of gender transgressions in sport among adolescent boys. *Men and Masculinities, 1*, 243-267.

Leit, R. A., Gray, J. J., & Pope, H. G. (2002). The media's representation of the ideal male body: A cause for muscle dysmorphia? *International Journal of Eating Disorders, 31*, 334-338.

Lenskyj, H. (1990). Power and play: Gender and sexuality issues in sport and physical activity. *International Review for the Sociology of Sport, 25*, 235-245.

Leszczynski, J. P., & Strough, J. (2008). The contextual specificity of masculinity and femininity in early adolescence. *Social Development, 17*, 719-736.

Lewin, M. (1984). "Rather worse than folly": Psychology measures femininity and masculinity. In M. Lewin (Ed.). *In the shadow of the past: Psychology portrays the sexes* (pp. 155-178). New York, NY: Columbia University Press.

Lippa, R. A. (2005). *Gender, nature, and nurture.* Lawrence Erlbaum: Mahwah, NJ.

Lips, H. M. (2005). *Sex & gender: An introduction.* McGraw Hill: New York, NY.

Ljungqvist, A., Patino, M. J. M., Vidal, A. M., Sanchez, L. Z., Pereira, P. D. (2006). The history and current policies on gender testing in elite athletics. *International SportMed Journal, 7*, 225-230.

Lorber, J. (1993). Believing is seeing: Biology as ideology. *Gender and Society, 7*, 568-581.

Lorber, J. (1996). Beyond the binaries: Depolarizing the categories of sex, sexuality, and gender. *Sociological Inquiry, 66*, 143-159.

Luciano, L. (2007). Muscularity and masculinity in the United States: A historical overview. In K. J. Thompson & G. Cafri (Eds.), *The muscular ideal: Psychological, social and medical perspectives* (pp. 41-67). Washington, D.C.: APA.

Martins, Y., Tiggeman, M., & Kirkbride, A. (2007). Those Speedos become them: The role of self-objectification in gay and heterosexual men's body image. *Personality & Social Psychology Bulletin, 33*, 634-647.

McGrath, S. A., & Chananie-Hill, R. A. (2009). "Big freaky-looking women": Normalizing gender transgression through bodybuilding. *Sociology of Sport Journal, 26*, 235-254.

Messner, M. A. (1988). Sports and male domination: The female athlete as contested ideological terrain. *Sociology of Sport Journal, 5*, 197-211.

Messner, M. A. (1990). When bodies are weapons: Masculinity and violence in sport. *International Review for the Sociology of Sport, 25*, 203-219.

Messner, M. A. (2002). *Taking the Field: Women, men and sports.* Minneapolis, MN: University of Minnesota Press.

Messner, M. A., Dunbar, M., & Hunt, D. (2000). The televised sports manhood formula. *Journal of Sport and Social Issues, 24*, 380-396.

Messner, M. A., Duncan, M. C., & Cooky, C. (2003). Silence, sports bras, and wrestling porn: Women in televised sports news and highlight shows. *Journal of Sport and Social Issues, 27*, 38-51.

Messner, M. A. (2011). Gender ideologies, youth sports, and the product of soft essentialism. *Sociology of Sport Journal, 28*, 151-170.

Metheny, E. (1965). *Connotations of movement in sport and dance.* Dubuque, IA: Brown.

Paechter, C. (2006). Masculine femininities/feminine masculinities: Power, identities, and gender. *Gender and Education, 18*, 253-263.

Pyke, K. D., &, Johnson, D. L. (2003). Asian American women and racialized femininities: "Doing" gender across cultural worlds. *Gender & Society, 17*, 33-53.

Plummer, D. (2006). Sportophobia: Why do some men avoid sport? *Journal of Sport and Social Issues, 30*, 122-137.

Potter, J. (1996). *Representing reality: Discourse, rhetoric, and social construction.* London: Sage.

Riemer, B. A., & Visio, M. E. (2003). Gender typing of sports: An investigation of Metheny's classification. *Research Quarterly for Exercise and Sport, 74*, 193-204.

Sartore, M. L., & Cunningham, G. B. (2007a). Weight discrimination, hiring recommendations, person-job fit, and attributions: Fitness industry implications. *Journal of Sport Management, 21*, 172-193.

Sartore, M. L., & Cunningham, G. B. (2007b). Explaining the underrepresentation of women in leadership positions of sport organizations: A symbolic interactionist perspective. *Quest, 59*, 244-265.

Sartore, M. L., & Sagas, M. (2007). A trend analysis of the proportion of women in college coaching. *International Journal of Sport Management, 8*, 226-244.

Scott, W. R. (1987). The adolescence of institutional theory. *Administrative Science Quarterly, 32*, 493-511.

Shaw, S. (2006). Scratching the back of "Mr. X": Analyzing gendered social processes in sport organizations. *Journal of Sport Management, 20*, 510-534.

Shaw, S., & Hoeber, L. (2003). "A strong man is direct and a direct woman is a bitch": Gendered discourses and their influence on employment roles in sport organizations. *Journal of Sport Management, 17*, 347-375.

Sidanius, J., Pratto, F., & Mitchell, M. (1994). In-group identification, social dominance orientation, and differential intergroup social allocation. *Journal of Social Psychology, 134*, 151-167.

Sidanius, J., Pratto, F., van Laar, C., & Levin, S. (2004). Social dominance theory: Its agenda and method. *Political Psychology, 25*, 845-880.

Slater, A., & Tiggemann, M. (2011). Gender differences in adolescent sport participation, teasing, self-objectification and body image concerns. *Journal of Adolescence, 34*, 455-463.

Smolak, L., & Murnen, S. K. (2008). Drive for leanness: Assessment and relationship to gender, gender role and objectification. *Body Image, 5*, 251-260.

Spence, J. T. (1993). Gender-related traits and gender ideology: Evidence of a multifactorial theory. *Journal of Personality and Social Psychology, 64*, 624-635.

Spence, J. T., & Hemreich, R. L. (1981). Androgyny versus gender: A comment on Bem's gender schema theory. *Psychological Review, 88*, 365-368.

Tajfel, H., & Turner, J. C. (1979). An integrative theory of intergroup conflict. In W. G. Austin & S. Worchel (Eds.), *The social psychology of intergroup relations* (pp. 33-47). Monterey, CA: Brooks/Cole.

Therberge, N. (1993). The construction of gender in sport: Women, coaching, and the naturalization of difference. *Social Problems, 40,* 301-313.

Turner, J. C., Hogg, M. A., Oakes, P. J., Reicher, S. D., & Wetherell, M. S. (1987). *Rediscovering the social group: A self-categorization theory.* Oxford, United Kingdom: Blackwell.

Vilhjalmsson, R., & Kristjansdottir, G. (2003). Gender differences in physical activity in older children and adolescents: The central role of organized sport. *Social Science & Medicine, 56,* 363-374.

Young, I. M. (1980). Throwing like a girl: A phenomenology of female body comportment, motility and spatiality. *Human Studies, 3,* 137-156.

Wackwitz, L. A. (2003). Verifying the myth: Olympic sex testing and the category "woman". *Women's International Studies Forum, 26,* 553-560.

West, C., & Zimmerman, D. H. (1987). Doing gender. *Gender and Society, 1,* 125-151.

Wiesemann, C. (2010). Is there a right not to know one's sex? The ethics of 'gender verification' in women's sport competition. *Journal of Medical Ethics, 37,* 216-220.

With-Nielsen, N., & Pfister, G. (2011). Gender constructions and negotiations in physical education: Case studies. *Sport, Education and Society, 16,* 645-655.

# CHAPTER 16

# SOCIAL CLASS AND SPORT

Kenneth Sean Chaplin

***

**Learning Objectives**

After reading this chapter, you should be able to:

1. Discuss the relationships between social class, stratification, and life chances.
2. Expound on the major theoretical perspectives of social class in sport.
3. Identify the patterns and practices of social class in sport.

## INTRODUCTION

In this chapter, I will explore some of the ways that sociologists study social class in sport and society. I begin with a conceptual approach to social class in society and then build on the concept of social class by describing and discussing social class's relationship to stratification and life chances. The discussion then moves to sociological theories of social class in society, followed by an overview of how some sociologists apply and explain social class in sport. I also demonstrate the influence of social class in sport involvement and close the chapter with some patterns and practices of social class in sport. I begin with an example of one of the ways in which social class is related to power, wealth, and income in U.S. Society.

In 2009 *Businessweek* magazine reported their annual list of the 100 most powerful people in sport - "The Power 100." Surprisingly, before 2009 all of the previous Power 100 lists were comprised of more than just professional players; the most powerful people on the list were almost always the team owners, agents, commissioners, and coaches, with the professional athletes trailing far behind. In 2010 and 2011 *Businessweek* refocused their attention towards the 'social power' of just professional athletes, specifically the power that professional athletes possessed inside and outside their respective sports. According to *Businessweek*, the social power of these 100 athletes was based on a two-year observation and tabulation of: (a) complex "on-field metrics" that measured how well athletes scored and played in their respective contexts, and (b) complex "off-field metrics" which included athletes' salary and total endorsement incomes, social awareness and responsibility, perceived honesty and trustworthiness, social appeal, and political influence. What is most telling about the Power 100 list is the ambiguous nature and indistinct bias that is awarded to the more popular sports and sensational athletes that ultimately granted some athletes greater weight and social power. This unpredictable bias is largely due to particular sports having more media focus and attention along with these sports' political appeal, profit and entertainment value, and perceived influence. The Power 100 list post-2009 demonstrates the complexity of 'social power' that is partially conceptualized in terms of class, status, power, wealth, and income and how all of these factors are almost always understood in austere economic terms. The 2009 list also shows strong evidence of a longstanding relationship between professional sports, athletes, and the mass media that is rooted in social and political power, wealth, and control of broader US social institutions inside and outside of sports.

## CLASS, STRATIFICATION, AND LIFE CHANCE

The Power 100 list pre-2009 is a statement of the social power of more than just professional athletes – it is a reflection of social class and the structure of US sports in society. Particular professional athletes and sports cannot be analyzed independently of the totality of sporting practices, and the space in which sporting practices occur is part and parcel of a broader social system whereby each element receives a distinct value (Bourdieu 1988). To understand a particular sport, one must locate the social position of that sport in the space of all other sports in that society. One must explore the relationship of that sport to social class via an investigation of the distribution of its practitioners, the distribution of the different social groups according to their number of members, their assets and social status of its practitioners, and the type of relation to the body that each sport favors or demands of its participants (Bourdieu 1988). The primary objective in a sociological analysis of sport is to explore and better understand the construction of the structure of the space of sporting practices in which an exploration of social class is paramount (Bourdieu 1978, 1984, 1988).

Social class is a fluid, malleable, and illusive concept, and few concepts in sociology are more contested and complicated (Marshall, 1997; McNall et al., 1991). There are many competing definitions, multifarious conceptualizations, and complex models of social class have not halted much of the superficial thinking about what social class is in society. Social class or "class" is a concept used by social and political scientists that they use to relate to specific models of social stratification in society. In this chapter, I conceptualize social class as a particular social position within a class-based stratification system that divides a community into a hierarchy of social positions. It represents a method of social ranking that involves wealth, power, culture, taste, identity, access, and life chances. Note that this is different than how people think about socioeconomic status, or the social and economic measurement of an individual's wealth and family background, education, occupation, and income, and the social and economic measurement and grouping together of different peoples based on these characteristics.

Inside and outside of the US, there are many social categorizations and variations in and between social classes, and even the best binary model of social class has too often characterized and summarized social class as a simple division between "the haves" and "the have-nots." Many of the more developed but still over-simplistic tripartite approach to social class have simply included the middle class as a social group between the "haves" and the "have-nots" (Winfrey 2006). These conceptualizations are problematic because they focus on the over deterministic nature of economics in the social structuring of contemporary society.

Some contemporary social class theorists have developed more adequate explanations of the arrangement of social groups in society that include the role and influence of particular individuals in social institutions, chiefly their influence on the family, education, politics, sport, and the economy (Bourdieu 1978, 1984; McNall et al., 1991; Wright 1997). These theorists have also advanced the understanding of the nature of conflict, structural inequality, and opportunities for intragenerational and inter-generational vertical mobility in society. Long ago Gordon (1949) described social class as the horizontal stratification of populations, and he conceptualized class as rooted in people's relationships to standards of wealth and income, occupation, status, group identification, levels and patterns of consumption, family background, religious affiliation, organizational ties and networks, and other innumerable social factors. Much of Gordon's (1949) conceptual approach to social class has remained and been developed, and more recent scholars of social class have explored with greater detail people's social, economic, educational, racial and ethnic, and political position and relationship to others inside and outside of others in their social class group.

In contemporary US society, social class is based on achieved status (not according to ascribed status like in a social caste system). From this perspective, social class includes an individual's possession of wealth (e.g., home ownership, stocks and bonds, trust funds, and so on), knowledge and access to education, culture, and opportunity to broader social circles and networks (Beeghley 2004; Bourdieu 1984; Coakley, 2006; Gilbert, 1998). In a social caste system, society is socially structured basis on kinship ties and associated occupations, which are clearly socially (and sometimes legally) separated, self-generating, and self-regulating. In social caste systems there are no life chances for intragenerational or intergenerational upwards mobility, no intercaste marriages, and no power over religious or divine interpretations. On the other hand, in a social class system, society is a socially structured basis on achievement and merit, where wealth, income, and occupation play a fundamental role in the structuring of communities or society. There are associated lifestyles and preferences and clear divisions of culture based on taste, identity, and social group ideology; however, upward social mobility is a possibility but not a probability. Both upward and downward mobility are possible due to the increase of interclass marriages and educational and occupational opportunities (Beeghley 2004; Gilbert 1998).

Wright (1997) suggested that the conceptualization of class is embedded in different theoretical agendas that involve asking and answering different kinds of questions reflecting the different social constructions and demarcations of the concept. Kerbo (1996) argued that the factors that determine social class vary widely from one society to another over time and place, and that even within a society, different people and social groups often possess very different ideas and theories about what makes one class 'higher' or 'lower' in a socially stratified hierarchal society. Wright (1997) and Kerbo (1996) proposed that a person's attitudes, ideology, and behavioral patterns are often related to a (mis)understanding of social class, class consciousness, and a broader understanding of social groups relations and the social organization of society. Wright (1997), Gilbert (1998), and Beeghley (2004) propose that people's understanding of social class in society is largely based on: (a) their perception of the similarities between each other, and (b) people's sharing of relatively similar economic, educational, and occupational goals, experiences, and backgrounds.

Kerbo (1996) helps to conceptualize social class by arguing that any analysis of individuals into social groups must include: (a) criteria for distinguishing classes, (b) a suitable amount of classes and social class divisions, (c) the extent to which individuals and groups are able to recognize class divisions and demarcations as meaningful, and (d) the everyday patterns and practices that reproduce these divisions. Bourdieu (1984), Wright (1997), Gilbert (1998), Beeghley (2004), Mantsios (2011), and others propose that the construction of class is rooted in the social, economic, and cultural categorization and division of individuals into social groups, which reflect more powerful and the less powerful individuals and social groups.

Given this background, I now shift to a broader context of social class by conceptualizing the social ranking and organized hierarchal arrangement of individuals and social groups in society. Sociologists use the term stratification to describe: (a) the classification of persons into social groups based on shared socio-economic classes, (b) the structuring of these unequal social groups into social class layers, and (c) the social organization of society. Gilbert (1998) and Beeghley (2004) argue that social stratification is the hierarchical arrangement of large social groups based on a group's control over basic resources. They describe social class stratification in the US as a social system that is "open" and allows for vertical mobility via achievement and merit. Vertical mobility in the U.S. is possible when individuals are able to move upwards or downwards in a social hierarchy from one level in the hierarchy to another level. Socioeconomic stratification is also sociologist's way of understanding and measuring social inequality and opportunity in society and individual's life chances.

Life chance is one way that sociologists have tried to explain the similarity of chance between individuals and social groups who share similar economic and cultural boundaries even when individuals in a social group might be different from each other. Life chance is the range of people's opportunity to improve their quality of life based on their (a) likelihood to turn out a successful venture, (b) social ties and networks, and (c) social interactions in a given social setting, based on particular social circumstances and situations. Individuals who share a similar life chance for obtaining and achieving social and economic success, mobility, and the potential for power is related to their social class background that is indicative of cultural tastes, lifestyles, social ties and network, and patterns of consumption (Bourdieu 1984; Swartz 1997). Life chance is difficult to tabulate because it is theoretically based on the extent to which an individual has access to basic resources (e.g., food, clothing, housing, mental and physical health) and the necessary resources (e.g., education, occupation, and employment opportunity) that can enable intragenerational or intergenerational upwards or downwards social mobility.

Life chance in an open class system allows for upward or downward social mobility because it offers individuals a range of chances to achieve their life goals and aspirations in a socially stratified system based on achievement and merit. Social change and mobility are based on individuals' opportunities for introduction and exposure to knowledge and experience outside of their social class location that can change and shape their pursuit of interests and quality of life (Marshall 1998). Social background is an important determinate of an individual's life chance, as well as a variety of lifestyles and behaviors, such as manner of speech, attire, type and style of haircut, residence, friendships, and other significant social ties and relationships (Bourdieu 1984, McPherson et al., 1989). Social class, stratification, and life chance are concepts that sociologists use to explain the social structure and organization of society, inequality, and social mobility.

## THEORIES OF SOCIAL CLASS

There are three main schools of thought about the creation and development of social groups into social class categories in society: the Durkheimian/Structural Functionalist Approach, the Marxist/Conflict Theoretical Model, and the Weberian/Critical Theory Paradigm. None of these approaches are exclusive in their thinking; however, each of these approaches is rooted in specific assumptions of society that undergird their orientation.

### Structural Functionalist Approaches

French sociologist Emile Durkheim approached society by exploring the social organization and integration of individuals into social groups. Durkheim theorized a structural and functional approach of society that accounted for the social division and specialization of labor, and changes in social order, stability, and consensus. His holistic approach and generic beliefs about social balance, harmony, coherence, and order in society and his proposition of these virtues operated as essential qualities, elements, and indispensable aspects of social order and stability (Grusky & Galescu 2005). According to Durkheim, social conflict, strife, division, and anomie are latent functions of society that are manifest in individual pathologies. Durkheim believed that very early in life, individuals came to internalize and accept ideologies, attitudes, and behaviors, which are collectively shared and formulate a consciousness of kind. In the *Division of Labor in Society* (1893), he argued that individuals function and interact with one another according to similar basic social norms and values that are rooted in beliefs, customs, and traditional rituals. Durkheim also believed that social action and interaction was a routine part of life that occurred customarily in particular social space and locations where the passing on of social rules and regulations are fundamental markers and the foundations of social life.

In *Suicide* (1897), Durkheim explored individuals' sense of belonging in society and the role of religion in integrating individuals into society. Durkheim believed that suicide existed in four theoretical forms (i.e. egoistic, altruistic, anomic, and fatalistic) and that a study of suicides and suicides rates in society is telling of patterns of religion and the social integration of individuals into society (Durkheim 1897; Freedman 2002).

In The *Elementary Forms of Religious Life* (1912), Durkheim explored religion and religious life, social solidarity, and the collective conscience among individuals who lived together in communal groups. According to Durkheim, society underwent structural and functional transformations due to social changes in the belief, interpretation, and practice of religion, specifically the shared collective beliefs in things 'sacred' and things 'profane.'

American sociologist Talcott Parsons supported and developed Durkheim's theoretical approach to society. He focused on the relationships between the social structure and the functional social actions of individuals. According to Parsons, social systems were comprised of the social actions and interactions of individuals, which in turn influenced social structures and forces. He believed that when individuals interact with one another, they do so based on expected interactive patterns and with imperfect internalized and idealized norms that structure social roles, action, and interaction. Social action and social roles in society support and undergird institutions and social structures that contribute to social order and stability. Social class, according to Parsons is part of a system of stratification that has positive functions in the stabilization of whole social systems. Four functional imperatives in all systems of action include: (a) adaptation, (b) goal attainment, (c) integration, and (d) latency/pattern maintenance (Parsons 1970).

Building on the aforementioned work, Davis and Moore (1945) proposed that social stratification and structured inequality in society was functionally necessary. Davis and Moore (1945) also suggested that stratification in society was a conscious evolving device that ensured that the most qualified people conscientiously filled the most important positions in society. Their functional and structural theory of stratification explained why social inequality is justifiable and legitimate in society: (a) some jobs and duties were not pleasant to perform in society, (b) particular jobs and duties needed to be done for the functional maintenance of society, and (c) some jobs required various degrees of talent and ability to perform them for the greater good and awards and for the proper functioning of society. Positions at the top of the social hierarchy require investments of time, money, and years of education in individuals and should therefore have higher rewards to encourage the best people. They also held that the most difficult jobs in society are the most necessary and require the highest rewards and compensation to sufficiently motivate individuals to fill them. Incentives are 'built-in rewards' of hierarchal social positions, which are necessary for the functional maintenance, and stability of scarce personnel.

Durkheim's, Parsons', and Davis and Moore's theoretical orientation to the development of social class, stratification, and society is applicable to sport because it can illuminate how individuals and social groups: (a) construct and develop collective values, beliefs, and consensus via sport, (b) undergo socialization into a smooth-running, smooth-operating, sports team and/or organization, and (c) adopt and internalize the positive attitudes and behaviors necessary for sport's play and participation. Other structural functionalist aspects of sport's participation are the development and maintenance of social bonds and solidarity in sporting communities, the relationship between sport success, academic achievement, and occupational attainment, and the positive aspects of sport on health and wellness and social class mobility. These perspectives also help to illuminate how and why sports teams are structured as they are, where there is a functional necessity for one leader and many obedient followers.

**Conflict Theories**

German philosophers, economists, and social theorists Karl Heinrich Marx and Friedrich Engels (1848) theorized that the historical foundation and most salient character of all societies was class struggle. They also proposed that in every society class struggle was a political struggle. According to these theorists, social class division is the result of economic conflict –a struggle over the goods and resources in society. They envisioned that economic conflict also possessed the potential for positive social change and transformation in society via the liberation of social class classifications and categorizations and the communal emancipation of goods and resources. Marx and Engels' asserted that social class is also based on the historical relationship of the ownership of goods, resources, the means of production, and the worker/labor relationships to others in society.

Marx envisioned the eventual dictatorship of the worker/labor class (the proletariat) over the ruling class (the bourgeois) and the eventual abolition of all classes to a classless society. According to Marx, it is not the consciousness of men that determines their being, but the social existence of a being that determined their state of consciousness. He later explained and expounded on the problems of class consciousness by illuminating the role of the Petite Bourgeois as a class of middle men in society. Marx proposed that the Petit Bourgeois was comprised of the educated elite and professional businessmen who worked for themselves and who also utilized economics and cultural ideology to socially control and subordinate the working class. According to Marx's theory, the ruling class produced and perpetuated itself by economically exploiting laborers and by structuring inequality based on pre-existing wealth, inheritance, and ownership over the means and mode of production. The working class lived and existed as long as they were able to find work and only because their labor increased the capital base and profits of the ruling class. The working classes, in Marx's view, are socially coerced to sell their labor (and thus themselves) as commodity, just like other articles of commerce in a capitalist market (Marx & Engels 1848).

While Marx never examined sport in society, his theoretical orientation towards the role and function of religion in society spurred other scholars to approach sport in a similar manner. Marx also proposed that religion was 'the sigh of the oppressed creature' and that religious suffering was the expression of 'real suffering' that is the heart-felt reaction of an economically heartless world (Marx 1844). According to Marx, religion operated as an opiate of working class peoples because it provided them the illusion of happiness and hope in an afterlife. Many sociologists of sport embrace this Marxists orientation and analysis of religion and have applied this theoretical orientation to sport. Sport according to some current conflict theorists, is an illusion and diversion from economic conflict, class struggle, and development of class consciousness in society

(Carrington & McDonald 2009). Some neo-Marxists scholars have also asserted that social stratification occurs in sport the same way that it does in broader society and that stratification is the intellectual driving force and ideological linchpin of the ruling class that undergirds the material distribution of goods and resources (Marx 1845).

Italian Marxist and Political Philosopher Antonio Gramsci embraced many of ideas and perspectives of Karl Marx; however, he focused more on illuminating the relationship between cultural and political leadership in advanced capitalists nation-states. According to Gramsci, the ruling class was able to control, maintain, and promote economic relationships between social class groups in society not just through violent political and economic coercion, but through the cultural ideology.

Neo-Marxist Philosopher Louis Pierre Althusser embraced many ideas and perspectives of Karl Marx, as he also focused on the role of ideology in the everyday operations and management of individuals under a capitalist's regime. Althusser theorized about how the ruling class was able to present their ideology to the greater mass of peoples utilizing social institutions in a nation-state as both social and institutional apparatus (Althusser 1970). According to Althusser, repressive state apparatuses ruled by force (e.g., fascist governments, military states, and state controlled police forces), but ideological state apparatuses rule by cultural discourse which is presents via the normalization of values, morals, and dispositions in religion, education, mass media, and sport (Althusser & Balibar 1970). These collective theoretical approaches to the ruling class as economically based and ideologically driven intertwine the means and modes of production, ownerships, and social control of the state with the cultural control of social institutions in society which shape social values and everyday practices.

Some recent sociologists of sport who have embraced a Marxist orientation have continued to ask insightful questions about the current relationship between sport and social class, and the role of sport in a Marxist vision of social change and transformation (Carrington & McDonald 2009; Edwards 1973; Hoch 1972). American historian and social critic Christopher Lasch (1977) represents one such example, as he noted:

> Among the activities through which men seek release
> from everyday life, games offer in many ways the purest
> form of escape. Like sex, drugs, and drink, they oblite-
> rate awareness of everyday reality, not by dimming that

awareness but by raising it to a new intensity of concentration. Moreover, games have no side-effects; produce no hangovers or emotional complications. Games satisfy the need for free fantasy and the search for gratuitous difficulty simultaneously; they combine childlike exuberance with deliberately created complications.

Other sociologists of sport have also applied a neo-Marxist orientation towards exploring and exposing specific problems and social issues in sport. They examine the intersection of social class conflict and struggle with racial, ethnic, and gender-based inequality and subordination in society (Edwards 1969; Hoch 1972). Sport Sociologist Paul Hoch (1972) developed and presented a neo-Marxist perspective of sport in capitalist societies as serving the function of "a safety-value." He asserts that in capitalist economies, the productive forces and the political power of the elite, which also promotes social class repression, domination, and athletic exploitation, control sport. Likewise, James presented a first-hand account of his involvement and participation in professional cricket during the 1950-60's, in *Beyond a Boundary* (1963/1993). In this book, he told of the salience and political significance of race and culture in the colonization and stratification of Cricket in the British Caribbean and in Europe. He also extended an analysis of his experiences in Professional Cricket to include some of the broader ways in which sport and social institutions work to subordinate people of color and lower social class backgrounds, and the racial and ethnicity stratification of people in sports.

Sociologist and former San Jose State University track star Harry Edwards (1969) illuminated the experiences of African-American athletes, specifically the lack of African American people in positions of corporate management and organizational influence in professional, collegiate, and Olympic sports. According to Edwards (1969) many Black American athletes were socialized to be nonpolitical, isolated, and overly committed to sport, but that many African American's struggle for basic resources, economic freedom, and political liberties and liberation from prejudice and discrimination in the 1960's resulted in overt political protest in the 1968 Olympic Games. The struggle for economic and political freedom on the part of African American peoples via sport is worldwide and manifest in (a) the life and experiences of African American professional boxer Muhammad Ali (born Cassius Clay), (b) African People's struggle to exclude Rhodesia and South Africa from the 1968 Olympic Games because of their overtly racist political policies and practices, (c) the segregated policies and social practices of racist and overtly discriminatory elite New York Athletic Clubs, and (d) the struggle to appoint African American coaches and administrators to the US Olympic Committee in the 1968 Olympics. Edwards' (1969) approach to sport reveals a variety of Marxist theoretical orientations, chiefly relating to racial and social class struggles for resources, access, and opportunity.

Another example of social class struggle in sport is Torre's (2009) account of the economic struggles and exploitation of professional athletes. Many professional athletes from The National Basketball Association (NBA), The National Football Association (NFL), and Major League Baseball (MLB) suffer from a financial pandemic and are inclined to lose most or almost all of their money in strikingly similar ways. These athletes begin earning income in school through illicit payments from sports agents, who usually end up taking advantage of them through blind, misguided, and imprudent investments. As a result, many professional athletes have filed for bankruptcy, sold their residences, and liquidated their assets even before their multimillion-dollar sports careers are over. Soon after retirement, about 80% of former NFL players have gone bankrupt or are under financial stress because of joblessness or divorce, and within five years of retirement an estimated 60% of former NBA players are broke. Torre reports that countless others who are retired NFL, NBA, NHL and MLB players frequently come forward claiming that they are financially ruined because their money is 'tied up' in bad investments, unproductive activities, and fraudulent financial ventures. According to Keyes (2011), lumping together NBA, NFL, and MLB professional athletes and their owners together as "millionaires and billionaires" obscures the real differences that exist between those who essentially own sports teams with those who are highly paid workers.

**Weberian/Critical Theoretical Perspectives**

German sociologist and political economist Maximilian (Max) Weber theorized social class in society by focusing on the role of religion in the everyday social and economic practices of individuals. From this perspective, social class is socially organized and based on a complex system of stratification with overlapping dimensions, factors, and relationships. Industrial capitalism spurned rationality and the specialization of individuals in bureaucratic structures and social institutions, which also spread the social values of religion to secular society. In *The Protestant Ethic and The Spirit of Capitalism* (1905/2002), Weber proposed that the spirit that undergirded capitalism evolved from a Calvinist belief in hard work and economic conservatism, which manifested itself in broad attitudes and behaviors of non-religious peoples in capitalist's societies. In *Politics as a Vocation* (1919), Weber illuminated the workings of the broader political institutions in the West, which he believed was rooted in the rational pursuit of economic interest, piety, devotion, faith, and frugality. According to Weber, the Puritans were opposed to idle games and early sports because they believed that it revealed the uninhibited expressions of uncontrolled instincts and idolatry. The Puritans also believed that sports encouraged the indulgence and arousal of naked ambitions, raw instincts, and the desire to gamble, and that sports were morally suspicious social activities (Weber 1905/2002). Over time religious leaders and the social and political of society eventually embraced sports because of the belief that sports could serve and reflect their interests. In many ways, sports evolved in a functional manner because they were used to promote order and stability, which served the interests of the elite class.

According to Weber, goods and resources are tangible and intangible and are laden with symbolic and material value. The unequal distribution of goods and resources in society involves power and status. Social class groups are important for the economic ordering, distribution, and allocation of goods and resources in society, status groups comprise the social and moral ordering of society, and powerful political groups are power-based parties which consist of the legal/political order of society. According to Weber, each order in society affects and is affected by the other, and power is most complex because it is conditioned by economic gain, it possesses some inherent value, and is attached to both social honor and prestige. Given the various ways in which power can be exercised, Weber was unable to reduce the organization of these orders to a single dimension such as the ownership over the means and modes of production (Gerth & Mills 1958).

Thorstein Veblen (1899/1994) theorized about social class in society by examining the economic patterns, cultural relationships, and behaviors of social groups. Key to this framework are issues pertaining to social stratification via status, social reproduction, exclusion, and manifestation of conspicuous leisure and consumption. The leisure class, according to Veblen, was also the ruling class, which demonstrated itself via social demarcation of frivolous consumption to demonstrate their economic abundance and high social location and position in society. Veblen proposed that sport was: (a) an ideal medium through which the ruling class was able to display their wealth and economic dominance, (b) a social setting premised on the conspicuous leisure of a 'non-productive' social group, (c) a social site where the ruling class is able to demonstrate its physical and social superiority over others, and (d) an imagined condition of warfare that is an extension of a more barbarous past (Sugden & Tomlinson 2000). Sports were also used to reflect the leisure of an elite leisure class and to evaluate and rank parvenus who sought to join the status of the elite leisure class. Veblen (1899/1994) also asserted that the social and political elites of past societies were able to retain and transform their power and privilege into authority by culturally controlling and separating forms of leisure and modes of consumption.

Herbert Marcuse theorized social class in society by looking at studies of the ideology of advanced industrial capitalist systems. In *One-dimensional Man*, Marcuse (1991) critiqued Marx's concept of the objectification and alienation of workers by suggesting that capitalism and industrialization caused working class laborers to resist objectification and alienation by envisioning themselves as extensions of the objects that they produced. Marcuse suggested that working class peoples in capitalist economies recognize and attach themselves to their commodities and the objects that they produce to resist conceptualizing labor relations as a new form of social control and domination. He also noted that the power of the ruling class is directed at promoting consumerism and false needs using advertising strategies and techniques in the mass media. Marcuse believed that this one-dimensional man who is a product of advanced capitalism could eventually lose the aptitude and ability for critical thought, action, and behavior that leads to the perpetuation of toil, aggression, misery, injustice and unjust inequality. The over consumption of sports and elevated esteem of professional sports teams and athletes are examples of the social extensions that working class people's make in their associations and affiliations to resist being objectified by their working class conditions. Resisting the objectification and alienation of working class conditions via obsessive sports association and practices also creates and contributes to the false consciousness and identification of misguided judgments about one's social location and positions in social class hierarchy.

French Sociologist and Philosopher Pierre Bourdieu borrowed many of the ideas and theoretical orientations of Marx, Weber, and Veblen in theorizing that social class is based on status and consumption. Bourdieu (1984) proposed that social class is rooted in the economic, social, and cultural relationships of individuals in social groups, which are connected to one another but are socially separate based on lifestyles, preferences, and life choices. Forms of material and symbolic capital mark social class, and inequality is based on the cultural division and distinction of habits, taste, predilection for leisure, consumption practices, education, and choices in foods, music, and clothing. Social subjects and objects are classified and distinguish themselves externally and internally by material and symbolic notions of beautiful, ugliness, vulgarity and appeal. Furthermore, culture and education reaffirm and reproduce an appreciation for particular kinds of foods, music, arts, and leisure. The endowing of honorary titles and the certification of talents and achievement are also used to bestow social status, prestige, and power/sanctioned authority, and social distinctions operate and are internalized in educational institutions and culture. Bourdieu proposes that young children and youth (a) internalize social habits and customs, (b) demonstrate a sense of awareness for expected social manners and behaviors, and (c) internalize the interactions they have with others in their social location and position in society via consumption choices that are related to their class position. He also proposed that sports are like any other social practice that is an object of struggle between fractions of the dominant class over the definition, meaning, and interpretation of sport.

## CONTEMPORARY PATTERNS OF SOCIAL CLASS IN SPORT

In the final section, I highlight contemporary examples of social class thinking in sport. Wilson (2002), Coakley and Dunning (2000), and Coakley (2006) report that people from a higher social class are more likely to be involved in sports, but that their involvement in sports are based on particular cultural choices that they make regarding the association of particular sports with higher and/or lower social class involvement. Not only does Wilson (2002) say that people from higher social class backgrounds have greater frequencies in organized sports, but they also have higher attendance rates at sporting events. This results in different sport experiences, interpretations, and patterns of participation from one social class to another. The choices of the upper class people are related to their cultural capital, which is demonstrated in their culturally appropriate preferences and tastes. People's choices and preferences for sports are reflective of their upbringing and education, which is a marker of social differences.

The contemporary social elites in capitalist societies are roughly comprised of individuals located in government, high ranking military officials, and the clergy, and those who are keepers of religious ceremonies and observances (Coakley 2006; Coakley & Dunning 2000; Sugden &

Tomlinson 2000). When it comes to participation in sport, the socioeconomic status of a family and a family's social background drives the preferences and tastes for participation of people in particular sports (Wilson 2002). Social class is strongly linked to choice of sports and regular and routine participation patterns in sports. Social stratification and economic inequality also correspond to participation of sports in certain areas and location, which are based on resources, lifestyles, wealth, and power (Bourdieu 1984; Coakley 2006). Those social class groups of high socioeconomic status who also possess power and have greater control over their life chances are routinely involved in individual sports (e.g. running/jogging, hiking, mountain biking, backpacking, etc.). They also possess more time and opportunities to attend live sport events and possess the discretionary funds, income, and networks for access to private social clubs and facilities.

On the other hand, people who are from lower, middle, and working class backgrounds are more likely to play sports in public places (e.g., local parks, schoolyards, and playgrounds) where the environment, facilities, and sports equipment are subpar, relative to elite sporting contexts. People from lower income groups do not play as much organized sports as those from higher income groups, and they do not possess the discretionary time or income to afford membership at elite social and sports clubs. Generally, people from the working class do not tend to cycle, run, swim, or hike by choice, due to economic constraints and cultural traditions associated with these sports. Working class sports are more often "prole" sports, which tend to include spectatorships and/of participation in these sports – prole sports are characterized by speed, physical aggression, and violence (e.g. UFC martial arts, boxing, football, basketball, bodybuilding.)

## CHAPTER SUMMARY

Businessweek's Power 100 list of 2009 illuminates the complexity of social class in sport, particularly the role and influence of professional athletes (and many important others) who influence sporting contexts. Sports cannot be examined or understood independently of social class. Sport is a mirror and reflection of society, and a deep investigation of social class in sport is needed to overcome what are otherwise simplistic approaches and understandings of how sport impact people's lives.

Conceptualizing social class involves asking and answering different kinds of questions and reflecting on the different social constructions and demarcations that complicate systems of social stratification, explanations of structural inequality, and understandings of social mobility. Discussions of social class must include much more than just economics; rather, it must also include an exploration and examination of culture, power, education, occupation, income and family's socioeconomic background. An exploration of life chances and opportunities for social mobility are also important dimensions of evaluating opportunity, structural, and social mobility. Establishing criteria for distinguishing classes, creating a suitable amount of classes and social class divisions, and exploring the extent to which individuals and social groups are able to recognize class divisions and demarcations as meaningful in their everyday social practices are important criteria for understanding social class in society.

## DISCUSSION QUESTIONS

1. What is the relationship between social class, stratification, and life chances?
2. How are Marx's, Durkheim's, and Weber's orientations of sport similar? How are they different?
3. In addition to the ones mentioned in the chapter, what are some other contemporary examples of sport in society that illuminate the importance of social class?

## RECOMMENDED READINGS

Bourdieu, P. (1978). Sport and social class. *Social Science Information, 17,* 819-840. (Bourdieu provides readers with an open and honest assessment of social class in sport and society and looks at some of the problems, issues, and patterns of social class in sport.)

Wilson, T. C. (2002). The paradox of social class and sports involvement: The roles of cultural and economic capita. *International Review for the Sociology of Sport, 37,* 5-16. (Wilson showed the difference between social class groups in sport and their preferences for sports.)

Wright, E. O. (1982). Class boundaries and contradictory class locations. In A. Giddens & D. Held (Eds.), *Classes, power, and conflict: Classical and contemporary debates* (pp. 112-129). Berkeley: University of California Press. (Wright explains the difficulty in conceptualizing and theorizing social class, and he explores some of the sociological perspectives of notable scholars on class.)

# REFERENCES

Althusser, L. (1970). Ideology and ideological state apparatuses. In B. Brewster (Translator), *Lenin and philosophy and other essays* (pp. 121-176). New York: Monthly Review Press.

Althusser, L. & Balibar, E. (1970). *Reading capital*. London: Verso Books.

Beeghley, L. (2004). *The structure of social stratification in the United States*. New York, NY: Pearson.

Bourdieu, P. (1978). Sport and social class. *Social Science Information, 17,* 819-840.

Bourdieu, P. (1984). *Distinction: A social critique of the judgment of taste*. Cambridge, MA: Harvard University Press.

Bourdieu, P. (1988). Program for a sociology of sport. *Sociology of Sport Journal, 2,* 153–161.

Carrington, B. & McDonald, I. (Eds.) (2009). *Marxism, cultural studies and sport*. New York: Routledge.

Coakley, J. J. (2006). *Sports in society: Issues and controversies* (9th ed.). New York: McGraw-Hill.

Coakley, J. J., & Dunning, E. (2002). *Handbook of sports studies*. Thousand Oaks, CA: Sage.

Davis, K. & Moore, W. E. (1945). Some principles of stratification. *American Sociological Review, 10,* 242-249.

Durkheim, E. (1893/1997) *The division of labor in society*. New York: Free Press.

Durkheim, E. (1912/1995). *The elementary forms of religious life*. New York: The Free Press, Simon & Schuster.

Edwards, H. (1969). *The revolt of the Black athlete*. New York: The Free Press.

Edwards, H. (1973). *Sociology of sport*. Homewood, IL: Dorsey Press.

Freedman, D. A. (2002). *The ecological fallacy*. Berkeley, CA: University of California Press.

Gerth, H., & Mills, C. W. (1958). *From Max Weber: Essays in sociology*. New York: Oxford University Press.

Gilbert, D. (1998). *The American class structure*. New York: Wadsworth Publishing.

Gordon, M. M. (1949). Social class in American sociology. *American Journal of Sociology, 55,* 262-268.

Grusky, D. B., & Galescu, G. (2005). Is Durkheim a class analyst? In J. C. Alexander & P. Smith (Eds.), *The Cambridge companion to Durkheim* (pp. 322-359). Cambridge, UK: Cambridge University Press.

Hoch, P. (1972). Rip off the big game: The exploitation of sports by the power elite. New York: Anchor Books.

James, C.L.R. (1963/1993). *Beyond a boundary*. Raleigh, NC: Duke University Press.

Kerbo, H. R. (1996). *Social stratification and inequality: Class conflict in historical and comparative perspective*. New York: McGraw-Hill.

Keyes, S. (2011). Why we can't dismiss the NBA labor dispute as 'millionaires versus billionaires.' In www.thinkprogress.com.

Lasch, C. (1977). The corruption of sports. *The New York Review of Books*. Retrieved from www.nybooks.com.

Mantsios, G. (2011). Media magic: Making class invisible. In T. Ore (Ed.), *The social construction of difference & inequality* (5th ed., pp. 93-101). New York, NY: McGraw-Hill.

Marcuse, H. (1991). Chapter 1: One-dimensional Man: *Studies in Ideology of Advanced Industrial Society.* London: Routledge.

Marshall, G. (1997). *Repositioning class: Social inequality in industrial societies.* London: Sage.

Marshall, G. (1998). "Life-Chances." *A Dictionary of Sociology.* Encyclopedia.com.

Marx, K. (1844). *Works of Karl Marx 1843: A contribution to the critique of Hegel's philosophy of right.* Written: December 1843-January 1844; First published: in Deutsch-Französische Jahrbücher, 7 & 10 February 1844 in Paris; Transcription: the source and date of transcription is unknown. It was proofed and corrected by Andy Blunden, February 2005, and corrected by Matthew Carmody in 2009.

Marx, K. (1845/1932). The German ideology - Part I: Feuerbach. Opposition of the materialist and idealist outlook B. *The illusion of the epoch in Marx-Engels collected works* (vol. 5). Moscow: Progress Publishers.

Marx, K., & Engels, F. (1848). Chapter I. Bourgeois and Proletarians, in *Manifesto of the Communist party* [German Original]. Retrieved from www.marxists.org.

McNall, S. G., Levine, R. F., Fantasia, R. (Eds.) (1991). *Contemporary and historical perspectives.* Boulder, CO: Westview Press.

McPherson, B. D., Curtis, J. E., & Loy, J. W. (1989). *The social significance of sport: An introduction to the sociology of sport.* Champaign, IL: Human Kinetics.

Parsons, T. (1970). *The social system.* London: Routledge.

Sugden, J., & Tomlinson, A. (2000). Theorizing sport, social class, and status. In J. J. Coakley & E. Dunning (Eds.), *The handbook of sports studies* (pp. 309-321). Thousand Oaks, CA: Sage.

Swartz, D. (1997). *Culture and power: The sociology of Pierre Bourdieu.* Chicago: The University of Chicago Press.

Torre, P. S. (2009). How (and why) athletes go broke. *Sports Illustrated.* Retrieved from www.si.com.

Veblen, T. (1899/1994). *The theory of the leisure class.* New York: Penguin Books.

Weber, M. (1905/2002). *Protestant ethic and the spirit of capitalism.* New York: Penguin Books.

Weber, M. (1919). *Politics as a vocation.* Retrieved from www.ne.jp.

Wilson, T. C. (2002). The paradox of social class and sports involvement: The roles of cultural and economic capital. *International Review for the Sociology of Sport, 37,* 5-16.

Winfrey, Oprah (2006) Class in America. *The Oprah Winfrey Show.* Retrieved from www.oprah.com.

Wright, E. O. (1997). *Class counts: Comparative studies in class analysis.* Cambridge: Cambridge University Press.

# CHAPTER 17

# POWER AND POLITICS

Akilah R. Carter-Francique and Michael Regan

*** 

**Learning Objectives**

After reading this chapter, you should be able to:

1. Discuss the various meanings of sport to societies.
2. Determine how sport and politics intersect.
3. Understand the role of ideologies and power in politics.
4. Explain the dominant issues of politics in sport.

## INTRODUCTION

In the cold winter of 1905, a group of concerned officials from thirteen colleges and universities came together to discuss the ever-increasing danger of football on their respective campuses. Students and non-students who participated in, and ran, the respective football squads were faced with the harsh realities of abundant injuries and deaths resulting from sport and competition. Subsequently, these intercollegiate realities caught the attention of the White House and President Theodore Roosevelt, and as a result, in 1906 the Intercollegiate Athletic Association of the United States (IAAUS) was formed under the order of President Roosevelt. The IAAUS, today known as the National Collegiate Athletic Association (NCAA), was created under the guise of protecting "young people from the dangerous and exploitive practices of the time," and thus, encouraged reforms in regards to the rules of play for football and rules in general for sports such as track and field and basketball (National Collegiate Athletic Association [NCAA], 2011).

We present this caveat to demonstrate how the world of sport can and does intersect with our respective societies. Within these societies and across generations, sport has played a significant role in the cultural milieu, for there are cultural differences in how communities and generations define sport and utilize sport in their daily lives (see Coakley, 2007). According to Coakley (2007), sport is defined as "institutionalized competitive activities that involve rigorous physical exertion or the use of relatively complex physical skills by participants motivated by internal and external rewards" (p. 6). In drawing from this perspective, we recognize how the institutionalization of sport can impact a society on various levels. Whether the issues reside with the physical nature of sport, entail the social injustices and inequalities based on race, gender, or class categorizations, or seek to empower and advocate for marginalized groups, sport and physical activity have the potential to reflect the issues of our greater society while directly serving the respective individual, group, organization, or industry in sport. Therefore, the purpose of this chapter is to discuss the role of power and politics in sports and physical activity.

Critical examination of the intersection of politics and sport is not new, as various authors have examined the espoused ideologies (see Black & Nauright, 1998; Sage, 1998), movements (see Edwards, 1969; Hahn, 1984; Wheeler, 1978), and experiences of groups (Abney, 2007; Anderson & South, 2007) within the sport context. So, how does this chapter add to or fill the gap of existing writings on politics and sport? Utilizing a critical theoretical lens (see Carter, 2010), our goal is to provide a generational vantage when we: (a) define the meaning of sport, (b) understand the relationship between sport and politics; and, (c) contextualize how the notion of ideologies and power in politics impacts sport and physical activity throughout time.

## THE MEANING OF SPORT IN SOCIETY

To better understand the relationship between sport and politics, we need to acknowledge the meaning of sport and the meaning of sport in various cultures and societies. While sport has a set definition, as described above, others define sport based on (a) the meaning given to the physical activities by their group or culture, or as (b) physical activities in which a culture or community values through their receipt of resources (Coakley, 2007). Thus, sport can be an institutionalized physical activity, like baseball, *and* sport can be a physical activity a society deems and values as sport, such as shuffleboard. Acknowledging how a society, culture, or community defines sport aids in determining their meaning of sport, along with understanding that specific society's values, ideas, and beliefs or ideologies.

As discussed in Chapter 1, sport is deemed as a microcosm of society and as a cultural institution, and as such has become an integral part of our daily lives. Thus sport, and all parties involved in the participation, production, and spectating of it, play a role in the development and maintenance of our cultures and values. Additionally, the underlying meaning of sport for the participants and the issues these sport organizations manage, play a role in the development and maintenance of valued ideologies within their respective societies. Hence, sport becomes a social construction, like race, class, and gender, and is subsumed by the dominant society, or those in power, to reiterate and justify social practices (Coakley, 2007; Sage, 1998).

Consequently, in addition to perpetuating prevailing practices and norms, sport can also serve as a site in which individuals and organizations can challenge dominant, or hegemonic, ideologies. These ideologies, or "a system of independent ideas that explain and justify particular political, economic, moral, and social conditions and interests, making them seem right or natural" (Sage, 1998, p. 2), can consist of race, gender, class, political, and/or national ideologies. Understanding how individuals and organizations define sport is significant in determining how their participation or service may speak to or be reflective of larger issues within their respective societies. For example, from the 1920's to the 1960's, sport was viewed as a way to foster fitness and fair play in the United States (U.S.) (Coakley, 2007). However, beginning in the 1950's, sport was utilized as a mode of social mobility, and people embraced the notion of competition and winning, or a capitalistic ideology. Accordingly, sport does have meaning for societies, organizations, and individuals; however, because sport is a microcosm of society, those in power have the authority to impose their own meanings to the role of sport and use sport as a platform for political purposes. These might include nation building, development of allies, silencing groups, and so on. This points to the political nature of sport organizations and the power they have over people's lives.

## POLITICS AND ITS RELATIONSHIP WITH SPORT

Expanding on the notion of the political nature of sport, it is important to note sport has been used as a platform globally to illuminate political unrest, social injustices, and practices of inequality. Embracing the notion that sport is political, individuals must understand that the decisions made on a daily basis impact groups, organizations, and societies in varying ways. However, the political impact is seen more readily in how the decision was made and where implemented (Coakley, 2007).

Thus, one might ask if the political decision was made to evoke power or to govern a society or group of people.

Accordingly, the relationship among politics, ideologies, and sport is synonymous with power and control over sport. From this perspective, politics is power. Whether the power comes from government, organization, or even ideology, the end result is an influence or control over sport. For example, consider the impact the government has over sport. According to Eitzen and Sage (2003):

> a) legislation has been passed exempting sports from antitrust laws; b) tax laws give special concessions to owners of professional teams; c) the blackouts of televised home games have been lifted for professional football under certain circumstances despite the protests of the commissioner and the owners; d) Congress decides which sport organization will have the exclusive right to select and train athletes for the Olympic Games; and e) Congress crafts legislation that exempts college sports and their benefactors from taxes. (p. 193)

These examples illustrate how intervention by the United States government can dictate the influence and/or direction of sport on an organizational level.

However, governmental motive for involvement can illustrate broader agendas. The broader agendas consist of sports utilization for (a) preparing the military, (b) facilitating social integration, (c) building a sense of national identity, (d) projecting a positive image of the nation abroad, and even (e) supporting economic development (Houlihan, 2000). These agendas demonstrate the complex relationship that exists between politics, power, and sport. Therefore, through these examples, one can understand how politics and sport are interwoven and agendas are initiated, which impact large-scale societal processes. However, what tends to be forgotten is how political decisions influence the opportunities for those within sport.

In the U.S., for instance, Blacks have faced a long and arduous struggle for political equality. These struggles stem from the history of slavery, to legalized racial segregation (see 1896 *Plessy v Ferguson*), and overt racism. Today, after legalized integration (see *Brown v Board of Education*), covert racial realities persist. This becomes apparent when comparing the employment rates for Blacks (15.4%) to the rest of the population (8.6%) (U.S. Department of Labor, 2011), or when examining the racial representation in social (e.g., education, economic, politic; Feagin, 2006) and cultural institutions like sport (Lapchick, 2011). Interestingly, when examining sport at the collegiate level, Blacks are overrepresented as participants in the highly visible revenue-producing sports, but underrepresented as administrators and coaches, or in key decision maker roles (Lapchick, 2010). Even as these disparities are illuminated and propositions for policy change have been put forward (e.g., Eitzen, 2000; Corbett & Tabron, 2007), Blacks and others (e.g., women, lower class) face similar representational disparities within sport.

When addressing the representational disparities for women and sport participation and leadership, Title IX of the Educational Amendments of 1972 comes to the fore. As outlined in Chapter 15, this law has positively impacted educational and sport opportunities for girls and women; yet, there are also unintended outcomes associated with the law's passage, including a decrease in the proportion of women in leadership positions (Acosta & Carpenter, 2010). In addition to Acosta and Carpenter's (2010) longitudinal assessment, others (e.g., Donnelly & Coakley, 2002) have argued general participation rates in physical activity and sport have increased; however, full inclusion has been relatively stagnant for historically excluded groups (e.g., racial and ethnic minorities, lower class).

From the outside looking in, sport presents itself as a progressive institution. However, as theses examples have illustrated, a deeper examination of the implementation and monitoring of policies are necessary when addressing the inequities in sport and physical activity. Thus, understanding the role of dominant ideologies and power dynamics in politics will elucidate how inequities result in the context of sport.

**Ideologies**

Sage (1998) defined ideology as a representation of societal values and ideas, which tend to explicate and justify the conditions and interests of those in power. In drawing from this perspective, it becomes apparent utilizing ideologies within sport is beneficial. Sport serves as an excellent backdrop to examine societies' dominant ideologies and power dynamics since societal phenomena are also observed in the sport context (Sage, 1998). Furthermore, sport as a cultural institution often aligns with the respective group, culture, or societies' dominant, or hegemonic, ideologies. For example, reviewing the historical progression of sport in the

U.S. during the rise of industrialization, organized sport adopted the dominant ideologies of society (e.g., success ideology) which aided in rationalizing and justifying the nature of other social institutions (Thompson, 1978). Hence, in sport, like society, ideologies can be utilized to push particular agendas forward, which can and have led to unequal benefit of one group over another based on their social categorizations (e.g., race, gender, class, religion).

Dominant power ideologies, for instance, promote the notion that one group is politically, economically, and socially superior to others. Therein lies the notion of hegemony, or "the condition in which certain social groups within a society wield authority – through imposition, manipulation, and consent – over other groups" (Whisenant etal., 2002, pp. 485-486). Thus, as one illustrative example, hegemonic masculinity illustrates men are both a social category structured by the gender system and they are dominant agents of social practices (Hearn, 2004).

Sage (1998) has argued sport represents one of the most hegemonic social institutions in society today. This perspective becomes relevant when examining the positions shared by women compared to men in sport, especially in their representation and advancement through sport leadership. Hegemonic masculinity has resulted in the dearth of women represented in sport administration and leadership positions at the high school (Whisenant, 2008) and collegiate (Acosta & Carpenter, 2010; Lapchick, 2010; Regan & Cunningham, in press) level. Due to the pervasiveness of this dominant ideology, women remain powerless and their access and advancement remain limited; thus, the ideological thinking that men are more dominant and deserving of sport's resources (e.g., positions, pay) continue to be reaffirmed (Theberge, 1987). Stemming from power ideologies, dominant racial ideologies also promote the notion of supremacy of one group over another. However, the supremacy being endorsed in this case is one's racial make-up.

When examining the dominant racial ideology in the United States, for instance, it becomes apparent why racial and ethnic minorities in sport are not fairing as well as their White counterparts. Racial ideologies and historical legislation (e.g., *Plessy v Ferguson*) have played a key role in justifying the unfair treatment towards Blacks (see also Chapter 15). For example, racial ideologies were used to: (a) validate slavery for U.S. political expansion, (b) rationalize why segregation was important after the abolishment of slavery, and (c) "scientifically" claim Blacks were naturally inferior to Whites (Coakley, 2008). These historic justifications, unfortunately, have placed Blacks today in a position of continual unwarranted access and treatment discrimination throughout society (Feagin, 2010). This is also prominent in sports where Blacks, in comparison with Whites, are unfairly treated and underrepresented beyond the playing field.

For instance, even in sports where Black athletes' numbers are overrepresented (e.g., college and professional basketball, college and professional football), research indicates Black athletes continue to be condemned and penalized by coaches, fans, officials, and the media for their conduct (e.g., taunting, celebrating) more than their White counterparts for similar behaviors (Simons, 2003). Additionally, the inferior status attributed to Blacks has relegated this group to particular playing positions in sport. This phenomenon is known as stacking and occurs when Blacks are relegated to positions assumed to require less intelligence, decision-making, and leadership (Smith & Henderson, 2000). The inequitable positioning of Blacks on the field of play has had a trickle up effect. For example, in 2000, Brooks and Althouse revealed a relationship between past playing position and positions as leaders (e.g., assistant coach, head coach, athletic director) and found fewer leadership roles were filled by those who were formally assigned to those positions deemed to require less intelligence, decision-making, and leadership.

Through these examples, the pattern and impact of dominant racial ideologies adversely affect Blacks in sport. Additionally, competing ideologies, such as color blindness, are transmitted through social and cultural institutions, including the mass media and popular culture (Leonard, 2004). Through this transmission, ideologies are justified and normalized, thereby concealing the gravity dominant racial ideologies have on the mistreatment of Blacks and other racial minorities. Thus, racial ideologies, and their competing ideologies, have the power to influence the way in which race is viewed throughout society. As such, this sheds light on the fact that there is no consensus to the severity of the race problem within the U.S.

Although the examples presented are brief, what should be understood is that dominant ideologies and power interests influence sport. And oftentimes these ideologies, coupled with individuals in power, will adversely affect those not belonging to the dominant group. Therefore, it is the alliance of the most powerful (e.g., government, big business, educational institutions, mass media) that have the most opportunity for embedding beliefs, values, and practices for their own interest in society and sport (Sage, 1998). Understanding how ideology impacts society, in this case sport, assists in grasping how decisions are made and power is asserted. Thus, the political decisions made, based on the advancement of dominant values, special interest, and ideologies, can become embedded in and throughout societies (Beamish, 2010).

## Power

In line with the previous discussion of ideologies, Sage (1998) has suggested that dominant individuals and organizations do not need to force or coerce subordinate entities to embrace or adopt hegemonic ideologies. Instead, these ways of knowing are embedded in people's everyday lives and oftentimes these ideologies are powerful enough to override their own cultural values and subvert their thinking. It is the pervasive operation of power by these dominant groups that can create conflict, silent voices, and present notions of inequality.

Thus, power, as viewed by social theorist Michael Parenti (1995), consist of "the ability to get what one wants, either by having one's interests prevail in conflict with others or by preventing others from raising their demands" (p. 5). People can use power as a tool for personal gain, self-interests, and limiting one's access and opportunities in various areas of sport and sport organizations. Furthermore, power is bets conceptualized as a process negotiated through interpersonal relationships and organizational structures; therefore, discussions of power and its relationship to sport must include the "ways that societies are organized and the ways that people determine what is important as they live with one another" (Coakley, 2007, p. 471). Hence, power plays a significant role in the perpetuation of ideologies and the ways in which ideologies enter, impress, and manifest in the sporting contexts.

As stated, much has been discussed about politics *and* sport from a national and global perspective (see Houlihan, 2000). While these issues are important, the goal of this chapter is to present the role of politics *in* sport, specifically highlighting how ideologies and power manifest in the lives of marginalized populations in the United States. According to Houlihan (2000), analysis of politics *and* sport includes how states and governments utilize sport as a resource and an aid in diplomacy; while examination of politics *in* sport is concerned with issues of "...access to, and the nature of, sports opportunities for individual sportsmen and women or groups" (p. 220). Therefore, when we consider issues of access to sporting opportunities in the U.S., there remains a sociopolitical history of limited access and inequity based on race, class, and gender (Acosta & Carpenter; 2010; Coakley, 2007; Lapchick, 1991, 2001; Oglesby, 1978; Sage, 1998).

Embracing grand notions of sport diplomacy and power (e.g., using sport to build strategic and political alliances) conceals the smaller, less visible, systems of domination (Collins, 1990, 2000; Sage, 1998). These inherent systems of domination, or matrix of domination (Collins, 1990, 2000), is what foregrounds many nations, for those in power were able to write the rules, institute the policies, and thus benefit from the structures they created. In turn, these individuals and organizations have the power to grant access, provide opportunity, and develop groups or not. This perspective, while limited, iterates issues of equity and equality.

On the other hand, examining issues of politics *in* sport, politics manifests with the aid of ideologies and power to determine "who gets what, when, and how" (Houlihan, 2000, p. 220), thereby governing individuals and instituting policies throughout organizations. Houlihan (2000) has argued that commercialization, gender, race and ethnicity are the dominant issues surrounding politics *in* sport. However, there are limited efforts to emphasize the connections between issues of access and opportunity to the political intersections within sport to include the meaning of sport, sport ideologies, and the use of power in these sporting contexts. In the next section, we will attempt to build a connection between the dominant issues and their political intersections in sport.

## POLITICS IN SPORT AND BEYOND

Coakley (2007) reminds us that "politics refers to more than issues concerning formal sport governing bodies; instead it refers to all forms of power relations in sport" (p. 446). Thus, the promotion and perpetuation of dominant ideologies, to include political ideology, can impact not only people's access and opportunities to sport, but the meaning of sport. Captivatingly, the Olympic Games are one of the most prominent global sporting events and have served as a platform for political ideology and nationalistic rhetoric. However, the political overtones and nationalistic rhetoric often overshadow the experiences of marginalization and social injustices for individuals and groups within the respective countries.

According to Guttmann (1992), the creator of the modern Olympic Games, French Baron Pierre de Coubertin, established the games as "the reconciliation of warring nations" and an opportunity to use sport competition to find common ground, or aid in diplomacy. Interestingly, de Coubertin would waiver on the purpose of the Olympic Games for he was "torn between a belief in individualism and the conviction that nationality is the indispensable core of individual identity" (Guttmann, 1992, p. 2). Thus, scholars suggest the promotion of nationalistic values and ideologies has the potential to "dilute political consciousness and diffuse feelings of rebellion" (Thompson, 1978, p. 83). Therefore, expounding on Houlihan's (2000) observation regarding politics *in* sport is significant, as individuals and groups may not challenge dominant ideologies and existing power structures.

Similar to the notion of politics and sport, examining the role of politics *in* sport can illuminate how dominant ideologies and power impact individuals, groups, and organizations access and opportunities in sport. More specifically, understanding the relationship between a global platform such as the Olympic Games and domestic governance will provide clarification of each influence on the other. Examining the dominant issues (e.g., race and ethnicity, gender, commercialization) of politics *in* sport may provide a more holistic understanding of the manifestation of politics *and* sport. In this final section we will examine how the perpetuation of (a) race and ethnicity, (b) gender and sex, (c) religion, (d) mental and physical ability, and (e) sexual orientation, ideologies have been utilized to marginalize the sporting experience and determine "who gets what, when, and how".

### Race and Ethnicity

Race and ethnicity are terms often used interchangeably. However, there is an important distinction between the two. Race is a socially constructed category; while, ethnicity refers to an individual's cultural background, heritage, and traditions (Coakley, 2007). Understanding these distinctions are important, for racial ideologies (e.g., white supremacy) in society *and sport* are rooted in the biological differences and are used to justify the power dynamics (i.e., organizational structure) and marginalization of groups (e.g., Blacks, Hispanics, Native Americans) (Coakley, 2007; Feagin, 2006).

In the 1936 Olympic Games, Jesse Owens, an African American, won four gold medals and set 3 world records in Berlin, Germany. Owens unprecedented feat challenged Adolf Hitler's racial ideology and notion of White athletic supremacy. Hitler's response to Owens achievements was the refusal to shake hands in congratulations, as he did with the

German champions. This global racial discriminatory act was acknowledged, but overshadowed by nationalistic success as the United States "won" the 1936 Olympic Games (Guttmann, 1992). In the U.S., the racial ideology of White supremacy was viewed as norm, and despite the Olympic victory by Owens, and Cornelius Johnson and David Albritten, the dominant racial ideology positioned Blacks as inferior in society, the workforce, and, in the realm of sport (Coakley, 2007; Cunningham, 2011; Lapchick, 2001, 2011). In sport, Blacks were deemed as intellectually inferior and athletically superior (Coakley, 2007; Edwards, 1973); however, some Blacks would refute this notion, while others chose not to challenge the status quo.

For example, Joe Louis' domination in the boxing ring in the late 30's and 40's made him renowned, but his quiet demeanor, which contrasted the great Black heavyweight boxer before him, Jack Johnson, made him more acceptable within the tumultuous era of Jim Crow (Deardorff, 1995). Although dominant racial ideologies were rampant throughout society at an elevated, unprovoked level, Joe Louis was embraced, even by the dominant society as Louis "assumed the more subservient role whites expected from members of his race" (Wiggins, 2007, p. 25). This historical illustration of a Black male being embraced at a society-wide level is significant as sport, similar to society, has the ability to create an illusion of equality.

The continual and overt combination of white supremacy and social injustices would trigger individual and group actions through protests (e.g., 1968 Mexico Olympics; see Edwards, 1969; Hartmann, 1996), boycotts, sit-ins, and the enactment of government legislation. At the height of desegregation, the impact of *Brown v Board*, and more specifically Title VII of the Civil Rights Act of 1964, created a shift and increase in Blacks enrollment to predominantly White college campuses. Their presence on these campuses, however, came with much resistance. The Black athlete, and Black non-athlete, experienced incidents of racism and discrimination from players on the same and opposing teams and faculty and students on campus and off-campus (e.g., obtaining housing) (Harris, 2000). These racial incidences were overt and widespread; therefore, President Truman developed and employed an interracial committee to study and find solutions to end racial discrimination on these campuses (Franklin & Moss, 1988).

Although Truman's efforts did not end racial discrimination on college campuses, the athletic programs appeared to be more progressive. More specifically, the realization of the benefits of integration created an atmosphere of progressiveness, subsequently, the athletic programs resulted in an increased number of Black participation and opportunities in sport in society (Harris, 2000). Black sport participation and opportunities also resulted in the dominant society embracing the high performing and record-breaking feats by Black athletes such as Lew Alcindor (later Kareem Abdul-Jabbar), O.J. Simpson, and Bob Beamon (Harris, 2000). Therefore, the combination of legislative acts and racial movements, newfound access and opportunity, and success of the Black athlete demonstrated how the power of sport could transcend racial ideology through political involvement.

**Gender and Sex**

Similar to race and ethnicity, gender and sex are often use interchangeably. However, gender is a socially constructed category based on role expectations; while, sex refers to one's biological attributes and physiological characteristics (Cunningham, 2011). Understanding these distinctions helps in understanding the prevalent gender ideology that excludes excluded women from participating in sport and physical activity, including the early Olympic Games. Coubertin stated that the inclusion of women would be "impractical, uninteresting, unaesthetic, and incorrect" (Guttmann, 1984). Therefore, it was not until 1900 when a limited number of women were allowed to participate in golf and tennis and in 1912 the addition of women swimmers and divers. But women's involvement in "strenuous" sports was resisted due to the belief that participation would lead to the development of masculine characteristics and/or that activity would cause harm to women's reproductive system (Cahn, 1994; Guttmann, 1992). This global ideology of masculine superiority would continue to influence the world.

In the U.S., the notion of girls and women's participation in sport and physical activity followed the hegemonic notion of masculine superiority, or patriarchy also. Despite this dominant ideology, U.S. women continued to make inroads in sport globally (e.g., Babe Didrikson, Althea Gibson, Wilma Rudolph) and domestically (i.e., Ladies Professional Golf Association (LPGA), Association for Intercollegiate Athletics for Women (AIAW)); as athletic success, industrialization, and the Civil Rights Movements lead to the enactment of Title IX of the Educational Amendment, or Title IX, was enacted in 1972.

Title IX addressed that no individual, regardless of sex, be denied the right to participate in any activity or educational program receiving federal financial assistance (Department of Education, 2011). Since Title IX's implementation, female sport participation numbers in both high school and college increased astronomically. However, women continued to face a power struggle with men in sport leadership roles (e.g., assistant coach, head coach, athletic director), where their numbers compared to men within four-year (Acosta & Carpenter, 2010; Lapchick, 2010) and two-year (Regan & Cunningham, in press) collegiate athletics, and high school sport (Whisenant, 2008) were underrepresented. This reflected the impact of gender ideology, or masculine hegemony, on the hiring practices within sport and society, which favored men over women. Hence, while politics may assist in sport participation access and opportunities, they had limited impact when the challenge is in the sharing of power (see Acosta & Carpenter, 2010; Cunningham, 2011; Lapchick, 2010).

According to Acosta and Carpenter (2010), more girls and women are participating in sports than before in the U.S. Scholars have found sport and physical activity to have several benefits for girls and women, including reduced stress and depression, increased academic success, enhanced mental health, and decreased risk for osteoporosis, certain cancers, and cardiovascular disease (Kane & Larkin, 1997). While the benefits are many, challenges still persist, as women continue to achieve and experience success in a masculine institution of sport. Cahn (1994) states "women's athletic success…is often perceived as a defeat for men and a threat to their masculinity" (p. 262). Therefore, the combination of increased participation rates (e.g., high school, college, professional sports), achievements (i.e., Olympic Medals, World Champions, Wimbledon Champion), and access (e.g., boxing, NASCAR) may threaten the notion of masculinity and increase implementation of organizational policies which provide access and opportunities.

Illustrative of these dynamics, in 2009 the success of South African 800 meter World Champion Caster Semenya raised suspicion as she became the subject of the IOC's sex verification testing. Sex verification testing, known as gender verification testing, is not a new policy. The first such test was at the 1936 Berlin Olympics, in which Helen Stephens, an American sprinter, was subjected to a physical examination and inspection of her external genitalia due to rumors that she was a man (Ritchie, Reynard, & Lewis, 2008). Thirty-two years later at the 1968 Mexico Olympics, a policy was written and a more humane sex verification test, or Barr body detection, was instituted forcing women to "prove" they were indeed females and did not have an advantage (Cahn, 1994; Ritchie et al., 2008). As time passed, women who were suspected as masquerading as men would be subjected to the IOC's, and International Association of Athletics Federation's (IAAF), authority; and in 2009 Semenya's success raised suspicion. Semenya underwent testing, and was banned from competition until the IAAF determined the findings. In July of 2010, the IAAF cleared Semenya for international competition, but chose not to release the findings, leaving the already tenuous issue with more questions.

While Semenya was cleared for competition, many stakeholders (e.g., South African civic leaders, Athletics South Africa coach Wilfred Daniels) and interested parties (i.e., commentators, politicians, activists, athletes) jeered the way in which the IAAF handled Semenya's sex verification citing her treatment violated her human rights and had racist undertones (Wonkam, Fieggen, & Ramesar, 2010). Ritchie, Reynard, and Lewis (2008) suggest sex verification testing is "humiliating and unproductive" in most cases and "detrimental to the sport" (p. 395). Nevertheless, the issue persists in the realm of intercollegiate athletics, as presented in the National Collegiate Athletic Association's (NCAA) implementation of a policy for the inclusion of transgendered student-athletes (see NCAA Office of Inclusion, 2011). This issue will be discussed in greater detail later in this section regarding sexual orientation.

### Religion

Houlihan (2000) noted race and ethnicity and gender as two dominant issues relevant for politics *in* sport; however, the religion, mental and physical ability, sexual orientation, and media are also marginalizing issues in sport. Religion is defined as "a socially shared set of beliefs and rituals that people use to transcend the material world and give meaning to important aspects of their lives" (Coakley, 2007, p. 530; see also Chapter 18). Thus, similar to race and gender, individuals and groups can be categorized based on their "socially shared set of beliefs". Coakley (2007) identifies that the shared beliefs (e.g., Christianity, Buddhism, Islam) may lead to (a) group unity or group conflict, (b) moral acceptance or judgment (i.e., marginalization), (c) adherence or rejection of social norms, and (d) use of policies and practices to marginalize and produce social inequities. Additionally, religion in sport has been used to (a) achieve religious goals and/or (b) achieve sport performance goals (Coakley, 2007). Thus, religion, like sport, is a cultural practice, and the meaning of each is determined by the time period and social location.

For example, in the 1936 Olympics, while Hitler's notion of White supremacy overshadowed the games, his religious anti-Semitic rhetoric was felt by Jewish athletes (Cashmore, 2005; Guttmann. 1992). Hitler's notion of White supremacy was not simply racial and ethnic ideology, but an overlapping subjugating religious undertone situating Aryan individuals as superior and excluding Blacks, mentally and physically disabled individuals, Gypsies, and Jewish individuals from German life (Bachrach, 2000). In this illustration, religious propaganda and rhetoric were used to create conflict, marginalize, and promote social inequities amongst non-Aryan individuals and participants. Thus, religion and/or religious rhetoric in sports can reaffirm hegemonic notions of race, gender, and sexual orientation. In addition, sport and religion overlap, reproducing and promoting dominant ideologies (i.e., matrix of domination), which can incite political dissention.

Conversely, religious rhetoric can be used to unite groups. For example, in the U.S., historically religion (i.e., Christianity) was used as a unifying tool for the preparation and development of men for war (Sage, 1998). In addition, organizations and fitness facilities such as the Young Men's Christian Association, or YMCA, Young Women's Christian Association (YWCA), and Jewish Community Centers (JCC) create community through the promotion of their respective fundamentalist principles through programming for sport, physical activity, and health and wellness. Organizations such as these serve individuals of all ages in local, regional, and national communities. Accordingly, the community beliefs may or may not extend into other organizations (i.e., professional sports) and institutions (i.e., high schools, colleges, and universities), and thus, influence the development and purpose for participation of coaches, athletes, and parents.

Akin to organizations, coaches and athletes utilize religion in competition to create team unity, reaffirm social norms, achieve competitive success, and nurture a sense of purpose or meaning. For example, according to Coakley (2007) followers of Christian faith use sport to (a) recruit members, (b) promote spiritual growth, and (c) promote religious beliefs informally or formally. Formally, organizations such as Fellowship of Christian Athletes (FCA) and Athletes in Action (AIA) embrace this notion. Athletes in Action, for instance, uses Christian principles as sport ministry espousing "sport is a universal language with the powerful ability to shape culture, heal a nation, break down political, racial, and economic barriers and restore national pride" (Athletes in Action, 2009). Acknowledging their "one language of sports," Athletes in Action's global following uses sport and religion in tandem to fulfill the afore-mentioned Christian principles to promote social change.

Issues arise when religious practice and an individual's and/or group's purpose for sport participation do not align (see Coakley, 2007). In par-ticular, conflict arises when religious practice is used to reaffirm hege-monic notions and power dynamics, and thus, justify marginalization. For example, Muslim women, or women who practice Islamic faith, have encountered challenges based on their religious doctrine (Sfeir, 1985; Walseth & Fasting, 2004; Walseth, 2006). More specifically, the Saudi Arabian government's stance on sport and physical activity for girls and women remains exclusionary, as sport is deemed strictly a male activity. Girls and women are allowed to participate in the "privacy of their homes", but beyond the scope of play (i.e., participation in public or pro-fessional sports), they are shamed for challenging the religious and cul-tural doctrine (see Reuters, 2012). In 2012, the Saudi Arabian government announced they would permit women to participate in the 2012 London Olympic Games in the sport of equestrian; however, only time will tell if this opportunity leads to additional opportunities for girls and women. Still, public opportunity comes at great cost, as Muslim women fall vic-tim to the overlapping constructs of domination with religion, gender, *and* social class simultaneously serving as limiting factors to access facili-ties and programs that can provide opportunities to participate beyond the privacy of their homes. Therefore, regardless of religious affiliation, religious beliefs and practices continue to permeate institutions and chal-lenge power structures in society and sports.

**Mental and Physical Ability**

Mental and physical ability, or disability, is another issue, which mar-ginalizes individuals and groups in society and sport. In the context of sport, mental and physical disability has segmented these individuals globally and domestically based on (a) attitudes towards athletes with disabilities, (b) barriers to inclusion, and (c) accessibility (Cunningham, 2011). Interestingly, international games have been created to allow these individuals to showcase their athleticism. In 1924, the first Deaflympics, affectionately called the "Silent Games", was held in Paris, France (see Deaflypics, 2012); in 1960, the first Paralympic Games was held in Rome following the Olympic Games (see International Paralympic Committee, 2012); and in 1968, the first International Special Olympics summer games was held in Chicago, Illinois (see Special Olympics, 2012). Again, each of these games allowed individuals with disabilities to showcase their athletic prowess, while also helping to build self-esteem, promote independence, achieve empowerment and acceptance, promote social interaction, and inspire. These are noteworthy benefits, as individuals with mental and physical disabilities have historically been stigmatized, stereotyped, and often shunned from mainstream culture due to an impairment which rendered them "undesirable, defective, and unwanted" (Cunningham, 2011, p. 157).

Nevertheless, people living with disabilities are finding ways to participate in sport and increase their physical activity levels. According to SportAbility (2011), 21 million people in the U.S. are living with disabilities, and one out of ten participates in daily physical activity. The inclusion of those with disabilities has steadily increased in this new era. For instance, the Special Olympics World Games, an IOC sanctioned athletic competition for those with mental disabilities, have participants from over 170 countries (Special Olympics, 2012 b). Similarly the Paralympics, the second largest multi-sport international competition trailing only the Summer Olympics (Miller & Washington, 2012) and, in addition to the Special Olympics, these events symbolize the significance sport can play for groups who have traditionally been excluded from participation.

With respect to the global and domestic relationship, the U.S. Department of Veterans Affairs have actively participated in supporting soldiers wounded in war. In particular, the Prosthetic and Sensory Aids Service (PSAS) provide a support for veterans to obtain medical equipment, sensory aids, prosthetic and orthotic services, and general support services based on the disability they sustained in service (U.S. Department of Veterans Affairs, 2012 b). This is noteworthy, as soldiers often return from war having experienced a mental disability (e.g., post traumatic stress disorder; see Richardson, Frueh, & Acierno, 2010; U.S. Department of Veterans Affairs, 2012 b) or a physical disability. Therefore, they have created numerous sport and educational programs for wounded veterans, such as the National Veterans Wheelchair Games, National Veterans Summer Sports Clinic, National Veterans TEE and Tournament, and the Wounded Warrior Amputee Softball Team. Similar to the benefits listed above, veterans with disabilities benefit in a number of ways, including reduced dependency on medication, less stress, higher educational attainment and employment, and more independence. Thus, despite the nature of disability, creating opportunities and providing access to individuals can be beneficial to all.

## Sexual orientation

The issue of sexual orientation, sexuality, in society and sport has also come to the fore. Sexual orientation is historically viewed as a binary construct, like gender, of heterosexual or homosexual, and not a continuum (Cunningham, 2011). Thus, there was no space for the inclusion of individuals who self identified as lesbian, gay, bisexual, or transgendered (LGBT). Traditionally excluded members of society, LGBT individuals, have typically hid their identity or joined communities with similar others. These individuals have experienced marginalization in society, the workplace, and in sport based on prejudices and discriminatory practices.

However, in 1980 Dr. Tom Waddell conceptualized the Gay Games (see Federation of Gay Games, 2012). The Gay Games have grown dramatically in recent years and is one of the largest sporting events in the world with fifteen thousand participants representing sixty-eight countries (Krane & Waldron, 2000). What is promising, according to Krane, Barber, McCung (2002), is the Gay Games has positively impacted its participants through their desire and work to promote social change, educate others, and work through political channels. Similar to the Special Olympics and the Paralympics, events such as the Gay Games continue to have increased participation and promote awareness. The benefit of these events for groups marginalized based on their sexual orientation have the potential to impress individuals in power (e.g., political agents) and those with key positions to use sport to promote social change.

On the domestic level, and as alluded to in the subsection on gender and sex, the NCAA's recent inclusion policy for transgender student-athletes comes after global and domestic ideologies regarding sport participation were challenged. In 2010, Kye Allums, a George Washington University basketball player's participation was brought to attention when he announced he was a transgendered male playing on the women's basketball team (USA Today, 2010). Acknowledging his biological genitalia and sex was female, Allums explicated, "feelings-wise, how it feels on the inside, I feel as if I should have been born male with male body parts" (USA Today, 2010). Therefore, he has not had any medical procedure; however, socially he identifies as male. This situation brought forth new challenges for the NCAA and the NCAA's Office of Inclusion.

In 2011 the NCAA Office of Inclusion drafted its handbook of policies and best practices to address the treatment and participation of transgendered athletes, as well as legal and medical information to help facilitate discussion and management amongst university programs, coaches, and athletes (see NCAA, 2011). Again, sport is a male-dominated cultural institution, and as such anyone identifying as an "other" is often subjected to prejudicial and discriminatory practices which limit and marginalize their sport and physical activity experiences.

## CHAPTER SUMMARY

The purpose of this chapter was to discuss the role of politics in sport and physical activity. In doing so, we defined sport, discussed the meaning of sport for groups, and described the relationship between sport and politics. In the latter sections, we further explained the ways in which politics function within the context of sport through the use of ideologies and power. The final section of the chapter focused on the relationship between global and domestic responses to politics *in* the sport contexts. This perspective provided an understanding of legislative acts and the institution of policies and their impact on the individuals and groups who have been historically or traditionally excluded from sport and sport participation.

## DISCUSSION QUESTIONS

1. Why is understanding the meaning of sports with various cultures and groups important?
2. What is the significance of power and politics in sport?
3. How are ideologies and power related to politics?
4. Compare and contrast the dominant issues of politics in sport.

## RECOMMENDED READINGS

Coakley, J. (2007). *Sports in Society: Issues and Controversies*, 9th edition. NY: McGraw-Hill, Inc. (Presents the sociological significance and meaning of sport for individuals and societies. Additionally, this text provides an understanding of race, gender, and class inequalities in sport and society.)

Cunningham, G.B. (2011). *Diversity in sport organizations*, 2nd edition. Scottsdale, AZ: Holcomb, Hathaway, Publishers. (Presents how individuals and groups experience prejudice and discrimination based on their diversity status (i.e., race, gender, mental and physical ability, religion) in society, and sport.)

Houlihan, B. (2000). Politics and Sport. In J. Coakley and E. Dunning (Eds.), *Handbook of Sport Studies* (pp. 213-227). Thousand Oaks, CA: Sage Publications Inc. (Presents an understanding of ways in which politics and sport intersect nationally and internationally.)

## REFERENCES

Abney, R. (2007). African American Women in Intercollegiate Coaching and Athletic Administration: Unequal Access. In D. Brooks and R. Althouse (Eds.), *Diversity and social justice in college sport: Sport management and the student athlete* (pp. 51-75). Morgantown, WV: Fitness Information Technology, Inc.

Acosta, V. & Carpenter, L. (2010). *Women in Intercollegiate Sport A Longitudinal, National Study Thirty Three Year Update: 1977-2010.* Retrieved on December 1, 2011 from http://www.acostacarpenter.org/.

Anderson, A. & South, D. (2007). The Academic Experiences of African American Collegiate Athletes: Implications for Policy and Practice. In D. Brooks and R. Althouse (Eds.), *Diversity and social justice in college sport: Sport management and the student athlete* (pp. 77-94). Morgantown, WV: Fitness Information Technology, Inc.

Athletes in Action (2009). *About.* Retrieved on March 1, 2012 from http://www.athletesinaction.org/about/.

Bachrach, S.D. (2000). *The Nazi Olympic: Berlin 1936.* Boston, MA: Little, Brown, and Company.

Beamish, R. (2010). Toward a Sport Ethic: Science, politics, and Weber's sociology. In E. Smith (Ed.), *Sociology of sport and social theory* (pp. 3-14). Champaign, IL: Human Kinetics.

Black, D.R. & Nauright, J. (1998). *Rugby and the South African Nation sport, cultures, politics and power in the old and new South Africas.* Manchester, United Kingdom: Manchester University Press.

Brooks, D. & Althouse, R. (2000). African American head coaches and administrators. In D. Brooks and R. Althouse (Eds.), *Racism in college athletics: The African American athlete's experience, 2nd edition* (pp. 85-117). Morgantown, WV: Fitness Information Technology, Inc.

*Brown v Board of Education.* (1954). *Brown v Board of Education, 347 U.S. 483.* Retrieved on October December 12, 2011 from http://www.nationalcenter.org/brown.

Cahn, S. (1994). *Coming on strong: Gender and sexuality in twentieth-century women's sport.* NY: The Free Press.

Carter, A.R. (2010). Using Social Theory. In G.B. Cunningham and J.N. Singer (Eds.), *Sociology of Sport and Physical Activity* (pp. 23-46). College Station, TX: Center for Sport Management Research and Education.

Cashmore, E. (2005). *Making sense of sports* (4th ed.). New York: Routledge.

Coakley, J. (2007). *Sports in society: Issues and controversies* (9th ed.). New York: McGraw-Hill.

Coakley, J. (2008). *Sports in society: Issues and controversies* (10th ed.). New York: McGraw-Hill.

Collins, P. (1990). *Black feminist thought: Knowledge, consciousness, and the politics of empowerment.* New York: Routledge.

Collins, P. (2000). *Black feminist thought: Knowledge, consciousness, and the politics of empowerment* (2nd ed.). New York: Routledge.

Corbett, D. R., & Tabron, M. J. (2007). An examination of athletic directors' perceptions of barriers to employment opportunities. In D. Brooks, and R. Althouse (Eds.), *Diversity and social justice in college sport: Sport management and the student athlete* (pp. 159-175). Morgantown, WV: Fitness Information Technology, Inc.

Cunningham, G.B. (2011). *Diversity in sport organizations* (2nd ed.). Scottsdale, AZ: Holcomb, Hathaway.

Deaflympics (2012). *About.* Retrieved from www.deaflympics.com/about/.

Deardorff, D. (1995, October 1). Joe Louis became both a black hero and a national symbol to whites after overcoming racism in the media. *St. Louis Journalism Review.*

Department of Education (2011). Title IX of the Education Amendments of 1972: 20 U.S.C. Sect. 1681. Retrieved from http://www.ed.gov/.

Donnelly, P., & Coakley, J. (2002). The role of recreation in promoting social inclusion. *Working Paper Series.* Toronto: The Laidlaw Foundation.

Edwards, H. (1969). *The revolt of the Black athlete.* Toronto: The Free Press.

Edwards, H. (1973). *Sociology of sport.* Homewood, IL: The Dorsey Press.

Eitzen, D. S. (2000). Racism in big-time college sport: Prospects for the year 2020 and proposals for change. In D. Brooks and R. Althouse (Eds.), *Racism in college athletics: The African American athlete's experience, 2nd edition* (pp. 293-306). Morgantown, WV: Fitness Information Technology, Inc.

Eitzen, D. S., & Sage, G. H. (2003). *Sociology of North American sport.* New York: McGraw-Hill.

Feagin, J. R. (2006). *Systemic racism: A theory of oppression.* New York: Routledge.

Feagin, J. R. (2010). *The White racial frame: Centuries of racial framing and counterframing.* New York: Routledge.

Federation of Gay Games (2012). *History.* Retrieved on February 26, 2012 from http://gaygames.com.

Franklin, J. H., Moss, A. A. (1988). *From slavery to freedom: A history of Negro Americans* (6th ed.). New York: Alfred A. Knopf.

Guttmann, A. (1984). *The Games must go on: Avery Brundage and the Olympic movement.* NY: Columbia University Press.

Guttmann, A. (1992). *The Olympics: A history of the modern games.* Urbana, IL: University of Illinois Press.

Hahn, H. (1984). Sports and the political movement of disabled persons: examining nondisabled social values. *ARENA Review, 8*(1), 1-15.

Harris, O. (2000). African American predominance in sport. In D. Brooks and R. Althouse (Eds.), *Racism in college athletics: The African American athlete's expe-*

393

*rience, 2nd edition* (pp. 38-52). Morgantown, WV: Fitness Information Technology, Inc.

Hartmann, D. (1996). The politics of race and sport: resistance and domination in the 1968 African American Olympic protest movement. *Ethnic and Racial Studies, 19*, 548-566.

Hearn, J. (2004). From hegemonic masculinity to the hegemony of men. *Feminist Theory, 5*(1), 49-72.

Houlihan, B. (2000). Politics and Sport. In J. Coakley and E. Dunning (Eds.), *Handbook of Sport Studies* (pp. 213-227). Thousand Oaks, CA: Sage Publications Inc.

International Committee of Sports for the Deaf (2012). *About.* Retrieved on February 26, 2012 from http://www.deaflympics.com/about/.

International Paralympic Committee (2012). *History of the movement.* Retrieved on February 26, 2012 from http://www.paralympic.org/TheIPC.

Kane, M.J. & Larkin, D. (1997). Physical Activity and Sport in the lives of girls: Physical and mental health dimensions for an interdisciplinary approach. *The President's Council on Physical Fitness and Sports Report.* Retrieved on February 22, 2012 from http://www.fitness.gov/girlssports.pdf.

Krane, V., & Walden, J. (2000). The Gay Games: Creating our own culture. In K. Schaffer & S. Smith (Eds.), *The Olympics at the millennium: Power, politics, and the Olympic Games* (pp. 147-164). Piscataway, NJ: Rutgers University Press.

Krane, V., Barber, H., & McClung, L. R. (2002). Social psychological benefits of Gay Games participation: A social identity theory explanation. *Journal of Applied Sport Psychology, 14,* 27-42.

Lapchick, R. (1991). *Five minutes to midnight: Race and sport in the 1990s.* Lanham, MD: Madison Books.

Lapchick, R. (2001). *Smashing Barriers: Race and Sport in the New Millennium.* Lanham, MD: Madison Books.

Lapchick, R. (2010). *The 2009 racial and gender report card: College sport.* Retrieved from http://www.tidesport.org/RGRC/2009/2009CollegRGRC.pdf.

Lapchick, R. (2011). *The racial and gender report card.* The Institute for Diversity and Ethics in Sport. Retrieved on December 10, 2011 from http://tidesport.org/racialgenderreportcard.html.

Leonard, D. L. (2004). The next MJ of the next OJ? Kobe Bryant, race, and the absurdity of colorblind rhetoric. *Journal of Sport and Social Issues, 28,* 284-313.

Miller, R. K., & Washington, K. (2012). Chapter 50: Events for athletes with disabilities. *Sports Marketing,* 381-384.

National Collegiate Athletic Association (2005, August). *NCAA executive committee subcommittee on gender and diversity issues report on references to American Indians in intercollegiate athletics.*

National Collegiate Athletic Association (2011). *NCAA inclusion of transgender student-athletes.* Indianapolis, IN: NCAA Office of Inclusion.

National Collegiate Athletic Association. *History.* Retrieved on October 29, 2011 from www.ncaa.org.

Oglesby, C. (1978). *Women and sport: From myth to reality.* London: Henry Kimpton Publishers.

Parenti, M. (1995). *Democracy for the Few* (6th ed.). New York: St. Martin's Press.

Plessy v Ferguson (1896). *Plessy v Ferguson, 163 U.S. 537.*

Regan, M. R., & Cunningham, G. B. (in press). Analysis of homologous reproduction in community college athletics. *Journal for the Study of Sports and Athletes in Education.*

Reuters, T. (2012). Saudi women push for the right to play sports. Retrieved on March 1, 2012 from www.nbcsports.com.

Richardson, L.K., Frueh, B.C., & Acierno, R. (2010). Prevalence estimates of combat-related post-traumatic stress disorder: Critical review. *Australian and New Zealand Journal of Psychiatry, 44* (1), 4-19.

Ritchie, R., Reynard, J., & Lewis, T. (2008). Intersex and the Olympic games. *Journal of the Royal Society of Medicine, 101,* 395-399.

Sage, G. (1998). *Power and ideology in American sport: A critical perspective* (2nd ed.). Champaign, IL: Human Kinetics.

Sfeir, L. (1985). The status of Muslim women in sport: Conflict between cultural tradition and modernization. *International Review for the Sociology of Sport, 20,* 283-306.

Simons, H. D. (2003). Race and penalized sports behaviors. *International Review for the Sociology of Sport, 38,* 5-22.

Smith, E., & Henderson, D. A. (2000). Stacking in the team sport of intercollegiate baseball. In D. Brooks and R. Althouse (Eds.), *Racism in college athletics: The African American athlete's experience, 2nd edition* (pp. 66-83). Morgantown, WV: Fitness Information Technology, Inc.

Special Olympics (2012 a). *Our history.* Retrieved on February 26, 2012 from http://www.specialolympics.org/history.aspx.

Special Olympics (2012 b). *Special Olympics World Games: A global stage to build awareness.* Retrieved from http://www.specialolympics.org.

Sport Ability (2011, September 11). *U.S. Paralympics and SportAbility of Iowa partner to create Paralympic sport-solon.* Retrieved from http://www.sportabilityofiowa.org.

Theberge, N. (1987). Sport and women's empowerment. *Women's Studies International Forum, 10,* 387-393.

Thompson, R. W. (1978). Sport and ideology in contemporary society. *International Review for the Sociology of Sport, 13,* 81.

United States Department of Labor. (2011). *Labor force statistics from current population survey.* Retrieved on December 10, 2011, from http://www.bls.gov/cps/

United States Department of Veterans Affairs. (2012 a). National Center for PTSD. Retrieved on February 27, 2012 from http://www.ptsd.va.gov/

United States Department of Veterans Affairs. (2012 b). Prosthetic and Sensory Aids Service (PSAS). Retrieved on February 27, 2012 from http://www.prosthetics.va.gov/.

USA Today (4 November 2010). *Transgender male Kye Allums on the women's team at GW.* Retrieved on February 29, 2012 from http://www.usatoday.com

Walseth, K. (2006). Young Muslim women and sport: The impact of identity work. *Leisure Studies, 25*(1), 75-94.

Walseth, K. & Fasting, K. (2004). Sport as a means of integrating minority women. *Sport in Society: Cultures, Commerce, Media, Politics, 7*(1), 109-129.

Wheeler, R. (1978). Organized sport and organized labour: The workers' sports movement. *Journal of Contemporary History, 13,* 191-210.

Whisenant, W. (2008). Sustaining male dominance in intercollegiate athletics: A case of homologous reproduction...or not? *Sex Roles, 58,* 768-775.

Whisenant, W., Pederson, P. M., & Obenour, B. L. (2002). Success and gender: Determining the rate of advancement for intercollegiate athletic directors. *Sex Roles, 47,* 485-491.

Wiggins, D. K. (2007). Climbing the racial mountain: A history of the African American experience in sport. In D. Brooks and R. Althouse (Eds.), *Diversity and social justice in college sport: Sport management and the student athlete* (21-47). Morgantown, WV: Fitness Information Technology, Inc.

Wonkam, A., Fieggen, K., & Ramesar, R. (2010). Beyond the Caster Semenya controversy: The case of the use of genetics for gender testing in sport. *Journal of Genetic Counselors, 19,* 545-548.

# CHAPTER 18

# RELIGION, SPORT, AND PHYSICAL ACTIVITY

## Calvin Nite and Michael Hutchison

***

## Learning Objectives

After reading this chapter, you should be able to:

1. Provide a definition for religion and explain the various theories relating to religion.
2. Identify the similarities and differences between sport and religion.
3. Assess the usage of religion in the sport setting at the organizational and individual level.
4. Assess the conflicts that arise between sport and religion.


## INTRODUCTION

From ancient times until the present, religions and religious institutions have played important roles in societies (Hulsether, 2007). For some, religious beliefs help them make sense of the events in their lives. For others, their religion serves as a social function that allows them to develop relationships with like-minded people. According to *Time Almanac* (2012), nearly 85% of the world's population claims to practice some form of religion, with Christianity (33%), Islam (22.4%), and Hinduism (13.8%) comprising the largest percentage groups. In many countries, legal systems and governments have foundations in the religious precepts and principles of the dominant religion in the region. Religion was one of the primary factors in the discovery and settlement of the "New World" and the eventual establishment of the United States of America. The Puritans and Quakers settled in what is now the New England region to escape religious persecution from the Church of England. Even in these present times, many of the laws and foundations of the US government still reflect religious traditions despite the supposed "separation of Church and State." Further, Islamic laws have historically governed many of the countries in the Middle East. In places such as Iran, Pakistan, and Saudi Arabia (and numerous other countries as well), Islamic law dictates punishment for crimes, people's work schedules, and, in some cases, how people may dress. Finally, religious practices are out-lawed in some countries. For instance, practicing Christianity and as-sembling for "church" is illegal in countries such as China, North Korea, and Vietnam.

Religion has also been one of the primary catalysts for many of the world's tensions. From Biblical times until the present, religious conflicts have been felt throughout the country/region known as Israel. Starting around 1000 AD, the Roman Catholic Church started the campaign known as the Crusades with the purpose of reclaiming the "Christian" lands of Jerusalem and other surrounding regions from Muslim people (The Crusades, n.d.). These campaigns lasted nearly 300 years, claiming millions of lives. Tensions in this region were revived post World War II, when Jews fleeing from the holocaust took refuge in Israel. These refu-gees eventually declared independence from Palestine and re-established the Jewish country of Israel (United Nations, 1949). Tensions from this have escalated throughout the years and Palestinians and Jews in the region still fight over these lands (The Israeli-Palestinian Conflict, 2007). The US has also been affected by religious conflicts. Religious extremists protesting the US presence in the Middle East carried out recent "terror-ist attacks," such as those on September 11, 2001. Clearly, religion and religious issues can be felt throughout the world.

With this in mind, it is only logical that the realms of sport and religion would intersect. Though religion and sport are seemingly different and unrelated, both are social institutions that are often parallel in design and, in many cases, are interconnected with one another. In this chapter, we will discuss the ways in which sport and religion affect each other. First, we will examine religion from a sociological and legal perspective in order to establish a foundation for subsequent sections. We will then examine the various ways people in sport use religion to enhance their lives and their sport. Further, we will also examine some of the ways religions and religious institutions use sport to advance their causes.

## WHAT IS RELIGION?

Prior to examination of the intersection between religion and sport, it is essential to provide a sociological foundation and definition for religion. From the sociological perspective, Durkheim (1965) defined religion as a set of common beliefs and practices of a community directed toward things that thought to be sacred which unite the collective members into a single community of faith (i.e., church) with all members following a common moral code. An important aspect of this definition is the collective nature of religion, wherein individuals live under the banner of an accepted view of a deity and the moral precepts that are theoretically drawn from their deity. For example, Judaism and Christianity have historically based their moral understanding on the Ten Commandments, which were written by the finger of God on stone tablets presented to Moses. As such, from the sociological and practical standpoint, religion serves as a means for maintaining order and good conduct among members of a given society. However, for members of communities of faith, religion is much deeper than a simple set of moral precepts governing a community. Through religion, people tend to feel they are somehow connected to something more mystical and powerful (i.e., God, see Exhibit 18.1) than they can ultimately explain. By this connection with God, many people find purpose and direction for their daily lives, and it is through this connection that people often attempt to make sense of the world in which they live.

Exhibit 18.1: Who or What is God?

The terms "God" or "god" can mean different things to different people. In the Christian and Jewish faiths, the consensus belief is that God is the eternal, spiritual being Jehovah. In the Islamic faith, God is known as Allah. Of course there are also numerous pagan religions as well. The ancient Greeks and Romans were polytheistic (believing in many gods) in their religious views. The modern day pagan religion, Wicca, adopts a dualistic view of God-ess, which is an impersonal deity that treats everyone as equal (www.wicca.org). Also, some religions are actually atheistic. Though many Buddhists do not necessarily deny the existence of gods or spirits, at its core Buddhism is a non-theistic religion. Thus, it is important to realize that the term "God" or "god" means different things to different people.

It is also important to understand the concept of spirituality, as spirituality and religion are often intertwined and sometimes used as interchangeable ideas. However, there is a distinction between spirituality and religion. Although many people have different definitions and conceptualizations of spirituality (see Cunningham, 2007; Mitroff, 2003; Schwartz, 2006), we have adopted the following definition for this chapter: spirituality is an individual's connection with those things that she or he considers to be sacred. Simply, spirituality is the individuals' connections with their diety, themselves, or nature. Although spirituality can be a part of religion, it is different in the idea that religion is a collective community and spirituality is more of an individual concept. It should be noted that many religions call for their members to pursue their own spirituality as they practice their religion. For many, this is done through prayer, meditation, and acts of charity. Thus, not only does the pursuit of spirituality benefit individuals by connecting them with their deity, it also enhances the religion. Individuals who are more connected with God strengthen the community of faith because they can offer better service to the community.

An important aspect of Durkheim's definition of religion is the idea of "sacred." Sacred has been defined as those things that "inspire awe, mystery, and reverence" (Coakley, 2007, p. 531). The sacred are believed to offer some type of connection with God. In various religions, the sacred can be written symbols, crafted figures, buildings, and even geographic locations. For instance, the city of Mecca is considered to be sacred in the Islamic faith. For Catholics and Christians alike, the symbol of the cross is sacred. Jews hold the Star of David as being a sacred symbol. In ancient Greece, the Parthenon was considered sacred, as it was the dwelling for the Greek goddess Athena. The meaning these examples provide for their religions are what make them sacred to their followers.

In contrast with the sacred is the profane. The profane are those things associated with everyday life and culture that are not viewed as having any type of religious or spiritual connection with a deity (Coakley, 2007). The profane can be morally neutral or can also be considered as a source of evil. Material possessions such as vehicles, houses, stadiums, and works of art can be considered profane, as would money. It is important to understand that religion is typically focused on the sacred, not the profane. Sport would typically fall into the latter category.

## RELIGION AND THE US LEGAL SYSTEM

As we previously noted, religion was a prominent aspect of the founding of the US. The First Amendment of the US Constitution addresses religion as it relates to the entire public sector and private sector state actors. According to the First Amendment, "Congress shall make no law respecting an establishment of religion, or prohibiting the free exercise thereof…" (US Const. Amend. I). In the court system, this initial portion of the First Amendment relating to religion has been divided into two clauses: the Establishment Clause and the Free Exercise Clause. The Establishment Clause ("Congress shall make no law respecting an establishment of religion…") determines a "freedom *from* religion." Within the public sector, an entity cannot legally endorse or promote a specific religion. For example, it is unconstitutional for a public institution such as Texas A&M University to endorse or support any form of religion. However, the Free Exercise Clause ("...or prohibiting the free exercise thereof...") is considered a "freedom *of* religion." This clause allows individuals the freedom to practice their religion of choice, thus prohibiting a governmental body from forbidding an individual to practice his/her respective religion. At Texas A&M, students are free to practice their chosen religion even amidst their attendance at a public institution. Due to their seemingly contradictory nature, these religious clauses comprise one of the most highly controversial interpretations and applications of Constitutional Law. As such, two primary questions concerning religious initiatives and sport warrant further understanding: (a) What are the boundaries of governmental involvement in religious activities, and (b) When is public religious activity allowed or prohibited?

As it relates to sport, particularly interscholastic and intercollegiate athletics, it is important to understand the difference in application within public institutions and private institutions. Public institutions receive government funding and act as representatives of the state (referred to as "state actors"), thus being subject to the Constitution. Private institutions, however, do not receive direct government funding and are usually not representatives of the state, therefore not being required to submit to constitutional standards. For example, higher learning institutions such as Louisiana State University, Mississippi State University, and the University of Florida are public institutions receiving government funding and are considered to be subject to the Constitution. These institutions are not at liberty to endorse or promote a specific religion because of their public, state actor status. On the other hand, private institutions such as Baylor University, Southern Methodist University, and Brigham-Young University do not receive direct government funding and are not required to abide by constitutional standards. Accordingly, these institutions have the freedom to establish and engage in their respective religious beliefs. For this reason, the application of Constitutional Law, and subsequent religious restrictions, is only applied to the public sector.

Having addressed the boundaries of governmental involvement with public-based religious activities, it is important to understand which religious activities are deemed constitutionally acceptable in the sport setting. Traditionally, professional sport teams and leagues have been categorized as private businesses, as opposed to public entities, within the legal setting (e.g., *Long v. National Football League*, 1994). However, with the intertwinement of municipal resources and tax-payer funds, professional sport teams and leagues have occasionally been deemed private entity state actors, thus subject to Constitutional Law (e.g., *Ludtke v. Kuhn*, 1978). The majority of examples relating to religious activities and the sport setting primarily occur within the education system. With particular relevance to the high school and intercollegiate athletics contexts, such examples include public prayer, religious organizations access to public resources and facilities, scripture reading, and religious clothing. Student prayer within the institutional setting has not traditionally been a matter of much constitutional concern. Unless a student is vocally praying in a disturbing or distracting manner, student-initiated prayer has limited unconstitutional implications. Examples of constitutionally permissible behavior include student-athletes meeting at center court to pray after a game, kneeling to pray after scoring a touchdown, or praying silently prior to an athletic contest. However, prayer initiated by authority figures (e.g., coach, teacher, administrator) is considered more ambiguous. Certainly, as established by the Free Exercise Clause, institutional authority figures have the freedom to pray individually within the confines of their office or classroom. Yet, authority figures who leverage their positions as a means of forcing or coercing student-athletes to pray is considered unconstitutional. An example of such behavior would be a high-school coach requiring members of the team to bow their heads for a pre-game prayer.

Religious organization access to public resources and facilities is another example of religious activities within the public school setting. Organizations such as the Fellowship of Christian Athletes (FCA) and Reformed University Fellowship (RUF) are widely known religious-based organizations within the collegiate setting. These student-led organizations are at liberty to constitutionally utilize public resources and facilities. However, such organizations are to be treated as any other campus organization, not receiving special or differential treatment. Additional examples such as scripture reading and displaying religious clothing are acceptable behaviors among students or student-athletes. As with student initiated prayer, these displays of religious activity are constitutionally permissible behaviors unless they result in widespread distraction or disturbance.

## COMPARING SPORT AND RELIGION

Many discussions of sport and religion focus on the influence of one or the other (discussed in later sections), yet there are also striking similarities and distinct differences between the two. Although they reside in different realms—religion in the sacred and sport in the profane—there are a host of similarities and differences between the two.

## Similarities between Sport and Religion

There are five striking similarities between sport and religion. They both: (a) have a devout following; (b) bring people together; (c) use symbolic rituals; (d) have elaborate structures; and (e) have heroines and heroes. We outline each of these in the following sections.

From an initial economic standpoint, there is a devout following for both religion and sport, with the largest followings generating the largest revenues. Patrons of a particular religion devote time and money in order to sustain that religion. Especially in Christianity, the clergy receive their salaries through donations made by members from their congregations. Notice that churches with the largest memberships tend to have the highest paid clergy. For example, Joel Osteen, pastor of Lakewood Church in Houston, Texas, which has more than 45,000 members, receives a large, six-figure salary from the church in addition to his book sales (Pinsly, 2007). Comparatively, sport teams, particularly collegiate and professional teams, are sustained through the devotion of fans' time and money. Game attendance is comparable to attending religious services, and season ticket holders are similar to church members. Teams with the largest fan bases tend to have the highest paid players and coaching staffs. For example, some of the most valuable Major League Baseball franchises (New York Yankees, Boston Red Sox, Philadelphia Phillies, Chicago Cubs) reported the highest payrolls for players and coaches (Badenhausen et al., 2011; USA Today, 2011). These teams further benefit from their popularity by earning revenue through the sales of their merchandise. This is similar to popular pastors and churches that benefit from book and merchandise sales.

Next, religion and sport are similar in their abilities to bring people into a focused social setting. In most religions, members have set times and days on which they gather in congregation to interact with fellow believers and worship their deity. It is through these gatherings that the traditions and messages of their religions are reinforced among the followers. The congregation also serves as a means to unite the followers with the purpose of continuing their religion. In sports, fans and spectators alike congregate at games and events to be entertained and to cheer on their favorite teams to victory. As previously mentioned, many teams have devout followings of fans who use sport as an avenue to socialize with people of similar interests. By their attendance at events, fans ensure the continued existence of the sport, much in the same manner as do religious patrons with their respective religions.

A third similarity between religion and sport is the symbolic rituals associated with both (Coakley, 2007). These rituals serve to unite the patrons and delineate "insiders" from "outsiders." That is, the rituals are typically well known by the insiders, and this inside knowledge brings a sense of belonging to members and fans alike. In most religions, members must perform rituals at their gatherings and, in certain sects, during their daily lives. In most Christian churches, there is a set order of events constituting a proper service. Although these may vary by denomination, typical worship services include opening and closing prayers, some type of music, a message or sermon delivered by a clergy member, and the taking of the Eucharist. In the Islamic faith, members are supposed to perform five daily prayers and travel to Mecca at some point in their lives in accordance with their religious traditions. This is comparable to the rituals that are performed at sporting events. At most sporting events in the US, the National Anthem is played prior to the start of the event. Many college football programs have traditional ceremonies at their games. For instance, The Ohio State University band performs a marching maneuver where they form the "script Ohio." It is considered a great honor at their school to be the person who dots the "i" during this ritual. Most sporting events on college campuses conclude with the singing of the school song. Another example is the singing of the song during the "7th inning stretch" at baseball games. When attending either religious or sporting events, a person can expect to see the performance of some type of ritual(s).

Another similarity between sport and religion is the elaborate buildings and structures in which events for both are held. Some of the most spectacular and beautiful structures in the world have been built for religious purposes. Some examples include the Cologne Cathedral in Cologne, Germany; Notre Dame in Paris, France; and Saint Patrick's Cathedral in New York, New York. Islamic mosques, such as the Dome of the Rock mosque in Jerusalem, also contain some of the more spectacular architecture the world has ever seen. Although typically not seen with the same reverence, sport stadiums reflect the same manner of architectural marvel and signify the level of importance that people often give sport. For example, Lambeau Field in Green Bay, Wisconsin, is a venue beloved by fans of the Green Bay Packers. The $1.2 billion dollar Dallas Cowboys

Stadium is one of the more recent sporting venues built that contains some of the most elaborate structures in sport (Mosley, 2009). The Beijing Olympic games were also a showcase of some of the more spectacular works of architectural art the Olympics and the world have ever seen. The main stadium, which had a capacity of 100,000 people during the 2008 Olympic games, was built to resemble a bird's nest (The Stadium Guide, 2004). The venue that was built for the water events, which was appropriately named the Water Cube, was built to resemble an ice cube (Mulvenney, 2008). Although these structures now house numerous non-sporting events, their initial purposes were strictly to house the Olympics in Beijing. Both sport and religion have some of the more marvelous venues seen in the world.

The final similarity is the presence of heroines and heroes in both sport and religion. Most religions have heroines, heroes, and legends who have either delivered transcending messages or who have fought against outsiders attempting to eradicate the religion. In the Jewish and Christian faiths, Moses is the hero who led the nation of Israel out of Egyptian slavery. Both faiths also hold King David in high regard because of the many battles he fought and won for Israel. Though rooted in Judaism, Christianity is based on the teachings of its hero, Jesus Christ. In the Islamic faith, the prophet Muhammad is one of the great heroes. His teachings and revelations from Allah are the foundations for the Qur'an. Gandhi is a renowned hero in India and the Hindu faith, and the Great Buddha is the hero and founder of Buddhism. As with religion, heroines, heroes, and legends abound in sport. Common examples are student-athletes on college campuses who have delivered legendary performances in athletic competition. At Texas A&M, former student-athletes Dat Nguyen and Acie Law IV are heroes on campus because of their athletic feats during their college careers. Further, soccer stars such as Ronaldinho are heroes in their home countries. National Basketball Association (NBA) stars such as Dirk Nowitzki and Yao Ming stars are legends in their home countries of Germany and China. For followers of particular sport teams in the United States, each fan base has particular people that they herald as being legendary. Some well-known examples include Michael Jordan, Babe Ruth, Joe Montana, and Wayne Gretzky. As such, both sport and religion contain their respective heroines, heroes, and legends.

## Differences between Sport and Religion

Although there are some striking similarities between sport and religion, there are indeed some pointed differences as well. We discuss two here: (a) the different realms in which they reside and (b) the nature of the experience.

Most notably, as highlighted previously, religion is considered to be a part of the sacred while sport is part of the profane (Coakley, 2007). Followers of any particular religion are typically seeking spiritual transcendence from the things of this world by connecting with their deity. Through their connection with their diety, religious people generally seek to live moral lives as they try to make sense of life in general. Sport is conceptualized as part of the profane because the end goal of sport is typically not connecting with a deity or attaining spiritual satisfaction. The goal of sport is generally entertainment and revenue generation. Although some athletes and organizations use sport to enhance their religious beliefs, most participants and consumers of sport are not typically seeking connections with the mystical and spiritual through the medium of sport. The one exception might be when people engage in sport or physical activity as a way to glorify their diety. This would especially be the case when people consider their body as a "temple" to do the Lord's work. While morality is often a preached emphasis in sport, sport is not seen as the vehicle or instrument though which morality and spiritual transcendence are created or attained.

Religion also differs from sport in regards to the nature of the experience. That is, religion is often an intangible experience typically experienced by the five senses of the body. It is more of a mental and emotional connection with something that is spiritual in nature, which is not seen, heard, smelled, felt, or tasted. While the tangible can be used to stimulate a heightened sense of emotion or mental awareness, when stripped down to its purest form, religion is ultimately an experience that is intangible in nature. For followers of religions, the idea of "faith" plays a vital role in sustaining their beliefs. Faith refers to knowing or believing in the existence of something that is typically not experienced by the five senses of the body. It is because of its intangibility and reliance on faith that religion is often described as mystical. Sport, however, is essentially a tangible experience for participants and spectators alike. Although sport can include some intangible concepts, such as faith in a player or team, it occurs in the physical realm where faith in a higher power is not typically required for involvement. Our five senses are able to detect and comprehend sport. We are not forced to believe that sport is occurring without the presence of physically experienced evidence of its existence.

## RELIGION IN SPORT

Religion and sport frequently intersect in societies across the world. Though religion is considered sacred and sport is considered profane, organizations and individuals alike have integrated the two entities for different purposes and for accomplishing different goals. In the organizational sense, religious institutions often use sport to spread and advance the teachings of their religion with the hopes of recruiting new members to the faith. At the individual level, sport participants often consider their performances in sport to be an act of glorifying their deities. These are just a couple of the many examples of the ways in which sport and religion have become intertwined with one another. In this section, we discuss the intersections of sport and religion at both the organizational level and at the individual level.

First, let us examine the ways in which sport and religion are intertwined at the organizational level. Often, sport is integrated into religious organizations with the purpose of using sport to spread the organizations religion to other populations. In the United States, different organizations have been formed using sport to spread religion across the world. One example of this is Athletes in Action (AIA), which is an extension of the religious organization Campus Crusade for Christ. David Hannah established AIA in 1966 with the purpose of spreading Christianity across the globe (Athletes in Action, 2011). AIA sends various sports teams across the world to play semi-professional and professional teams on what they call tours. These tours usually last about two weeks, with the AIA teams playing as many as 10 games on a tour. During each tour, the AIA athletes often host youth camps where they focus on developing the sport among the local children, but they also use the camps as opportunities to spread their religion. Further, at some point during each game, the AIA athletes will convey their stories of how they came to follow their religion to the spectators at the event. This is just one example of an organization using sport to promote its religion.

The spreading of religion through sport also occurs locally in many communities across the country. The Young Men's Christian Association (YMCA) is one of the more prominent religious organizations intended to provide a positive environment for family and children to enjoy sport. In 1844, George Williams founded the YMCA in London, England, with the hopes that young men would pursue religious activities instead of delinquent lifestyles on the streets of the city (YMCA, 2011a). Once the YMCA spread to the United States during the Civil War, sport became part of the YMCA. The YMCA claims to be responsible for introducing millions of people to sport as well as inventing some of the popular modern sports (i.e., basketball). YMCAs remain prominent in countless communities and still host numerous adult and youth sport leagues along with other sport initiatives to promote physical activity to their members. In recent years, the YMCA has deemphasized its religious traditions, yet their mission of building strong communities still exists (YMCA, 2011b). Other local organizations also use sport to promote their religion. Church sport leagues are common in many metropolitan areas throughout the United States. Although these leagues may have numerous stated objectives for their formations, a common theme in most is the spreading of religion through participation in sports. These are all examples of the intersection of sport and religion at the organizational level.

There are also various intersections of religion and sport on the individual person level. Athletes and coaches use religion in their sport participation for a variety of different purposes. We highlight two common usages here. First, religion can be used for therapeutic purposes, such as reducing anxiety, avoiding troublesome behavior, and focusing the efforts and lives of the individual. Secondly, individuals have used their participation in sport as a means for glorifying their deities. Common examples of these behaviors include praying prior to and at the conclusion of games, reading religious texts during travel to games, and referencing religion during competition. There are numerous professional athletes who provide fitting examples for how religion can be used for both therapeutic purposes as well as for the glorification of God.

Hakeem Olajuwon, a former professional basketball player and current NBA Hall of Famer, is a devout follower of the Muslim faith. Throughout his playing career, Olajuwon adhered to the mentality of "God comes first." As a professional athlete, Olajuwon was committed in following his religious practices, consistently displaying his commitment to his beliefs by such acts as always carrying a compass in order to make sure he could pray towards Mecca, read the Qur'an on airplanes between cities, visit the local mosque in any city he was playing, and arrange his daily errands around ritual prayer times. Olajuwon further displayed his devout beliefs by honoring the traditional Muslim holy month of Ramadan, which requires fasting from both food and liquid from dawn to dusk, during the latter half of every NBA season.

Tim Tebow, a professional football player, is also well known for using his participation in sport as a platform for spreading his religion. Tebow routinely referenced his religion in interviews and press conferences during his time in the collegiate and professional ranks. Tebow was known to put Bible verses on his "eye black" stickers during games in college (such practice has been disallowed by the NCAA). During Super Bowl XLV, Tebow became one of the first athletes to use his position in sport to convey his religious beliefs through commercials on television.

Boxing legend Muhammad Ali was also known for incorporating his religious beliefs in the boxing ring. A devout Muslim, Ali would begin each match with a prayer to Allah prior to competing with his opponent (for more related to Ali and other athletes, see Exhibit 18.2).

Finally, Tony Dungy, a former professional football coach, has been outspoken in his theological Christian beliefs. More importantly, Dungy utilized his foundational Christian beliefs in order to promote daily values, such as hard work, discipline, and service, in his interactions with his coaching staff, players, and fans.

Exhibit 18.2: Athlete Name Changes

A particularly visible expression of athletes' religious beliefs is their name changes. A common practice of athletes who convert to Islam is for them to change their names. This can be for a variety of reasons. Some athletes, especially African American athletes, change their names as a symbolic rejection of their given slave names. Also, athletes change their names in order to glorify God. Many prominent athletes have changed their names. Kareem Abdul-Jabbar, who was originally known as Lew Alcinder, and Muhammad Ali, who was originally known as Cassius Clay are two of the greatest athletes in their sports of basketball and boxing that have garnered name changes. Other examples of people in sport that have changed their names include sports caster Ahmad Rashad (formerly Bobby Moore), Mahmoud Abdul-Rauf (formerly Chris Jackson), and Bison Dele (formerly Brian Williams).

## CONFLICTS BETWEEN RELIGION AND SPORT

As discussed in the preceding section, sport and religion intersect at the organizational and individual levels for different purposes. However, there are some apparent conflicts and contradictory occurrences between religious ideals and the world of sport. In this section, we will discuss some of the conflicts between religion and sport.

To begin, participation in sporting events on holy days presents a conflict for many religious people. In most religions, certain days, months, and times of year are considered particularly sacred. In the Christian faith, Sunday is considered the Sabbath day, while Jewish people hold Saturday as the Sabbath. In both faiths, the patrons are instructed through their teachings and writings to "remember the Sabbath day by keeping it holy" (Exodus 20:8, NIV). Thus, performing in athletic competitions often poses conflicts for the athletes that subscribe to these particular beliefs. In fact, some athletic programs at certain universities do not allow their teams to participate on Sundays. Brigham Young University (BYU), an affiliate of the Church of Jesus Christ of Latter Day Saints, is one such example. In the event that BYU's basketball teams make the NCAA tournament, they are always scheduled to play on the Thursday/Saturday games so that they do not have to participate on Sundays, which is in accordance with their Church doctrines. As discussed earlier in this chapter, during the Islamic month of Ramadan, Hakeem Olajuwon would not eat or drink during the time when the sun was out, and this frequently caused him to be physically ill and dehydrated during basketball games. Sandy Koufax, who is considered by many to be one of the greatest pitchers of all time in Major League Baseball, made headlines during the 1965 World Series when he declined to pitch in Game 1 because it fell on the sacred Jewish holiday of Yom Kippur. Koufax maintained that his personal religious beliefs outweighed his professional beliefs (Brody, 1996). For more information, see Exhibit 18.3.

Another conflict between religion and sport is the participation of professed religious athletes in violent sports or deviant behaviors. Most religions in the world place a general emphasis on living a peaceful life. Yet many professed religious athletes participate in sports that are especially violent. There are many professed Christians and Muslims who participate in boxing and football who routinely acknowledge God during their participation in these sports, and it could be argued that their participation in these sports is contrary to the teachings of their religions. Also, as discussed throughout this chapter, one particular function of religion is to provide a moral code for its followers. Problems arise when professed religious adherents engage in deviant behaviors that are contrary to the teachings of their particular religions. Many popular sports figures have struggled with maintaining the moral teachings of their religions, including struggling with infidelity and drug use. Some of these athletes have been included in various steroid scandals and have been caught using other performance enhancing drugs. More serious examples are the athletes that have been convicted of violent crimes such as rape, manslaughter, and assault.

Exhibit 18.3: Prayer at Sporting Events

In the United States, a particularly heated topic has become prayer in school and prayer at school sponsored sporting events. Traditionally, sporting events have been preceded by prayers in locker rooms and in some parts of the country over the loudspeakers at games. There has been much debate over whether or not this is an act supported by the United States Constitution. Those against such prayers cite the idea of separation of church and state; while advocates claim that prayer at sporting events is well within their first amendment rights. Recent Supreme Court decisions have disallowed representatives of schools to lead their teams in pregame prayers and school equipment is not to be used as a means to broadcast prayers (Batista, 2002). However, students, athletes, and fans are still allowed to exercise their religious beliefs as protected by the First Amendment. Prayer at sporting events and in school has been and likely will continue to be an area of much debate.

A final conflict between sport and religion is the self-promoting of individuals in sport. These days, even in team sports, a recent trend has been athletes trying to distinguish themselves as individuals. Although this may not be necessarily negative in today's society, self-promotion, from a religious standpoint, is typically not considered proper. Many religious teachings emphasize virtues of humbleness and humility. In the Christian and Jewish faiths, the scriptures devote many texts to the purpose of instructing followers of the faith to be humble and not self-serving. The Qur'an also speaks to the idea that humility and humbleness are the paths to greatness. These teachings are quite conflicting with the self-promoting nature of sport, especially in the United States. Athletes that actively promote themselves and their brands, while professing their religious beliefs, are the most common examples of this conflict.

## CHAPTER SUMMARY

In this chapter, we focused on the use of religion in the sport environment, beginning with a definition of religion and spirituality. Although sometimes used interchangeable, the concepts of religion and spirituality do have distinct meanings. According to Durkheim (1965), religion is a set of common beliefs and practices of a community directed toward things thought to be sacred that unite the collective members into a single community of faith (i.e., the Church) with all members following a common moral code. Contrarily, we defined spirituality as an individual's connection with those things he or she considers to be sacred. We concluded by acknowledging the difference between the sacred (i.e., religion) and the profane (i.e., sport). Following the introduction, we discussed religion and the U.S. legal system. Specifically, we discussed the religious freedoms provided by the First Amendment of the Constitution. We further provided objective sport-based examples of constitutionally acceptable and unacceptable actions.

This section was followed by a discussion of the similarities and differences between sport and religion. Among the similarities between sport and religion, we discussed how both sport and religion as institutions bring people together, the devout followings among sport fans and religious groups, symbolic rituals of sports fans and religious groups, places of gathering for sport fans (e.g., stadiums) and religious groups (e.g., churches), and heroes/legends of sports fans (e.g., Michael Jordan) and religious groups (e.g., Jesus Christ). Additionally, we addressed the differences between sport and religion, focusing on tangible connections within the sport setting, as opposed to the intangible connections in the religious environment.

Following the similarities and differences apparent between sport and religion, we discussed the usages of religion in the sport environment from both the organizational and individual levels. We began by addressing the spread of religion in the sport setting by such organizations as Athletes in Action, the YMCA, and generic church leagues. In addition, we examined the usages of religion from the individual level, discussing the use of religion for therapeutic and glorification of God purposes. Finally, we closed with an examination of the conflicts between religion and sport, focusing on athletic participation on sacred days or periods of time, religious athletes who participate in violent sports, deviant behaviors of professed religious athletes, and the self-promotion aspect of the sport environment.

## DISCUSSION QUESTIONS

1. After reading this chapter, do you think there is a difference between religion and spirituality? Describe the similarities and differences between both concepts.
2. The chapter describes several similarities and differences between sport and religion. Can you think of any additional similarities or

differences between sport and religion? List and describe each additional similarity and difference.
3. In your opinion, what are the positives and negatives of the use of religion in sport? Do you think it is acceptable for athletes to use religion (e.g., prayer, glorification of a higher being) in the sport environment? Why or why not?
4. In your opinion, do you think it is acceptable for professed religious athletes to participate in perceived violent sports (e.g., football, hockey, wrestling)? Explain.

## RECOMMENDED READINGS

Durkheim, E. (1965). *The elementary forms of religious life*. New York: Free Press. (Durkheim's theories and studies of religion are fundamental to understanding religion from a sociological standpoint.)

Putney, C. (2003). *Muscular Christianity: Manhood and sports in Protestant America 1880-1920*. Boston: First Harvard University Press. (Putney details the historical emergence of the movement in the late 1800s and early 1900s that saw Protestant leaders promote competitive sport among men to achieve an ideal status of manhood.)

## REFERENCES

Athletes in action. (2011). Retrieved on November 13, 2011 from http://www.athletesinaction. com.
Badenhausen, K., Ozanian, M. K., & Settimi, C. (2011). Baseball's most valuable teams. Retrieved on November 14, 2011 from http://www.forbes.com.
Batista, P. J. (2002). Prayer at Public School Athletic Events: Clarifying Misperceptions of *Santa Fe ISD v. Doe*. *Texas Entertainment and Sports Law Journal, 11*(3), 23-25.
Brody, S. (1996). Sandy Koufax. Retrieved on October 27, 2011 from http://www.jewish virtuallibrary.org.
Coakley, J. (2007). *Sports in society: Issues and controversies* (9th ed.). New York, NY: McGraw-Hill.
Cunningham, G. B. (2007). *Diversity in sport organizations*. Scottsdale, AZ: Holcomb-Hathaway.
Durkheim, E. (1965). *The elementary forms of religious life*. New York: Free Press.
Hulsether, M. (2007). *Religion, culture, and politics in the twentieth-century United States*. New York, NY: Columbia University Press.
*Long v. National Football League*, 870 F. Supp. 101 (N.D. Pa. 1994).
*Ludtke v. Kuhn*, 461 F. Supp. 86 (S.D. N.Y. 1978).
Mitroff, I. I. (2003). Do not promote religion under the guise of spirituality. *Organization,10*, 375-382.

Mosley, M. (2009). Cowboys Stadium: A tribute to excess. Retrieved from
    http://espn.go.com.

Mulvenney, N. (2008). Beijing's bubble-wrapped "Water Cube" unveiled. Re-
    trieved from http://www.reuters.com.

Pinsly, M. I. (2007). Televangelist Joel Osteen shuns lavish lifestyle. Retrieved
    from http://www.religionnewsblog.com.

Schwartz, M. S. (2006). God as a managerial stakeholder? *Journal of Business Eth-*
    *ics, 66,* 291-306.

The Crusades. (n.d.). Retrieved from http://history-world.org.

The Stadium Guide. (2004). Beijing Olympic Stadium. Retrieved from
    www.stadiumguide.com.

United Nations. (1949). Plenary meetings of the general assembly. Retrieved
    from http://domino.un.org.

U.S. Const. amend. I.

USA Today. (2011). 2011 Major League Baseball salaries by team. Retrieved from
    http://content.usatoday.com.

YMCA. (2011a). The story of our founding. Retrieved from
    http://www.ymca.net.

YMCA. (2011b). Our focus. Retrieved from http://www.ymca.net.

# AUTHOR INDEX

**E**

Eagleman, A. N.   335
Eccles, J. S.   74, 75, 82, 193, 261
Eckstein, R.   115
Edensor, T.   104
Edwards, H.   84, 300, 309, 362, 363, 364, 374, 383
Edwards, M. B.   70, 77, 85
Eimer, D.   178
Eitle, T. M.   86
Eitles, D. J.   86
Eitzen, D. S.   5, 6, 8, 9, 10, 11, 12, 13, 14, 15, 25, 27, 28, 31, 45, 47, 50, 51, 71, 85, 108, 109, 146, 149, 154, 157, 159, 160, 214, 216, 217, 218, 220, 221, 223, 225, 226, 229, 300, 314, 317, 319, 376, 377
Elder, J. P.   80, 81, 85
Ellaway, A.   70
Elling, A.   338
Emmers-Sommer, T.   76
Engels, F.   108, 114
Engels, F.   360, 361
Engh, F.   272
Engstrom, C. M.   291
Entine, J.   305
Ericsson, K. A.   258
Escobedo, L. G.   75
Estabrooks, P. A,   3
Evanovich, J. M.   24
Ewald, K.   215

**F**

Fahey, J. F.   8
Falcous, M.   129
Falk, W. B.   225
Fantasia, R.   354, 355
Farrell, M. P.   75
Fasting, K.   300, 388
Fausto-Sterling, A.   331
Feagin, J. R.   298, 377, 379, 382
Federation of Gay Games   390
Feinsand, M.   76
Fellmeth, L.   257

Felton, G. M.   80, 81, 85
Ferraro, K. F.   70
Fidler, D. P.   318
Fieggen, K.   386
Field, A. E.   80
FIFA History of Football   124
Fifer, A. M.   270, 271
Fink, J. S.   37, 163, 343
Fisher, A. T.   238, 239, 244
Flegal, K. M.   74
Fletcher, D.   177, 229, 248
Fletcher, T.   122
Floyd, M. F.   70, 74, 77, 80, 83, 85
Foer, F.   209
Football 4 Peace   199
Foucault, M.   333
Fox, T.   134
Frankenberg, R.   302
Franklin, J. H.   383
Fraser-Thomas, J. L.   270, 271, 272
Fredricks, J.   261
Fredrickson, B. L.   336
Freedman, D. A.   359
Freeman, M.   216
Frey, J. H.   108, 109
Friedman, T.   121, 126
Frisby, W.   64
Frommer, D.   146
Frueh, B. C.   389
Fulks, D.   280
Fuller, R. D.   24

**G**

Gaertner, S. L.   342
Gaesser, G. A.   74
Gahagan, S.   80
Galescu, G.   358
Galli, N.   335, 341
Gangwich, J. E.   75
Garcia, M.   44
Gardiner, A.   57, 63
Gardner, D. E.   218
Gatto, M.   170
Gearlds, A.   311, 316
Gerth, H.   365

# SUBJECT INDEX

## A

*A League of their Own*  262-263
ABC  4, 99, 142, 148, 150, 285
Abdul-Jabbar, Kareem  384, 409
Abdul-Rauf, Mahmoud  409
Aboriginals  195
Academic Success Rate (ASR)  289
ACT test  289
African Americans  22
   and integration into sport,  308-309
   Black-White binary and,  303-304
   increase in visibility,  299
   male athletes,  344
   racism toward,  86, 298, 303, 312
underrepresentation as coaches and
   sport administrators,  55,  310, 311
   women and sport participation, 310, 344
AIDS, *see* HIV/AIDS
Albritten, David  383
Alcindor, Lew  384, 409
Alfred University  228
Ali, Muhammad  195, 207, 363, 409
Allen, Paul  105
Allums, Kye  390
Almonte, Danny  267
Amateur Athletic Union (AAU) 257-258
Amenorrhea  78
American dream  12-13, 299
American values in American sport 9-16
   competition,  9, 11
   external conformity  14-15
   materialism,  13-14
   progress,  12-13
   success,  9-10
   valued means to achieve,  9, 11-12

Amhurst College  256
Annan, Kofi  197
Anorexia athletica  78
Anorexia nervosa, *see* Eating disorders
Apartheid  128
Arena and stadium funding  29, 112-117
   Bradley Center,  113
   Cincinnati Bengals,  115
   Comiskey Park,  113
   consequences of public subsidization,  115
   Corpus Christi case study,  115-117
   Dallas Cowboys Stadium,  14, 112, 159, 404
   Ebbets Field,  113
   Fleet Center,  113
   New York Yankees Stadium, 112
   opportunity cost,  115
   Philadelphia Union,  115
   public funding,  114
   public-private partnership,  113
   Target Center,  113
Arsenal (soccer)  111
Artest, Ron  201
Asian American Journalists Association (AAJA)  319
Asian-German Sport Exchange Programme (AGSEP)  198
Asians  198, 307
   and race matters,  297-298, 300, 304
   discrimination against,  319-320
   in American professional sport, 318-319
   LPGA "English only" policy, 319
   sport values,  9
Aspen Institute  206

431

values, 47
Eucharist 404

## F

Facebook 143, 159, 161
Favre, Brett 223
Federer, Roger 107
Femininity
and female-appropriate sports, 337
and sport media, 30, 143, 158, 344
and sport participation, 340
and the gender binary, 331-332
and the human body, 334-336
as a gender category, 331
intercollegiate sport and, 341
physicality and, 342
questioning of, 330
youth ideals of, 337
Feminist theory 29-30
Black 310
Fellowship of Christian Athletes (FCA) 387, 402
FIFA 2, 124, 177
World Cup, 2, 177
Finch, Jenny 159
Florida State Seminoles 314-315
Focus on the Family 23
Football 4 Peace (F4P) 199
Football Bowl Subdivision (FBS) 226, 280, 287, 311
Forbes Celebrity 100 List 106-107
FOX 4, 151, 285
Free agency 14, 51, 149, 312
Freeman, Cathy 195
Functionalism theory 25-27, 32
Functionalist approach 45-46, 70-72, 82, 87, 89, 263, 358
Functionalist perspective 45-46
approach to health, 70-72

## G

Gatorade "Punt, Pass, and Kick" contests 10
Gay Games 155, 390
Gender
and body image, 334-336, 338
and college sport, see Intercollegiate sport
and consumption of sport, 154
and inequality, 363
and notions of femininity, see Femininity
and notions of masculinity, see Masculinity
and physical activity levels, 76
and sport media, 144-145, 338
and the human body, 334-336
and Title IX, see Title IX
and youth sport, see Youth sport
capital, 334
differences in perceived competition, 245-246
equity mandates, 52
experiences of Black female athletes and, 310
hiring practices and, 310-311
identity, 330, 333
influence on sport marketing, 30
Olympic Games and, see Olympic Games
performance of, 336-337
sex and, 330-333
social construction of, 83, 330, 332-333, 337
stereotypes, 333
traditional gender roles, 157, 261, 331, 333, 338
verification tests, 329
Gender verification testing, see Sex verification testing
George Washington University 390
Gibson, Althea 384
Gilbert, Dan 312-313

Moses 399, 405
Muhammad Ali Center 207
Muhammad the prophet 405
Muscular Christianity movement 71
Muslim women, opportunities for sport participation 388

## N

Nadal, Rafael 107
NASCAR 385
National Association of Intercollegiate Athletics (NAIA) 280, 289-290
National Basketball Association (NBA) 10, 53, 58-59, 61, 107, 109, 111, 124, 149-150, 196, 224, 311-312, 314, 364, 405, 408
  history of, 124
  international reach of, 129, 131-133, 152
  labor disputes, 44, 61, 111
  NBA Cares initiative, 201
  regulation of steroid use and testing, 53, 224
  sport media and, 150
  success of Asian athletes, 319
National Christian College Athletic Association (NCCAA) 280
National Collegiate Athletic Association (NCAA)
  and hazing, 227-228
  and policies concerning sexual orientation, 386, 390
  and student-athlete criminal records, 226
  and student-athlete injuries, 221
  and the commodification of college sport, 110
  and the idea of amateurism, 109-110, 288
  and wrestling weigh-in rule changes, 229
  as a governing body, 56-57, 62-63, 163, 229, 231, 280, 282, 287-290, 292, 314-315, 373, 409-410
  as a nonprofit organization, 109, 112
  athletic conferences within the, 147
  hiring practices of member institutions, 311
  men's basketball championships, 10, 99
  Native American mascots and, 315
  Office of Inclusion, 390
  organizational structure, 56-57
  regulation of steroid use and testing, 53
  scholarships, 258
  television contracts, 285-286
  women's basketball championships, 10
National Federation of High Schools (NFHS) 25, 227, 257
National Football League (NFL) 107, 149, 155, 314, 364
  athlete behavior and conduct, 62
  athlete health and participation, 61, 221-222, 229-230
  average salary, 100
  commodification, 51
  corporate social responsibility, 201
  deviant behavior, 216, 220, 225-226
  fines, 231
  history of, 124
  international reach of, 131-133
  labor disputes, 44, 61, 111
  personal conduct policy, 62
  Play 60 campaign, 75-76
  regulation of steroid use and testing, 53, 224
  television rights, 99, 146
National Football League Players Association (NFLPA) 61

Pecuniary emulation 102-103
Penn State University 44, 225
Performance enhancing substances
9, 52-53, 216, 222-225, 263, 410
Person-environment fit research
241
Petersen, Chris 162-163
Petite Bourgeois 361
Philadelphia Eagles
fan violence, 227
green initiatives, 185-186
Philadelphia Phillies 403
Philadelphia Union 115
Phoenix Coyotes 105
Physical activity
and critical race theory, *see*
Critical race theory (CRT)
and ethics, *see* Ethics
and Feminist theory, *see*
Feminist theory
and functionalism, *see*
Functionalism theory
and sport, 2-4
consumer spending, 4
definitions of, 3, 73
health benefits, 27, 75
prevalence of, 4
sociology of, definitions of, 6
Physical activity and health theories
26, 34-35
social ecological theory, 34-35
Physically Active Youth (PAY)
198, 206
Pittsburgh Steelers 220, 225
*Plessy v. Ferguson* 376, 378
Polamalu, Troy 201
Police Athletic League (PAL) 257
Politics
and African-American
participation in sport, 377-379
and female representation in
sport, 377
and its relationship with sport,
375-381
motives for government
involvement in sport, 376

power, *see* Power
Pop Warner Football 257
Portland Trailblazers 105
Power
and commodification, 51
and deviant behavior, 231
and gender, 333-334, 339, 342-
343, 385
and health, 71
and massification, 50
and politics, 375-382
and privilege of men in sport,
8, 39
and race relations, 298-302, 305,
310, 312-313, 315-316, 379, 382,
384
and religion, 387-388, 406
and sexual orientation, 390
and social change, 203, 205
and sport media, 141, 148, 152
as related to conflict theory, 26-
27, 72
as related to critical theories,
28-30
definitions of, 380
social class and, 102, 353, 355,
357, 363, 365-368
structures in sport, 15, 125-126,
135, 312, 382
Princeton University 256, 281
Professional athlete salaries 100
Professional Golfers Association
(PGA) 100, 107, 124, 152, 158,
168, 176
Proletariat 108-109, 361
Proposition 48 (NCAA) 289
Prosthetic and Sensory Aids Service
(PSAS) 389
Psychic income 248
Public prayer 402
Puritans 12, 71, 365, 197

**Q**

Quakers 397
Qur'an, the 405, 408, 411

# R

Race
  increasing significance in sport
    of,  299-301
  relationship between ethinicity
    and,  305-308
  social construction of,  304-308,
    382
Race matters  297-298, 301, 304-305,
  308-309, 315, 316, 320
Racial formation theory  297
Ramadan  408, 410
Rampone, Christie  159
Rangers Football Club  79
Rashad, Ahmad  409
Reese, Jeff  229
Reform environmentalism  173
Reformed University Fellowship
  (RUF)  402
Religion
  and intercollegiate athletics,
    401
  and material possessions,  400
  and sport at the individual level,
    408
  and sport at the organizational
    level,  407
  and sport, conflicts between,
    409-411
  and the NCAA, *see* NCAA
and the structural functionalist
  approach  359
  and the US legal system,  400-
    402
  as sacred,  400
  athlete name changes,  409
  church sport leagues,  408
  conflicts,  398
  definitions of,  398-399
  differences between sport and,
    406-407
  displays in sport,  402
  faith in,  406-407
  persecution  397-398

role in society  397
similarities between sport and,
  403-405
Religious fundamentalism  23-24
Research methods  35-39
  Qualitative,  38-39
  Quantitative,  37-38
Rickey, Branch  31
Riggs, Bobby  196
Right to Play  198
Robinson, Jackie  31, 195, 208, 302-
  303, 307
Rodriguez, Alex  53, 107
Roethlisberger, Ben  225
Roll Back Malaria Partnership  76
Roman Catholic Church  398
Ronaldo, Cristiano  107
Roosevelt, Theodore  184, 281, 373
Rudolph, Wilma  384
Rugby World Cup  196
Rugby's Six Nations Tournament
  181-182
Rupp, Adolph  31
Rutgers University  256, 281, 297
Ruth, Babe  405

# S

Sabathia, CC  201
Sabbath, the  410
San Francisco Forty-Niners  79
San Francisco Giants  176
San Jose State University  363
Sandusky, Jerry  225
SAT test  289, 292
Schottenheimer, Marty  221
Scripture reading  402
Seattle Seahawks  105
Seattle Sounders  105
Seattle Super Sonics  149
Self-objectification theory  335
Semenya, Caster  329, 344, 385-386
Sense of Community Theory
  (McMillan and Chavis)  240-
  241, 244
influence,  240-241

442

446